A Functional Theory of Government, Law, and Institutions

A Functional Theory of Government, Law, and Institutions

Kalu N. Kalu

LEXINGTON BOOKS
Lanham • Boulder • New York • London

Published by Lexington Books
An imprint of The Rowman & Littlefield Publishing Group, Inc.
4501 Forbes Boulevard, Suite 200, Lanham, Maryland 20706
www.rowman.com

6 Tinworth Street, London SE11 5AL, United Kingdom

British Library Cataloguing in Publication Information Available

Library of Congress Cataloging-in-Publication Data Available

ISBN 978-1-4985-8702-0 (cloth : alk. paper)
ISBN 978-1-4985-8703-7 (electronic)

∞™ The paper used in this publication meets the minimum requirements of American National Standard for Information Sciences—Permanence of Paper for Printed Library Materials, ANSI/NISO Z39.48-1992.

To the
Ndukwe Kalu Family
Past, Present, and Future

Contents

List of Figures

Preface

My scholarly interest in functional theory arose from my article on the subject matter titled "Institution-Building, Not Nation-Building: A Structural Functional Model," which was published in the *International Review of Administrative Sciences* in 2011. This publication followed an earlier presentation of the same article at the 5th Specialized Conference of the International Institute for Administrative Sciences (IIAS) in Helsinki, Finland, in July 2009. Since then and drawing from the outcome of the conference, I have developed an unwaning research interest that seeks to address the persistent question of how social and political structures reinforce specific functions in such a way that sustains equilibrium states. On a practical level, much of this has to do with how (political) systems maintain a sense of order, stability, and continuity, even as subsystemic elements break away from each other and recombine here and there. But it still begs the question: How do systems manage or regulate the ever-present tensions that arise out of the interactions of their multiple parts?

It is true that structural-functionalism as a framework for the study of social and political systems has been with us since its anthropological/sociological roots in the works of Herbert Spencer, Durkheim, Weber, Malinowski, Radcliffe-Brown, and Talcott Parsons. But its most prominent application in Sociology, particularly in the works of Parsons and his contemporaries, shows the richness of the intellectual history. A common mistake we make in social scientific inquiry is that we are too quick to discard our foundational philosophies in a rush to embrace new and often romanticized fads that seem all too-pleasing. Structural-functionalism (or functionalism if you prefer) has been with us for some time, but then and to the contrary, it has never left us. This work is an effort to reawaken us to the potentials of functional theory in understanding the key drivers of social and political systems, the interrelationships among the parts, and how institutionalization processes work to moderate the inherent tension arising from the functional relationships.

The building block of any theory lies in its ability to inform the researcher of the characteristics of the object or phenomenon of inquiry, how specific variables relate to each, and how we can conceptualize the series of actions or explanations in an attempt to understand it, to enrich it, or generate new pathways for creating new knowledge. This is the contribution this work makes. By drawing from an array of interdisciplinary orientations, it offers novel and interesting ways for understanding social and political action both at the individual or social/group levels of analyses. Institutions and institutionalization processes play a central role in functional analysis because they provide the bond within which social and political action takes place. This is even more relevant in the contemporary modern state as we witness a continuous break-down in the regulatory authority of critical institutions of state and government, in the customs, practices and social mores that have kept society together for decades and on. Interactions within and between social or political systems are of different kinds and also generate different and oftentimes conflicting effects. All interactions generate some kind of tension, but then it is a matter of degree. Tension can originate in the form of disagreements, resistance, by application of brute force, or in unilateral defection from agreed upon social practices and conventions. But whichever way it manifests, the bottom line is that a primary function of states and governments is the maintenance of law and order and the management of tension in such a way that it does not get out of hand or disrupt ongoing processes of governance.

In the process of completing this work, I have been exposed to various epistemological traditions but also on the utility of the interdisciplinary approach in the search for explanation. Because no single framework or episteme can cover all that may apply in the explanation of social phenomena, I believe that we gain more by investigating the object or phenomenon from various different but complementary angles or premises. We need to address issues concerning causation and inference, questions about ontology (what is) and epistemology (how we come to know about what is) and other path-dependent relationships that may apply to specific objects or phenomenon. The modern state is under enormous stress and is changing very rapidly but without complementary foundations for such change. The change and stress comes from many different sources of inspiration that includes but is not limited to economic downturns, declining rate of political tolerance within the body politic, ideological extremism, interstate and intra-state wars, civil strife, narco-and-human trafficking, changes in values and rising expectations, an increasingly frustrated and agitated mass, and a clamor to change existing social norms and practices just for the simple sake of changing them.

Political leaders construct competing social realities about pressing environmental problems and climate change such that policy debates generally end in disagreements and disagreements become public policy. Bad political judgments often lead to war between states; but war is a mid-range phenomenon between rationality and irrationality depending on which side of the divide you are. Technology and innovation are increasing at a pace where the ability of states and governments, or even society as a whole, is inadequate to cope with. Illegal immigration that has seen thousands crash through sovereign borders of several western countries end up delegitimizing state authority and independence; but the long-term consequences arising from its politicization means that competing issues of national identity, cultural hegemony or neutralization, and a de facto territorial conquest by foreign aliens will become the centerfold of power and contestation in national politics now and in the foreseeable future. The boundary between who is elected to govern and who actually governs has become blurred as organized resistance seeks to take over the public space without any form of alternate discourse. Increasing dissatisfaction breeds anger, and anger oftentimes breeds violence. Ongoing events in our social world cannot continue as it is without attaining critical mass, sooner or later. How do we understand these processes before they become institutionalized; and even then, how do we develop effective social structures in the effort to contain or preempt them?

I am very grateful to the various anonymous reviewers of the manuscript for the insightful suggestions that have enriched this work. I am also thankful to the editorial committee for their role in this work and for keeping to the publication timeline much earlier than expected. Finally, I am highly indebted to my greatest fans Renee, Joy, and Glory, for their generosity and untiring support in effectively managing all the daily routines while I toiled away on this project. And to Sebastian and Mira, we love you.

Kalu N. Kalu
Montgomery, USA
May 27, 2019

Chapter 1

The Framework of Functional Theory

A basic assumption of functional theory is that each part of society contributes something to the overall maintenance of the social order and stability in the system. But it also raises a question as to how each of the parts contributes to the maintenance of that order, its adaptation to internal and external changes, and the sustenance of the whole system state. While much of the emphasis has been about understanding social relations at the macro-level structure, it is equally important to focus on the micro-level structure for the simple fact that cause-and-effect relationships often draw upon complex subjective and objective factors. Because "the relation between cause and effect in nature is often reconstructed as a deductive relation between premise and conclusion";[1] we therefore, rather mistakenly, assume a unidirectional path in the sequence of actions that generates specific outcomes.

In social scientific inquiry, we generally deal with multiple variables (at least those that we are able to deduce from general principles or from what is already known); and for this reason, an outcome could have multiple causal relations or reciprocal causality, in some cases. And this is why functional analysis as a method is less about causal questions (the "what") as opposed to the "how" and "why" things occur the way they do. The "how" question seeks answers about how a specific phenomenon, structure, government, or institution works (the process) and also why it works the way it does (epistemology). The traditional conception of functional theory maintains that governments exist to enforce norms, law and order, and stability is achieved because "each aspect of society depends on each other and each contributes to the overall maintenance and functioning of that society."[2] But this premise can be questioned in the sense that not every part of society functions in ways that contribute to its overall stability and well-being. There are those who break the law, renege on their contributions to the social order, or engage in actions that seek to undermine the general functioning of state and society. There are also other factors that emanate within the general system of relations and interaction of the various parts of society in such a way that the tension they generate can, in and of itself, become a destabilizing force to the well-functioning of society. This is a theoretical gap that continues to exist in contemporary scholarship on the subject matter of functional analysis.

Rather than looking only at the outcome of the system of relationships and interdependence (manifest functions), the premise of this work is also to understand the logic that undergirds the interactions (how the parts work together), and how the structural tension or friction from the interaction (latent functions) affects the functioning of the whole system. To this end, this work takes the structural-normative approach to functional analysis. First, I seek to illuminate our understanding of the functional properties of social systems and how they play out in the context of social action. Secondly, drawing insights from central arguments in general systems theory, cybernetics, philosophy of science, and sociological theories of human institutions, I illustrate the utility of functional theory in the analysis of states, governments, and institutions, as well as its relevance to the framework of this work. States and governments are more likely to maintain stable conditions based on the ability to manage the tension resulting from the interaction of their constituent parts, the complementarity of prevailing institutional structures, and the structure of order that govern social action.

The role of functional analysis is to educate us on what the government does, and how it goes about doing it and for what ends. We can specify certain building blocks of functional theory as an input-process-output relationship, and while this seems to follow a straightforward logic, it still begs the question as to why some states succeed in achieving their specified ends and others do not. How does a state evolve and why do people come to accept and respect its laws and regulations? And in what ways does acceptance become institutionalized as a practice? One way to attempt these questions is to view the state as an aggregation of ideas and belief systems. Because of its emphasis on individual perceptions, social systems contain micro- (subjective) and macro (objective)-level structures; "and these structures might have causal effects on the identities and interests of state actors."[3] "Causal questions inquire into the antecedent conditions or mechanisms that generate independently existing effects; and these are generally what we want to know when we ask the question as to 'why' something happened or 'how' a process works."[4] On the other hand, "constitutive questions inquire into the conditions of possibility that make something what it is or give it the causal powers that it has; hence by asking how social kinds are put together to have the causal powers that they do, constitutive questions show us the role that our own practices play in sustaining the seemingly objective social facts"[5] (institutions such as laws, regulations, conventions, and norms).

Although more difficult to address, there are other questions that we need to ask, such as what makes a law a law, what makes a regulation a regulation, and what do we mean when we say that something is a convention? Because the effect of all of the above can only be known through their functions (how they actually work out in real life), we cannot know them as having any form of ontology expect by their functions. Because functional analysis seeks to explain a feature of society in terms of the beneficial consequences it has for the larger society;[6] it offers a more effective means for analyzing the relative or reciprocal effects that each element or unit of the social structure contributes to the maintenance of the whole. Functional analysis therefore requires an understanding of the dynamics of the interaction process involving critical elements of the social system, the constitutive properties, constraints, and the types of relational structures (visible or not) that could predict different types of effects and possibilities for the system as a whole. This is the theoretical building block for the *interactionist* emphasis of this work.

From a somewhat different angle, this approach could also be used to illuminate some of the insights demonstrated in Ostrom's Institutional Analysis and Development (IAD) framework in which a key requirement is the identification of an *action situation* (typically characterized by reciprocity, exchange, or by team problem-solving, or command) and the resulting patterns of interactions and outcomes, and evaluating these outcomes.[7] And her reasoning was that the "problem of the *action situation* could be at an operational tier where actors *interact* in light of the incentives they face to generate outcomes directly in the world."[8] There are a lot of things (both objective and subjective) that could affect the outcome of interaction between objects or system elements; hence, each analytical approach offers only a slice of a much larger pie. While the IAD framework seems to focus on how structure might affect interaction and outcomes, I am particularly concerned about how interaction shapes the nature of outcomes. The key to functional analysis is to understand the underlying principles that help to explain the processes by which independent effects of system elements contribute to a functional whole. In the following sections, I will attempt to further illustrate the relationship between ontology, causation, and inference, particularly as it applies to the properties and functional analysis of social systems.

ONTOLOGY AND CAUSATION

It would be very difficult to view the individual and the state in isolation from each other, mainly for the reason that people have always lived and existed together in the form of a social institution. While much of classical and contemporary philosophy have generally seen man as a social animal; it is equally true that society is the product of the individual and the individual is also the product of society. The individual identity and character cannot be expressed or even understood by the individual in his own internalized subjective world; it requires a social reference group, but the "unity of the person (in relation to others) requires the unity-enhancing perspective of a life-world that guarantees *order* and has both cognitive (communicative) and moral-practical significance"[9] (norms and shared values). Human society therefore could be understood as the facilitation of ideas through language; and when these are directed to serve a specific purpose, the ensuing socialization processes and action results in identity formation (structure). The framework of this shared identity is sustained by norms, values, religion, ideology, language, belief systems, and social conventions "in such a way that the contingencies of an imperfectly controlled environment (social system) could be processed simultaneously with the fundamental risks that confront human existence within it."[10]

By way of shared identity, social systems constitute or rather construct a structure that turns around and regulates behavior within the social system so that it can survive to achieve its stipulated objective. The stability of social systems is pretty much conditioned by the way existing functional relationships are structured and how the various parts interact with each other. On the premise that the state as a social system does not create itself and cannot be understood a priori except by an analysis of the elements that constitutes it and their relative functions (properties) in sustaining an independent life-force that is external, dynamic, and non-deterministic, we should be able to have a better understanding of the nature of states when they function in ways prescribed by the functional properties of the elements and the causal relations between them. To this effect, a more appropriate analogy would be Rene Descartes' dictum *Cogito Ergo Sum* (I think, therefore I am), which in a way, resurfaces the age-old argument about the primacy of *existence* over *essence*, or in a more mundane reference to the chicken and egg problem (which one comes first).

I have always believed that Descartes was wrong in asserting his own experience (I think) before affirming his existence or being (I am). I base such disagreement on the simple premise that to be able to think, one either must have been in existence and would also have had the prior knowledge or idea that the present activity one is engaged in is an activity known as *thinking*. To *think*, therefore, presupposes a body, context, language, and temporality (as a priori conditions). Even if this condition is an expression of Descartes' self-doubt, but then the very act of *doubting* something, ipso facto suggests a foreknowledge of that which is being doubted. And certainly, one has to exist in some form (or body) to be able to express the cognitive sensation of doubting—which in itself is a form of reflection or an activity of thinking. How do we acquire knowledge or ideas about things or events if we do not have a prior existence through which we have come to associate specific qualities and properties to those things or events? Descartes' fault therefore was that he seemed to put essence before existence, epistemology before ontology—both of which are views that could somehow be suggestive of scientific realism.

In fact, if we follow the simple logic of deductive inquiry which is most typical in the social sciences (because we do not come to know things as they exist in themselves expect by their functions and the meanings we attach to them), we can easily debunk Descartes' hypothesis on the premise that we only come to know that a person thinks if he already exists as a person or an object. The idea of *thinking* is not a phenomenon that could be understood separately on its own except as an ontological property that qualifies an object as a person or as a manifestly conscious being. "Pains, tickles, itches, emotions and thoughts have a mode of existence which is ontologically subjective in the sense that they only exist insofar as they are experienced by human or animal subjects."[11] Ontological issues also raise causal and epistemological questions. They are causal in the sense that specific objects are naturally wired in specific ways to perform specific functions. In other words, objects or things are what they are notwithstanding whether we see it differently or not. While it may be easier for positivist science to draw inferences based on what has been observed and studied about the behavior of specific objects or phenomenon, but social scientific inquiry is much more difficult and complex.

In social science research, most phenomena of investigation are objects that lack any scope of deep structure that makes it possible to establish an ontological foundation. What makes a community a community? What makes an organization an organization? A simple and more tempting answer would be that they are made up of people (individuals), who share similar ideas or values, and who seek the attainment of the same goal or objective. But this still does not address any ontological question, because the sharing of ideas, values, and similar objectives do not explain what a community or an organization is, they only serve as the constitutive properties around which the notions of community or organization are constructed and organized. Communities or organizations do not have a life of their own separate or independent of their constitutive properties, because it is these that determine the means by which the community or organization functions as well as the ways we make distinctions between them. This is the perennial problem of ontology—to what extent it can be used effectively as a framework to understand and interpret behaviors as well as cause-and-effect relationships within social systems?

Ontology and Institutionalization

One of the basic arguments of "classical ontology which it inherited from Parmenides and Plato, was its belief in immutable, seemingly external ideas or substances that either preexist or inhere in the appearances of reality and rule it."[12] But this should not preclude the fact that "the function of ontology is strictly analytical; it provides the taxonomy which serves to systemize and clarify our knowledge about the universe."[13] Plato's hypothesis about dualism in nature fits very much into this picture, in the sense that the body (corporeality) can only move and act in accord with the dictates of the mind (soul), but neither can exist alone without the other. We only come to develop our knowledge of the mind through its association with the body, and its ability to direct it in specific directions and toward particular ends.

We can equally say this about states that they cannot exist in isolation apart from the individual members. "The domain of personal or individual values lies in the fact that it is almost inextricably intertwined either with society or with artifacts which it uses as material carriers to express or manifest itself, either as personality or, collectively, as social consciousness."[14] In the same way that man is constitutive of mind and body, states are constitutive of the individual members and the social or functional relationships that bind them together. "Ontology, therefore, can be seen in two ways: through observation and reasoning, or through experience and judgement."[15] The first constitutes factual truth (there is day and night), the second, rational or logical truth (deductive reasoning anchored on universal principles); although we recognize the fact that while "factual truth satisfies our daily empirical needs, it is logical truth which constitutes strict theory as well as ontology."[16]

As individuals, what we do on a daily basis may have a purpose to which it is directed; but then there may be circumstances where other factors beyond our control may lead to outcomes that were never contemplated. Logical truth therefore provides us with a framework within which to either make excuses or rationalize why events happened to turn out the way they did. Individuals live in a social world (social structure) in which they relate to each other in various ways such as family members, coworkers, fellow students, fellow church members, or simply fellow citizens; but for the fact that "social structures constitute actors with certain identities and interests,"[17] the role of government therefore becomes one of coordination and regulation of the various interests and identities. Such coordination does not necessarily come about because the government approaches it with a heavy hand; rather it is more effective and enduring when the people have come to internalize its virtues as an obligation and as a necessity for living in a larger world beyond the individual horizon.

It is by doing all the little things that help to serve the collective interest that we also derive a sense of accomplishment and fulfillment as individuals. "When I fulfil my obligations as a brother, husband, or citizen, and when I execute my contracts; I have also performed duties which are defined, externally to myself and my acts, in law and in custom."[18] And "even if they conform to my own sentiments and I feel their reality subjectively, such reality is still objective, for I did not create them; I merely inherited them."[19] When individuals perform their social roles voluntarily and when "collective beliefs are in accord with the prevailing institutional framework,"[20] common values become motivationally integrated into action without any overt compulsion.[21] I have argued in chapter 6 of this work that institutional effects are the result of cognitive and noncognitive structures that guide social action. Collective beliefs and values do not development overnight; they manifest overtime in institutionalized form through practice, rule of thumb, imitation, and/or social learning. The key takeaway from this is that collective beliefs and practices, to the extent they are "successfully produced and reproduced, are *functional* in various ways; not least in contributing to social coordination, stability and predictability, but usually also carries connotations of normativity."[22] They acquire normative properties that imbue and reinforce social action.

As long as prevailing institutional frameworks facilitate solutions to recurrent problems of social interaction, they are more likely to be continuously validated within the social structure in which they apply. But then this still begs the question: What of if an existing institutional framework does not solve any or most of the social problems? It would be rather tempting to suggest that either the institution fails on its own or it would be abandoned by the social community. Neither of these answers makes much sense, unless we are able to answer the question: Why did the institution fail? Starting from the purpose (function) for which the institution is supposed to serve, we can deductively begin to build a systematic argument that could help us to address various causal questions as to why the institution as currently constituted or upheld, did not seem to serve its *function* in a predictable and excepted manner? In fact, it is even possible that the institution may be working perfectly, but evolving changes or contradictions within the general social environment may be more to blame for the institutional failure. This is what Elinor Ostrom seems to be suggesting when she argued that "the challenge for institutional theorists is to know enough about the structure of a situation to select the appropriate assumptions about human behavior that fit the type of situation under analysis."[23]

A study of the efficacy of institutional frameworks also requires an even greater understanding about how they are made to adapt to variations in their operational environment; but to address the *how* question, it is also important that we understand what causes institutions to adapt or change the way they do? Because institutions also raise causal questions, I therefore deem it quite necessary to provide further discussion on the prevailing *episteme* about causal questions, particularly as it applies to social systems and social scientific inquiry. I believe that this attempt would be very helpful as I continue to build up the framework of functional theory and the central arguments retained in this book.

CAUSAL QUESTIONS AND THEIR EPISTEMOLOGY

In scientific analysis, there are two types of phenomena (complex and simple) and two types of reasoning (inductive and deductive); but to do this, we often rely on existing theories as a frame of reference or as a basis for inferring causal relations between two or more phenomena if and where they exist. We construct sets of hypotheses linking one variable to the other as a guide to addressing the central thesis of our theory. But for the fact that most variables in social systems are unpredictable, unobservable, non-discrete, and generally in flux, social scientific analysis deals mostly with complex phenomena. Because "factors outside the scope of our theory could provide crucial links in the causal sequence of events";[24] the logic of social scientific inquiry also demands us to "consider the environmental factors, the structures of power, the forces of conditioning, the real dimensions of choice that people face in social situations, and the material possibilities people actually have of solving their own problems."[25] In other words, how do the structure of activities and the relationships between them help to serve the primary purpose for which those activities are meant to serve? In what ways have the various activities become functional—that is, serve their purpose?

In his *The Function of General Laws in History*, Carl G. Hempel postulates that "the causal analysis of an event establishes an explanation for it, and since this requires reference to general hypotheses, so do assumptions about relevance, and, consequently, so does the adequate analysis of the historical development of an institution"[26]—in this case the *state* as a system of social relations. As a way of seeking to establish a logical cause-and-effect relationship between a phenomenon and action, we therefore rely first, on our understanding of universal principles (such as "If there is daylight, what comes after would always be the night"; "If I throw an object upwards, it will always fall down"). Because these have become *givens* that always meet expectations, we therefore take them for granted without actually engaging further in any act of investigation or experimentation. We engage in deductive reasoning, drawing from universal or general laws, rationalizing the logical sequence in which events occur, and eventually accepting and validating those events as practices and as a condition of our own individual and social existence. We become more confident in making both prediction and inference such that: If $A = B$ and $B = C$; then it would always mean that $A = C$. And furthermore, wherever there is A, there will also be B, and there is always the greater likelihood that there will also be C.

The above logical synthesis would seem to hold true in situations where humans have little or no control, and/or where social reality and the way the world operates makes the predicted outcome a certainty. But then there is always an exception to the rule, particularly in situations where individuals are involved. It is very difficult to predict human behavior in situations where the motives are unknown; and even when they are made known, still yet we cannot be too sure that they are sincere or are simply strategic ruses meant to elicit specific responses or information. Because individuals can change their minds at any moment in a deliberation, and as state actors, they also bring with them a high level of uncertainty and unpredictability. While we can design the best of constitutions, systems of government, laws, and regulations, it will take individuals to manipulate or violate them. Laws and constitutions do not violate themselves; they are violated because individuals refuse to abide by the stipulations. At the center of state action is the individual, hence a study of state behavior is, invariably, also a study of individual behavior broadly construed. But since we cannot capture the full essence of the state by way of its individual elements, it is therefore important to discuss the state in the context of its constitutive and ontological properties.

The structural-normative approach of this work holds that states and governments are more likely to function better when they strike a balance between the friction generated by the interaction of systemic elements (tension management), and the imperative of a structured or induced order. That is, the ability of governments to maintain contingent stable states and to serve their primary purpose is dependent on their ability to resolve the tension between input-output (cause-and-effect relationships). To the extent that institutions help in the maintenance of a structured order, they are also part of the systemic elements and the relational architecture within which the parts interact with each other. We can only know things and their relative functions as a result of the outcomes they generate as well as the meaning (and importance) we attach to those outcomes. Because the interaction between systemic elements raises ontological questions for both cause-and-effect relationships, we are often confronted with a situation where what we assume to be the cause may actually be an effect of some other things that may have occurred a priori. What is it about a particular *cause* and its constitutive properties that makes it to generate a particular type of effect and not something else?

Mistakes are often made when we erroneously attribute context and body to abstract or descriptive notions of events that we have lived through or imagined; and the mistake may come from the fact that what we term as a cause, may actually be part of the constitutive properties (ontology) of a phenomenon that happens to manifest itself to us. "Causation is a relation in nature not in logic,"[27] and unless we actually know the inner workings or the deep structure of which the cause is made of, the consequent inferences we draw as causal inquiries are only about their relational properties but not causal origins. This view is consistent with Wendt's argument that "internal structures do not cause the properties associated with them, in the sense of being antecedent conditions for independently existing effects, but rather they make those properties possible."[28] As Daniel Little points out, these generalizations or claims should depend on analysis of the specific causal mechanisms (ontology) that connect cause and effect;[29] but to do so also requires that we understand the functional properties that link the cause to the effect.

Making law-like generalizations are most useful if the premise is based on what I would call *universal givens*—that is, they exhibit a pattern recognition that is already evident in human or social experience. Such *universal givens* could be such that "If am thirsty and I drink water, there is no doubt in my mind that the water would be able to perform its *function* of quenching the thirst. If there is night, I am under no illusion that within a few hours, there will be daylight." Ontological questions therefore require that we can only understand what a piece of chalk is made of, by knowing the function or the purpose for which we need a chalk. The chalk cannot truly reveal itself to us except by what it does for us—its *function* as a writing material. If we are trying to look for what makes a chalk a chalk, obviously we cannot find it in the object itself; we can only find it in the *interaction* between a chalk and the activity of *writing* on the board. And that is why we say that "a chalk is an object for writing"; and nothing more would be needed to know what a chalk is, except through its *function* or the role it plays.

One of the reasons why we do correlation analysis or t-test of means in social scientific research is that we wish to establish a relationship between two or more variables, but it is not necessarily about the causal sequence between the sets of variables. A high correlation between two or more variables does not tell us that variable x causes variable y or vice versa; rather what it tells us is that x and y are related in some ways, and there is an underlying phenomenon (that we cannot see) that is bringing x and y together in fundamental ways. Depending how we chose to frame our hypothesis, the underlying dimension should thus manifest itself as harboring aspects of both the cause (x) and the effect (y). The constituent properties of an object are critical to determining how it will behave or function in real life. Our assumptions and predictions (at least theoretically), therefore must rely on an a priori understanding of what those properties are (their ontology). While this requirement may be impossible, at least from the standpoint of empirical realists or nominalists; we just cannot be too sure that we know what we believe we know no matter how hard we try. The *object of knowledge*, what Tony Lawson refers to as being in the intransitive domain (by not giving itself out too readily) is not the same as *knowledge of the object* (which exists in the *transitive domain*).[30] But to ensure the latter, our conceptual framework must allow us to differentiate whether the knowledge we have of an object is an essential part of its ontology, or whether it is one that has been imposed on it as a necessary condition that satisfies human or social needs. And this is one of the justifications for the importance of covariance in social scientific research—because it enables us to attempt an explanation of a specific phenomenon or object of inquiry within a range of probabilities and margins of error. And by this, we readily make allowance for what we do not know or may never know as a result of the complex nature of the social variables we have to deal with.

Because some social scientists hold the view that there are several modes of explanation that are distinct from causal explanations and are particularly pertinent to social phenomena;[31] they see *functional explanations* as dependent essentially on the availability of a causal explanation establishing the postulated functional relationship. Because causal questions also raise ontological questions (What is *this* A that causes B?); it would thus mean that we can be able to address both ontological and causal questions by looking at the *function* of particular objects or phenomena. Functional explanations therefore are constitutive of the ontology (life world) and the cause-and-effect relationships that emanates from an object; that is, the ontology of an object is *partially included* in that which drives the characteristic function associated with the object. I believe this to be what Roy Bhaskar may have alluded to when he talked about the inexorability and all-inclusiveness of ontology in everything.[32] When we say that a child looks pretty much like the father; we are already implying that there are certain visible characteristics of the father that have transferred to the child. We are also saying that variants of the father's ontological properties (imprinting) have been inherited by the child; and for the simple fact that (using a minimalist argument in this case) the father is the *cause* and the child the *effec*t, the *function* is constitutive of the ontological and cause-and-effect relationships (interactional friction) inherent in the activity of having a child.

In the following sections, I will attempt a broader discussion of the literature on functional theory, and its application and utility to dealing with the central issues raised in this work. I also provide preliminary discussions of the three elements of functional theory (interactionalism, institutionalization, and the notion of structured or induced order) as developed in this book, as well as how they collectively offer novel approaches to understanding the principles and institutional structures that govern social order and the notion of stable states.

FUNCTIONAL THEORY: BETWEEN AND WITHIN STATES

The interdependence of two or more elements of a system creates a relationship; but their interaction creates a unique structure that is ontologically independent of each of the system elements. As a result, systemic stability or failure (dysfunction) is a function of the magnitude of *interaction* between the elements or parts, not their interdependence. In social systems, various factors such as social order, economic efficiency, or homogeneity of value systems are structures within the system that are interpreted as contributing to the maintenance of equilibrium or stable states.[33] Due to the complexity of social systems, random perturbations do not evolve in a linear fashion; they can occur from anywhere and at any time. They can originate from sudden variations in the internal characteristics of system elements, inertial or environmental forces, or as the natural effect of the entropic process which, as argued in chapter 4 of this book, is a continuous process of incremental degeneration even when system states may seem to be functioning under stable conditions.

The richness of functional theory lies in its versatility and broad appeal in many disciplines ranging from the behavioral sciences, sociology, anthropology, biology, environmentalism, political science, physics, and the humanities. It has its origins in the works of the French sociologist Emile Durkheim who was particularly concerned with the maintenance of social order and relative stability within societies over an extended period of time. It also holds the view that society consists of different but interrelated parts, each of which must serve a specific purpose for the whole to survive. Others such as Hebert Spencer, Talcott Parsons, Robert Merton, Alfred Radcliffe-Brown, and Bronislaw Malinowski have all been associated with pioneering the development of functionalist thought and turning it into a major paradigm shift in the way we study and understand social systems as well as organisms. In the social sciences, the term *functionalist* is generally used interchangeably with functionalism or structural functionalism, hence in this work, the meaning and conceptualization of the term should be considered the same.

Functionalism is a "theory based on the premise that all aspects of a society—institutions, roles, norms, and so on—serve a purpose and that all are indispensable for the long-term survival of the society. A social system is assumed to have a functional unity in which all parts of the system work together with some degree of internal consistency. What is called functionalism today in the social sciences is closely related to structuralism, with the term structural-functional a common one, especially in sociology or anthropology. Function refers to the way in which behavior takes on significance not as a discrete act but as the dynamic aspect of some structure."[34] The British anthropologist Alfred Radcliffe-Brown[35] explored the theoretical implications of functionalism as a relationship between a social institution and the *necessary conditions of existence* of a social system. He saw the function of a unit as the contribution it makes to the maintenance of a social structure—the set of relationships among social units. "Others have used the concept of function to mean the interrelationships of parts within a system, the adaptive aspect of a phenomenon, or its observable consequences. Distinctions have also been made between manifest functions, those consequences intended and recognized by participants in the system, and latent functions, which are neither intended nor recognized."[36]

In an attempt to develop a more dynamic analysis of social systems, the American sociologist Talcott Parsons[37] introduced a structural-functional approach that employs the concept of *function* as a link between relatively stable *structura*l categories, with a particular focus on the conditions of stability, integration, and effectiveness of the system. Hence, any process or set of conditions that does not contribute to the maintenance or development of the system is therefore said to be dysfunctional. For Parsons, an established state of a social system is a process of complementary interaction of two or more individual actors in which each conforms with the expectations of the other in such a way that reciprocal reactions serve to reinforce given need dispositions and thus fulfill given expectations.[38] But for the system to work and remain functional, each action set must be directed to a purpose that contributes to the welfare of the whole. A corollary to this hypothesis is its useful application in systems theory, cybernetics, and in illuminating the inertial principles that govern feedback loops and homeostatic equilibrium. This aspect will be explored further in chapter 4 of this book.

Functionalism also found application in political science particularly in the works of David Mitrany and that of later neo-functionalists such as Ernst Haas and L. Lindberg. Mitrany was more concerned about the problem of international order and how increasing the levels of interdependence and cooperation (transnational cooperation) between the federating units of the European Community, would lead to a *functional* supranational entity that would sustain peace and unity within the federation. In his *The Functional Theory of Politics*, Mitrany argued that "functionalism is of use particularly to those students of international conflict who seek to understand the general underlying causes of violence, rather than the circumstances of a particular quarrel."[39] "Functionalism holds that violence has its roots in the social and economic circumstances of people, and that if we give them a moderate sufficiency of what they want and ought to have, they will keep the peace."[40] On the rather optimistic premise that national governments do not have interests that are immutable, the functionalist argument suggests that cooperative engagements that yield mutually beneficial gains are bound to be repeated and sustained to a point in which state interests give way to the collective multinational interest. By seeking to "link authority to a specific activity, and to break away from the traditional link between authority and a definite territory,"[41] this argument therefore was used to provide a philosophical support in the case for European integration as well as global international relations.

Even within states and to the extent "that stability in society is the result of consensus about the broad ends of social action";[42] "functionalism can also help to create attitude change that cements the bonds of intercommunity relations."[43] Hence, "in order to deal with political problems it would be necessary first to tackle and solve functional problems"[44]—in the sense that necessary amenities and provisions must be made to serve the physiological, and security needs of the people; create an enabling environment for economic entrepreneurship, and enough space for the expression of specific liberties and engagement in public civic discourse without let or hindrance. However, and unlike Mitrany's emphasis on the relationship between states, my functionalist argument focuses on what happens within states and how the nature of interaction and exchange between various actors and institutions can enable functional processes that reinforce system continuity, stability, and effectiveness. My argument is not necessarily about states and how they relate to each other; rather it is about states and how they govern within themselves; and how the various units of the state system interacts or ought to interact in a functional way. The definition of function here relates to the activities, roles, and the design protocols necessary to keep the state functional—in the sense of carrying out that which states are supposed to do, as well as meeting the expectations of the people. There is therefore a practical distinction between the application of *functiona*lism in this work and that of Mitrany.

Functional analysis is "most appropriate in systems that have a tendency toward self-regulation or self-correction, with the result that the system preserves some equilibrium state (stable state) against random perturbations of the environment."[45] It deals less in matters of cause-and-effect relationships (although causal questions are important), rather it is more about how various activity sets and their interaction creates the possibility that a desired end state would be sustained in a predictable manner without much variation from original expectations. Although functional accounts do not exclude multiple causes in the absolute sense of the term, functionalism in this regard could be construed as an effort to "search for specific self-regulatory aspects of a social system and to examine the ways in which various traits of the system might contribute to its particular mode of self-regulation"[46] and durability. Social systems like states, often, are able to do this because of the level of slack already built into their mechanisms of operation. Slack provides an element of redundancy that allows system elements to continue to function even when unexpected or dramatic deviations from the norm occur. As a tool of adaptation, slack creates *functional equivalents* in the sense that "for a given functional problem (such as a rise in interest rates), there are usually a variety of possible solutions."[47] Using the American state as an example, the Federal Reserve Board could by means of its monetary policy lower its discount rate (prime lending rate) to commercial banks; the government could lower taxes to generate more disposable and investment incomes; or increase government spending to create more liquidity for private investment and reduction in unemployment. Because each of these macroeconomic tools could be used simultaneously or individually, they are "functional equivalents" that could help to sustain the state system in times of economic anomalies.

In the end, we are still left with some pressing but profound questions: Is the state system as currently understood serving all the needs for which it was created? Should we continue to engage the debate on which organizational forms could be more adaptable to contemporary or future political processes and public needs? How could rules, procedures, or functional relationships be made to self-adjust in times of dramatic change and systemic turbulence. While I do not assume that all the propositions put forth so far in this work will solve all of humanity's social, political, and organizational problems, there are nonetheless two essential reasons for this—the inability to judge and know in advance what really motivates individual actors to behave the way they do, or to make one choice instead of the other? Secondly, while choice-making reflects, to an extent, the nature and character of interests sought, it is difficult to determine in advance which specific interests or advantages are reconcilable to what ends and in what form? Nonetheless, these difficulties should not prevent us from seeking novel approaches for understanding the structural and institutional processes at work in matters that affect the ability of the state as an institutional mechanism for social control and political order.

ELEMENTS OF FUNCTIONAL THEORY

The maintenance of stable states is dependent on the ability of a government to legislate, enforce, and induce the structure of order which serves its own interest. It matters less what specific regime type the government is; rather this is based on the premise that all states have basic existential, foreign, and domestic policy objectives (although these may differ in terms of application, context, and culture). When citizens concede to or abide by the existing tenets of law and order as stipulated by the state and to the extent they continuously reinforce this behavior, the order thus acquires a life of its own and becomes a regulatory device. Because they have achieved the status of an objective reality that is collectively shared and assumed as important to the functioning of the social community, regulatory devices create structures of order that also turn the same regulatory devices into institutional facts. They become the normative symbols that undergird social behavior and conduct.

The three elements of functional theory that would be elaborated below and in consequent chapters are that states and governments function and adapt more effectively based on their ability to manage the friction or tension resulting from the interaction of system elements, including feedback loops (chapters 4 and 10); when prevailing institutionalization processes accommodate both cognitive (informal) and noncognitive (formal) categories (chapters 5 and 6); and in designing a system of structured or induced order applied consistently by way of requisite structures, communication, and sanction systems (chapter 6).

Interactionalism

The interactionist emphasis made here is drawn from the premise that social interaction is in part a causal process of mutual adjustment that may lead to intended but also unintended consequences.[48] One of the central features of social interaction is the enduring "conformity to collective practices, where the later are everywhere to be found in human societies."[49] And because collectively intentioned behaviors can be used to legitimize various status declarations that carry community-wide recognition, these collective practices serve to constitute a pattern of behavior that is acknowledged as the "*way we do things here*." Drawing from the tenets of general systems theory and cybernetics, I make the argument that the inherent problem of social systems does not result directly from the *interdependence* of the parts that make up the system; rather it derives from the friction or tension generated as a result of the *interaction* of those parts. The focus is not on the interdependencies that may exist between the parts of a system, but on the *interactional effects* or outcomes that result from their functional relationships.

It is also important to note that we cannot always expect to predict with certainty what the outcome of the interaction process (social or technical) would be since much of this is contingent on the magnitude of friction between the parts or units as well as other environmental or contextual factors that may dictate the interactional process itself. Oftentimes, these may generate negative externalities or unexpected contingencies that work against optimal expectations; but they also generate new demands to create new structures or institutions that eliminate or minimize the negative externalities so that positive outcomes would ensue.[50] As new problems or solutions emerge from the interactional process, it "may force actors (policy makers, administrators, or the public) to consider alternative ways of dealing with the problem; and by thought, borrowing, diffusion, trial and error, innovation, imitation, or luck, they create a sociocultural patterns or structures that resolves the problem, thereby facilitating adaptation."[51]

In human or social interactions, friction or tension is manifested in the form of conflict, competition, contradictions, adaptations, realignments, failures, or even victories that are generated at the point of contact between two or more system elements or properties. Although structural functionalism focuses on the implications of function on structure, the notion of *interactional functionalism* as advanced here focuses on the reciprocal effects of the interaction (friction) on the function itself. If the interactional process continuously yields positive outcomes and is constitutive of the relative interests of the various social actors, then that is all the more a reason to justify the application of more resources and continuous improvement (new learning and innovation) to stabilize and sustain the process. In this regard, I see the notion of *interactionalism* as a meta-theoretic device and one in which I have developed a specific interest within the general scheme of functional analysis, as will be demonstrated later. In the following sections, I will try to provide further illustrations to reinforce the central thesis advanced above.

When two or more variables (e.g., x, y, and z) or phenomena *collide* or rub against each other, they often generate a level of *friction* or tension; and how we manage the friction will determine whether the effect manifests in the predicted or expected way. It is by assessing the magnitude or intensity of the friction (from the interaction) that we are able to understand how changes in specific structural and institutional features (alignments and realignments) can reinforce existing stable states. Drawing from Newton's Laws in the physics and application of friction, drag, and elasticity between two competing forces, I offer further illumination on the central tenets of *interactionalism* and its theoretical application in functional analysis. How can two opposing or complementary forces come together to create a *function* (or *motion* in the Newtonian case)? According to Newton,[52] friction is a force that opposes relative motion between systems in contact, but then we still need to understand its more elementary general characteristics and the circumstances in which it unfolds. One of the characteristics of friction is that it is parallel to the contact surface between systems and always in a direction that opposes motion of the systems relative to each other. When two systems or objects are in contact but remain stationary, only static friction can act between them. There is little or no change in the properties of both objects except for the usual wear and tear, necessitated more by the magnitude, duration, or the amount of time it takes for the friction to come to an end. Alternatively, if two systems or objects are in contact and moving relative to one another, then the friction between them is called *kinetic friction*.

The concern of this work is focused on the two types of force structure, although more on kinetic friction which occurs at the interface where two parts or objects are in contact with each other and moving toward a specified direction (function), than on *static friction* (where the two parts or objects are stationary). I illustrate the same line of thought following the schematic equation as adapted from Urone and Hinrichs:[53] When there is no motion between two systems or objects, the magnitude of static friction f_s is:

$$f_s \leq \mu_s N$$

where μ_s is the coefficient of static friction and N is the magnitude of the normal force (the force perpendicular to the surface point or edge of the interaction between two objects or activity sets). The symbol ≤ means less than or equal to, implying that static friction can have a maximum value of $f_{s(max)} = \mu_s N$. Static friction is a responsive force that increases to be equal and opposite (has adaptive properties) to whatever force is exerted, up to its *maximum* limit $f_{s(max)}$. Once the applied force exceeds $f_{s(max)}$, the object will move, that is, achieve the *function* of motion. Once an object is moving, the magnitude of kinetic friction f_k is thus given by:

$$f_k = \mu_k N,$$

where μ_k is the coefficient of kinetic friction. A system in which $f_k = \mu_k N$ is described as a system in which friction behaves simply. The direction of friction is always opposite that of motion, parallel to the surface between objects, and perpendicular to the normal force. The objective here is to determine whether the coefficient of friction which is normally taken to be the ratio of the frictional resistance force to the normal force which presses the surfaces together (the surface being the edge or point of contact or interaction between two objects; or as conceived here, two activity sets) is equal to 1 (normal stable state) or greater than 1 (unstable or turbulent state). The coefficient of friction has a value between 0 and 1 but can in fact be greater than 1.[54] That is, there is essentially no limit. While a value of 1 means that the frictional force between two objects is equal to the normal force needed for specific functions, a coefficient of friction greater than 1 means that the friction is stronger than the normal force. Alternatively, a value of 0 means that there is no friction between the two objects, although this may not always be the case in real life because all contacts between objects always involve some kind of friction even if hard to notice.

Interactional Functionalism: A Frictional Metaphor

To begin to provide context and to demonstrate the applicability of the physics of friction to the phenomenon of interaction in functional analysis (construed in this regard as *interactional functionalism*), I will do two things here. First I will draw insights from the idea of *superadditivity* as illustrated by Scott Page in his logic of diversity and heuristics in the work place.[55] In developing his framework, Page argued that by seeing problems differently (diverse perspectives) and by looking for solutions in different ways (diverse heuristics), teams, groups, and organizations can achieve greater outcomes and innovations. Because combination of tools can be more powerful than the tools themselves, individual improvements in work processes can be combined in such a way that *superadditivity* is created when the total exceeds the sum of the parts. This is represented mathematically as 1+1 = 3 (this being the common outcome or heuristic resulting from the combined effort of 1 + 1). The notion offered here may not convey mathematical clarity or correctness in the conventional sense, but Page explains this by making the point that when we add heuristics, either of the two point to the same solution (in which case 1+1 =1) or the two heuristics differ (in which case 1+1 = 3); hence anytime you have two heuristics, you can create a third by *combining* the two heuristics.[56]

Secondly, utilizing the general equation of kinetic friction, I will attempt to generate a set of functional equations that could be employed in the determination of the level of friction, drag, or disturbance that we would normally experience when two corresponding or competing functions or activity sets interact with each other in the social world of human experience. Following Page's illustration, I assume the premise that1+1 =3; where 1 is an individual or an activity set, and 3 is the constitutive outcome (sum or heuristic) that is achieved by the combined effort of the two individuals or two different activity sets. In the above illustration, there are two individuals (1+1) and when they work effectively together, they will generate a functional structure, outcome, or heuristic (3) that is neither wholly related to each of the two individuals or activity sets but is a combination of both; hence, it is unique.

Let us consider each of the two individuals or activity sets as x and y, then the equation would be: $x + y = 3$, where 3 is the combined outcome of x and y. As already indicated above, the magnitude of kinetic friction f_k is given by $f_k = \mu_k N$; hence we can readapt this equation for our current purpose to construct a new equation between x and y, in such a way that:

$$F = \mu xy \geq 0 \qquad \text{Equation 1}$$

Where

μ = the coefficient of the friction (interaction) generated by x and y; and for instance:
x = the first individual or activity set, and
y = the second individual or activity set.

We therefore get $F_f = \mu(1)(1) \geq 0$; which mathematically translates to

$$F_f = \mu 1 \geq 0$$

The magnitude of the friction is normal, hence the interactional effects between x and y should be able to maintain a stable state or functional equilibrium.

Drawing insight from Scott Page's illustration of *superadditivity* (1+1 = 3); I reconstitute the equation as $x + y = 3$, where 3 is the combined outcome or heuristic value of the combined interaction of x and y, such that $F_f = 3(x)(y) \geq 0$

Where

$x = 1$

$y = 1$

3 = (the constant coefficient of the outcome or heuristic value derived from the interaction or combined effort of x and y), such that:

$$F_f = 3(1)(1) \geq 0$$

$$F_f = 3 \geq 0 \qquad \text{Equation 2}$$

The magnitude of the friction is greater than 1, hence the interactional effects between x and y is more than normal and may lead to increased tension or dysfunction in current activities.

But in situations where there are more than 2 individuals or activity sets interacting with each other to produce a particular outcome, we can still adapt this situation by way of *substitution*. Let us then say that there are 3 individuals (x_1, x_2, x_3) performing a specific activity set and another set of 4 individuals (y_1, y_2, y_3, y_4) also performing another set of complementary activity sets; but the activities or individuals must always interact simultaneously so as to effect a required outcome. To capture this situation and the interactional effects, this would lead to the following function (figure 1.1):

Assume K = 3 (constant from the *superadditivity*), n = 3 individuals or activity sets m = 4 individuals or activity sets

$$\sum_{i=1}^{n} x_i \sum_{i=1}^{m} y_i$$

Figure 1.1 Summation of Interactional Effects between Individuals and Activity Sets.
Source: Author.

Note: We are using K as a surrogate for μ since it represents the base outcome of any interaction between two individuals or activity sets if we follow the principles illustrated in Scott Page's thesis on superadditivity.

Equation 3

$$F_f = K(x_n)(y_m) \geq 0$$

$$F_f = 3(3)(4) \geq 0$$

$$F_f = 36 \geq 0$$

Where

x_n = 3 individuals or activity sets
y_m = 4 individuals or activity sets
K = 3 (constant).

Because one cannot interact with oneself and an activity set cannot interact with itself but must do so with others, it would thus suggest that the minimum threshold of 1 + 1 will naturally and always yield 3 (which is the combined product or outcome of at least two individuals or activity sets engaged in an interactional episode). For the purpose of this formulation, the product or outcome of 1 + 1 will be such that 3 will always be held as a *constant* or a *given*. The magnitude of the combined friction of the seven individuals or activity sets is 36 (greater than 1), hence the combined interactional effects between x_n and y_m though greater than normal would still be sufficient to maintain a stable state and efficient functioning of the various activity sets. This is so because the independent effects of each of the individual participants or activity sets is within the range of normality at 36/7 = 5.14 (within the tolerable range of normal friction). I admit though that there may be some exceptions to the rule, particularly in situations where some of the individual participants or activity sets may involve greater responsibilities and influence more than the others, hence there could be larger variations in their independent contributory effects. Large variations can also occur as a result of the natural process of negative entropy (the tendency for systems to gravitate toward disorder or a state of ultimate dissolution), but this is always the case in matters concerning most systems and objects in the physical world of human experience and action situations. But the larger point made here is that "whenever interdependent individuals are thought to be acting in an organized fashion, several layers of universal components create the structure that affects their behavior and the outcomes they achieve."[57] These outcomes have causal properties in the sense that they could also lead to results that play complementary or dysfunctional roles in the structural arrangements within which these roles are played out.

There are also factors inherent in the very notion of friction or interaction, such as drag, which could resist the smooth functioning of the process. Within individual participants, drag force could manifest as a function of differences in motives or interests, technical specialization, attitude to work, cognitive structures, different idiosyncratic behaviors, or other psychosocial anomalies. And from the standpoint of objective activity sets, drag could also be a result of procedural or technical issues, timing, resource scarcity, inadequate skill sets, or a declining complementarity of roles. Although agencies, participants, or other social actors could arbitrarily set their own tolerance range based on their unique features or structural forms; they can adjust the number of individual participants, activity sets, or functional units accordingly to fit within their tolerance range. But what I have done here nonetheless is to establish a minimum baseline of the independent effects on the magnitude of the interactional friction, and this should be a key consideration in any effort at functional analysis.

The interactional perspective as developed here could also be useful in interstate negotiations, game theoretic decision making, in the governance of multilateral treaties or regimes, or as a tool for understanding some of the games people play in diplomatic negotiations. What this suggests, at least in the context of interaction within and among social systems, is that interaction can either be observable or not, but either way, they do generate institutional effects that have the tendency to branch out in different directions. As John Searle points out, "all institutional effects (including those cases that seem to have an abstract or free-floating ontology) still do bottom out in *brute facts* as reflected in actual human beings and the sounds and marks that constitute their linguistic (language) representations."[58] These representations could already be seen in various forms of social, economic, or political interactions. We have diplomatic interactions (foreign policy), economic interactions (trade policy), military interaction (warfare), humanitarian interaction (relief aid), cross-border interaction (legal and illegal immigration), political interaction (electoral competitions), and on to infinite regress. In each of these structures of interaction, there are positive or negative consequences—some of these tied to the interactional episodes themselves or to different types of idiosyncratic baggage and interests people bring into the process. And oftentimes, the language of interaction can affect the structure of interaction (and vice versa) in such a way that we not only do more than represent particular interests, but "we also simply create that which is represented."[59]

Language usage is at the center of most social, political, and economic transactions, but it is also a crucial factor in the development or mitigation of tension between and among interacting social actors. So far, what I believe we can have an agreement on is that any form of interaction has the potential to generate some form of friction or tension, and this could be physical, psychological, or emotional. It could be a benign tension (in which case the purpose of the interaction is sustained) or it could be a hostile one (in which case the objective of the interaction is undermined). Benign tension often leads to compromise and accommodation, while hostile tensions generally result in disagreement and conflict. The basis for the conflict could be tied to the nature and magnitude of the interaction itself and the implied sets of disparate interests that are lodged within it. Apart from the fact that human actors oftentimes can be cognitively conflicted within themselves in their choice-making, but then that is a different kind of conflict. I am talking about conflict between two or more actors in the search for some kind of mutual or collective accommodation.

What I have therefore argued in this regard is that any grand theory of conflict must also of necessity draw upon a frictional theory of interaction. This postulation can also be considered in the context of an interactional engagement under bilateral or multilateral conditions. Bilateralism generates a single dyad (interaction between two parties), while multilateralism generates multiple dyads (interaction between three or more parties). Because multiple dyads are more likely to harbor multiple competing and disparate interests, they are more likely to abrade against each other with greater intensity—thereby creating multiple sources of conflict, acrimony, and oftentimes sustained regression from the existing norm. It could also lead to higher transactions costs in terms of coordination problems, compliance issues, and increased propensity for unilateral defection. In the end, although interacting social actors may seek to establish recognizable and enduring patterns of behavior that overtime become institutionalized into a form of structured or normative order, the magnitude of the tension generated as a result of the interaction often lead to the opposite effect in which selection pressures force actors to dig in their heels (refuse to compromise) in their choice-making calculus. Institutionalization therefore can be an essential factor in the mitigation of tension or conflict.

Institutionalization

Institutions are guideposts and constraints that shape the nature of individual and social actions, and in most cases, the context within which social interactions takes place. They can come in the form of norms, values, practices, customs, contracts, laws and regulations, formal and informal structures of order. As a working premise, people also carry institutional facts (knowledge of those things, artifacts, or symbols that we collectively attribute to and are uniquely associated with particular institutions) in their heads, such that consequent actions are initiated when representations of these institutional facts are cognitively triggered in the person. It also initiates a process of self-awareness and reflective search on the part of the individual to justify the fact that a specific behavior is consistent (pattern recognition) with the collective intention on how the object or subject matter ought to or should be handled.

I have argued in chapter 6 that institutions comprise of cognitive and non-cognitive categories, which essentially implies that at any particular point in time, human beings and what they do or think about in particular situations are consistently shaped by forces spread across a widening spectrum of competing institutional matrix. Institutional effects may be context-specific or they may be context-free; but to the extent that what we know about them or their constitutive properties (that which belongs to specific institutions and what they represent) are embedded in human cognition, institutions can be said to be everywhere. The government is an institution as well as an organizing system, and so are the political culture, the economy, the law, and the prevailing social mores and norms. "Institutions do not cause outcomes on their own, but they set the framework within which contending interests engage each other; hence interests and the ideas that lie behind them are the fundamental drivers in political life."[60] "Social institutions and the conventions they embody, therefore contribute to the integration, stability, and maintenance of the social system as a whole";[61] and "because institutional patterns consist of norms defining what action and attitudes are legitimately expected of people,"[62] "they are causal insofar as they regulate behavior."[63]

In the normal process of state governance, it is important for citizens to understand the structural framework within which old norms and new practices would converge and how the emerging new normal would affect their daily lives, thereby making adaptation more acceptable as well as tolerable. "Social institutions economize reasoning by making activities routine and computationally easier";[64] thereby reinforcing existing standards of order and control in a more predictable way. However, this is not to suggest that the dynamics of the political system could not work in unexpected directions. To the contrary, it is quite possible that the prevailing institutional architecture could be the source of continued misunderstanding between parties, in the same way that societal and cultural differences do. But then this is much easier to overcome in circumstances where there is already an implicit understanding (institutionalized norms) among the political elites on the importance of preserving the unity and sovereignty of the state; and where practice and precedents have already acquired a life of their own by shaping prevailing beliefs and behaviors in a supportive way.

When individual behaviors become routinized and are seen as essentially conforming to an acceptable social convention and established rules of appropriate behavior, they help to validate the functional role of institutions. There is a practical example that could help to illuminate the hypothesis that I seek to construct here. For example, we can have a situation where four cars suddenly arrive at a crossroad all at the same time. This situation can only be resolved by a consideration of the law, common sense, and ordinary human reciprocity (practice)—all intervening at the same time. If none of the drivers decide to heed to any of the above three considerations, then they would most likely hit and wreck each other. But what this situation requires is a shared understanding that it would be in the mutual interest of all concerned, and in fact, of society as a whole, for this situation to be negotiated in such a way that each of them gets the right of way one after the other. It might take a few seconds, but then what is important is that this habit be repeated several times and always in similar contexts.

Institutions (e.g., laws, contracts, Departments, or Agencies) have *status functions* in the sense that they are broadly recognized, but also because they are the product of collective intensions, aspirations, and objectives. Because status functions carry "*deontic powers*, they objectively and from a distance impose rights, duties, obligations, requirements, permissions, authorizations, entitlements, etc, on us."[65] The simple recognition of prevailing institutions and the individual temperament required to obey them can, in and of itself, become a regulatory and an ordering device that reinforces the durability and efficacy of the social system. To the extent that such behavior serves as an *ordering device* and is constantly repeated in situations of this nature, we can then begin to say that the process of institutionalization has taken place—but in a functionally supportive way. The central arguments advanced here would be further explored in the forthcoming chapters 5 and 6.

Structured or Induced Order

In his conceptualization of the functional prerequisites of social systems, Talcott Parsons argued that the functional problem of all social systems is the "motivational problem of order"[66]—the aggregate effort to minimize potentially disruptive behavior and the motivation to it. This latter fact may develop when disruptive tendencies become randomly organized as a sub-system in such a way as to impinge on strategic points in the social system itself, but still not constitute an existential threat to its stability. The notion of structured or induced order is, in and of itself, an organizing principle. But it would also require other factors such as individual attitude, civility, citizenship roles and responsibility on the part of the individual to routinize these practices as an ongoing normative obligation. If a "practice is introduced and sustained by the fact that it produces the expected benefit (*hygienic conditions, safety, comfort*, etc.) and its disposition to produce the benefit leads to its selection by intentional actors; the consequent disposition of the practice to produce the benefit *causes* its persistence because it leads agents (*participants*) to adopt this practice"[67] "Rules, however strict, would simply be ignored if the agent had no motivation for following them; but because human agents are capable of thinking and acting under the presupposition of freedom, a system of rules or orders will work only if there is some reason to obey them."[68] And reasons there are, such as to contribute to public welfare, self-interest, legal conformity, or simply to avoid sanctions, or popular rejection. But then there are also many occasions where one does not and should not have these kinds of choices, and where compliance may be non-negotiable.

Drawing upon insight from cognitive psychology, I delineate in chapter 6 the central elements of a structured or induced order, and how it is reinforced in the broader context of the structural-normative aspect of this work. I make the case that social institutions (such as the habit of taking out one's garbage to the curbside for the truck pick-up every Friday morning) "basically consist of a norm system and a system of *social practices* conducive to the satisfaction of these norms."[69] Among these social practices is that people seemingly and involuntarily engage in what I would call *"initiating structures"* on a routine basis prior to actually taking the garbage out to the curbside. They put everything in plastic bags (sometimes sorted by category—plastics, paper, bottles, etc.), tie them up, put them in the garbage bin, and take them out for the collection (instead of just throwing them out there). People rarely think about or reflect on these mundane activities simply because they have become part of the collectively intentioned social practices. What is also very important is that the various instruments of induced order and their applications be continuously updated as the practical conditions and tolerance levels change over time. I will elaborate on this in greater detail in chapter 6. In the following sections, I will diverge a bit to explore the nature of social systems and their functional properties, and then discuss how states as social systems help to shape or structure the processes by which social action become institutionalized. In the end, we should be able to get a deeper sense of the evolving nexus between social practices, the structure of order, and their mutual reinforcement as they journey (or are dragged) along toward the path in which they become increasingly institutionalized.

THE STRUCTURE OF SOCIAL SYSTEMS AND ACTION

A state is an organizational construct representing an aggregation of three elements: *structure, process, and individuals*. It is only when the three elements work together in such a way that the purpose for which the state exists is preserved, that we can then say that the state is functional. The problem of states, therefore, revolves around "how to create a stable political system; how to make such a system effective in meeting the demands placed upon it; and how to adapt to changing external environments or to internal changes within a society."[70] Although many states face the challenge of state-building in different ways and under different conditions; but the very structure of government and the ways and means of engagement in the political system, could undermine the ability of the state to deal decisively with most pressing issues of national interest. In the analysis of the structure of any social system, one has to look seriously at the prevailing value pattern—the basic orientation of the system to the situation in which it operates, which, invariably, guides the activities of participant individuals.[71]

There are three main objectives of this book: to explore the processes by which the structure of states can create mutually reinforcing and self-regulatory functions that sustain system stability and purpose; how states can adapt to environmental changes and feedback loops yet stay on course to serve their primary purpose; and the integration of specific theoretical models and the linkages between them in the analysis of state action. In this regard, my conceptualization and analysis draw from three broad theoretical frameworks such as structural functionalism, general systems theory/cybernetics, and organizational theory and behavior. Because the central arguments are framed around technical and subject matter orientations generally associated with disciplines such as political science, biology, physics, and sociology; it is hoped that the interdisciplinary orientation and the underlying assumptions embodied in these theories and the operational linkages between them would be able to provide a level of explanatory power critical to a greater understanding of why some states have done quite well and remained relatively stable over time, and why it has not worked out so well for others.

There are several uses of theory in social science, but among these are that theories supply frameworks within which concepts and variables acquire specific significance; which ultimately enables us to interpret the larger meaning of our findings as well as in making "fundamental assumptions about human behavior."[72] The point of any science is to develop a set of theories to explain the events within their range of observation; hence a theory is only as good as its present and potential uses in explaining observations."[73] To the extent that a theory helps us to generate ideas for research and when it leads to other theoretical ideas, it can thus be seen as having heuristic value.[74] Since much of my work and training has been in the political and social sciences, but less so in matters that mainly concern the physical sciences; I have always believed that both spectrums of the sciences stand very much to be enriched by one another, and that theoretical integration across the board (where possible) can be very useful in designing novel and innovative approaches to dealing with the problems of human and social organization. The title of this book is *A Functional Theory of Government, Law, and Institutions*. I emphasize the "A" in the title for the simple fact that we are dealing with a social system in which many events are somewhat unpredictable, and where the psychology of the human mind can oftentimes betray the outward expression one observes. The claim made here is, therefore, driven more by the practical and logical implications of the everyday experience of life in a social system and the reciprocal demands they impose on each other.

The idea of a social system is not necessarily about the independent units that make it up, but rather, it is about the *relational scheme* that binds one unit to the other, and how it enables the whole to evolve and endure. Analysis of social systems should therefore be concerned about the "structure and processes of the system built up by the relations of such units to their situations; but less about the internal structure of the units except so far as this directly bears on the relational system."[75] The existence of any social system or collectivity is based on the nature of pattern maintenance and a cultural or normative system that reinforces continuity within the pattern. Reduced to its barest minimum, "a social system consists in a plurality of individual actors interacting with each other in a situation which has at least a physical or environmental aspect, actors who are motivated in terms of a tendency to the 'optimization of gratification' and whose relation to their situations, including to each other, is defined and mediated in terms of a system of culturally structured and shared symbols."[76] Structure, in this regard, "refers to the structuring properties allowing the binding of time-space in social systems, the properties which make it possible for discernibly similar social practices to exist across varying spans of time and space and which lend them 'systemic' form."[77] The "flow of action across time continually produces consequences which are either intended or unintended by actors; and these unintended consequences also may form unacknowledged conditions of action in a feedback fashion."[78] By "engaging in certain practices individuals produce and reproduce the social structures that constitute and regulate those practices and their associated identities."[79] In "reproducing structural properties, actors also reproduce the conditions that make such action possible."[80] And this suggests that "the moment of the production of action is also one of reproduction in the contexts of the day-to-day enactment of social life."[81]

What this therefore tells us is that, contrary to what most literature may suggest, the idea of structure can be analyzed based on two orientations—the external process reinforced by laws, rules and regulations, hierarchy, and routines; and the internal subjective orientation involving the individual actor in terms of knowledge, beliefs, idiosyncrasies, and obedience to the established standards of conformity. Once individual behavior develops a standard pattern or logical sequence in a regularized and formal manner, then it becomes an implicit part of the existing structure and relationships. What we think, always and in most cases, dictates what we do. "Mental states and events are representational states and, as such, are what they are by virtue of what they are about."[82] Structure, therefore, has no existence independent of the knowledge that agents have about what they do in their day-to-day activities—even when they may know little of the ramified consequences of the activities in which they engage.[83] Social systems, once in existence, tend to reproduce themselves while maintaining internal and external checks and balances for system stability and durability, on the collective assumption that the various activities within the system will serve a positive end or utility. Part of this is "rooted in the human need for ontological security—which creates a generalized preference for order and predictability; and the other is based on the internalization of roles and identities, which generates subjective commitments to objective positions in society."[84] Although external sources of instability are less predictable, "internal sources of stability refer to sources within actors that make them not want change."[85]

While it is necessary to make analytical distinctions of the various components that make up the social system, yet we cannot understand its identity and function outside of its constitutive properties. But above all, there are involuntary impulses that enable social systems to maintain a sense of *being* and identity, particularly when actors have come to embrace the collective notion of "we" as opposed to "me." The idea of "we" suggests the existence of shared norms, purpose, culture, and collective interest. "Collective interests mean that actors make the welfare of the group an end in itself, which will in turn help them overcome collective action problems; hence when their culture is threatened, well socialized actors will tend instinctively to defend it."[86] Social systems seek to fuse constraint and enablement in such a way that individual actors become more self-disciplined in following established protocols of appropriate and acceptable behavior. Although "role expectations organize in accordance with general value-orientations, the reciprocities, expectations, and responses to those expectations in the specific interaction systems of ego and one or more alters; but it is in this reciprocity or complementarity that sanctions enter and acquire their place in systems of action."[87] In this regard, enablement encourages individuals toward positive and system-enabling actions, while "constraint presupposes a range of normative sanctions which may be deployed against those whose conduct is condemned or disapproved of by others."[88] Enablement and constraint impose passive rule-conformity as well as deterrence in the orientation of behavior as well as action; hence it is by these *functional* properties that we have come to know and appreciate them.

Functional Properties of Social Systems

A relationship between two or more individuals ordinarily involves a kind of interaction or communication; but when it involves a community or a large society made up of many people, the nature of the interaction becomes more complex and differentiated. When sustained overtime with increased regularity and as patterns of social ordering emerge, the interactional process develops structures or activity patterns that take up a life of their own. By designating both the process by which social life is created and recreated into recurrent patterns with identifiable outcomes or products;[89] they become social organizations through which members attach meaning to their daily lives and experiences. At the cultural level, while beliefs and ideas can shape societies, change personalities, and even produce heroes; it also concurrently reflects the social life, personality structures, and organic characteristics of their components.[90] "Regardless of its size, location or particular form, social organization develops whenever individuals create stable social relationships that display patterns of social ordering and become infused with shared cultural ideas."[91] Although the process of social organization can assume or produce unlimited specific forms such as friendships, schools, churches, interest groups, nuclear families, governments, societies, gangs, cartels, caste systems,[92] the emphasis of this work is on one specific type of social organization—the state, and by implication the government. I consider the state as an overarching social organization while the others previously mentioned are considered as sub-units or sub-social organizations—all of which are encompassed or exist within the state. In this context, the development of social organization involves the interdependence of individual personality, social order (community), and culture all of which are sub-systemic elements. In the same way that "communities exercise many constraints upon the actions of their members, the sustenance needs and personality characteristics of individuals also continually affect the nature and scope of community activities."[93] In most cases, it is important to note that when we refer to a social organization as having a character, we are simply referring to the nature of the relationships and interactions between the various components. Sometimes these could be referred to as activity sets (the mode of production) or processes which help to secure the necessities for mutual coexistence and stability within the social organization.

On the premise that the mode of production of material life conditions the social, political, and intellectual life processes within the social system (the state),[94] we can compare two illustrations of the means by which social organizations acquire their character as well as function. I draw upon Auguste Comte's positivist politics and the Marxian thesis founded on a materialistic interpretation of history. In Comtean terms, there are three main structures of society and they are built around power, class, and occupation; but then this is presided over by a superstructure (the state) by virtue of its controlling influence on power, property, and labor.[95] Power therefore grants wealth, control, and autonomy. But for Karl Marx, "no society survives without an appropriate means of subsistence (division of labor and production), a mobilizing action driven by an ideological superstructure, and without the invention and use of artifacts or symbolisms (which it must use as material carriers to express or manifest itself)."[96] Orthodox Marxism has always laid greater emphasis on what is referred to as economic reductionism—"which interpreted the dynamics of history primarily in terms of economic development in the base that supposedly controlled developments within the superstructure. It was therefore deterministic in two ways, in that while the economic base determined the superstructure, laws of history, rooted in the economy, determined the trajectory of social life."[97] By locating power and property in the domain of the bourgeoisie, and labor as the preserve of the proletariat, Marx argued that the structure of relations between the two classes is based on the nature and mechanism of exchange (an institutional artifact). On the one hand, the bourgeoisie (owners of the factors of production) offer monetary rewards or compensation to the proletariat (workers) in exchange for their labor; but this is done in such a way that while the bourgeoisie creates surplus value for itself (which it uses to control the economic superstructure of the state or what Marx calls "monopoly or state capitalism"), it at the same time pauperizes the proletariat through exploitation and a structure of dependency. Casting the framework of his argument on the premise that "relations of production exist in order to promote the forces of production and the state exists in order to protect the interests of the capitalist class, Marx could also be said to have made functionalist claims."[98]

There are a few assumptions that could be drawn from the above. One is that social relations create a pattern of order, and in most cases a hierarchy. The second is that any pattern of order creates a structure of advantage and disadvantage, and depending on where one is located on the continuum, advantage is oftentimes a function of power, control, and authority. Depending on the nature of the relations between the state and the economy, it is also the case that when private bourgeoisie interests morph into the sphere of political authority, radical social change becomes more difficult, although not impossible. We can therefore make the case that in social systems, variations and change occur as a result of changes in the structure of relations between the constituent units, in the scope and magnitude of interactions between the units; or as a result of "differentiation in functional systems such as the economy, the state, or in cultural spheres such as religion, ideology, and custom."[99] In the above section, I have tried to explain the structure and functional properties of social systems broadly construed; but what I seek to do in the following section is to recast the idea of the state and to discuss it more tightly in the context of its role as a social system.

THE STATE AS SOCIAL SYSTEM

As a rule, social systems also follow the general principles of all systems (including mechanical and biological systems). Since they are literarily exposed to the larger environment of which they are a part, social systems are also open systems. While this is a framework that will be explored further in chapter 4 of this book, what I want to point out is that states can equally be construed as organizations and as open systems. Through the institution of government, the state engages in the same types of actions one would see in typical bureaucratic organizations—such as agreements concerning policy decisions and objectives, allocation of roles and functions, systems of accountability, and coordination for implementation and results. Social systems in the context of states "comprises of unit acts in which status roles are connected to each other through *interaction systems* comprised of a plurality of actors occupying statuses and enacting normatively presented roles."[100] Faced with the constant struggle in the search to maintain system stability and continuity, states as social systems must also satisfy several structural and functional imperatives. The most important single condition of the integration of an interactive system is a shared basis of normative order, common culture or a symbolic code (such as a language);[101] the allocation of human capacities and human resources among tasks;[102] the allocation of facilities for the performance of roles;[103] emphasis on the achievement of goals through collaboration in complementary role situations;[104] and ensuring that the distinction between rewards and facilities is not one between the intrinsic properties of the relevant objects, but concerns rather their *functional* relations in the system of action.[105] The last point is very essential and will be engaged at every corner and intersection throughout the rest of this book.

A functional social system requires a degree of compatibility between the various elements of the action system (individuals, the interactive systems, and the cultural orientation) that make it up. By exploring Parsons's detailed account of the *Social System*,[106] I am able to draw out a series of foundational propositions. His account which I will summarize below provides a solid sociological basis and a mirror through which we can begin to understand why some states succeed and why others fail; and why internal incompatibility of system elements can play a destabilizing role in the fate of nations or states. The eight items below pretty much summarize Parsons' functional prerequisites of social systems.[107]

1. A social system cannot be structured as to be radically incompatible with the conditions of functioning of its component individual actors (as biological organisms and as personalities) or of a cultural system.

2. A social system depends on the requisite minimum of support from each of the other systems.
3. It must have a sufficient proportion of its component actors adequately motivated to act in accordance with the requirements of its role system, positively in the fulfillment of expectations and negatively in abstention from too much disruptive or deviant behavior.
4. It must avoid commitment to cultural patterns which, either fail to define a minimum order; or which place impossible demands on people and thereby generate deviance and conflict to a degree which is incompatible with the minimum conditions of stability or orderly development.
5. The minimum needs of individual actors constitute a set of conditions to which the social system must be adapted. However, it is not the needs of all the participant actors which must be met, nor all the needs of anyone; but only a sufficient proportion for a sufficient fraction of the population.
6. There is a need to secure adequate participation of a sufficient proportion of the individual actors in the social system; that is to motivate them adequately to the performances which may be necessary if the social system is to persist or develop.
7. The significance of an action is to be understood not directly and primarily in terms of its motivation but of its actual or probable consequences for the system.
8. The functional problem of all social systems is the "motivational problem of order"—minimizing potentially disruptive behavior and the motivation to it.

It should now be quite obvious that many contemporary states do not meet some or most of the above stipulations. It can also be used to illuminate our current understanding concerning the role that regime types, ideological differences, ethnicity, historical experiences, cultural practices, and power asymmetries play in the stability of states, mechanisms of social control, as well as the durability of existing institutions. When different cultural or ethnic groups make up a social system (Stipulation 4), it is important that emphasis be placed on building cross-cutting cleavages that reinforce the mutual progress and development of all parties. A social system therefore "is not possible without certain minimum patterns of culture; such as empirical knowledge necessary to cope with situational exigencies and sufficiently integrated patterns of expressive symbolism and value orientations."[108] Most of the crises that have befallen some developing and underdeveloped states are that they have allowed cultural or religious differences to dominate and become the center of gravity in national politics. When such differences become the basis for political power and majority rule in a country, it also tends to sow the seeds of resentment on the part of the ethnic groups that are in the minority. This can generate either discontent or outright hostility with enormous consequences for the functioning of the social system.

Another example that fits quite well with Stipulation 7 (above) would be the phenomenon of corruption and other types of political and official malfeasance. Most of the people (or probably all of them) who engage in corruption do not consider as much how it affects the system as opposed to how it benefits or serves their own independent ends. The same applies to regime types or countries in which much of the civil liberties have been proscribed. If majority of totalitarian regimes that have existed or exists today in the world ever contemplated the consequences of their actions before they undertook them, perhaps the damage to the emergent political society would have been more limited. The above illustrations also point to a larger phenomenon; that the problem of the state is also a problem of the social system within which it operates or evolves. And at the center of the argument is that which should make states function in such a way that they are able to serve the ends for which they were created. It can also help us in addressing "questions about the once-and-for-all causes of events—so that by knowing how things got the way they are, we would be in a better position to judge whether that is the way they ought to be; and questions about functions of institutions—so that we would have a better idea of what we would be up against if we tried to change them."[109] These questions are asked, not as ends in themselves, but as a means for eliciting guides for judgment and action within social systems and for reaching consensus on competing policy preferences.[110] We can therefore draw on "the insight that action systems are structured in three ways: the individual actor, the integrative system, and the system of cultural patterning. And to the extent that each implies the other, the variability of any one is limited by its compatibility with the minimum conditions of functioning of each of the other two."[111] To remain functional, the internal properties of a social system must be able to permeate each of the units in such a way that the push-pull of inertial forces always tilts the balance in a positive and system-maintaining direction.

In their much referenced piece *Why Nations Fail: The Origins of Power, Prosperity, and Poverty*,[112] Acemoglu and Robinson argue that structural differences within societies and the prevailing institutions can provide causal explanations for poverty and inequality between and within states. They sought to demonstrate how "political and economic institutions interact in causing poverty or prosperity, and how different parts of the world ended up with such different sets of institutions."[113] And they came to the conclusion that although "the political process may determine what economic institutions people live under; it is the political institutions that determine how this process works. Hence as institutions influence behavior and incentives in real life, they forge the success or failure of states."[114] In his own account, Jared Diamond offers sets of behavioral and ecological reasons why some societies have failed while others succeeded.[115] Among some of the reasons he cites are that of societies failing to anticipate problems of which they lacked prior experience, failure to perceive a problem that has actually arrived until it is too late, failure to solve perceived problems because of conflicts of interest, inability to detect slow trends concealed within noisy fluctuations (*creeping normalcy*), persistence in error and refusal to draw inference from negative signs (*mental stagnation*), holding on to core values even when changing times necessitate otherwise. He also points to differences among environments, and environmental problems such as catastrophic deforestation, loss of arable lands, and overpopulation.

In addition to the structural and behavioral arguments already made, I am of the view that states do not actually fail; rather it is the institutions empowered to serve its public purpose that fail. What we erroneously refer to as *state failure* is actually a mask for *institutional failure*, and this includes failure in leadership structure and capacity or what I would call *imaginative entrepreneurship*—the ability to rationalize or take bold initiatives even when all the square pegs have not yet been comfortably placed into square holes. Institutional failure therefore is a function of:

- The inability of some countries to utilize that which nature has endowed to create a transformative economy consistent with the sociopolitical and cultural imperatives of the society.[116]
- The inability to address contingent market failures, as well as guarantee of property rights
- Limited or absence of critical vision shaped by great revolutionary ideas
- Limited human and capital resources including expertise and leadership skills
- Indecision in selecting policy priorities and lack of political will or consensus in their implementation
- The failure to see the activity of *learning* (including *mimetic* learning) as a means, but not as an end in itself.

In the final analysis, what comes across in all of these is that the sources of "state failure" are everywhere and can come from anywhere, both internally and externally. Many of the reasons, therefore, are not too far removed from each other. For example, when *societies* fail (as envisioned above by Diamond), they more often than not, take the *state* with them. Contemporary examples abound of states such as the former Soviet Union, Somali, Yemen, Iraq, Liberia, Syria, Libya, and Afghanistan in which much of the institutional architecture, for one reason or the other, disentangled and imploded from within. Although some of them may still be in existence today so to say, but they are barely as functional as the skeletal remains of a bygone civilization.

There are ten chapters in this book each of them dealing, in their own ways, with specific themes surrounding the functional role of the state as a social system, the role of government in providing the institutional framework within which social action takes place, and how ontological and philosophy of science considerations helps to illuminate our understanding of the objective and subjective phenomena that shape the social and political world of human experience. In chapter 1, I set the stage with an extended discussion of the epistemological and philosophy of science issues, the method of social scientific inquiry, as well as address several ontological questions and causal processes that often lead to different system outcomes. In addition to discussing the functional properties of social systems, and the utility of functional theory in the analysis of state action, the chapter also delineates the central elements of functional theory (interactionalism, institutionalization, and the notion of structured or induced order) which informs the central theses and several arguments made in this work.

In the following chapter 2, I discuss the distinction between the state and government as well as the ontological issues associated with both. In addition to delineating the characteristics and obligations of the modern state and the contemporary challenges it faces, I also focus on some central thematic areas such as the complexity of social systems, conformity and obedience to authority, and processes of legitimation. Further, I delve into the issue of values, the enduring ruptures in public and private values, and how emerging tensions between and within value premises breeds increased complexity and uncertainty in the role of the modern state as an organizing symbol for system-wide stability, social order, and mutual coexistence in an increasingly turbulent world characterized by the pursuit of power, interest, and preeminence.

NOTES

1. Wendt, Alexander. 1999. *Social Theory of International Politics*. New York: Cambridge University Press, 79.
2. http://www.thoughtco.com/functionalist-perspective-3026625. Accessed on December 2, 2018.
3. Wendt, Alexander. 1999. *Social Theory of International Politics,* 371–372.
4. Wendt, Alexander. 1999. *Social Theory of International Politics*, 373.
5. Wendt, Alexander. 1999. *Social Theory of International Politics*, 373–375.

6. Little, Daniel. 1991. *Varieties of Social Explanation: An Introduction to the Philosophy of Social Science*. Boulder, CO: Westview Press, 91.

7. Ostrom, Elinor. 2011. "Background on the Institutional Analysis and Development Framework." *The Policy Studies Journal* 39, no. 1: 7–27, 10. Accordingly Ostrom, "*action situations* are the social spaces where individuals interact, exchange goods and services, solve problems, dominate one another, or fight (among the many things that individuals do in action situations," 11.

8. Ostrom, Elinor. 2011. "Background on the Institutional Analysis and Development Framework," 39, 10.

9. Habermas, Jurgen. 1975. *Legitimation Crisis*. Boston, MA: Beacon Press, 118.

10. Habermas, Jurgen. 1975. *Legitimation Crisis*, 118–119.

11. Searle, John R. 2006. "Social Ontology: Some Basic Principles." *Papers 80*: 51–71, 55.

12. Mueller, Get H. 1989. *Sociology and Ontology: The Analytical Foundations of Social Theory*. Lanham, MD: University Press of America, 4.

13. Mueller, Get H. 1989. *Sociology and Ontology: The Analytical Foundations of Social Theory*, 4.

14. Mueller, Get H. 1989. *Sociology and Ontology: The Analytical Foundations of Social Theory*, 26.

15. Mueller, Get H. 1989. *Sociology and Ontology: The Analytical Foundations of Social Theory*, 4.

16. Mueller, Get H. 1989. *Sociology and Ontology: The Analytical Foundations of Social Theory*, 5.

17. Wendt, Alexander. 1999. *Social Theory of International Politics*, 78.

18. Durkheim, Emile. 1994. Social Facts. In *Readings in the Philosophy of Social Science*, edited by Michael Martin and Lee C. McIntyre, 433–440. Cambridge, MA: The MIT Press, 433.

19. Durkheim, Emile. 1994. Social Facts. In *Readings in the Philosophy of Social Science*, 433.

20. Faundez, Julio. 2016. "Douglas North's Theory of Institutions: Lessons for Law and Development." *Hague Journal of Rule of Law* 8: 373–419, 394.

21. Parsons, Talcott and Edward A. Shils. 2001. *Toward a General Theory of Action: Theoretical Foundations for the Social Sciences*. New Brunswick, NJ: Transaction Publishers, 203.

22. Lawson, Tony. 2012. "Ontology and the Study of Social Reality: Emergence, Organization, Community, Power, Social Relations, Corporations, Artefacts and Money." *Cambridge Journal of Economics* 36: 345–385, 361–362.

23. Ostrom, Elinor. 2005. *Understanding Institutional Diversity*. Princeton, NJ: Princeton University Press, 7.

24. King, Gary., Robert O. Keohane., and SidneyVerba. 1994. *Designing Social Inquiry: Scientific Inference in Qualitative Research*. Princeton, NJ: Princeton University Press, 10.

25. Hoover, Kenneth., and Todd Donovan. 2011. *The Elements of Social Scientific Thinking* (10th Edition). Boston, MA: Wadsworth, 132–133.

26. Hempel, Carl G. 1994. "The Function of General Laws in History." In *Readings in the Philosophy of Social Science,* edited by Michael Martin and Lee McIntyre, 43–53. Cambridge, MA: MIT Press, 51.

27. Wendt, Alexander. 1999. *Social Theory of International Politics,* 81.

28. Wendt, Alexander. 1999. *Social Theory of International Politics*, 83.

29. Little, Daniel. 1991. *Varieties of Social Explanation: An Introduction to the Philosophy of Social Science*, 13.

30. Lawson, Tony. 2003. "Theorizing Ontology." *Feminist Economics* 9, no. 1: 161–169, 165.

31. Little, Daniel. 1991. *Varieties of Social Explanation: An Introduction to the Philosophy of Social Science*, 91.

32. Bhaskar, Roy. 2007. "Theorising Ontology." In *Contributions to Social Ontology*, edited by Clive Lawson, John Latsis, and Nuno Martins, 192–204. London: Routledge, 198.

33. Little, Daniel .1991. *Varieties of Social Explanation: An Introduction to the Philosophy of Social Science*, 92.

34. https://www.britannica.com/topic/functionalism-social-science. Accessed on November 30, 2107.

35. https://www.britannica.com/topic/functionalism-social-science. Accessed on November 30, 2017.

36. https://www.britannica.com/topic/functionalism-social-science. Accessed on November 30, 2017.

37. https://www.britannica.com/topic/functionalism-social-science. Accessed on November 30, 2017.

38. Parsons, Talcott. 1951. *The Social System*. Glencoe, IL: The Free Press, 204.

39. Mitrany, David. 1975. *The Functional Theory of Politics*. New York: St. Martin's Press, xi.

40. Mitrany, David. 1975. *The Functional Theory of Politics*, xi.

41. Mitrany, David. 1966. *A Working Peace System*. Chicago, IL: Quadrangle Books, 27.

42. Mitrany, David. 1975. *The Functional Theory of Politics*, xiv. See also John W. Burton. 1975. "Functionalism and the Resolution of Conflict." In *Functionalism: Theory and Practice in International Relations*, edited by A. J. R. Groom and Paul Taylor, 238–249. New York: Crane, Russak & Company. He argues that the application of functionalism at the inter-state level can also be applied at the domestic level within states; pointing out that just as there are certain system properties common to all social organizations, so also there are organizational properties common to all.

43. Mitrany, David. 1975. *The Functional Theory of Politics*, xxiii.

44. Mitrany, David. 1948. "The Functional Approach to Organization." *International Affairs* 24, no. 3: 350–363, 362.

45. Little, Daniel. 1991. *Varieties of Social Explanation: An Introduction to the Philosophy of Social Science*, 92.

46. Hempel, Carl G. 1994. "The Logic of Functional Analysis." In *Readings in the Philosophy of Social Science,* edited by Michael Martin and Lee McIntyre, 349–375. Cambridge, MA: MIT Press, 371–372.

47. Hempel, Carl G. 1994. "The Logic of Functional Analysis," 349–375, 359. See also Robert K. Merton. 1957. *Social Theory and Social Structure*. Glencoe, IL: Free Press, 19–84; and Talcott Parsons. 1949. *Essays in Sociological Theory, Pure and Applied*. Glencoe, IL: Free Press, 58.

48. Wendt, Alexander. 1999. *Social Theory of International Politics*, 82.

49. Lawson, Tony. 2012. "Ontology and the Study of Social Reality: Emergence, Organization, Community, Power, Social Relations, Corporations, Artefacts and Money." *Cambridge Journal of Economics* 36: 345–385, 361.

50. Turner, Jonathan H. 2003. *Human Institutions: A Theory of Societal Evolution*. Lanham, MD: Rowman & Littlefield Publishers, Inc., 15.

51. Turner, Jonathan H. 2003. *Human Institutions: A Theory of Societal Evolution*, 16. See also Herbert Spencer. 1898. *The Principles of Sociology*, 3 Volumes. New York: D. Appleton.

52. Urone, Paul Peter, and Hinrichs, Roger. 2017. *College Physics*. Houston, TX: OpenStax, 174

53. Urone, Paul Peter, and Hinrichs, Roger. 2017. *College Physics*, 175.

54. http://physics.bu.edu/~duffy/semester1/c6_measuremus.html. Accessed on December 31, 2018.

55. Page, Scott. 2007. "Making the Difference: Applying the Logic of Diversity." *Academy of Management* 21, no. 4: 6–20, 6–8.

56. Page, Scott. 2007. "Making the Difference: Applying the Logic of Diversity," 6–20, 8.

57. Ostrom, Elinor. 2005. *Understanding Institutional Diversity*. 6.

58. Searle, John R. 2010. *Making the Social World: The Structure of Human Civilization*, 108–109.

59. Searle, John R. 2010. *Making the Social World: The Structure of Human Civilization*, 113.

60. Macintyre, Andrew. 2003. *The Power of Institutions: Political Architecture and Governance*. Ithaca, NY: Cornell University Press, 169.

61. Burrell, Gibson and Gareth Morgan. 1979. *Sociological Paradigms and Organizational Analysis*. Aldershot, UK: Ashgate, 53.

62. Parsons, Talcott. 1954. *Essays in Sociological Theory*. New York: The Free Press, 147.

63. Wendt, Alexander. 1999. *Social Theory of International Politics*, 82.

64. Tuomela, Raimo. 2013. *Social Ontology: Collective Intentionality and Group Agents*. New York: Oxford University Press, 215.

65. Searle, John R. 2010. *Making the Social World: The Structure of Human Civilization*, 9.

66. Parsons, Talcott. 1951. *The Social System*, 27–30.

67. Little, Daniel. 1991. *Varieties of Social Explanation: An Introduction to the Philosophy of Social Science*, 100–101.

68. Searle, John R. 2010. *Making the Social World: The Structure of Human Civilization*, 143.

69. Tuomela, Raimo. 2013. *Social Ontology: Collective Intentionality and Group Agents*, 214.

70. Verba, Sidney. 1965. "Comparative Political Culture." In *Political Culture and Political Development*, edited by Lucian W. Pye and Sidney Verba, 512–560. Princeton, NJ: Princeton University Press, 512.

71. Parsons, Talcott. 1960. *Structure and Process in Modern Societies*. Glencoe, IL: The Free Press, 20.

72. Hoover, Kenneth, and Todd Donovan. 2011. *The Elements of Social Scientific Thinking* (10th Edition). Boston, MA: Wadsworth, 30.

73. Hoover, Kenneth, and Todd Donovan. 2011. *The Elements of Social Scientific Thinking,* 30.

74. Shoemaker, Pamela J., James William Tankard, Jr., and Dominic L. Lasorsa. 2004. *How to Build Social Science Theories*. Thousand Oaks, CA: Sage Publications, 176.

75. Parsons, Talcott. 1951. *The Social System*, 4.

76. Parsons, Talcott. 1951. *The Social System*, 5–6.

77. Giddens, Anthony. 1984. *The Constitution of Society: Outline of the Theory of Structuration*. Berkeley, CA: University of California Press, 17.

78. Giddens, Anthony. 1984. *The Constitution of Society: Outline of the Theory of Structuration*, 27.

79. Wendt, Alexander. 1999. *Social Theory of International Politics*, 342.

80. Giddens, Anthony. 1984. *The Constitution of Society: Outline of the Theory of Structuration*, 26.

81. Giddens, Anthony. 1984. *The Constitution of Society: Outline of the Theory of Structuration*, 26.

82. Fay, Brian. 1994. "General Laws and Explaining Human Behavior." In *Readings in the Philosophy of Social Science,* edited by Michael Martin and Lee McIntyre, 91–110. Cambridge, MA: MIT Press, 100.

83. Giddens, Anthony. 1984. *The Constitution of Society: Outline of the Theory of Structuration*, 26.

84. Wendt, Alexander. 1999. *Social Theory of International Politics*, 339.

85. Wendt, Alexander. 1999. *Social Theory of International Politics*, 339.

86. Wendt, Alexander. 1999. *Social Theory of International Politics*, 337.

87. Parsons, Talcott and Edward A. Shils. 2001. *Toward a General Theory of Action: Theoretical Foundations for the Social Sciences*, 190–191.

88. Giddens, Anthony. 1984. *The Constitution of Society: Outline of the Theory of Structuration*, 173.

89. Olsen, Marvin E. 1978. *The Process of Social Organization: Power in Social Systems* (2nd ed). New York: Holt, Rinehart and Wilson, 6.

90. Olsen, Marvin E. 1978. *The Process of Social Organization: Power in Social Systems* (2nd ed), 10.

91. Olsen, Marvin E. 1978. *The Process of Social Organization: Power in Social Systems* (2nd ed), 6.

92. Olsen, Marvin E. 1978. *The Process of Social Organization: Power in Social Systems* (2nd ed), 6.

93. Olsen, Marvin E. 1978. *The Process of Social Organization: Power in Social Systems* (2nd ed), 10.

94. Tucker, Robert C. *The Marx-Engels Reader*. New York: Norton, 4.

95. Mueller, Get H. 1989. *Sociology and Ontology: The Analytical Foundations of Social Theory*. Lanham, MD: University Press of America, 25.

96. Mueller, Get H. 1989. *Sociology and Ontology: The Analytical Foundations of Social Theory*, 25–26.

97. Kellner, Douglas. 1989. *Critical Theory, Marxism, and Modernity*. Baltimore, MD: The Johns Hopkins University Press, 11.

98. Kincaid, Harold. 1994. "Assessing Functional Explanations in the Social Sciences." In *Readings in the Philosophy of Social Science,* edited by Michael Martin and Lee McIntyre, 415–428. Cambridge, MA: MIT Press, 415.

99. Kellner, Douglas. 1989. *Critical Theory, Marxism, and Modernity*, 4.

100. Turner, Jonathan H. 1982. *The Structure of Sociological Theory*. Homewood, IL: The Dorsey Press, 44.

101. Parsons, Talcott. 1977. *Social Systems and the Evolution of Action Theory*. New York: The Free Press, 168.

102. Parsons, Talcott and Edward A. Shils. 2001. *Toward a General Theory of Action: Theoretical Foundations for the Social Sciences*, 198.

103. Parsons, Talcott and Edward A. Shils. 2001. *Toward a General Theory of Action: Theoretical Foundations for the Social Sciences*, 199.

104. Parsons, Talcott and Edward A. Shils. 2001. *Toward a General Theory of Action: Theoretical Foundations for the Social Sciences*, 200.

105. Parsons, Talcott and Edward A. Shils. 2001. *Toward a General Theory of Action: Theoretical Foundations for the Social Sciences*, 201.

106. Parsons, Talcott. 1951. *The Social System*, 27–34.

107. Excerpted from Parsons, Talcott. 1951. *The Social System*, 27–30.

108. Parsons, Talcott. 1951. *The Social System*, 34.

109. Dore, R. P. 1994. "Function and Cause." In *Readings in the Philosophy of Social Science,* edited by Michael Martin and Lee McIntyre, 377–389. Cambridge, MA: MIT Press, 387.

110. Dore, R. P. 1994. "Function and Cause," 377–389, 387.

111. Parsons, Talcott. 1951. *The Social System*, 27. See also Talcott Parson. 1960. *Structure and Process in Modern Societies*, 35–36.

112. Acemoglu, Daron and James Robinson. 2012. *Why Nations Fail*. New York: Crown Business.

113. Acemoglu, Daron and James Robinson. 2012. *Why Nations Fail*. Cited in J. Tyler Dickovick and Jonathan Eastwood (Eds). *Comparative Politics: Classic and Contemporary Readings*. New York: Oxford University Press, 11.

114. Acemoglu, Daron and James Robinson. 2012. *Why Nations Fail*. Cited in J. Tyler Dickovick and Jonathan Eastwood (Eds). *Comparative Politics: Classic and Contemporary Readings*. New York: Oxford University Press, 10.

115. Diamond, Jared. 2015. *Collapse: How Societies Choose to Fail or Succeed*. New York: Viking, 419–440. See also Barbara Tuchman. 1984. *The March of Folly: From Troy to Vietnam*. New York: Ballantine Books.

116. Sica, Alan. 2000. "Rationalization and Culture." In *The Cambridge Companion to Weber*, edited by Stephen Turner, 42–58. Cambridge, UK: Cambridge

University Press, 57. Max Weber was very critical in his reference to this issue pointing to the fact that "peoples in other parts of the world who have begun imitating the general model of behavior and social organization of modernized/rationalized western humans have also become childish in their demands upon each other and upon their environments." And his main concern was the observation that "when it suits their private short-term desires, they exhibit 'rationality' in the purest economic meaning of the term; yet after their material and status needs are more or less satisfied (at least temporarily), they turn for relief from regimentation and predictable tedium to those very realms of social life (those zones of solace) wherein rationality has the least play and the least likely influence."

Chapter 2

State and Government

Ontology and Function

The modern state system has been the traditional means for organizing world geopolitical and governing institutions based on specific ideological or cultural distinctions. Although made up precisely of individuals, groups, and interests, there are many other factors that make it rather difficult to fully address the perennial issue of why some states succeed and others fail in the enterprise of governance. Part of this could be due to differences in ideology, structural design, institutional relationships, or in the nature of distributive politics and rights of citizenship. But if the essential purpose of states is to serve the best interest of their citizens, and even where there are some exceptions to the rule, there ought to be a baseline that should work well for each state (as a social system) despite differences in regime types, institutional design, or ideology.

Today, we are yet to develop a new method of governance beyond what the Treaty of Westphalia offered in 1948; but it still remains a fact that the Treaty did not address most of the internal problems of organization and conflict resolution that befell the new states. And to address the ontological question of what the state is or is not, it is therefore important to understand how it works, as well as make "assumptions about what it is made of and how it is structured."[1] As in most other areas of social scientific inquiry, "it is important that we address the initial conditions that inform key operational constructs as well as linkages between nominal terms, their inherent qualities, and the specific functional relationships that serve as building blocks for many of the grand theories in the field."[2] My aim in this chapter is to define the character and obligations of the modern state, the contemporary challenges it faces, and to raise a few questions whether the state system as currently constituted will endure for the foreseeable future and for how long? It is not necessarily a call to move away from the current form of sociopolitical organization; but it is an awakening to the necessity for us to begin to think about how we can adapt as well as reengage what currently obtains with the prospects and challenges that tomorrow may bring. As a social organization, the state is made up of various functional properties such as the personality subsystem, the cultural subsystem, and the interactional subsystem. "At their point of intersection lies the legal order that regulates the privilege of disposition of the means of production and the strategic exercise of power, which, in turn, requires legitimation."[3] The problem of the state, therefore, is partly a problem of coordination of the internal subsystems, the integration of the subsystems as a basis for the preservation of the collective interest and identity, and of stability in the social structure of relations critical to the maintenance of the whole system.

DEFINING CHARACTERISTICS

Ideally, "a defining characteristic of the genuine state is the preservation of the common interest (*utilitas communis*)—interpreted here in terms of protection, security, and well-being—essential values which originate from the people as their natural desire to preserve themselves and their possessions."[4] Some states treat their citizens fairly equitably with basic guarantees of civil liberties, dues process, and economic opportunity; but many others are predatory toward their citizens. Unless in the most extreme of circumstances, it is very rare for the state and the government to work at cross-purposes with each other; more often than not, state and government use each other to reinforce their power and strategic advantage in the course of political governance. The courts cite legal precedents in making judicial rules, while legislatures draw upon specific sections of the Constitution to justify new regulations or the abrogation of existing ones. While governments use the security agencies to implement measures for safeguarding internal security, the armed forces exist as instruments of both the state and the government to use in securing the territorial integrity of the state as well as the national interest.

In the sense that "different responses from within the state mean that we cannot simply assume that as a whole it acts in a rational and coherent fashion, or strategically follows a defined set of interests";[5] but this assumption does not always extend to authoritarian states with limited liberties and freedoms. To the extent that the "basic uniformity in the structure of groups is not incompatible with the range of variations in the character of the structure of authority within it";[6] states have different institutional arrangements in which capabilities and responsibilities are assigned either based on proven expertise or political expediency. In plural democratic societies, the government is a temporary caretaker of the affairs of the state and governance of its institutions. The government's legitimacy derives from the "adoption of a constitution which lays out the basic structures, procedures, powers, and limitations of government, and with explicit formal rules that govern the decision making process,"[7] including the electoral process. But in totalitarian regimes, the government is technically the state with minimal distinction between them. The legitimacy of the government stems from the indoctrinatory ideals of the ruling oligarchy and the degree of authoritarian control exercised in the regulation of public and private lives. Taken together, it becomes quite illustrative when considered in light of Raadschelders' postulation that "government is both politics and administration, and as such, is deeply involved in the selection and realization of publicly defined societal values and policies."[8]

In the end, both liberal democratic societies and totalitarian regimes are based on the essential platform of the state and government; it is just that they do things differently when it comes to the issue of governance and the way they treat their citizens. The state does not exist except as a schematic abstraction, but we only have a sense of it by virtue of its policies and the activities of individuals who are engaged in the seemingly endless process of implementing state laws and statutes. We also conceive of a state as being the sole sovereign authority over a particular geopolitical territory, hence has the power and authority to reward and to sanction, and to decide who comes in or goes out as well as the specific laws and jurisdictions that apply in different cases and under varying situations. For Weber, in addition to having legal authority, "the state is a compulsory association with a territorial basis; and its claim to the monopoly of the use of force is as essential to its character of compulsory jurisdiction and of continuous organization."[9] As a regulatory agency the state makes laws governing activities or civic behavior within its territory; but while it requires individuals to obey the laws, the reality is that most of the time they do not. Individuals are required to pay taxes for the sustenance of the state, but some individual do not, preferring, perhaps for reasons of self-interest, to free-ride off the sweat of others.

ORGANIZATION AND THE COMPLEXITY OF SOCIAL SYSTEMS

Social systems do not have permanent non-malleable structural fixtures, in the sense that there are equally no permanent interests. The structure of interests is a function both of the nature of the realistic situations in which people act and of the definitions of those situations which are institutionalized in the society.[10] Some interests, particularly from those in controlling positions of authority are already vested, hence maybe "oriented to the maintenance of objects of interest which have already become established."[11] But other groups may be driven by either resentment, rejection, or an attempt to recalculate the existing structure of interests in such a way that a group's fortunes are advanced much further than what currently obtains.

As a result of the differential forces that drive each of the various parts of a social system (the personality subsystem, the interactional subsystem, and the cultural subsystem), the ability to maintain overall system stability will depend on the extent to which the various interests bridge and mimic each other. If the issues separating one group from the other are minimal, then it is possible that the incentives generated as a result of agreement on critical issues would be enough to give each group a stake in the sustenance of the social system as a whole. In this regard, collective agreement and obedience to the rules of the game enable institutional patterns to be reinforced "by the behaviors of members of the society, whose behaviors are also determined by the existing institutional patterns."[12] Among the forces that help shape institutional conformity and durability are the shared cultural norms, the nature of social and economic organization, and the role of law in judicial adjudication and as a form of social fact.

In multiethnic societies, cultural patterns are often disaggregated, hence they confront each other in an adversarial manner; but as aspects of cultural patterns fuse into each other overtime, the bases for the institutionalization of a new form of social control emerges. For example, I would like to believe that every culture views thievery and cheating as bad, and benevolence and philanthropy as good, hence these could serve as unifying symbols that help to bridge existing differences. Cross-cultural learning and diffusion therefore is a form of institutionalization. The same applies to the nature and pattern of social and economic organization—the arrangement of the social structure and authority relationships and the processes of economic aggregation and productivity. Weber points to "two interdependent strategic sectors of the social structure of the modern economy: those impinging on the use of money (as a medium of exchange and acquisition) and the structure of markets and relations of economic units to them on the one hand, and those connected with the relations of appropriation (property), on the other."[13] By viewing the economic and social aspects of the social system in the context of an organizational framework, Weber seems to suggest that the organization itself could only be sustained through appropriate division of labor and the structure of relationships between the units. On the premise that "every rational course of political action is economically oriented with respect to provision for the necessary means, and it is therefore always possible for political action to serve the interest of economic ends."[14]

Even though money is instrumental in the facilitation of exchange and appropriation, yet its utility lies in the structure and modes of orientation of rational economic action. The first is the "rational allocation of available resources as between the various uses to which they may be put by an individual or any sort of collectivity; and the other, is the exploitation of opportunities for profit, that is of the increase of available resources, directly in exchange or through production for exchange."[15] This is one of the reasons why advocates of Keynesian economics and the more restrained supply-siders tend to disagree on the most effective mechanism for economic growth and wealth accumulation. While Keynesians take a macro demand-driven approach, the supply-siders take a micro fiscal incentive perspective—although with the common objective of growing the economy, reducing unemployment, and generating enough disposal income to create increases in the demand for goods and services.

Although Weber did not actually perceive that "it was possible by functional analysis to develop a generalized outline of social systems of action; but invariably, such an outline was, in fact, to a large extent implicit in the structure of his own system of ideal types."[16] For him such a system must meet the exigencies of its external situation (both human and nonhuman), and also must be integrated so that its parts function in a certain degree of harmony. It can thus be said that while Weber's central argument tends to accommodate the role of structure as well as functional analysis in understanding the way social systems operate as well as endure overtime; and to the extent that we may not fully know what is it that motivates individuals to act the way they do, but at least, "some generalizations could be made about the manner in which economic interests tend to result in social action of a certain type"[17] and the possible consequences of those actions.

As an instrument of social control and legitimate order, the law also helps to ensure conformity both through direct application of sanctions and deterrence. The law is an ordering device, "a mode of structuring human relationships in such a way that it is *functionally* related to the necessity of integrating the activities of many people, both by preventing disruptive activities and by coordinating actions in the interest of goals which could not be achieved by individuals acting independently."[18] As I indicated earlier, the legitimacy of a law depends on the extent to which people are willing to obey it; but ceteris paribus, the reality of the matter is that most people do not obey the law. Legitimate and social control is achieved not necessarily because of the fact that a law has been made, but its efficacy lies in the fact that people can see what social *function* the law serves (adjudication, affirmation, punishment, and/or sanctions) in terms of reinforcing social order. Such is the case that the legitimacy of a legal order or law may derive from a rational belief in the absolute validity of the order as an expression of ultimate values; or entirely by self-interest, through expectations of specific ulterior consequences which are, more or less, particularized to particular groups or individuals.[19] Even when it is not invoked or applied in a situation, the mere thought that any willful contravention of the law would attract specific sanctions or disapproval, in and of itself, may be enough to extract restraint and conformity to the prevailing norms of social interaction and exchange.

Ideational Properties

In the state of nature and prior to the advent of civil political society, Thomas Hobbes argues that the *war-of-all-against-all* is partly a result of the fact that the human inclination and desire for power is never satiated by the acquisition of more power. For their safety and preservation, the people therefore must seek an independent sovereign—"a person authorized by the community to act on their behalf, for their peace and security, so that what that person does counts as an act of the whole community."[20] For Hobbes, "the state is an abstraction of the will of the sovereign, which is in turn an abstraction of the originating compact of the social order."[21] Hence "what is relevant is not the process by which the sovereign acquired power, but the fact that he has it";[22] and as such, it becomes incumbent on the people, once they have consented to his rule, to obey him. Such obedience transcends for all practical purposes, a divine and legitimate authority for the sovereign to preside over the affairs of society. In the typical Hobbesian state, sovereignty therefore resides in the individual leader partly through "the socializing effects of state power on individual identities,"[23] while in democratic states, sovereignty is conferred on the people, first through their elected representatives, and second, through the power of the vote during elections. The latter is what seems to have made Locke's natural rights democracy more appealing an ideal in the emerging western political thought of the seventeenth century.

While Locke also held the view of the crisis of mutual-fatality that characterized the state of nature, he also held out the promise that a well-constructed representative legislature should be able to account in a measurable way the welfare and interests of the people. While he does not condone the exercise of arbitrary or absolute power over the affairs men, but still he was of the view (contrary to Hobbes) that where the state does not live up to its promise, then the people deserve the prerogative to dissolve it since such a state governs only by the people's consent. While we can argue about what constitutes a state with regard to the internal processes and functions that characterize different regime types, we can also agree that what applies to each regime type equally is that all share in the exercise of power, authority, and identity. Identity is very important to states in the sense that *identity* and *preservation*, oftentimes, go hand in hand. States go to great length to protect or reshape their identity because that is what they wish to present to the rest of the world about themselves, and it is also the way they want the world to see them.

The existential problem of the state, however one may look at it, is a problem of identity without which it could not survive as a constituted and homogenous entity. "Understood as centralized authority structures with a territorial monopoly on the legitimate use of organized violence, the typical variation among states is in how their political authority is organized domestically in their regime types."[24] But it is also about how the structure of social relations and material production are related to each other in a functional way and how they cumulatively serve the collective interest of the state and the people. This has been a defining issue of political debate even in classical times. Plato's preoccupation in his quest for the ideal form of state was based on his understanding of society and how occupational relationships could be structured to achieve the best possible outcome for the people. In situations where men lacked a common or universal education for political duties, Plato's central argument rests on "the belief in a natural social hierarchy based upon natural human differences; and one in which innate differences between people should provide a natural basis for functional specialization" or "division of labor in society."[25]

Drawn out in greater detail, Plato was of the view that there are three groups of people in any society, and as such, we should assign labor or public responsibilities to each according to his natural God-given capabilities. He was among the earliest classical thinkers to suggest the idea of functional division of labor as a basis for organizing the affairs of government and society. "His was a vision of a united and harmonious community (state) with which the individual is perfectly identified, and in which he has the full opportunity to develop and be realized";[26] and this he considers as the defining characteristic of justice. Although Plato's contemporary Aristotle favored a state governed by an aristocracy defined by wealth and socioeconomic status; it was more of a recognition that only those who are able to contribute to the welfare and security of the state should have the legitimate basis for charting the course of its political destiny. The wealthy are able to pay their taxes for the maintenance and security of the state and also create opportunity for others in the polity to flourish. Aristotle does not necessarily suggest that other less disposed members of society be denied the opportunity for active participation in politics; after all, even in liberal democracies, the vote of the poor and ordinary folks have generally been used to enshrine and legitimize aristocratic rule at the top. And this very point helps us to reinforce the notion that who governs is quite different from the notion of how we govern.

GOVERNANCE AND OBEDIENCE TO AUTHORITY

The concept of governance has been utilized to explain various sets of activities connected to the functional role of the state and government in the exercise of public service, domestically as well as in matters of international relations.

On the one hand, it can apply to the activities of formal administrative institutions, the involvement of various nongovernmental agencies in public service delivery, obedience to law and authority as exhibited by individuals, the manner in which justice and jurisprudence are applied; and on the other hand, international regimes of rules and processes that govern state behavior in its relations with other states in the international system. But in whatever context it is used, governance is the *ways* and *means* by which we get certain things done in order to achieve a particular end or objective—mostly in the public interest. It often includes "global and local arrangements, formal structures and informal norms and practices, and spontaneous and intentional systems of control."[27] On a broader scale, this conceptualization nonetheless seeks to "link constitutional institutions with the realities of policymaking and public management,"[28] but also recognizes "governance as involving the various means for achieving coordination and control of individuals or organizational units on behalf of their common interests."[29]

The structure of governance allows for a systematic maintenance of social and economic order. It also provides the essential character of the political system, the rules governing participation, representation, and the distributive incentives of association (in the Lasswellian sense of "who gets what, when, and how much"). While some administrative institutions of government (parliaments or legislatures, courts, electoral systems, and bureaucracies) provide ideas about the structure and method of governance, others such as the mass media, the schools, interest groups, and nonprofit organizations provide mechanisms for socialization as well as cultural diffusion and assimilation. Governance is a balancing game. It is a search for the *golden mean* in which every veto point, more or less, gravitates toward the middle. However, meeting in the *middle* does not necessarily mean that everyone gets all of what they want to the degree they want it; it simply means that each and every interest has the opportunity to secure for itself, at least the basic minimum necessary to sustain it and to make continued participation more meaningful and rewarding. If they happen to get more than they hoped for, then that is all the more reason to aspire continuous participation as well as the sustainability of the mechanisms within which these distributive opportunities are negotiated. It was for this reason that Durkheim had argued that the "distribution of things among individuals can be just only if it be made relative to the social deserts of each one."[30]

As a process, governance requires two competing premises, that of a *directive* (the way things are or should be done) and *legitimation* (when people accept, validate, or buy into the principles or ends that governance seeks to secure). The tendency to consider the notion of governance as a vertically directed set of directives for which those at the lower rungs of the administrative hierarchy ought to respond is operationally false. The process of governance is both hierarchical and horizontal, and sometimes simply organic. For the fact that it can incorporate malleable sets of institutional designs, rules and procedures, individuals and their behaviors, roles and routines (all taking place at the same or at different times), governance as a process, can be said to be everywhere. It does not matter whether it is in the public or private sectors, the art of governance is also imbued with such values as planning, organizing, staffing, budgeting, directing, coordinating, and reporting—central elements of a typical managerial function. But "where it is not a matter simply of maintenance of an established routine; but of where the commitment is thus to undertake types of action contingent on circumstances as they develop, then the risk to be minimized is that such contingent commitments will not be carried out when the circumstances in question appear."[31] The structure of governance therefore, is a function of the end to which it is directed at any particular point in time, as well as the social and political imperatives surrounding that end.

Beyond service provision, governance also involves the application of best practices, sound macroeconomic and fiscal policymaking, efficient budgetary management, promotion of equal opportunity and access, and an adequate regulatory framework.[32] While governance may lead to the securing of instrumental ends, it is oftentimes designed to achieve normative ends that serve specific arrays of values. For this reason, it has become a catch-all phrase for all sorts of characterizations about *what* and *how* government needs to do certain things to make life better for its citizens. And this is where the problem lies: the relentless fervor to glamorize governance as possessing form, context, and character, hence capable of generating novel approaches to doing the same things we have always done before. While it may seem as a fluid construct, we are also told that good governance helps us "to recognize and fill the growing gaps between the formal constitutional order and the way order is produced and reproduced in everyday life."[33] Governance therefore is a mechanism of control, a process for the distribution of incentives, and cannot function effectively without regard to the political order within which it must operate.

Although it is generally construed within the context of the state, it is a mistake to think of governance as the exclusive preserve of the juridical state, nongovernmental or international organizations. By paying taxes, by obeying the law, by obtaining licenses for businesses or for other government-provided services, by standing in the queue at the local bank, by obeying traffic conventions including speed limits, individuals are also participating in and validating the process of governance. In fact, much of governance is about individuals, coordinating and regulating their behavior, and directing it toward a specific *telos* or objective. Rules and regulations do not obey themselves; they require individuals to obey them, thereby granting the basis for judging their efficacy. And because "rules and regulations go away under interpretation unless they are objectively sustained by other human beings or organizational structures; a rule has less of a reality base than the objective presence of another human superior"[34]—(the abstract imagery of the overriding boss is always around as a reminder even when he is not present). This is where existing authority structures (in the objective sense that they exist and are recognized by everyone) serve as a basis for the conditioning of individual behavior.

Authority structures can take the form of physical positions, laws, and artifacts or recognized symbols, and because they imbibe the power of sanction or reward, they also generate institutional effects. My take on authority in this regard is not one based on some kind of natural or divine designation (like parents, pastor, bishop, or the pope), but one vested in the sovereign laws of the state and prevailing institutions for the maintenance of social order and exchange (like the president, directors, and administrators of key administrative institutions or positions). The efficacy of authority (in the administrative sense) does not come from within, but it arises from the effects or obligations it imposes on those to whom it applies. In other words, our understanding of an authority structure is based on its relational property (how it affects us and what it commands us to do and under what circumstances), and how these conform to or validate the expressed will of the state. Obedience to such authority can also be conditioned by a sort of *cognitive preference ordering* (what Herbert Simon refers to as *area of acceptance*) in terms of the ratio of transaction cost between obedience and disobedience to authority, and between potential reward and punishment.

Oftentimes people simply obey because it is more widely accepted as the appropriate thing to do, or when such actions arise as a collectively intentioned and accepted norm or practice. An important point, though, that has been attributed to Simon, is the sense that the "exercise of authority involves a *willingness* to obey; thus implying that until an order or proposal is accepted or complied with, it is not authoritative."[35] But to view authority structures in this way is to rely on a seriously flawed premise. The mere fact that an order exists or has been issued consistent with the law or legal position, in and of itself, implies a sense of authoritativeness and legitimacy as an a priori condition. The *authoritativeness* or *legitimacy* does not depend on whether it is obeyed or not; but it depends on the body of existing laws or statues within which the provisions of such order can be argued and defended. What makes an order *authoritative* is the legal foundation that it carries with it; and in fact, it is this legal property that makes it imperative and obligatory that we should obey the order even if we disagree with its core premise. To suggest otherwise is to imply that the legal basis upon which the order is based is not itself legitimate, until people concede to its precepts. Because some people are less likely to obey the law (or will violate it at specific moments of opportunity), and if we base the authoritativeness of such laws or orders on peoples' willingness to obey them as they chose, then we would have a society in constant turmoil and disorder.

Authority structures (once created or changed) are what they are irrespective of what we think or do about them in our own dispositions or responses to them. "Once authority is established through law or position, obedience to the authority is mandatory."[36] In democratic systems (but much less so in totalitarian states), people are permitted, to an extent, to challenge existing authority structures; but we must note that much of this challenge is not because those authority structures should not exist, rather it is part of a continuous debate about what they mean and how they are used to address competing issues of public discourse and political action. When some people disagree with the president of the United States (and I will surmise as in most other countries around the world), they are not disputing that he does not have such *authority* to do this or that (since these are already stipulated in the Constitution as belonging to the *position* or *office* of the presidency and not to the individual who occupies it); but what they may be disagreeing is in the way they feel the authority *should not have* been exercised. And because these disagreements can be seen as a result of differences in ideology, partisanship, interest group or individual preferences, or as Raadschelders and Stillman explain it, as a result of the "interaction between people with motives, values, beliefs, and interests,"[37] it is not unusual to hear accusatory expressions such as *abuse*, *disregard*, or *circumvention* of constituted authority.

But of even greater import is that the primary reason for resistance or challenge to authority may result from generational issues based on broader "changes in social life and the way in which identity formation both affects and is affected by patterns of authority in society."[38] Because there are a lot of variables (objective and subjective) at work when it comes to matters concerning authority relations, obedience can partly be explained as a function of the individual, the context, and the particular period of time in which social life is experienced. While some may dismiss this development "as a sign of the times," I think that it goes beyond the implied rhetoric. Many states are going through various forms of economic and political crisis necessitated by drastic changes in the domestic character and interest articulation as well as unexpected shifts in the structure and priorities of the international system. While both developments may seem like existential threats, they reflect, on the one hand, issues of cultural and geopolitical realignments in state formation; and on the other, a profound reevaluation of the *state* and its ability to address ongoing issues of value change, interest articulation, representation, trans-border immigration, and the challenge of rising expectations within the civic polity.

LEGITIMATION AND ACTION

Theoretically, we can say that the state exists to serve the collective interest of the citizens,[39] but we all know that all states (or at least some of them) do not serve the collective interest of all their citizens no matter how well-intentioned political leaders may be. Because the "modern liberal state requires widespread consent and popular support in order to have its decisions obeyed without resort to coercion, it can function with a minimum of force as long as the majority of its citizens acquiesce; but if the majority does not, then the state cannot survive for long."[40] The role of "legitimation is crucial for the functioning of the state and government because political power requires some degree of collective recognition or acceptance."[41] But even when the state does not seem to overtly exercise its power, legitimation combined with collective recognition and acceptance grants it a form of *deontic power* or what I would call *latent or passive power*—the power to influence or induce obedience without any actual or physical manifestation of the power. But it still begs the question as to who owns the state and to what extent should it be obligated to the welfare of its citizens and vice versa? It is by addressing these normative questions that political leaders are able to build the ownership commitment needed to advance the course of statehood, governance, and citizenship.

The issue of state and government must be seen as reciprocal as well as mutually reinforcing; the first concerned with constructing effective institutions and constitutional processes critical for a functional system, while the latter focuses on carrying out the legitimate administrative obligations of the state in service of the citizens. Through its actions and the existing socialization processes, the state thus creates awareness within the citizenry of the reciprocal nature of duty, obligation, and responsibility. Set apart from everything else, the state provides the framework for a formative political society, deciding its form, as well as the nature of relationships between its various elements. It is the prime locus of loyalty and satisfaction of needs, and it is to it that individuals and groups turn to for protection and well-being in times of crisis.[42] It conforms to a specific philosophy of ideas about human nature, habit, and logic in both time and space; hence as an ideal, it offers a crucial pathway and justification regarding how people within a particular geopolitical territory can coexist in the context of what we refer to as *nationality*. Mutual coexistence thus becomes a value that needs to be safeguarded for its own sake as well as for political stability. While state and government cannot be the same, they complement each other; the former setting down the principles, and the latter implementing them. The government therefore becomes the institutional agency responsible for realizing the normative ideals of the state.

Though the term "state" is oftentimes "dismissed as a vague abstraction from the past having little empirical meaning or researchable features, the term can refer to concrete structures and observable relationships among them."[43] When particular governments assume control and authority over a state, they utilize standing institutions and laws to advance and consolidate their legitimacy and political power. Such institutions include the legislature, the executive structure, the judiciary, and existing bureaucratic systems—a methodological emphasis generally referred to as the "legal-institutional-descriptive" approach. While the *state* ought to be considered as something more than the *government*, its integrative function derives from the continuous administrative, legal, bureaucratic, and coercive systems that are used not only to structure relations between civil society and public authority, but also in structuring many other crucial relationships in the broader society.[44] Because institutional designs serve different purposes tied to specific regime types, the problem of the modern state has been "the failure of intermediary institutions (democracy, majority rule, party politics, interest groups, etc.) to provide a linkage between the state and the individual."[45] In light of the segmented nature of individual and/or group needs; and to the extent that this situation can be construed as inevitable, an appraisal of how well and effective the state is in meeting peoples' needs and expectations would always be segmented, and at other times contingent.

In *On Duties*, Cicero likens the government to a guardianship or tutelage committed to the welfare of those to whom the trust is created (the people), but not of those (public officials) to whom it is entrusted.[46] While the "state, regime, and government may or may not overlap empirically, but in concept, they are quite distinct."[47] By enforcing obedience, power, and authority over all activities within a defined geographical space combined with recognition by members of the international community, a state acquires legitimacy both within and beyond its borders. Through the use of symbols (flags), anthems, insignias, myths and legends, and other artifacts that invoke the power and nostalgia of a people's history, myths, ceremonies, and legends, a *state* stands in parallel relation to the people and culture it represents. In fact, "what has distinguished the modern state from most other large-scale political organizations in history, such as empires, has been its insinuation into the core identities of its subjects. It aims to shape people's entire moral order—the content of the symbols and codes determining what matters most to them."[48] It is to preserve this moral order, identity, and the cultural history which they embody that governments are created to manage and coordinate the affairs of the state. Hence, when we discuss the issue of "state-society relations," it ought to be seen rather as an issue of "government-society relations"; since as a matter of fact, states do not govern, but governments do.

As a form of social and economic organization, the state is made up of three critical elements such as *structure*, *individuals*, and *function*. While the *structure* delineates the design and methods by which authority and relationships are organized, *function* stipulates the various activities and processes that must be undertaken in order to serve the primary end for which the state exists. But at the center of this arrangement are the individuals, groups, or coalitions of interests who are engaged in the various programs of the state and who serve and are also served by these programs. The state, broadly construed is thus an organizing formula or symbol; but it is organized, more or less, for a shared purpose. Among these are the protection of sovereign authority, territorial integrity, national security, and on a comparative level (since some states guarantee these more than the others) life, liberty, and equality of opportunity for citizens in civic, political, and economic matters. Idealistically, while I assume this to be the normative role of the state, I am also not oblivious to the fact that some states do not guarantee these liberties and opportunities to all of their citizens; and some states, in fact, do not provide for these at all.

When some states deviate from *what ought* to *what is*; they often become self-serving, predatory, and sometimes rapacious. Consistent with the broader thesis of this book, it is therefore argued that states become dysfunctional when, as a result of systemic anomalies, it becomes exceedingly difficult to fulfill the primary role for which they were created. From classical antiquity to the modern era, the state has been used as a framework for affirming geopolitical and cultural distinctions, organizing national defense, politics, and for the development of what has come to be known as national interest. The Treaty of Westphalia (1648) introduced the modern state system as a primary institution in interstate relations. "It was a major shift in world order, one that brought about legal equality and increasing secularism within and between states. It was a treaty of mutual and peaceful co-existence but one that did not go far in deciding how each state would organize internally with respect to the grants of specific freedoms, rights, and responsibilities."[49] Rather, "it was left to each state to decide for itself the type and character of government it wanted, be it monarchy, aristocracy, or democracy."[50] As a consequence of these choices, we now have competing arrays of state institutions and structures, states at different levels of development, perennial tensions within and between states as a result of ideological or policy differences, wars within and between states, states refusing to abide by international regimes and conventions for reasons that serve their own specific interests, and an international system in which power projection has become more of a virtue than taking care of the collective needs of the citizens.

If an opinion poll is held for all citizens of the world at this very moment, my best guess would be that less than 50 percent would agree that their own country is doing well at what it is supposed to do as a state. Even within established industrial democracies like the United States and much of continental Europe and the developed countries of Asia, there are disagreements on almost every indices of policy success, national security, trade relations, unemployment, climate change, illegal immigration, and illicit economies that challenge the supremacy of the formal economy at every stage. With this much disagreement and chaos the world over, there is a growing anxiety and tension among various global publics that the world of the twenty-first century continues to cast a dark shadow on the fate and future of mankind in an evolving social world.

As would be discussed latter, the ideational foundations for the state system that was envisaged in 1648 has been severely eroded. States are not created simply to go to war but for the sake of peaceful mutual coexistence and preservation. On the premise that "social forces are oftentimes directly responsible for injury to or destruction of some individuals and some of the wants or needs of all individuals; it is equally understood that a war cannot be won without casualties and acceptance of war is sometimes a condition of survival of a social system,"[51] but not necessarily a sufficient condition or rationale for its existence. But ironically, for one reason or the other, states do go to war, sometimes as a means for achieving peace, but also for motives that are quite ulterior. States spend huge sums of money seeking the acquisition of new weapons of war including nuclear weapons and chemical-biological systems, either as a deterrence or with the expectation of using them in time of necessity. But yet, going to war or developing the capacity to use nuclear weapons is not the main reason why states are created. It is also true that states see it as their responsibility to build up their military infrastructure as a way of defending themselves in times of aggression or war; but this is a matter of political expediency founded on the framework of an anarchic state-system in which neighbors rarely trust each other's motives, hence making their potential behaviors unpredictable. I know of no state, at least in the modern era, which was created simply to go to war. War has always been a means to an end, although for most states, war did not yield a glorious end.

States exist to deliver public goods (including security), law and order, as well as to satisfy the basic needs of associational ownership to their members. When they "function as they ideally should, they mediate between the constraints and challenges of the international arena and the dynamic forces of their own internal economic, political, and social realities."[52] But in societies where strong associational groupings have emerged, they tend to provide alternative sources of advocacy for disenfranchised groups to vent their frustrations against the state and its institutions. Ironically, instead of serving as an avenue for advancing a more pluralist form of political engagement and interest articulation, advocacy groups oftentimes end up creating a situation that seeks to undermine the very system they aim to safeguard. "The government is supposed to have the responsibility, the will and the power to restructure society in whatever way maximizes social welfare";[53] but then that is always the easiest part. Competing interests and ideological formations lodged within the state, either blame the government for all that ails society, or they take out their frustrations on both the government and state by advocating a radical overhaul even though the alternative they propose has no practical guarantee that it would work as they profess. Hence state and government end up pleasing some people all of the time, others some of the time, and still others at no time at all.

Everywhere one looks there are civil protests, official malfeasance, boundary disputes, internecine strife, poverty, homelessness, hunger, insurgencies, civil wars, aggression and threats of aggression, decay, and abandonment. This is not to suggest that much of this never existed in history; but in most countries particularly the United States, the existing sentiment stokes of a continuing breakdown of trust between the government and those who are governed. For instance "in 1964, 77 percent of Americans trusted the federal government most or all of the time; but as of December 2017, that number was 18 percent, nearing and all-time low."[54] They harbor a palpable fear that "the consensus that holds the nation together—*objective truth*—is breaking down,"[55] as demonstrably reflected in the contentious nature of public discourse. While there does not seem to be a light at the end of the tunnel anytime soon, the real take-away from all these is what it tells us about what may be in store for the state system—the most important form of social and political organization utilized the world over. It also raises a profound question as to how we get to govern, under what conditions, and with what. I will attempt to illustrate below some of the dysfunctional issues that affect the modern state system, and which also would help to illuminate the utility of functional analysis as a central element in the theoretical premise of this work.

CHANGE AND FLUX: ORDER AND DISORDER IN STATE SYSTEMS

Some people may see the state as a constructed experience in which various roles and functions transact with or across each other; but at the center of this dynamic is the individual as both principal and as agent. States do not only have to coordinate and manage the functions or activities that serve the interest of the citizens, but ironically, they also have to manage the activities that serve their own existential interests and instincts for survival. But the number and magnitude of demands and imperatives placed on the contemporary state are enormous and daunting.[56] There are now "more independent states than ever before—almost 200, as compared to about 50 at the end of World War II—but that has not made the international system any more stronger or cooperative."[57] There was a time when states used to have the capacity to determine the conditions under which their citizens live and the ability to develop safety nets that minimize the economic inequality that development generates; but in "an unregulated global economy, those nets are sagging and becoming frayed."[58] It used to be the case that states have some control over movements of people and exchanges of ideas; but the prominence of the Internet, Facebook, Twitter, Google, and other technological gadgets have undermined that ability, such that it is harder now than it used to be for states to monitor the activities of those individuals, gangs, non-state actors, and espionage activities from those who are their enemies.[59]

Today, "we are gradually moving out of a world of sovereign states toward new forms of overlapping jurisdictions,"[60] as demonstrated in "the growing foreign populations in Western Europe and in the United States, the growing proportion of person with dual citizenship and multiple state membership. The increase in cross-national marriages suggests that traditional models of the melting pot, of a unitary and bounded civil society, are, at best, in question."[61] Across the Americas, Europe, Asia, and the rest of the world, there seems to be a growing category of ambivalent population groups advocating one issue or the other, some relatively peaceful, others more or less violent. It thus would seem that most people have become rather immune to the pressing problems of the world, and by default, have accepted the idea of living in a world without peace as a modern day interpretation of the human condition. While political leaders may seem overwhelmed by the daily surge of problems and expectations, their pessimism is nonetheless aided by the continuous weakening of political and administrative institutions of the state, economic recession and decline in funding mechanisms, as well as rise in debauchery and official malfeasance within the ranks of the political elite and their surrogates in the general public.

To the extent that "the duality of state and society has been the organizing frame of political debate and practice since, arguably, the Peace of Westphalia in 1648, then there are signs that we are reaching another *Westphalian moment*."[62] Yes, there are a growing number of borderless multinational corporations that have developed economic and somewhat political footprints in various parts of the world; but while these have been beneficial to growth and development of some countries, it has not been so redeeming for the others. I am not advocating a dramatic shift or replacement from the current state of political and economic organization anchored on the Westphalian state system; but what I wish to point out is that the strains that have been heaped on it over the years would of necessity call for drastic adjustments to the trajectory in which the system is currently heading. It is important that we help to redefine and adjust to the evolving parameters; rather than for it to be imposed on us based on a logic that is antithetical to the existential interests of respective states, their sovereignty, and citizenship.

The modern state is undergoing a relentless siege both from within and from without, hence "its role is no longer exclusively to protect the national interest, but to assist in the process of adjustment to change that is an increasingly demanding one in the modern complex and rapidly altering world society."[63] Even among contemporary thinkers and idealists, there is a constant barrage of new interpretations and reconceptualization regarding what the modern state is, is not, or should be. Across the world, authoritarian and illiberal regimes have developed a rising sense of impunity when it comes to human rights and the rule of international law; and behaviors once forbidden anywhere now happens even beyond borders in full view of public scrutiny.[64] The frantic yearning for answers to vexing social and political problems of the state, and "the trend toward impunity comes as voters in many countries seem more attracted to strongmen and dictators"[65] than the more politically accountable alternative.

On the singular premise that no single entity can withstand this much pressure for as long as the state has endured it; at some point in the not so distant future, the pressure will generate its own critical mass. Either the state succumbs to it in one crystalizing burst of energy or it fizzles on its own accord in a slow but gradual process of atrophy and decline. While everything around it and within it is changing rather rapidly, there has to be a simple realization that the modern state will also change from what we know of it today. What I want to do in the remaining parts of this chapter is to explore the dynamics of that change as well as the factors that will drive it. From within, criminal gangs have taken over sections of major cities and imposed their law and justice on its inhabitants, laws and regulations are broken at will, and law enforcement agencies, so legitimized by the authority of the state to enforce the rule of law in the maintenance of social peace have unfortunately been made to become the problem rather than the solution. In contemporary jurisprudence, the criminal who willfully breaks the law has more public sympathy and rights than the law enforcement officer who made the interdiction. Hence as law and order becomes to each according to your own interpretation, the state continues to unravel at the seams and everywhere anarchy reigns supreme.

The customary norms that have bound the framework of social life, and invariably citizenship, have been sidelined in preference for new seemingly arcane traditions that have no history behind them. The distinction between morality and immorality has become blurred such that the most odious of vices are celebrated as virtue under the hubris of disguised progressivism bereft of theoretical or moral foundation. The political rhetoric of the cliché "big government" has become a household euphemism for an attack on the state as the ruthless and all-encompassing behemoth bent on taking away individual rights as well as imposing more demanding tax regimes on society as a whole. In its lonely and paradoxical situation, the state receives little or no accolade when things are going well and people are happy; but when things go wrong (as it always does), the state as well as the government in power is visited with an unceasing opprobrium. "Contested issues are adjudicated on the basis of the merits of the case, as defined by international human rights codes, and not on the basis of national interest or how the state defines its scope of jurisdiction."[66] The news media by virtue of specific constitutional guarantees has essentially taken over the role of setting the state's political agenda by, for better or for worse, focusing and reinforcing some issues and not others; but at the same time attacking and impugning the integrity of the state and its institutions at the slightest opportunity. For the state, there is no place to hide.

Criminal cartels within the state in complicity with cartels outside of the state have developed a network system of their own that enables them to import drugs, narcotics, adulterated and counterfeit products in contravention of state laws. Within and between states, human trafficking, transborder prostitution, slavery, money laundering, credit card fraud, identity thefts, Internet hacking, and all sorts of financial crimes have run amok—and the state does not have the ability to control them. The territorial sovereignty and authority of the state has also come under attack as terrorist groups seize chunks of territory and impose their will on it including collecting taxes and informal rents from hapless citizens. Children, men, and women under the guidance of terrorist groups can now blow themselves up in a crowd of innocent citizens as long as they take hundreds with them. Instead of celebrating peace profound, the world has become numbed by uncommon violence.

A subterranean economy in the form of currency counterfeiting, child pornography, kidnapping for ransom, sale of contraband drugs, and other illicit vices have continued to operate in tandem alongside the formal economy, such that both are now viewed as contributory factors in economic growth, employment, and development. Equally unsparing of itself, the state nonetheless, harbors an implicit paradox. While it seeks to serve as an institutional and legal basis for the execution of public polices and the law, it ironically, also offers a placeholder for uncommon corruption, hoodlumism, and official malfeasance that has seen public funds siphoned away or diverted to serve narrow private interests. High-handed corruption and debauchery have become second nature to the existence of most contemporary states. In a world in which the few are more than ever willing to take advantage of the many, how we ever get to celebrate our commonness may stand as the greatest riddle of the century. In our daily encounters, mob rule and elevated agitation have overtaken sane discourse in the public space leaving little room for reciprocity and mutual exchange of ideas; and zero-sum game has become the new calculus for engaging competing issues of public policy. But the more ominous prospect is that none of these shows any sign yet of abetting either now or in the near future. And for better or for worse, most citizens and public officials seem to have accepted it as part of living in the modern state.

In the United States particularly, there are over 200 "sanctuary cities" that harbor and protect people who break the laws of the state and enter the United States illegally and in contravention of federal law. In a brazen act of political daring, some states, municipal, and local authorities under whatever guise and political expediency, seek to undermine not only the power but also of the constituted authority of the juridical state. As illustrated by Steve Salvi,[67] despite a 1996 federal law [the Illegal Immigration Reform and Immigrant Responsibility Act (IIRIRA) that requires local governments to cooperate with Department of Homeland Security's Immigration and Customs Enforcement (ICE), many large urban cities (and some small ones) have adopted so-called "sanctuary" policies. Generally, sanctuary policies instruct city employees not to notify the federal government of the presence of illegal aliens living in their communities. The policies also end the distinction between legal resident aliens and illegal aliens—so illegal aliens often benefit from taxpayer funded–government services and programs too.

As human traffickers continue to smuggle illegal migrants across state borders with impunity, authorities are also handicapped by their own laws that prevents them from enforcing who comes in and who gets out. State institutions are used to undermine the very policies they are supposed to enforce. In the United States, the court system itself, in certain respects, has not been spared. As more "liberal" judges increasingly engage in acts that I would qualify as *political jurism*, some court rulings have sought to or ended up undermining the strategic interests and foreign policies of the state, and oftentimes are used to nullify executive authority in matters that are clearly stipulated in the Constitution. They have refused or are unable to balance judicial interpretations with the ever-changing imperatives of politics and political expediency; and as such, have left most people confused as to what various aspects of the Constitution may actually mean both in law and in practice. As runaway partisan judges wade continuously into the realm of executive prerogative and office, they also invariably, seem to be destroying the democratic project one ruling at a time. And for this, many citizens have either chosen to disengage from the *public*, or they have remained frustrated at not knowing to what and where they are being herded.

Many people will take comfort in not paying their taxes to the state if the possibility of not being caught ever presents itself; and many will free-ride on the sacrifices of others where the penalty for non-contribution is minimal or nonexistent. The moral principles upon which foundational institutions of state and society have endured for centuries are ceaselessly undermined when any flimsy and irrational excuse can be manufactured to deny responsibility and accountability for wrongdoing. In the search for absolute freedom and a moralizing idealism that seems to operate above the practical manifestations of everyday realities of the human condition, one is always reminded of the three words: "What's the catch?". Unfortunately, the modern state and what it stands for is the *catch*. The state as a social system is eating itself from the inside out, while the people whose arbitrary actions undermine the stability of the social order continue to give little or no credence to the existing laws and other institutional mechanisms of social control. In a world of unfolding moral decline, where the boundary between decency and vileness is becoming narrower at each passing day, and unfortunately so, citizenship cannot be immune nor can it be an exception to the new normal that surrounds it. As things currently stand, state and society both seem to be heading in a direction very few can predict, and they are speeding toward it with reckless abandon. One of the indisputable facts of life in today's modern and modernizing societies is the relentless erosion of values both at the individual and systemic levels. But then things could get no worse.

VALUES AND IDEOLOGY: FRAMING SOCIAL RELATIONS

The importance of values in shaping the nature of social relations is due mainly to the fact that they often form the basis for consensus on some issues, but not in others. Values, in its ethical connotation, "are beliefs that are the basis for personal judgments about what is true, just, virtuous, or appropriate."[68] They are oftentimes emotion-laden, spiritual, and for most people transcendental, particularly in such cases as ideology, religion, and secularism. And this is what makes values as a framework not only for guiding behaviors, but also in providing self-justification or legitimation for behaviors whether popularly recognized or not. To the extent they are broadly shared, "values give institutional norms special significance and thus increase the probability of conformity."[69] Politically, values could be ideological, cultural, or economic; hence to the extent they help shape political preferences and decision making, values play instrumental roles in the exercise of political action. Because expressions of values "are characterized by both cognitive and emotive elements,"[70] value conflicts have become the bane of collective action, competition for power, and in some cases, domination of one value premise over another.

In such situations where it may be difficult to separate personal values from public values; it is because personal values are cognitively constructed and oftentimes hidden from public notice until they are overtly manifested in action. It can equally be argued that the foundation upon which individuals come to accept, understand, articulate, or legitimize public values, is based on its receptivity to their own personal values. People oftentimes engage in selective attention and are more likely to act and live by that which fits more appropriately to their preconceived notions or world views; or they can reject a value premise that seeks to undermine belief systems and practices that have endured and been effective over time. Personal values therefore, "are not purely individual events, but are relational in time and space."[71]

Alternatively, public values reflects a society's "normative consensus about the rights, benefits, and prerogatives to which citizens should or should not be entitled, the obligations of citizens to society, the state, and to one another, and the principles on which governments and polices should be based"[72] (such as democracy, majority rule, due process, equal treatment under the law, innocent until proven guilty, trial by jury, etc.). Because they specify the normative principles on which governments and polices should be based, public values provide direction to the behavior of public servants; hence can be expressed and safeguarded at the individual as well as systemic levels.[73] "Values are internally anchored in the actor, to be committed to and, more or less, effectively implemented; while norms on the other hand, are anchored in the structure of the situation to be taken into account or to be conformed with."[74] But the difference between personal and public values often gets blurred as soon as it becomes the basis for political disagreements and contestation over who gets what, when, and how much. And this is a key problem with values, when we are unsure about which one is operating and at what level—particularly in matters concerning the expression of rights, beliefs, and associational groupings.

Although *public values pluralism* (the notion that several competing values and orientations are tenable and can mutually coexist in society)[75] is a cherished ideal within democratic circles, but it is also a source of the inherent difficulty in achieving normative consensus. And the simple reason is that "for any given issue, people may have only one position but many interests, some more important than the others,"[76] but all nonetheless motivated by implicit or extrinsic value domains. Because we do not know what we do not know and because we cannot be too sure of the motivations behind them, "most administrative decisions cannot be determined to be appropriate and ethical simply based on the content of their final action."[77] Rather, such a determination can only be seen not as a search for the absolute truth of why administrators make one choice over the other, but as a frame of reference for mitigating the odds (not eliminating them) that personal values would transcend public values. The tenacity with which some people hold on to their value premises can be so powerful as to transform such values into a form of ideology, particularly in matters concerning politics and policymaking.

Political ideology is a value that can be shared by many people, under various formulations such as conservatism, liberalism, anarchism, and/or libertarianism. In the above regard, political ideology is a *public value*. It is also a *personal value* to the extent that individuals, in their own self-interest, have come to accept the tenets of one political ideology over another as the basis and justification for their political preferences. As an illustration, let me dwell a little bit on the ideological difference between conservatism and liberalism on almost all indicators of political governance, including rights and obligations. While there are many variations regarding the definition of ideology, the more predominant view is that *ideology* represents the "nature of political thinking people develop about how government should work and how it actually works." It provides a set of concepts or cognitive (mental) models through which people view the world around them as well as express their own political beliefs concerning the structure and institutions of government, the ways and means by which public policies are made, and the social forces that shape them. Hence, among and within political systems or regimes, you will find that different sets of ideologies persist over time (some more dominant and pronounced than the others, and some less vociferous but equally competitive).

As a concept, ideologies involve ideas and belief systems that relate to the social and political world, and that provides a philosophical basis (or conviction) for specific expressions of rights. Ideologies therefore help to shape political attitudes and the nature of political competition within a country. In other words, ideologies are highly organized and rationalized systems of ideas that directly bear on the political character of a country, as well as its political culture.[78] Conservatives generally "place more emphasis on respecting institutions and traditions and are not sure they (or others) are capable of devising a better system."[79] They seek to maintain the status quo or the way things are, particularly if there is no genuine reason for change. Alternatively, "liberalism includes a belief in human potential, in the ability of individuals to change institutions for the better, in human rationality, and in human equality and freedom."[80] For liberals, change is desirable not only for its own sake but as a means of adaptation to changing social and political values. But for both ideologies, the challenge is therefore a question of either/or; whether to maintain the status quo or change—if not for the sake of change but for the fact that the existing order of things around us is also changing.

So, What Has Changed?

The twenty-first century, long-touted as the era of great discoveries and technological innovation has left an air of uncertainty about the direction in which evolving and undeliberated value change is taking the world and humanity with it. Identity politics has created a situation where fiction becomes fact and facts become alternative truths. Traditions, institutions, and social mores that have kept society as a functional whole are being torn apart and replaced with whatever comes up in someone's imagination. Truth is questioned and ambiguity is celebrated, if for nothing but to arbitrarily inject neutralizing effects into existential questions tied to common issues of the human condition. Gender identity and the institutions that surround it has become anything you deem to call it, you own it, you evolve it, and you can recreate it despite immutable evidence to the contrary. The distinction between normality and abnormality has become deliberately blurred, and those who question what is being aimlessly heaped on everyone else without their consent are castigated and bullied into oblivion. Sane democratic debate has willfully been turned into a shouting match in which individuals and groups disrupt legislative proceedings in the "attempt to thwart democratic processes so that the people could not listen and make their own judgements."[81] Argument for the sake of argumentation has become the new collective reality, and ontology has become tautology—leaving in its wake a disenchanted and confused mass.

In our public discourse, incivility has replaced civility, and words and language are being manipulated and reinterpreted at whim to fit an evidently erroneous narrative in the inglorious attempt to justify wrongdoing and reckless behavior. Organized *mobbery* and stand-in-your-face rascality has become the new method of political expression and civil discourse in a fast-changing but uncertain world of public discourse. And this does not seem to be of much concern to many, particularly when considered in the context of the increasing level of acidity that seems to characterize an increasingly contentious American political firmament. In a new brand of authoritarian streak, alien values are being imposed on everyone else without their consent, without deliberation, and without any form of democratic discourse, yet most countries in the Western world still hold up the banner and continue to profess unceasing fidelity to the democratic ethos.

People and groups, oftentimes without so much of a reflection or hindsight, have arbitrarily arrogated to themselves specific "rights" that have no precedents or history behind them; nor were such "rights" claims ever deliberated as part of a robust democratic discourse. Acquiring "rights" have now become a function of simply stating the motion: "I have the *right* to so, so, and so," and it automatically becomes a binding fait accompli on everyone else. "We have norms because they safeguard foundational principles, such as due process, the presumption of innocence, and freedom from unreasonable and unwarranted police prying,"[82] but this can only work if society at large is beholden to it. If society is to function the way it has been designed to function, then each and every one must hold on to your values and reject that which has been imposed on you without your consent.

A creeping revisionism aimed at changing the historic American narrative, and erasing the past to reconstruct an uncertain future has emerged in the United States. We now see much of this in the new fervor to pull down historic monuments by casting problematic narratives on them, the drive to change historic names such as Columbus Day, and so on. But what has been forgotten in this modern day puritanical truth-seeking is the famous words of the Spanish poet George Santayana, that "*those who cannot remember the past are condemned to repeat it*." Should we therefore erase all historical monuments to the savagery of slavery because it reminds us of an immoral and heinous act? Would it then not be better to remind ourselves and posterity about the past evils of this world so that we could learn not to repeat it? To the extent that the future may promise new learning and knowledge, we must also not forget that it is history that provides it the foundation upon which to learn and to seek the truth.

I therefore "find it hard to resist the conjecture that we are witnessing a transformation in democracy as fundamental and lasting as the change from institutions of popular government,"[83] to a form of absolutism and value revisionism yet to be understood in all its manifestations. I see much of this happening throughout continental Europe where citizens are up in arms against their own governments as well as against each other over matters that range from the prevailing economic crisis, taxes, terrorism, unbridled immigration (legal and illegal), Brexit, resurgent political illiberalism, and cultural irredentism. Some governments are now considered by their own people as the problem as opposed to the solution; and unmistakably so, some of the governments simply turn around and stick it to their citizens by imposing on them values and policies for which there is no popular consensus. As social discontent continues to brew underneath (as was witnessed in Venezuela in January and much of the early months of 2019), the agitation for rebellion assumes a collective temperament with a potentially explosive undercard. But how benign will this be?

POWER, INTEREST, AND PURPOSE: A RECONSIDERATION

The state exists, so to say, to secure the common interest of its citizens; but different states may also have different interests in their relationships with other states in the international system. There is the recognition among realists that the source of mistrust, conflict, and anarchy that explains the structure of the international system is a result of the pursuit of different and oftentimes incompatible interests by state actors. In a situation of self-help, each state is on its own when it comes particularly to matters of national interest and sovereignty. Powerful states seek to project their own power and views onto the international system, while weaker states are, more or less, handicapped by their status in the overall structure of relations between states. Alternatively, liberal institutionalists assert that states willfully seek the collective interest of the international system, and by increasing levels of interdependence (economic or multilateral), the evolving structure of cooperation and interests would deepen to the extent that every state would seek its preservation and maintenance beyond what their own individual national interests may suggest. Peaceful coexistence and mutual trust are cherished virtues by most states and they will work to achieve them given the right conditions and incentives, suggesting, in this case, that cooperative structures and institutions could lead to *functional* outcomes.

Amid a history of recurrent conflicts and rivalry between states,[84] "the Cold War spanned not only military and strategic issues but filtered into competition over the international economy, technology (the race to outer space, nuclear arms race) sports competitions, and virtually all aspects of society."[85] Even without any external impulse to the effect, internal disequilibrium within states can also generate their own pathologies. Contemporary examples abound in the form of failed state institutions (like Somali, Libya, Yemen), insurgency movements (like the Taliban in Afghanistan and Boko Haram in Nigeria and Cameroon), and the economic crisis and market failures like the 2015 Greek *tragedy* (the debt crisis of 2015), and China's stock market crash also in 2015, that saw individual and institutional investors lose billions of dollars if not more. Today as in earlier periods, rivalries, competition, outright hostilities, and acrimony abound everywhere between and within states: between the United States and Russia over Putin's more muscular foreign policy and militarism regarding Crimea and separatists in Ukraine, between Iran and Saudi Arabia over Yemen and the evolving balance of power in the Middle East, between the United States and Iran over the latter's nuclear brinkmanship, between India and Pakistan over Jammu and Kashmir, between India and China over territories adjoining their common borders, between Israel and the Arab world over the enduring issue of Palestine, between Sunnis and Shias in almost every country where they coexist, between Sudan and South Sudan, and between North Korea and the rest of the world.

Even within countries like Libya, Syria, Iraq, South Sudan, Central African Republic, Yemen, Mali, Burundi and many others, things seem to have fallen apart and the center could not hold anymore. There was a time when piracy on the high seas was the de facto economic policy of a state (and may still be today); and as the world watched helplessly, the state known as Somali, bruised and battered, became synonymous with all that can go wrong when state, citizenship, and its institutions disconnect from each other. The restlessness of the global state system remains unabated. In some cases, the plane of political interaction between states reflects enduring conflicts between belief systems and a recurring motif in what seems to be the impossibility of understanding and reconciliation.[86] Ongoing geo-strategic realignments and power-balancing has seen a resurgent Russia under Putin as well as a rising China. With one of the world's most powerful growth economies under its control and the continuing flexing of its military muscle in the South Pacific and Asia geo-strategic hemisphere, it is unclear whether China's rise would be aggressive or peaceful—hence adding more uncertainty to the power politics of the post–Cold war era. Amid a continuing crisis of rationality, the contemporary world seems to be faced with profound problems of moral and epistemological incommensurability that refuses to be assuaged neither by manifest differences and the similarities or identities that persist through them.[87]

The current revolution in military affairs (RMAs) and the rise of asymmetric warfare and tactics has made interstate and intrastate conflicts more lethal and deadly with devastating consequences. "When asymmetric warfare is implemented, traditional defensive barriers such as military power and deterrence (that has kept the peace for the last fifty plus years) often declines in value."[88] In this regard, the deck of cards is stacked against the state, in the sense that while "terrorists or insurgents might have no reservation in killing large numbers of innocent civilians; the modern state which often operate under legal, public, and ethical constraints may be enjoined from responding in kind."[89] There is an intriguing paradox that seems to confront humanity on earth. While technological breakthroughs in medicine, nutrition, and health care have ended up securing and extending the quality of human life; the same technological breakthroughs have also unleashed unto the world so much destructive power, all marshaled for a quick and sudden obliteration of the same humanity that it seeks to preserve. After two atomic bombs were dropped during World War II on Hiroshima and Nagasaki in 1945; and for all the devastation, yet rather than evoking eternal moments of somber reflection on many countries, the lethality of the bomb has ironically become an endless fatal attraction for many countries as they seek to develop their own nuclear capabilities. And they will go to great length to get it without thinking as much about the potential consequences to their own survival.

As historical animosities and disputes endure and reinvent themselves, they have become the bane of global peace; such that peaceful resolution of conflicts has become a rare commodity. If the case can be made that citizenship can exist in "different axis of social and political life, such as in the relations between individual and the state, in the bonds that link states together in an international society, and in the much looser realm consisting of the ties between individuals and humanity,"[90] it is even more sobering when we learn that the state of the world in which we wish to embed the moral foundation of global citizenship is a world in which many states are in a seemingly perpetual crisis. While states may differ in terms of what may be in their national interests, they all seem to display similar characteristics both in structure and in function. "Each is a hierarchical structure of power over a defined membership and territory, consisting of a network of recognized rules, centralized administrative apparatus, an army for the maintenance of internal and external security, a means for appropriating and redistributing surplus labor, and a mechanism for the resolution of disputes."[91] "So conceived, any state, therefore can be analyzed in a number of related ways—legally and institutionally, politically, sociologically, and economically."[92]

While this work discusses the above approaches in great detail, it focuses more particularly on the structural-functional approach. How design systems shape and reinforce the ways and means by which states carry out their duties or obligations to their citizens. It is therefore less a matter of differences in regime types or level of development; rather it is about delineating effective structures and institutions for doing the same things that all states normally do on a basic level. Without casting judgment on the merits of a particular Constitution over others, the point is that Constitutions provide a sense of structure that defines the nature of the country and the procedural mechanisms needed to carry out its political and social functions. While structure helps to reinforce "functional specificity and division of labor, patterns governing personal status and rights, and those governing the treatment of ability and achievement,"[93] it is the insistence on treatment of all men by the same generalized, impersonal standards (ethical universalism)"[94] that differentiates democratic from totalitarian states. In the same way that states provide structure for the organization of functions or activity sets, they also provide the basis for shaping political experience and civic attitudes consistent with the type of political regime. Because of the constitutional design and the emphasis on specific freedoms and liberties, Americans mostly identify with the tenets of their egalitarian republican government. In the same vein, the design structure and institutions of the Chinese state pretty much dictate the character of the relationship between the people and the state as well as in their cultural and collectivist orientation.

For liberal states with multiparty systems, it is an empirical fact "that the organizational characteristics of parties have a profound impact on policy making and the overall functioning of democracies,"[95] but in totalitarian one-party states, it is difficult to discern where the *state* ends and the *party* begins, since both are interwoven into each other in a symbiotic marriage of convenience. In liberal democracies, the party system functions based on the institutional constraints provided by the state; but in totalitarian one-party systems, the state functions based on the institutional constraints and ideological doctrines imposed by the party. Historical examples abound in terms of Hitlerite Germany, Fascist Italy, Castro's Cuba, North Korea, or in such theocratic (de facto authoritarian) states as Iran and Saudi Arabia. It matters less whether political authority is vested in one man, an oligarchy, or on the people; the obvious fact is that the location of power and authority in both democratic and totalitarian regimes is a function of the design structure to which all forms of activities and expressions must submit. While this may change overtime in most democracies; but in totalitarian regimes, they remain obdurate (as long as the regime continues to hold on to power).

In the end, we are left with some pressing but profound questions. Should we now begin a crucial debate on how novel political and administrative processes could be made more objective and germane (one size fits all), and how the law, regulations, and social relationships could be made to self-adjust in times of dramatic change, uncertainty, and systemic turbulence? At the same time, I am persuaded to point out that while I could not pretend that the propositions put forth in this work would alone solve all of mankind's problems; my tempered reservation is nonetheless driven by two central observations: First, the inability to know and to judge in the absolute sense of the term that which really motivates individuals to behave the way they do, or to make one choice instead of the other. Secondly, while choice-making may reflect the nature and intensity of interest and advantages being sought, it is difficult to determine in advance which interests or advantages are reconcilable to each other, to what extent, and in what form.

Because "virtually all social relationships evidence conflict at one time or another, conflict is thus ubiquitous in organized social life."[96] Oftentimes conflict situations arise as a result of the constant jostling for power and influence over the incentives derived from social relationships. "Although there is a common tendency to equate conflict with the breakdown of social organization, conflict is neither identical to nor indicative of social disorganization."[97] And while it is important to know that conflicts do occur and to anticipate that they will occur, it is the analysis of these events and the ramifications they bring in the context of existing social relations that is at the core of understanding the whole system within which these social relations must take place. I have always maintained the fact that the character of a state is a function of the particular institutional design as well as the political culture and values that bind citizens to each other. Conflicts occur, not because people disagree on the merits of these values or the necessity for their continued applicability in social life; but because people disagree on how these values should be validated within the political system, or made more meaningful by serving a broader or specific end than was originally anticipated.

In the next chapter, I provide an extended review of the literature on structural functionalism. In the sense that through established mechanisms of role differentiation and action, there is a mutually reinforcing relationship between structure and function; this work draws from the structural-functional approach and the role functional contingencies play in the various activity systems that constitute state action. The chapter also illustrates the applicability of the sociotechnical systems framework in the coordination and integration of activity systems around people, technology, and process.

NOTES

1. Wendt, Alexander. 1999. *Social Theory of International Politics*. New York: Cambridge University Press, 370.

2. Kalu, Kalu N. 2008. *State Power, Autarchy, and Political Conquest in Nigerian Federalism*. Lanham, MD: Lexington Books, 11.

3. Habermas, Jurgen. 1975. *Legitimation Crisis*. Boston, MA: Beacon Press, 19.

4. Wood, Neal. 1988. *Cicero's Social and Political Thought*. Berkeley, CA: University of California Press, 137.

5. Midgal, Joel S. 1994. "The State in Society: As Approach to Struggles for Domination." In *State Power and Social Forces: Domination and Transformation in the Third World*, edited by Joel S. Midgal., Atul Kohli., and Vivienne Shue, 7–34, 9.

6. Weber, Max. 1947. *The Theory of Social and Economic Organization* (Translated by A. M. Henderson and Talcott Parsons). New York: The Free Press, 57.

7. Smith, Alan G. 2017. *A Comparative Introduction to Political Science: Convention and Cooperation*. Lanham, MD: Rowman & Littlefield, 92.

8. Raadschelders, Jos C. N. 2003. *Government: A Public Administration Perspective*. Armonk, NY: M. E. Sharpe, 48.

9. Weber, Max. 1947. *The Theory of Social and Economic Organization*, 156.

10. Parson, Talcott. 1954. *Essays in Sociological Theory* (Revised Edition). New York: The Free Press, 241.

11. Parson, Talcott .1954. *Essays in Sociological Theory* (Revised Edition), 241.

12. Parson, Talcott. 1954. *Essays in Sociological Theory* (Revised Edition), 239.

13. Weber, Max. 1947. *The Theory of Social and Economic Organization*, 33.

14. Weber, Max. 1968. *Economy and Society: An Outline of Interpretive Sociology* (Edited by Guenther Ross and Claus Wittich). New York: Bedminster Press, 65.

15. Weber, Max. 1947. *The Theory of Social and Economic Organization*, 34–35.

16. Parsons, Talcott. 1947. "Introduction: Weber's Methodology of Social Science." In *The Theory of Social and Economic Organization,* edited by Max Weber, 8–29. New York: The Free Press, 20.

17. Weber, Max. 1968. *Economy and Society: An Outline of Interpretive Sociology*, 341.

18. Parsons, Talcott. 1947. "Introduction: Weber's Methodology of Social Science," 8–29, 22.

19. Weber, Max. 1968. *On Charisma and Institution Building* (Edited by S. N. Eisenstadt). Chicago, IL: The University of Chicago Press, 11–12.

20. Hobbes, Thomas. 1994. *Leviathan* (edited with Introduction and Notes by Edwin Curley). Indianapolis, IN: Hackett Publishing Co, Inc, xxxiii.

21. Bates, Clifford Angell, Jr. 2003. *Aristotle's "Best Regime:" Kingship, Democracy, and the Rule of Law*. Baton Rouge, LA: Louisiana State University Press, 63.

22. Hobbes, Thomas. 1994. *Leviathan* (edited with Introduction and Notes by Edwin Curley), xxxiv.

23. Hanson, Donald. 1984. "Thomas Hobbes' Highway to Peace." *International Organization* 38: 329–354.

24. Wendt, Alexander. 1999. *Social Theory of International Politics*, 353.

25. Sayers, Sean. 1999. *Plato's Republic: An Introduction*. Edinburgh, Great Britain: Edinburgh University Press, 24.

26. Sayers, Sean. 1999. *Plato's Republic: An Introduction*, 53.

27. Ingraham, Patricia W., and Laurence E. Lynn, Jr., eds. 2004. *The Art of Governance: Analyzing Management and Administration*. Washington D. C: Georgetown University Press, 4. See also Oliver Williamson. 1996. *The Mechanisms of Governance*. New York: Oxford University Press.

28. Ingraham, Patricia W., and Laurence E. Lynn, Jr., eds. *The Art of Governance: Analyzing Management and Administration*, 6.

29. Ingraham, Patricia W., and Laurence E. Lynn, Jr., ed. *The Art of Governance: Analyzing Management and Administration*, 6. See also Laurence E. Lynn, Jr., Carolyn J. Heinrich, and Carolyn J. Hill. 2001. *Improving Governance: A New Logic for Empirical Research*. Washington D.C: Georgetown University Press.

30. Durkheim, Emile. 1957/1992. *Professional Ethics and Civic Morals*. London: Routledge, 214.

31. Parsons, Talcott. 1967. *Sociological Theory and Modern Society*. New York: The Free Press, 313.

32. Brinkerhoff, Derick W. 2005. "Rebuilding Governance in Failed States and Post-Conflict Societies: Core Concepts and Cross-Cutting Themes." *Public Administration and Development* 25: 3–14, 6. See also the World Bank. 2000. *Reforming Public Institutions and Strengthening Governance: A World Bank Strategy*. Washington D.C: World Bank's Poverty Reduction and Economic Management Network.

33. Levi-Faur, David. 2012. "From Big Government to Big Governance?" *The Oxford Handbook of Governance*, Online, September 2012, 2.

34. Hummel, Ralph P. 1987. *The Bureaucratic Experience*. 3rd ed. New York: St. Martin's Press, 158.

35. Simon, Herbert A. 1957. *Administrative Behavior: A Study of Decision-Making Processes in Administrative Organization*. New York: The Free Press, 126. See also Jos C.N. Raadschelders and Richard J. Stillman II. 2007. "Toward a New Conceptual Framework for Studying Administrative Authority." *Administrative Theory & Praxis* 29, no. 1: 4–40, 22.

36. Eagan, Jennifer L. 2007. "Is Authority in Public Administration Separable from Authoritarianism? Personalities, Institutions, and Resistance." *Administrative Theory & Praxis* 29, no. 1: 83–101, 84.

37. Raadschelders, Jos C. N., and Richard J. Stillman II. 2007. "Toward a New Conceptual Framework for Studying Administrative Authority." *Administrative Theory & Praxis* 29, no. 1: 4–40, 29.

38. Marshall, Gary S. 2007. "Commanded to Enjoy: The Waning of Traditional Authority and Its Implications for Public Administration." *Administrative Theory & Praxis* 29, no. 1: 102–114, 102–103.

39. This sub-section titled "Legitimation and Action" is based on a revised and updated excerpt from an earlier work of the author Kalu N. Kalu. 2008. *State Power, Autarchy, and Political Conquest in Nigerian Federalism*. Lanham, MD: Lexington Books, 11–16.

40. Macridis, Roy C., and Steven L. Burg. 1991. *Introduction to Comparative Politics: Regimes and Change*. New York: Longman, 5.

41. Searle, John R. 2010. *Making the Social World: The Structure of Human Civilization*. Oxford, UK: Oxford University Press, 163.

42. Groom, A.J. R. 1975. "Functionalism and World Society." In *Functionalism: Theory and Practice in International Relations*, edited by A. J. R. Groom and Paul Taylor, 93–111. New York: Crane, Russak & Company, 94.

43. Stepan, Alfred. 1978. *The State and Society: Peru in Comparative Perspective*. Princeton, NJ: Princeton University Press, xi.

44. Stepan, Alfred. 1978. *The State and Society: Peru in Comparative Perspective*, xii.

45. Turner, Bryan S. 1957/1992. "Preface to the Second Edition: Interpreting Emile Durkheim." In Emile Durkheim. 1957/1992. *Professional Ethics and Civic Morals*. London: Routledge, xiii–xlii, xxxviii.

46. Wood, Neal. 1988. *Cicero's Social and Political Thought*. Berkeley, CA: University of California Press, 134.

47. Chazan, Naomi, Robert Mortimer, John Ravenhill, and Donald Rothchild. 1992. *Politics and Society in Contemporary Africa*. Boulder, CO: Lynne Rienner Publishers, 39.

48. Migdal, Joel S., Atul Kahli., and Vivienne Shue. 1994. *State Power and Social Forces: Domination and Transformation in the Third World*. New York: Cambridge University Press, 13.

49. Kalu, Kalu N. 2017. *Citizenship: Identity, Institutions and the Postmodern Challenge*. New York: Routledge, 30. See also P. Beaudry. 2003. *The Economic Policy that Made the Peace of Westphalia*. Washington, D.C.: The Schiller Institute.

50. Kalu, Kalu N. 2017. *Citizenship: Identity, Institutions and the Postmodern Challenge*, 30.

51. Parsons, Talcott. 1951. *The Social System*. Glencoe, IL: The Free Press, 28.

52. Rotberg, Robert. 2006. "Failed States in a World of Terror." In *Global Politics in a Changing World*, 3rd Ed., edited by Richard W. Mansbach and Edward Rhodes, 131–137. Boston, MA: Houghton-Mifflin, 134.

53. Ostrom, Elinor. 1990. *Governing the Commons: The Evolution of Institutions for Collective Action*. Cambridge, UK: Cambridge University Press, 215.

54. Calabresi, Massimo. 2018. "The Spy Masters." *Time* 191, no. 22 (June 11), 43.

55. Calabresi, Massimo. 2018. "The Spy Masters," 44.

56. This section of the chapter is a revised and updated excerpt from an earlier work *Citizenship: Identity, Institutions, and the Postmodern Challenge,* 115–119.

57. Gaddis, John Lewis. 2004. *Surprise, Security, and the American Experience.* Cambridge, MA: Harvard University Press, 79.

58. Gaddis, John Lewis. 2004. *Surprise, Security, and the American Experience.* 79.

59. Gaddis, John Lewis. 2004. *Surprise, Security, and the American Experience,* 79.

60. Carter, A. 2001. *The Political Theory of Global Citizenship.* New York: Routledge, 19.

61. Jacobson, David. 1998. *State and Society in a World Unbound. In Public Rights, Public Rules: Constituting Citizens in the World Polity and National Policy,* edited by Connie L. McNeely, 41–57. New York: Garland Publishing Inc., 42.

62. Jacobson, David. 1998. *State and Society in a World Unbound. In Public Rights, Public Rules: Constituting Citizens in the World Polity and National Policy,* edited by Connie L. McNeely, 41–57, 41.

63. Burton , John W. 1975. "Functionalism and the Resolution of Conflict." In *Functionalism: Theory and Practice in International Relations*, edited by A. J. R. Groom and Paul Taylor, 238–249. New York: Crane, Russak & Company, 246.

64. Steward, Dan. 2018. "Autocrats Grow Bolder." *Time* 192, no. 16: 21–22, 22.

65. Steward, Dan. 2018. "Autocrats Grow Bolder," 21–22, 22.

66. Jacobson, D. 1996. *Rights Across Borders: Immigration and the Decline of Citizenship*. Baltimore, MD: The Johns Hopkins University Press, 119. See also Harvard Law Review. 1990. "Constructing the State Extra-Territorially: Jurisdictional Discourse, the National Interest and Transnational Norms." *Harvard Law Review* 103, no. 6: 1273–1305, 1297.

67. Salvi, Steve .2015. The Original List of Sanctuary Cities, USA. http://ojjpac.org/sanctuary.asp. Accessed on October 13, 2015.

68. Hill, Carolyn J., and Laurence E. Lynn, Jr. 2016. *Public Management: Thinking and Acting in Three Dimensions* (2nd Ed.). Thousand oaks, CA: Sage Publications, 285.

69. Turner, Jonathan H. 2003. *Human Institutions: A Theory of Societal Evolution.* Lanham, MD: Rowman & Littlefield Publishers, Inc., 72.

70. Hill, Carolyn J., and Laurence E. Lynn, Jr. 2016. *Public Management: Thinking and Acting in Three Dimensions*, 2nd ed., 285.

71. Rutgers, Mark R. 2015. "As Good as It Gets? On the Meaning of Public Value in the Study of Policy and Management." *American Review of Public Administration* 45, no. 1: 29–45, 35.

72. Bozeman, Barry. 2007. *Public Values and Public Interest: Counterbalancing Economic Individualism.* Washington, D.C.: Georgetown University Press, 13. See

also Carolyn J. Hill, and Laurence E. Lynn, Jr. 2016. *Public Management: Thinking and Acting in Three Dimensions*, 2nd ed., 287.

73. Andersen, Lotte Bøgh, Torben Beck Jørgensen, Anne Mette Kjeldsen, Lene HolmPedersen, and Karsten Vrangbæk. 2012. "Public Values and Public Service Motivation: Conceptual and Empirical Relationships." *The American Review of Public Administration* 43, no. 3: 292–311, 294.

74. Parsons, Talcott. 2007. *The American Society: A Theory of the Societal Community*, edited and introduced by Giuseppe Sciortino. Boulder, CO: Paradigm Publishers, 205.

75. Nabatchi, Tina. 2012. "Putting the 'Public' Back in Public Values Research: Designing Participation to Identify and Respond to Value." *Public Administration Review* 72, no. 5: 699–708, 700.

76. Nabatchi, Tina.2 012. "Putting the 'Public' Back in Public Values Research: Designing Participation to Identify and Respond to Value." *Public Administration Review*, 701.

77. Van Wart, Montgomery. 1998. *Changing Public Sector Values*. New York: Garland Publishing, Inc, 23.

78. Mahler, Gregory S. 2013. *Principles of Comparative Politics*, Upper Saddle River, NJ: Pearson, 40–44.

79. Mahler, Gregory S. 2013. *Principles of Comparative Politics*, 40.

80. Mahler, Gregory S. 2013. *Principles of Comparative Politics*. 40.

81. Noonan, Peggy. 2018. "Voices of Reason—and Unreason." *The Wall Street Journal*, October 13–14, A17.

82. Melloan, George. 2018. "Is 'First, Kill All the Lawyers' the Democrats' New Credo?" *The Wall Street Journal*, October 13–14, A17.

83. Cited comment is quoted from Dahl, Robert A. 1982. *Dilemmas of Pluralist Democracy: Autonomy vs. Control*. New Haven, CT: Yale University Press, 80.

84. The following section of the chapter is a revised and updated excerpt from an earlier work *Citizenship: Identity, Institutions, and the Postmodern Challenge,* 117–118.

85. Quackenbush, Stephen L. 2015. *International Conflict: Logic and Evidence*. Thousand Oaks, CA: Sage-CQ, 319.

86. Bhaskar, Roy. 2007. "Theorising Ontology." In *Contributions to Social Ontology*, edited by Clive Lawson, John Latsis, and Nuno Martins, 192–204. London: Routledge, 200.

87. See Bhaskar, Roy. 2007. "Theorising Ontology." In *Contributions to Social Ontology*, 200–201.

88. Kay, Sean. 2015. *Global Security in the Twenty-First Century: The Quest for Power and the Search for Peace*. Lanham, MD: Rowman & Littlefield Publishers, 246.

89. Kay, Sean. 2015. *Global Security in the Twenty-First Century: The Quest for Power and the Search for Peace*, 247.

90. Linklater, Andrew. 2007. *Critical Theory and World Politics: Citizenship, Sovereignty and Humanity*. New York: Routledge, 76.

91. Wood, Neal. 1988. *Cicero's Social and Political Thought*. Berkeley, CA: University of California Press, 124.

92. Wood, Neal. 1988. *Cicero's Social and Political Thought*, 124.

93. Weber, Max. 1947. *The Theory of Social and Economic Organization*, 82.

94. Weber, Max. 1947. *The Theory of Social and Economic Organization*, 80.

95. Mayhew, David. 1974. *Congress: The Electoral Connection*. New Haven, CT: Yale University Press. See also Mathew McCubbins and Frances Rosenbluth. 1995. "Party Provision for Personal Politics: Dividing the Vote in Japan." In *Structure and Policy in Japan and the United States*, edited by Peter Cowhey and Mathew McCubbins, 35–55. Cambridge, UK: Cambridge University Press; and Marcus Kreuzer. 2001. *Institutions and Innovation: Voters, Parties, and Interest Groups in the Consolidation of Democracy – France and Germany*, 1870–1939. Ann Arbor, MI: The University of Michigan Press, 163.

96. Olsen Marvin E. 1978. *The Process of Social Organization: Power in Social Systems*. New York: Holt, Rinehart and Winston, 307.

97. Olsen Marvin E. 1978. *The Process of Social Organization: Power in Social Systems*, 309.

Chapter 3

Structural Functionalism

Stable States and Organizational Forms

In the previous two chapters, I have tried to focus on a detailed elaboration of the nature of states (as social systems) and how they are able to maintain a sense of order and functionality over time. Through established mechanisms of conduct and the differentiation of various roles, social systems create a pattern of institutional relationships that have enduring value; that is, they are able to reproduce and function through the organized system of its several parts. In that there is a mutually reinforcing relationship between structure (the way things are organized) and their *functions* (the processes by which they satisfy specific objectives); this work draws from the richness of structural functionalism in the analysis of the state, government, and its institutions.

Although structural functionalism and functionalism are essentially considered to have the same epistemological foundation; structural functionalism sees society as a structure with interrelated parts, while functionalism sees society as a whole in terms of the functions played by its constituent parts. "They have frequently merged not only because of their symbiotic implications, but because both perspectives emphasize a number of other conceptual features that make them highly compatible";[1] hence, both terms are generally used interchangeably. The premise of functional theory used in this work is also equally grounded in the structural functional framework. The utility of structural functionalism in this work is very useful for the systematic analysis of complex sets of activities that are mutually reinforcing as well as the pattern maintenance structure that helps to sustain them. It is also useful as a framework for analyzing the distribution of functions or activities and their relative implications within a social system (state or government), and how adjustments or adaptations to system outcomes can be made in such a way that stability or systemic equilibrium conditions is achieved.

Functional analysis examines the social significance of phenomena, that is, the *function* they serve a particular society in sustaining the whole."[2] The application of the term *function* has disciplinary overlaps, but we can recognize the fact that while "functions are performed by occupants of designated positions, they are also shaped by a wide range of standardized activities, social processes, culture patterns and belief systems found in society."[3] "Since it was first introduced by Leibniz, the word *function* has its most precise significance in mathematics, where it refers to a variable considered in relation to one or more other variables in terms of which it may be expressed or on the value of which its own value depends."[4] Though with distinct connotation, social scientists generally view the term *function* as involving the notion of interdependence, reciprocal relations, or mutually dependent variations."[5]

However, "functionalism as a school of thought in anthropology emerged in the early twentieth century as a reaction to the excesses of the evolutionary and diffusionist theories of the nineteenth century and the historicism of the early twentieth century. Its premise sought to view society as a whole by looking at the contributions of its constituent parts to the maintenance of the whole. Two versions of functionalism developed between 1910 and 1930: Malinowski's biocultural (or psychological) functionalism, and Radcliffe-Brown's structural functionalism.[6] For Malinowski, individuals have physiological needs (food, shelter, etc.); hence, social institutions exist to serve those needs.[7] Malinowski sees functional analysis as the "part which social or cultural items play in the society. His was an attempt at the explanation of anthropological facts at all levels of development by their *function,* by the part which they play within the integral system of culture, and by the manner in which they are related to each other within the system."[8] Drawing from a biological analogy, Radcliffe-Brown asserts that "the function of a recurrent physiological process is thus a correspondence between it and the needs (the necessary conditions of existence) of the organism."[9]

But in the social sphere where individual human beings are connected by networks of social relations into an integrated whole, "the *function* of any recurrent activity is the part it plays in the social life as a whole and therefore the contribution it makes to the maintenance of the structural continuity."[10] Radcliffe-Brown suggested that "a society is a system of relationships maintaining itself through cybernetic feedback, while institutions are orderly sets of relationships whose function is to maintain the society as a system."[11] On his part, Talcott Parsons held that "the social system is made up of the actions of individuals";[12] and as behaviors are repeated in more interactions, expectations are entrenched or institutionalized, and formal roles develop—thus creating stability across social interactions. "The collectivities of roles complement each other in the fulfilment of functions for society as a whole."[13] While some roles are bound up in institutions and social structures (economic, education, legal), they are functional in the sense that they assist society in operating and fulfilling its functional needs so that society runs smoothly.[14] For the fact that most functional arrangements have the virtue of technical self-determination, the value neutrality they embody ought to make them more readily acceptable.[15] Functional analysis, therefore, "is an attempt to explain stability by discovering how practices fit together to sustain that stability; hence the function of a practice is its role in sustaining the overall social structure."[16] Although this work draws heavily from the sociological approach, what would be reflected in latter chapters is an effort to integrate several grand theories in the discipline in such a way that they complement the richness of functional analysis in the understanding of state action.

In this chapter, four critical arguments will be advanced. First, that effective institutional and organizational outcomes can be achieved when conceived as part of a broader structural-functional framework of social action; secondly, that Talcott Parsons' GAIL framework offers a crucial pathway for the development of structural capabilities that could advance the functional effectiveness of government and the constitutional rules of administrative behavior and accountability. Thirdly, that the overwhelming focus on "functional outcomes" as an objective can be more successful when *functional contingencies* and the *interactional effects* of system elements have been properly addressed; and the fourth illustrates the utility of the sociotechnical systems approach as a working model in the design of key administrative institutions.

THEORETICAL AND PRACTICAL EXPLANATIONS

By building on the central tenets of Parsonian structural-functionalism, this work focuses on *structure*, *process*, and *norms* as critical to the development of enduring states and institutions.[17] The concept of *function* utilized here is derived from both macro (social organization) and micro (individual) level of analyses on how a series of actions, practices, and differentiated roles are able to sustain a level of organic equilibrium over time. While equilibrium suggests a type of "stable state," it helps to reinforce the argument that effective institutions (including individual behaviors, norms, and values) can provide the structural foundation needed for successful state-building initiatives. Hence by drawing from the theoretical premise of structural functionalism, this work helps to address the "how" question as well as shed more light on the design processes conducive to effective functional outcomes. Functions do not carry themselves out; they are influenced and constrained by a system of structures and regulatory mechanisms (including cognition or thought processes) that define what is or is not technically or normatively permissible under prevailing conditions.

As the dominant perspective of cultural anthropologists[18] and rural sociologists,[19] structural functionalism takes the view that society consists of parts (i.e., police, hospitals, schools, and prisons) each of which have their own functions and work together to promote social stability. It assumes that society is a system comprised of social structures, institutions, or roles. While "structure" refers to a system of organized parts, the "function" reflects the expressed contribution made by any of those parts to the fulfillment of the goal of the larger system of which they are a part. In structural-functionalism, the goal of any system is to maintain unity of the functional parts in such a way that it leads to a stable equilibrium condition. Because the parts could represent individuals who participate in social life and occupy statuses within the system, the social network is made up of social relationships between individuals of a society—all of whom are, in turn, controlled by norms and patterns that govern behavior as well as serve as a template that helps to return society to a normal state of affairs in the case of a disturbance. These eventually help to create a sense of shared awareness or common understanding among members of a society such that the cohesion of common experience creates a sense of organic solidarity and unity of purpose.

Like earlier cultural anthropologists such as Durkheim and others, Parsons was concerned with the problem of social order, cooperation, and social integration. He held that while this comes from the values of society and of social actors, when people act on the basis of their values their actions are oriented and also constrained by the values and norms around them. Hence these norms and values are the basis of social order.[20] To the extent that they have enduring and practical value, I view norms and values as institutions in terms of their integrative potentials and regulatory capacity. It does not matter how much effort is spent reconstructing the structural and administrative infrastructure of the state, the effort would sooner or later crumble if hitherto existing norms and values (social institutions) are not rehabilitated first. It is on the foundation of these social institutions (norms and values), especially when they are resilient, that we can hope to reconstruct other structural elements critical to government effectiveness. By focusing on stability, equilibrium, and survivability, the structural-functional model illustrates four elemental features that would help state and society to achieve the "stable state" or goal being sought. These are structure, function, interdependence and equilibrium, and evolutionary change, all of which are further elaborated below:[21]

Structure

Structure refers to enduring relations between individuals, groups, and larger units including role assignments (authority and responsibility), grouping of positions in divisions, departments, standard operating procedures, job design, and physical arrangements.[22] Social systems have certain needs and society is a system of social structures made up of economic, legal, educational systems, and groups or associations. If and when the needs of society are met, it is the social structures that shape the boundaries within which these needs are met. In the sense that they help society to operate, the structures are therefore functional. And because interconnections exist within and among these structures, individual and group actions are constrained by them. While structure helps to moderate aberrant behavior, it also helps to establish a sense of predictability in the potential outcome of social action.

Function

Each society has certain needs that must be met for social life to survive and develop. Goods and services must be produced and distributed, and in order for people to survive, there must be some administration of justice, a political system must exist, and some family structure must operate so as to provide a means to reproduce the population and maintain social life on a daily basis. In the structural-functional model, individuals carry out each of these tasks in various institutions and roles that are consistent with the structures and norms of society. Robert K. Merton calls these *manifest functions*[23]—those objective consequences contributing to the adjustment or adaptation of the system which are intended and recognized by participants in the system. Because the shared values and norms, the institutions of the family, and the generally agreed-upon means for accomplishing ends are functional for the operation of society as a system, societies and political structures decay or atrophy when existing values and procedural norms of social action and engagement fall apart or are severely disturbed.

Interdependence and Equilibrium

The roles taken on by people as well as the various institutions and organizations of society are interdependent. A change in one part affects the others, requiring other parts to take account of the changes, modify their actions, and adapt as necessary. So long as roles are performed, the structures should function smoothly, and it is individuals carrying out their functions and roles properly within the structures that make the structures work. Disturbances in the structure and roles (system or society) trigger a series of adjustments in the various parts of the system that attempts to return it to a state of equilibrium. Parsons' central premise is that for any system, "there is a tendency toward seeking equilibrium, but such a tendency is not automatic or necessarily predictable."[24] Because "no particular pattern of interaction can simultaneously satisfy all the needs of all the individuals and groups involved;

unsatisfied needs are more likely to becomes sources of tension and possible conflict within given systems."[25] As a result, the notion of equilibrium does not necessarily suggest a "static" condition nor does it suggest the existence of stability or the negation of instability; rather equilibrium conditions are simultaneously recurrent and continuous.

Evolutionary Change

In the structural-functional framework, conflicts or external factors stimulate adjustment of the parts as they move toward a new equilibrium. As changes occur, the various parts of societies become more differentiated, with these parts adapting to new needs and problems. Societies become more complex, with new institutions and subsystems developing that perform the new functions required to make them (societies) operate smoothly. But what is essential is also a realistic and timely analysis of what these changes would mean and what type of new resources and capabilities would be needed to adapt them to the evolving structure of social relationships. From the viewpoint of the political system, structural functionalism sees the polity as an overall system of interacting parts. By adapting an organic metaphor, it views the social, psychological, and cultural attributes of individuals as the parameter driving much of the systems operation;[26] hence political outcomes are a response to the competing needs of the system.

Because the dynamic *interaction* of differentiated roles aim towards the achievement of a specific objective (a stable state system), the existing cultural norms of society also serve as "check points" or self-corrective mechanisms that helps to maintain balance and continuity in the process. "Once a body of rules or norms is firmly established in authority they can remain intact through a considerable shift in motives—for there develops an interlocking of interests in the maintenance of the system."[27] Because he was so much concerned about the problem of social order and how pattern variables become institutionalized over time, it is important to illuminate further the defining characteristics of Talcott Parsons' structural functionalism and its practical utility in the context of state action and system stability.

PARSONS' "GAIL" AS ACTION FRAMEWORK

The Parsonian approach accepts the fundamental premise that problems of social organization arise in all forms of human society. But what these problems are can be determined by analyzing the various requirements of cooperation through a rational ends-means process. In this regard, the actors must thus deal with two analytically distinct problem areas: that of determining the technically effective method of cooperation for attaining chosen ends, and secondly, that of maintaining efficient cooperation.[28] Because the main goal of government is to maintain the normal functioning of the administrative, institutional, and economic roles of the state, it is therefore important that we understand the system of social action within which these roles must take place. As stated by Morse,[29] a system of social action is composed of three types of subsystems: the *personality systems* of at least two individual actors, consisting of internalized "need dispositions" and the requisite "motivational commitment" to various types of goals and patterns of behavior; the *social system*—consisting of defined roles and their associated and institutionalized role expectations; and the *culture system*, consisting of the heritage of knowledge, beliefs, ideas, technologies, mores, customs, habit, laws, together with the symbols and languages that represent them. While the culture system serves as the major binding element, no system of action could survive unless the three subsystems are mutually consistent within some relative degree of tolerance.[30]

Because the success of social action is dependent on the relationship between structure and process, Parsons hypothesized that a *process* in any social system is subject to four independent functional imperatives (system requisites for all actions systems) which must be resolved adequately if equilibrium and/or continuing existence of the system is to be maintained. "Functional imperatives generate the fault lines along which a social structure becomes differentiated; and differentiation between functional requirements is due to the fact that various functional needs are often in conflict, in ways that efforts directed at solving one functional problem interfere with efforts directed toward the others."[31] Structural differentiation therefore helps to reduce social frictions. The four functional imperatives are:[32] Goal attainment, Adaptation, Integration, and Latency:

Goal Attainment

This is the objective of the social action cycle—when the subsystem (i.e., education or culture) has "completed" its contribution to the functioning of a larger system (state)—that is, when the subsystem has attained a goal that is "intermediate" (not final) from the larger system standpoint. But in this case, what is important is that the process of goal attainment remains active as a means of keeping the action system moving steadily toward its goals. In figure 3.1, the various administrative institutions (education, health, defense, agriculture, environment, transportation and communication, etc.) are subsystems and they, in one way or the other, contribute continuously toward the goal of providing public services. They exist because they serve vital and different roles in the functioning of society, without which the state loses its primary purpose for being. To the extent that social or policy institutions enable the state to provide public services to the citizens, they can be said to be functional. Of specific note is that the development of institutions such as education, health, and agriculture are most effective in the early and mid-stages of institutional development.

For example, while agriculture provides the basic means for subsistence and feeding the people, health programs helps in the maintenance of physical vitality and quality of life. Education provides the foundation for learning, the preservation of values, and the acquisition of new knowledge for the political and economic advancement of both state and society. In the evolution of modern societies from primitive to advanced industrialized systems, education also "evolved progressively as a formal system of instruction, imparting a particular curriculum or the other, notions of the civic culture, and establishing a highly ritualized passage through the system; thereby helping in the reproduction of societal members who can participate in, and fit into, other

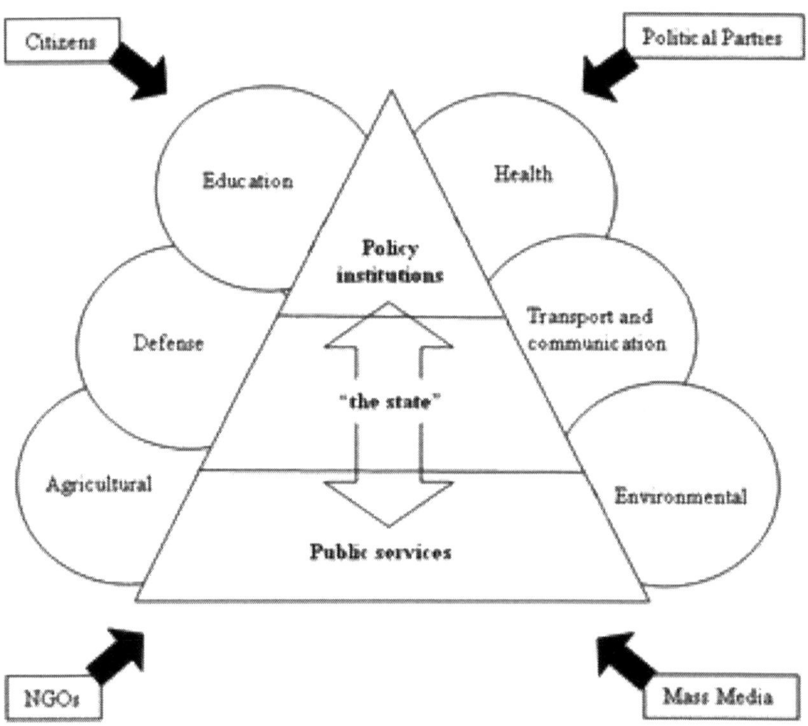

Figure 3.1 An Organic Framework for System Development and Consolidation. *Source*: Adapted from Helge Godo, et al., *The System of Innovation in the Public Sector* (2008). p. 168.

institutional spheres of public and private lives."[33] Collectively, and because the various social or policy institutions depend on and reinforce each other in specific ways, they help to create a pattern of order and stability through which basic institutional structures and social frameworks are stored, learned, and passed on to future generations.

Adaptation

This is the process of mobilizing the technical means required for goal attainment. While it is also a continuous process, the problem of adaptation is that of properly perceiving and rationally manipulating the object world for the attainment of ends, including cooperation and unity of purpose. In figure 3.1, policy institutions (by making new laws and regulations, and providing funding) can help in the process of adaptation. There may also be other roles performed by nongovernmental organizations (NGOs), and the citizens at large (public opinion, issue advocacy, or by participating in the electoral system)—all of which can provide stabilizing effects toward system continuity and performance.

Integration

This is the process of achieving and maintaining appropriate emotional and social relations among those directly involved in the goal attainment process, the "satisfactory resolution of conflicts among the various units of the system,"[34] in a system of action viewed as a continuing entity. This would involve both internal and external stakeholders (media, NGOS, citizens, political parties) who have different roles to play in the goal attainment process of providing various public services and ensuring state legitimacy. The problem of integration therefore is that of holding the various actors and agencies in line, of creating and maintaining solidarity, and devising a fair procedure for sharing the spoils of cooperation (distributive justice).

Latency

This is the period of time between successive goal-attainment processes and is not necessarily a period of inactivity. The activities may consist in restoring, maintaining, or creating the energies, motives, and values of the cooperating actors or units as a desirable end. While this may not advance the larger system toward any specific goal, these activities perform a pattern maintenance function that keeps the "wheels" of the system continuously "greased and warmed up"—so that the various units can be effectively activated when needed or at opportune moments in time. In this regard, every unit or institution (citizens, media, political parties, NGOs, administrative agencies, and political institutions) must be expected to perform their latency functions if the whole system is to survive intact. The importance of *latency* as a stabilizing force lay in its expediency. Latency offers an ability to call up various adaptive mechanisms to deal with unexpected and unrecognized situations that may come up during periods of change and turbulence. Oftentimes, latency requires the building of excess capacity into the framework of functional relationships across all spectrums of existing work processes (both vertically and horizontally).

In the final analysis, the utility of adapting the GAIL framework as an action framework for effective governance initiatives is that it serves two main purposes: one of "task performance" (goal attainment and adaptation), and the other of system maintenance or survivability (integration and latency). It also helps us to analyze key problems of social action from both a micro and macro perspectives, in such a way that the emotional and expressive components of individual action are factored as highly consequential for overall system integration and efficacy. By adapting the "GAIL" framework to the resolution of the problems of the state or government as a social system, I believe that we can be able to achieve a greater understanding of the forces at work and how interdependent (interactive) institutional processes could be adapted to provide the enabling condition for system stability, administrative accommodation, and functional effectiveness despite prevailing contingencies.

FUNCTIONAL CONTINGENCIES: HOW BENIGN?

As a way of satisfying the primary requirement for system maintenance, every part of a system must perform its designed function. I argue that this assumption, though tenable to an extent, is not a sufficient condition for the achievement of stable states. The notion of *functional contingencies* developed here, provides the missing link as to why specific functions or actions do not always lead to their desired ends; why institutions fail, or why some states keep getting worse while others get better. But it also helps to illuminate specific areas in the literature where functional analysis could be enriched, whether one views it as a hypothesis or as a theory.

Functional contingencies are those things or situations that have a direct influence on whether a function or activity set achieves its purpose or not. When they contribute in a positive way, they are known as *facilitators*, but when they create conditions where the function prevents or does not contribute to the desired end, they are then known as *inhibitors*. As a phenomenon, a *function* is an activity set with an intrinsic requirement for energy, nourishment, and renewal. Such requirements include individual knowledge base or skill, rationality, effort, dexterity, motivation, needs, and expectations. Every activity (or function) requires a certain amount of skill or dexterity, and it matters no less whether it is the activity of cooking and cleaning, the writing of a book, or the building of a house.[35] But when viewed in its elemental properties, the *function* itself always requires some material (or idea) upon which it will be performed and which through fabrication (or adaptation) is transformed into a worldly object as an outcome that satisfies a desired end.[36] Hence, the outcome of a particular function is the materialization "whose end has come when the object of necessity is achieved, ready to be added to the common world of things."[37] Hannah Arendt argues that a *function* itself "regardless of historical circumstances and independent of its location in the private or public realm possesses indeed a necessity or need of its own, no matter how futile and non-durable its products may be."[38] The individual who occupies a specific role or functional position within a social system (state or an organization) should be expected to have the knowledge base, cognitive capacity, and motivational level critical to performing the functions or actions required of the position.

But where all or some of these functional requirements does not exist, the function no matter how well designed would not be able to achieve the desired end. If and when it seems to have done so, the outcome or result could either fall short of expectations or reflect a less than optimal outcome. In the worst case scenario, it would lead to system failure. Many states and organizations have failed not because they lacked the formal processes or structural design to get the job done; they failed because the individuals assigned to specific positions do not have the requisite capabilities or the motivational desire critical to performing well in the positions they have been assigned. But at other times, a function or activity fails to achieve a set object not because individuals are not capable, but because the operational environment has decayed, hence is not able to provide the needed and adequate supporting mechanism. In functional analysis, the nature and type of environment is also consequential. Social systems much like organizations are considered open systems with competing obligations imposed on them by both internal and external environmental contingencies. The close internal environment which includes the various actors, roles, and activity sets that help to satisfy the conditions for the system's well-being and stability provides the institutional basis for the maintenance of identity as well as its legitimation. The general environment, on the other hand, includes other sub-systems such as "the economy, the legal and political systems, social institutions such as the family, population distribution and composition, and local or national cultures within or along which the system (a *state*) operates."[39] In the case of states, and just like organizations, a friendly and munificent environment is also a functional contingency.

By taking a macro-organic view of the state as a social system, I will also like to point out that functional analysis does not necessarily lay absolute claim to the fact that there is a linear path toward the maintenance of stability in the social structure. "Societies, like individuals, have their moral crises and their spiritual revolutions; and though inherited dispositions may be constant from generation to generation, the system of valuations, preferences and ideals, and the social environment within which individual character functions—is also in process of continuous change."[40] Dysfunctions within the social structure could arise as a result of forces of nature for which we are not able to control or account for. Prima facially, social structures make for differentiated access to existing opportunity structures in the larger society. "While elimination of politics from functional decision-making may help overcome many sources of tension, mal-administration, and injustice, functional institutions like all institutions have within them their own sources of inefficiency."[41] Part of this could be due to the role of human agency, antiquated structures, and changes in the distribution of opportunity structures overtime.

Opportunity structures reinforce class distinctions in such a way that may lead to resentment which undermines the stability of the social system itself. Opportunity structures therefore are functional contingencies. We need to know how variations in systems are accounted for by variations in constituent parts; and how the properties of the parts can be more properly understood outside of their functions and their roles in system integration and stability.[42] In the sense that they represent a specific experience and reality, functions and their relational properties (what they contribute to the maintenance of the whole system) can be influenced by the nature and quality of task structure, mechanisms of adaptation, and enrichment. This is perhaps an area that, though quite germane, has not been fully explored in the literature on functional analysis.

Task structure imposes a sense of order on the nature of functional relationships between different activities and their collective orientation to a specific goal. It is therefore important to engage in a continuous reassessment of the task structure, individual roles, and the capabilities necessary to fulfill specific functions and to ensure that unexpected deviations from the norm can be corrected in a timely manner. Although "deviation amplifying causal loops often cause trouble because their variables are moving in the wrong direction; but then even small deviations can be amplified into complex homogeneous events."[43] All social systems are essentially open systems and so they have to deal with a lot of variability, uncertainty, and environmental turbulence. As a result, social systems that endure over time are those that are able to develop adaptive mechanisms to deal with sudden and unexpected changes that undermine existing functional relationships. Part of the adaptation mechanisms include creating functional redundancies, building slack into the structural framework of the system, and duplication (building the whole into the parts)—including partial inclusion into other environmental sub-systems.

Enrichment involves the provision of additional resource inputs into the functional relationships, providing support mechanisms, encouragement and recognition, and a more effective utilization of outcomes. The relevance of this approach is that all three elements (task structure, mechanisms of adaptation, and enrichment) "are capable of concrete measurement, and are therefore capable of concrete adjustments in keeping with changes in the conditions of the function."[44] It is therefore important that "adequate epistemological analysis must focus on the total system as a complex on-going whole, for the information selection, transformations, or codings that occur at any point or linkage in the system depend not only on prior events and processes, but also on feedbacks from later points."[45] In this regard, they are *functional contingencies* or facilitators of action.

For example, a car cannot drive without gasoline or electric energy, but just because you have a car filled with gasoline does not necessarily mean that you are guaranteed that it will drive well for as long as you want it to. For a rolling wheel to function better, or even function at all, you have to constantly lubricate it by applying grease to it. For both the car and the rolling wheel, the gasoline and grease are functional contingencies, respectively. As a contingency, they have to work quite well, in order to ensure the effective functioning of the car or the rolling wheel. But then, even though we may have developed the means for the sequencing of activities and events, we cannot be too sure that things will work out well as designed until the provisions are put into action. As they say, the best laid plan of a military strategist is written on paper, but it is a different story when the plan is exposed to the practical realities of battlefield exigencies.

There is a reason why medical doctors are required to go for recertification after a few years on the job, and various occupational categories require employees to undertake career development programs to hone in their skills or accommodate impending changes in task structure or job orientation. In the following sections, I will provide further insights into the role of functional contingencies in functional analysis. There are three aspects of functional contingencies—active, reactive, and organic dimensions, all of which relatively correspond to the processes of task structure, adaptation, and enrichment:

Active Dimension

A common property that social systems, in fact, all systems share in common is the distribution of activities, or a division of labor in which people or units perform unique and repetitive functions. Each of these activities follows an ordered sequencing of actions in such a way that a rationalized pattern emerges as long as the units perform their different roles in the order in which they were established. I refer to this as the task structure or orientation. A task structure is directly related to the function—the cumulative series of steps or processes by which specific tasks are carried out. In any functional relationship, the task structure is also a functional contingency in the sense that to achieve a desired outcome, things ought to work well as designed. But this cannot be guaranteed, at least, all of the time. Because a particular function has relational properties associated with other activity sets in the overall sequencing of action templates, it cannot therefore be sealed-off from itself, but can influence or be influenced by changes in the relational properties of other associated activity sets.

To the extent that every function is a task, but it is not a task unto itself, except that its reality becomes obvious (is felt) only in its relationship with other tasks to which it is associated. To bake a good tasting bread requires the satisfying of a set of conditions among which are having the right flour, yeast, making the dough and letting it rest, the right amount of heat, and the skill of a baker. Although the function is the activity of baking bread, the final product (a good bread) involves more than just baking the bread. It involves the availability of all the previously mentioned ingredients and techniques plus the temperament and status of well-being of the baker. A break-down in (or negation of) any of these conditions may not yield edible bread; hence the function or activity of baking bread would not have worked out well or achieved optimal outcome.

Various tasks have different types of interdependent relationships to other tasks; and the nature of the relationship could be either sequential or reciprocal. "Sequential interdependence means the output of one department goes to the next department, and reciprocal interdependence means that departments mutually exchange materials and information."[46] Greater interdependence means that employees must communicate frequently, and as differences in goals and attitudes surface, conflict is likely to occur when agreement is not reached about coordination of services to each other.[47] This would have an effect on whether the various functional categories (structures) or activity sets have made positive contribution to the desired objective or have weakened the ability of the whole system to do so. Task structures function within a larger systemic framework (task environment) "in which the organization interacts directly and that have a direct impact on its ability to achieve its goals."[48] Task structures are also very sensitive to the degree of formalization and complexity to which the various activity sets are subjected to within organizations. Regulations, statutes, and legislative and bureaucratic politics can hamstrung a public organization from performing its function in a manner that would achieve better and effective results. While "the heavy emphasis on the accountability of public organizations to external authorities may impede the use of some flexible (task) structures in government agencies,"[49] it may also weaken the ability of these organizations to innovate or to find alternative and less costly routes for doing the same things they have always done.

Reactive Dimension

Reactivity is a form of response to an occurrence or a sudden change in the expected pattern of behavior, where such response is either *adaptive* or corrective so as to mitigate potentially harmful deviations from the norm. By building in redundancy, slack, and excess capacity (even when not immediately in use), organizations or social systems are able to draw upon a reservoir of capabilities to address emerging challenges to system operations. Because social systems are, more or less, exposed to their general environment, they are oftentimes subjected to the effects of variables that are fluid and unpredictable. A particular function or activity set can always achieve the desired end if there is more than one way of doing the same thing, so that if one approach fails, another one can be used as an alternative or self-adjusting mechanism so that the functional operation of the whole system continues uninterrupted. Every function therefore should have an associated latent function (alternative options) that could be put in action once the necessity arises or system failure becomes imminent. They should embody "*functional equivalents*—in which two or more functions (functional sets) are able to overlap almost completely in their contribution to the system."[50]

One of the complaints about rule rigidity in the public sector is that they do not permit administrators to address evolving contingencies or to change the established protocols of formalized administrative routines in a timely manner. As a result, the same routine and methodology is applied to functional categories continuously, even as the functions themselves demand change, perhaps as a result of changes in applicable technologies in use, or emerging political and economic shifts in the larger environment. Innovation as a form of adaptation, for obvious reasons, is thus more limited in the public sector than in the private domain. And this is why building slack into the handling of resources, including information, is not only inevitable, but also essential to the smooth functioning of operations in both public and private sectors.[51] "All operations require a margin of error that must be built into the system—an allowance for mistakes, waste, spoilage, and similar unavoidable accompaniments of work."[52] This would allow social systems or organizations to function in ways that make allowance for unexpected and potentially disruptive contingencies by taking proactive actions "to periodically assess and continue improvement."[53] Nonetheless, the case that I have tried to make is that functional analysis should not be only about a set of activities that leads from A to B; but it should also be about the occurrence of events that may have a positive or negative influence on A and B, both internally and externally. As they say, we know things only by knowing the things in themselves and in their different relationships to other things.

Organic Dimension

The idea of organic dimension is based on the fact that most functions or activity sets are carried out by individuals (although others are carried out exclusively or partially by machines). But as human beings, individuals have their own internal problems (physical, psychological, cultural, economic, and ideological) which may, one way or the other, induce specific behaviors or attitudes that affect their roles in a particular function or activity. The biological metaphor implied here draws on the very notion that like living organisms, a function also has a life of its own, thereby requiring a set of functional imperatives without which a role could not possibly be carried out. It includes forces that originate or are inherent to the personality subsystem. Ordinarily people have to feel well; they also have to eat food to feel well or even to stay alive, and also be emotionally undetached to the work at hand in order to perform well in it. Individuals receive, comprehend, and process information differently, and even when there is a standard operating procedure in the way specific activities are performed, functional outcomes are more likely to be different from one activity set to the other. For example, "the information attended to or selected for processing during activity is continually changing as a function of the on-going intentions, decisions, and actions of the individual";[54] hence there is a "difference between the general state of knowledge in some domain and the particular manner in which this knowledge is deployed and embedded in a given work situation."[55] "Only if the body is not irritated and, through irritation, thrown back upon itself, can our bodily senses function normally, and receive what (instructions) is given to them."[56]

There are lots of reasons given as to why some people are fired or relieved of their job responsibilities or moved to another unit or location. Among these are that "they did not do their jobs well, they are not qualified, they are not up to speed, or that they were simply not meant for the job." There are two conclusions that could be gleaned from the litany of reasons. First is that the reason why the person was relieved of his duties or received negative evaluation has nothing to do with the *function* or the job itself; the *function* failed because the *person* who was designated to carry it out was, for whatever reason, unable to satisfy the requirements of the *function*. The individual in this regard, therefore is a functional contingency. The second point is that the failure or distress resulting from the individual's low performance sent signals that reverberated throughout the whole system in such a way that other functional relationships were negatively affected or disrupted. It is therefore by correcting the error (replacing the position with a more competent and better performing person) that the particular function or set of functions would have the chance of succeeding and meeting expectations. This very point can further be illuminated by drawing from the sociotechnical framework because of its implicit integration of the structural functional and open systems approaches.

SOCIOTECHNICAL SYSTEMS: APPLICATION OF SYSTEMS SCIENCE TO POLITICAL PROBLEMS

The application of sociotechnical systems framework in functional analysis is essential to our continued understanding of the dynamic complexities of social systems, particularly in the political sphere. "Sociotechnical systems consist of components, which are social structures, and artifacts, which are technical elements that contribute directly or through other components to common system goals."[57] That is, sociotechnical systems include technical systems but also the operational processes and people who use and interact with the technical system. When we conceive of the state as a sociotechnical system, we are simply recognizing the fact that it is made up of social, political, economic, and technical components, arranged in such a way that they work collectively to advance a common goal; but at the same time provide feedback loops which enable us to establish the degree of correspondence or divergence between actual system outputs and formal system goals.

Because the type of wicked problems that affect social systems are unpredictable, variable, and have ill-defined shifting definitions and multiple conflicting elements;[58] solutions to such wicked problems have arisen from approaches that incorporate variants of sociotechnical systems theory.[59] Following the end of "World War II, the Tavistock Institute of Human Relations in England began to focus on the study of work systems on the basic premise that work involves a combination of social and technical requisites and that the object of design is to jointly optimize both components—not sacrifice one for the other." By emphasizing both individual tasks as well as organizational features, the key assumption was that work groups, properly structured, can provide workers with an ongoing source of incentives, error correction, assistance, learning opportunities, and social support that would not be tenable under the rational systems approach where technical systems were designed and human workers "fitted in" to their requirements.[60] "Organizations therefore are systems that respond to social, economic, and technological imperatives that have to be satisfied for effective operation of the system."[61] It also includes the ability to adapt to environmental variations such that "in periods of disturbances, the system moves to a new point of equilibrium—a new ongoing pattern of interrelated social and technical processes."[62] To the extent that "designing the organization to meet human needs while ignoring the technical systems, or changing technology to improve efficiency while ignoring human needs, may inadvertently cause performance problems";[63] "the sociotechnical systems approach attempts to find a balance between what people want and need and the technical requirements of the organization's production system."[64]

Sociotechnical systems characteristics fit quite nicely to the analysis of political systems. The theory embraces the concepts and metaphors of general systems theory as a way of analyzing, and designing systems with *joint optimization* in mind, particularly those that embody some degree of linearity within themselves as well as the environment they reside in.[65] Based on the notion that "human and technical imperatives must be satisfied in the interest of the system as a whole, people, technology, and resources, are thus, regarded as *inputs* to a purposively rational process geared to the achievement of *end states*."[66] It can therefore serve as a model for analyzing the administrative challenges of the modern state. The following characteristics of sociotechnical systems provide analytical metaphors for the study and understanding of social and political systems such as the state:[67]

- Emergent properties—that is, properties of the system as a whole that depend on the systems components and their relationships. There are two types of emergent properties such as *functional properties*—which appear when all the parts of a system work together to achieve some objective; and *non-functional properties*—which relate to the behavior of the system in its operational environment (i.e., reliability, performance, safety, and security).
- Non-deterministic—they do not always produce the same output when presented with the same input because the system's behavior is partially dependent on human operators, and
- Complex relationships with organizational objectives—the extent to which the system supports organizational objectives does not just depend on the system itself.

In general, sociotechnical systems theory is founded on two basic principles. "One is that the *interaction* of social and technical factors creates the conditions for successful (or unsuccessful) system performance. The other is that these interactions are comprised partly of linear *cause and effect* relationships (the relationships that are formally designed), and partly from non-linear, complex, and unpredictable relationships (those that are often unexpected)."[68] For political systems (the *state*), a greater burden therefore is placed on the role of system monitoring, coordination, and integration.

Because sociotechnical systems provides a way for monitoring system elements and mediating the functional boundaries or linkages between them, it thus offers a trip-wire or early warning signal to potential or existing dysfunctions before they reach critical mass. It offers a basis for developing activity systems that spontaneously reorganize toward states of greater heterogeneity and complexity and achieve a "steady state" at a level where critical functions are not disrupted.[69]

Without doubt humans make mistakes, but so do machines (we call these "errors"), but the utility of the sociotechnical systems thinking is how to avoid most mistakes that could represent radical departures from predictable expectations. One way to do this is to design functional roles and work units (simple structures) in such a way that they can respond flexibly to changing demands related to tasks performed and the environment.[70] The point of using simple sociotechnical structures or sets of interlocked behaviors "as building blocks of organizational (or state) action is that they function with only incomplete knowledge among the participants."[71] The attractive feature though is that while "we know most social systems or organizations function quite well even when very few people may know little about what actually goes on; the coordination is built into simple structures, the assemblage of which creates units that become more complex."[72] It is "this greater complexity that allows these simple structures to be used to cope with, manage, and resolve issues that are more complex than participants can visualize or articulate."[73] The idea is not necessarily meant to equate humans with machines but to illustrate that most work situations require the effective integration of both human and technological systems either in complementary or sequential roles.

The other approach is to develop both internal and external congruence in critical work systems, by providing "a structure and a purpose around which to exercise power and control."[74] "System congruence requires interrelated attempts delivered in a coordinated fashion to improve organizational functioning and impact such as production, productivity, and quality of work life."[75] It also "implies the need for a fit among culture, reward, and control systems of an organization and the design of specific work processes, employee roles, and departments."[76] Viewing state institutions from the perspective of structure and functional work processes offers us the opportunity to draw from those areas of organizational analysis where public and private sector organizations, even though they may be unalike in certain respects, yet are not mutually exclusive. It is therefore important to elaborate on the six functional components of the sociotechnical systems approach and their applicability to the workings of state institutions. In this regard, I speak of the state as a *social system* and also as an *organization*, and in some cases drawing upon analogies from formal bureaucratic organizations.

Functional Components

Goals Metrics

Goals are "conceptions of desired ends. They not only supply criteria for choosing among alternative activities; they also guide decisions about how the organization structure itself is to be designed; they specify what tasks are to be performed, what kinds of personnel are to be hired, and how resources are to be allocated among participants."[77] Goals provide criteria for identifying and appraising selected aspects of organizational functioning, and it is the standard or metrics upon which functional outcomes are measured. However, "the various functions of goals—guiding, motivating, symbolizing, justifying, and evaluating behavior—do not coincide because they not only serve different purposes but also emanate from different sources."[78] In states and governments, because most goals seem to be very stable over time, it becomes more difficult to adapt them to changing administrative and political imperatives. It is thus important to adapt existing goals to changes in the key objectives to which the goals are directed.

People

The people are the individuals or groups who carry out various activities directed at achieving the organizational goals and objectives. Besides these activities, individuals also bring with them their own skills and knowledge, values, attitudes, idiosyncrasies, preferences, and needs to the work environment. These "behaviors and attitudes over time become interrelated with such factors as organizational tasks, structures and processes, leadership, and culture";[79] such that "with all these factors impinging on people, motivating employees and stimulating effective attitudes in them become crucial as well as sensitive."[80] Furthermore, the demographic characteristics of individual participants—their age, gender, and ethnic backgrounds (general health conditions and quality of life issues)—also have important consequences for many aspects of organizational structure and functioning.[81] Just as the larger environment, individuals also bring with them a certain level of unpredictability and uncertainty to the governance or work situation.

Process and Procedures

The *process* includes "prevailing patterns of interaction between individuals and groups, which may contribute directly or indirectly to transforming inputs into outputs."[82] Some processes or procedures, particularly in formal bureaucratic organizations or government agencies, are routine and already programmed into fixed operational schedules. This makes the process inflexible and less amenable to individual discretion or novel approaches to doing the same work in different ways. "Subcomponents of behavior and processes that are particularly important for handling functional challenges include cooperation, leadership, coordination, communication, problem solving, self-criticism, evaluation, and group learning."[83] But then these are only possible depending on the extent to which rule rigidity and goal displacement impedes the exercise of due diligence in functional relationships. The process itself, to the extent that it prescribes sets of actions that should be carried out where, when, and by whom may pose an inherent problem of mismatch—when process mechanisms or protocols become archaic or weak, or when changing operational conditions dictate otherwise.

Culture

The idea of "culture refers to shared norms, values, beliefs, and assumptions and the behavior and artifacts that express these orientations, including symbols, rituals, stories, language, myths and legends"[84] among members of a society or organization. It is built on sets of assumptions underlying the relationships between the members of a community and the larger social environment of which they are a part. Culture therefore "provides people with a sense of organizational or social identity and generates in them a commitment to beliefs and values that are larger than themselves."[85] Like organizations in the private sector, national institutions or government agencies cannot escape the influence of the broader political culture of which they are a part. It is thus incumbent on them to adhere or in most cases become ambassadors or advocates for the merits of the extant political culture. Agency actions are impacted by cultural values and ideals such as equality, due process, work force diversity, social equity, meritocracy, neutral competence, efficiency, non-discrimination, and political responsiveness. All of these impose their own independent and/or collective constraints that oftentimes impede the effectiveness of administrative action as well the functional outcomes they generate. Every state action is, implicitly, non-value neutral; hence the price of adherence is oftentimes at the expense of effectiveness and efficiency.

Technology

Technology "refers to the tools, equipment, and techniques used to process inputs and transform them into outputs."[86] However, most organization theorists embrace the broader view that technology includes not only the hardware used in performing work, but also the skills and knowledge of workers which they carry in their heads, and even the characteristics of the objects on which work is performed."[87] In other words, technology refers to "the physical combined with the intellectual or knowledge processes by which materials in some form are transformed into outputs."[88] The pace of change in the application of technology (particularly computer applications) in both public and private sectors means that administrators would need to be constantly updated with new skills and training, as well as new approaches to doing their work. For effective results, the job function should be commensurate with the technology in use as well as applicable human resource skills.

Infrastructure

In state administration as well as in private enterprise, the role of infrastructure[89] is that it provides the underlying foundation or basic framework within which work is performed. While it includes the permanent installations required for the system of public works of a country, state, or region (such as personnel, buildings, or equipment) required for an activity; I would argue that the larger notion of infrastructure includes the skills and knowledge of the personnel, leadership roles, rules and procedures, the structure of functional relationships and their interdependencies, the personnel system, the incentive and sanctions systems, and the technology in use. For a social system such as the *state*, functional stability or "stable state" is achieved as a result of the ability to coordinate the existing network of infrastructures and the evolving patterns of relationship in a systematic but stability-inducing fashion.

Because the "effects of the technological subsystem upon the social subsystem and upon the environment are more often than not delayed, subtle, or secondary; we must also consider how systems impact on one another and on the environment, how they collide, conflict, and may be irreconcilable no matter our best intents and effort."[90] Standard operating procedures, though part of the functional structure of organizations or social systems like the *state*, can overtime take on a life their own; hence oftentimes generate competing imperatives that puts additional stress and tension that could undermine existing functional relationships. When individuals become attuned to their established routines on a regular basis, they may also become oblivious to subtle changes in functional outcomes, and this makes timely detection of operational anomalies very difficult—until they result in partial or whole system failure.

In chapter 4, I will continue the discussion by focusing on the implication of general systems theory in terms of how systems are able to maintain stable states or homeostatic equilibrium conditions in the face of uncertainty and environmental complexity. Drawing from the science of cybernetics, I propose the concept of the *cybernetic state*. A case is made regarding design structures and self-regulatory control mechanisms in which imprinted signals and feedback loops allow for error detection and correction in ongoing routine operations or in situations of unexpected deviations from the norm. One way of doing this is to construe the feedback loop as a subsystem within a much larger system, but one in which the logic of the loop pretty much duplicates as well as complicates the inner workings of the main system.

NOTES

1. Abrahamson, Mark. 1978. *Functionalism*. Englewood-Cliff, NJ: Prentice Hall, Inc, 17.
2. Jarvie, I. C. 1973. *Functionalism*. Minneapolis, MN: Burgess Publishing Company.
3. Merton, Robert K. 1968. *Social Theory and Social Structure*. New York: The Free Press, 75.
4. Merton, Robert K. 1968. *Social Theory and Social Structure*, 75.
5. Merton, Robert K. 1968. *Social Theory and Social Structure*, 75.
6. http://anthropology.ua.edu/cultures/cultures.php?culture=Functionalism. Accessed on December 8, 2017.
7. http://anthropology.ua.edu/cultures/cultures.php?culture=Functionalism. Accessed on December 8, 2017.
8. Merton, Robert K. 1968. *Social Theory and Social Structure*, 75.
9. Merton, Robert K. 1968. *Social Theory and Social Structure*, 76.
10. Merton, Robert K. 1968. *Social Theory and Social Structure*, 76.
11. http://anthropology.ua.edu/cultures/cultures.php?culture=Functionalism. Accessed on December 8, 2017.
12. Parsons, Talcott, and Edward A. Shils, eds. 1976. *Toward A General Theory of Action*. Cambridge, MA: Harvard University Press, 190.
13. Parsons, Talcott. 1961. *Theories of Society: Foundations of Modern Sociological Theory*. New York: Free Press, 41.
14. Gingrich, P. 1999. "Functionalism and Parsons." In *Sociology 250 Subject Notes*, November 9. Canada: University of Regina. http://uregina.ca/~gingrich/n2f99.htm. Accessed on December 13, 2017.
15. Mitrany, David. 1948. "The Functional Approach to World Organization." *International Affairs* 24, no. 3: 350–363, 358.
16. https://en.wikipedia.org/wiki/Alfred_Radcliffe-Brown. Accessed on December 8, 2017.
17. This section is an extensively revised and updated version of an earlier work by the author that appeared under the name *Institution-Building, not Nation-Building: A Structural-Functional Model*, by Kalu N. Kalu, as published in *International Review of Administrative Sciences* 77, no. 1: 119–137, Copyright 2011 Sage Publications Limited, UK.
18. Radcliffe-Brown, Reginald. 1952. *Structure and Function in Primitive Society*. New York: The Free Press. See also Emile Durkheim. 1933. *Division of Labor in Society*, Translated by G. Simpson. New York: Macmillan.
19. Merton, Robert. 1957. *Social Theory and Social Structure*. London: The Free Press. See also Parsons, Talcott. 1951. *The Social System*. Glencoe, IL: The Free Press.
20. Knapp, Peter. 1994. *One World-Many Worlds: Contemporary Sociological Theory*. New York: Harper-Collins, 191–192.
21. http://uregina.ca/~gingrich/n2f99.htm. Accessed on November 15, 2017.

22. Harrison, Michael I. 2005. *Diagnosing Organizations: Methods, Models, and Processes*. Thousand Oaks, CA: Sage Publications, 29.

23. Merton, Robert K. 1968. *Social Theory and Social Structure*, 105.

24. Simmons, Robert H., and Eugene P. Dvorin. 1977. *Public Administration: Values, Policy, and Change*. Port Washington, NY: Alfred Publishing Co., 446.

25. Simmons, Robert H., and Eugene P. Dvorin. 1977. *Public Administration: Values, Policy, and Change*. Port Washington, NY: Alfred Publishing Co., 446.

26. Hall, Peter, and Rosemary C. R. Taylor. 1998. "Political Science and the Three New Institutionalisms." In *Institutions and Social Order*, edited by Karol Soltan, Eric M. Uslander, and Virginia Haufler, 15—43. Ann Arbor, MI: The University of Michigan Press.

27. Durkheim, Emile. 1968. "The Development of the Theory of Social Control." In *The Structure of Social Action: A Study in Social Theory with Special Reference to a Group of Recent European Writers*, edited by Talcott Parsons, 376–408. New York: The Free Press

28. Morse, Chandler. 1961. "The Functional Imperatives." In *The Social Theories of Talcott Parsons: A Critical Examination*, edited by Max Black, 100–152. Englewood Cliffs, NJ: Prentice-Hall, Inc, 104.

29. Morse, Chandler. 1961. "The Functional Imperatives." In *The Social Theories of Talcott Parsons: A Critical Examination*, edited by Max Black, 100–152, 105.

30. Morse, Chandler. 1961. "The Functional Imperatives." In *The Social Theories of Talcott Parsons: A Critical Examination*, edited by Max Black, 100–152, 105.

31. Scott, W. Richard, and Gerald F. Davis. 2007. *Organizations and Organizing: Rational, Natural, and Open Systems Perspectives*. Upper Saddle River, NJ: Pearson-Prentice Hall, 78. See also Parsons, Talcott. 1951. *The Social System*; and Talcott Parsons., Robert F. Bales., and Edward Shils. 1953. *Working Papers in the Theory of Action*. Glencoe, IL: Free Press.

32. Morse, Chandler. 1961. "The Functional Imperatives." In *The Social Theories of Talcott Parsons: A Critical Examination*, edited by Max Black, 100–152. Englewood Cliffs, NJ: Prentice-Hall, Inc, 113. See also Parsons, Talcott. 1951. *The Social System*.

33. Turner, Jonathan H. 2003. *Human Institutions: A Theory of Societal Evolution*. Lanham, MD: Rowman & Littlefield, 89.

34. Simmons, Robert H., and Eugene P. Dvorin. 1977. *Public Administration: Values, Policy, and Change*. Port Washington, N. Y: Alfred Publishing Co, 454.

35. Arendt, Hannah. 1958. *The Human Condition*. Chicago, IL: The University of Chicago Press, 90.

36. Arendt, Hannah. 1958. *The Human Condition*, 91.

37. Arendt, Hannah. 1958. *The Human Condition*, 98.

38. Arendt, Hannah. 1958. *The Human Condition*, 88.

39. Harrison, Michael I. 2005. *Diagnosing Organizations: Methods, Models, and Processes*, 3rd ed., Thousand Oaks, CA: Sage Publications, 29.

40. Tawney, R. H. 1926. *Religion and the Rise of Capitalism: A Historical Study*. New York: Mentor Books/Harcourt, Brace & World, 227.

41. Burton, J. W. 1975. "Functionalism and the Resolution of Conflict." In *Functionalism: Theory and Practice in International Relations*, edited by A.J.R. Groom and Paul Taylor, 238–249. New York: Crane, Russak & Company, 243.

42. Turner, Jonathan H., and Alexandra Maryanski. 1979. *Functionalism*. Menlo Park, CA: The Benjamin/Cummings Publishing Company, 95–96.

43. Weick, Karl E. 1979. *The Social Psychology of Organizing*. New York: McGraw-Hill, 81–83.

44. Mitrany, David. 1948. "The Functional Approach to World Organization." *International Affairs* 24, no. 3: 350–363, 358.

45. Buckley, Walter. 1972. A Systems Approach to Epistemology. In *Trends in General Systems Theory*, edited by George J. Klir, 188–202. New York: John Wiley & Sons, Inc, 189.

46. Thompson, James D. 1967. *Organizations in Action*. New York: McGraw-Hill, 54–56.

47. Daft, Richard L. 2016. *Organization Theory & Design*, 12th ed., Boston, MA: Cengage Learning, 517.

48. Daft, Richard L. 2016. *Organization Theory & Design*, 12th ed., 142.

49. Rainey, Hall G. 2009. *Understanding and Managing Public Organizations*, 4th ed. San Francisco, CA: Jossey-Bass, 223.

50. Abrahamson, Mark. 1978. *Functionalism*. Englewood-Cliff, NJ: Prentice Hall, Inc, 5.

51. Scott, W. Richard, and Gerald F. Davis. 2007. *Organizations and Organizing: Rational, Natural, and Open Systems Perspectives*, 135.

52. Scott, W. Richard, and Gerald F. Davis. 2007. *Organizations and Organizing: Rational, Natural, and Open Systems Perspectives*, 135.

53. Ziegenfuss, James T. Jr. 2002. *Organization & Management Problem Solving: A Systems and Consulting Approach*. Thousand Oaks, CA: Sage Publications, 21.

54. Buckley, Walter. 1972. "A Systems Approach to Epistemology", 88–202, 189.

55. Scott, W. Richard, and Gerald F. Davis. 2007. *Organizations and Organizing: Rational, Natural, and Open Systems Perspectives*, 125.

56. Arendt, Hannah. 1958. *The Human Condition*, 113.

57. https://www.researchgate.net/publication/240239070_A_Review_of_Sociotechnical_Systems_Theory_A_Classic_Concept_for_New_Command_and_Control_Paradigms, 3. Accessed on December 21, 2017. See also Walker, Guy H., Neville A. Stanton, Paul M. Salmon, and Daniel P. Jenkins. 2008. "A Review of Sociotechnical Systems Theory: A Classic Concept for New Command and Control Paradigms." *Theoretical Issues in Ergonomics Science* 9, no. 6: 479–499; Trist E. L., and K. W. Bamforth. 1951. "Some Social and Psychological Consequences of the Longwall Method of Coal Getting." *Human Relations* 4: 3–38; and Fred E. Emery and E. L. Trist. 1965." The Causal Texture of Organizational Environments. " *Human Relations* 18: 21–32.

58. https://www.researchgate.net/publication/240239070_A_Review_of_Sociotechnical_Systems_Theory_A_Classic_Concept_for_New_Command_and_Control_Paradigms, 3. Accessed on December 21, 2017. See also H. W. J. Rittel and M. M. Webber. 1973. "Dilemmas in a General Theory of Planning." *Policy Sciences* 4, no. 2: 155–169.

59. https://www.researchgate.net/publication/240239070_A_Review_of_Sociotechnical_Systems_Theory_A_Classic_Concept_for_New_Command_and_Control_Paradigms, 3. Accessed on December 21, 2017. See also H. Hasan and C. Dwyer. 2010. "Was the Copenhagen Summit Doomed from the Start? Some Insights from

Green IS Research." Paper presented at the Americas Conference on Information Systems (AMCIS 2010), Lima, Peru.

60. Scott, W. Richard, and Gerald F. Davis. 2007. *Organizations and Organizing: Rational, Natural, and Open Systems Perspectives*, 144–145.

61. Rainey, Hall G. 2009. *Understanding and Managing Public Organizations*, 44.

62. Rainey, Hall G. 2009. *Understanding and Managing Public Organizations*, 44.

63. Daft, Richard L. 2016. *Organization Theory & Design*, 12th ed. Boston, MA: Cengage Learning, 291.

64. Emery, F. 1959. Characteristics of Sociotechnical Systems. Tavistock Institute of Human Relations, Document 527; See also Daft, Richard L. 2016. *Organization Theory & Design*, 12th ed. Boston, MA: Cengage Learning, 291.

65. https://www.researchgate.net/publication/240239070_A_Review_of_Sociotechnical_Systems_Theory_A_Classic_Concept_for_New_Command_and_Control_Paradigms, 4. Accessed on December 21, 2017. See also Walker, Guy H., Neville A. Stanton, Paul M. Salmon, and Daniel P. Jenkins. 2008. "A Review of Sociotechnical Systems Theory: A Classic Concept for New Command and Control Paradigms." *Theoretical Issues in Ergonomics Science* 9, no. 6: 479–499.

66. Burrell, Gibson and Gareth Morgan. 1979. *Sociological Paradigms and Organizational Analysis: Elements of the Sociology of Corporate Life*. Aldershot, UK: Ashgate, 160.

67. http://mysite.du.edu/~lbarne28/SE/Slides/Ch2.pdf. Accessed on December 21, 2017. See also Ian Sommerville. 2006. *Software Engineering*, 8th ed. (chapter 2). Boston, MA: Addison Wesley.

68. https://www.researchgate.net/publication/240239070_A_Review_of_Sociotechnical_Systems_Theory_A_Classic_Concept_for_New_Command_and_Control_Paradigms, 3.Accessed on December 21, 2017. See also Walker, Guy H., Neville A. Stanton, Paul M. Salmon, and Daniel P. Jenkins. 2008. "A Review of Sociotechnical Systems Theory: A Classic Concept for New Command and Control Paradigms." *Theoretical Issues in Ergonomics Science* 9, no. 6: 479–499.

69. http://moderntimesworkplace.com/archives/ericsess/sessvol2/STS_Emery.pdf. Accessed December 2, 2017.

70. Ziegenfuss, James T. Jr. 2002. *Organization & Management Problem Solving: A Systems and Consulting Approach*. Thousand Oaks, CA: Sage Publications, 19.

71. Weick, Karl E. 1979. *The Social Psychology of Organizing*. New York: McGraw-Hill, 109.

72. Weick, Karl E. 1979. *The Social Psychology of Organizing*, 109.

73. Weick, Karl E. 1979. *The Social Psychology of Organizing*, 109.

74. Taylor, James C., and David F. Felten. 1993. *Performance by Design: Sociotechnical Systems in North America*. Englewood Cliffs, NJ: Prentice Hall, Inc., 7.

75. Ziegenfuss, James T. Jr. 2002. *Organization & Management Problem Solving: A Systems and Consulting Approach*. Thousand Oaks, CA: Sage Publications, 20.

76. Nadler, D., and M. Tushman. 1980. "A Model for Diagnosing Organizational Behavior." *Organizational Dynamics* 9, no. 2: 35–51. See also James T. Ziegenfuss,

Jr. 2002. *Organization & Management Problem Solving: A Systems and Consulting Approach*. Thousand Oaks, CA: Sage Publications, 20.

77. Scott, W. Richard, and Gerald F. Davis. 2007. *Organizations and Organizing: Rational, Natural, and Open Systems Perspectives*, 36.
78. Scott, W. Richard, and Gerald F. Davis. 2007. *Organizations and Organizing: Rational, Natural, and Open Systems Perspectives*, 185.
79. Rainey, Hall G. 2009. *Understanding and Managing Public Organizations*, 243.
80. Rainey, Hall G. 2009. *Understanding and Managing Public Organizations*, 243.
81. Rainey, Hall G. 2009. *Understanding and Managing Public Organizations*, 24.
82. Harrison, Michael I. 2005. *Diagnosing Organizations: Methods, Models, and Processes*. Thousand Oaks, CA: Sage Publications, 28.
83. Harrison, Michael I. 2005. *Diagnosing Organizations: Methods, Models, and Processes*, 28.
84. Harrison, Michael I. 2005. *Diagnosing Organizations: Methods, Models, and Processes*, 29.
85. See Schein, Edgar H. 1992. Organizational Culture and Leadership, 2nd ed. Homewood, IL: Richard D. Irwin. See also Richard L. Daft. 2016. *Organization Theory & Design*, 12th ed., 387.
86. Harrison, Michael I. 2005. *Diagnosing Organizations: Methods, Models, and Processes*, 28.
87. Scott, W. Richard, and Gerald F. Davis. 2007. *Organizations and Organizing: Rational, Natural, and Open Systems Perspectives*, 125.
88. Hulin, Charles L., and M. Roznowski. 1985. "Organizational Technologies: Effects on Organizations' Characteristics and Individuals' Responses." In *Research in Organizational Behavior* 7, edited by L L. Cummings and Barry M. Staw, 39–84. Greenwich, CT: JAI Press, 47.
89. https://www.merriam-webster.com/dictionary/infrastructure. Accessed on December 24, 2017.
90. Greene, Kenyon B. 1973. *Sociotechnical Systems: Factors in Analysis, Design, and Management*. Englewood Cliffs, NJ: Prentice-Hall Inc., 10.

Chapter 4

The Cybernetic State

Of Homeostasis, Entropy, and Feedback Loops

The modern world, particularly the world of the twenty-first century has become increasingly more bureaucratic and complex. It is a world that is ever more dependent on the production and dissemination of large amounts of information, but also a world in which the control and utilization of such information has become a shared responsibility between man and machine. It is a phenomenon that seeks a purposeful end, the control of the processes that lead to that end, and the continuity and stability of the various structures and tasks that serve as a means for producing that end. The task of processing the daily deluge of information and the cognitive capacity to make sense of them surpasses whatever ability the human mind can muster; hence the increasing reliance on technological assets to balance the odds in our favor. The notion of cybernetics is a useful analogy that captures the current and evolving state of human society and the structural orientations to which technological development and bureaucratic complexity has forced upon it.

While "cybernetics is concerned with the communication and manipulation of information and its use in controlling the behavior of biological, physical and chemical systems; it is also the basic science underlying the process of homeostasis (whereby an organism acts or self-adjusts so as to restore its internal equilibrium) in biological systems and automation in industry and increasingly its implications are being applied in economic and social planning."[1] The cybernetics framework is built around the concept of information flows between key variables in a process, the control or regulatory mechanism that characterize the framework itself, and the feedback loops that warn of deviations from predicated pattern orientations. In order words, the notion "of feedback loop is essentially involved in steering or controlling behavior (governance) through which the output of the system is linked to its input in such a way that variations in output from some *programmed* norm results in compensatory behavior that tends to restore the system output to that norm."[2]

It was the "recognition that the basic mechanisms of adaptation are analogous to the mechanisms involved in automatic control systems (servomechanisms) and in many physiological processes (i.e., homeostasis) that led to cybernetics being recognized as a universally applicable concept, and as a subject so fundamental to man and his biological and social evolution."[3] Such classical works as Cannon's *Wisdom of the Body* is "an illustrative exposition of these phenomena in the autonomic processes of men; the *self-regulatory* aspect of neurophysiological phenomena as reflected in the works of Sherrington on *reflexes*, McCulloch in his analysis of *neural networks*, and Arturo Rosenbluth in his studies of *psychomotor disorders*."[4] By the early 1940s, a broad range of disciplines including physicists, electrical engineers, and mathematicians were at work on servo-mechanisms, self-regulating systems that could be used for such military purposes as gun laying, and for other purposes.[5] But in its broader appeal, cybernetic science is about communication, the application of computerization in information processing and pre-programmed automatic control devices—all reflecting the potential in the use of scientific concepts drawn from natural or engineering sciences in social sciences and political action.[6]

CONCEPTUAL APPLICATIONS

My attempt here is not necessarily to illustrate what may, or may not, have been most evident in the governance of modern societies; but to the extent that we are stuck in this symbiotic relationship between man and technology, what I want to do is to shed more light on what this seemingly but inescapable relationship is, and how it could be made more functional both in conceptualization as well as in practice. When there is crisis or disagreement between factions in the political system which may result in conflict, and when the possibility of peace may have become a forgone conclusion; is it possible to develop a governance system that would disseminate the appropriate signals within its internal elements so as to initiate corrective or preemptive measures before things get worse or result in outright violence?

To the extent that states are social systems, "they not only respond to an existing environmental challenge, but they may also foresee such challenges and plan to forestall them or cope with them in the future. Hence, societies respond not only to perceptions of reality but to the extrapolation of that reality into possible future states."[7] And as given future goals become more concretely defined, social behavior may increasingly resemble that of a *servomechanism* in which guidance is reduced to control—by the margin of error at which the object stands at a given time with reference to a relatively specific goal, hence action may then become a routine problem of technical administration.[8] It is therefore by detecting deviant norms in a timely manner that states are able to maintain the critical balance necessary for continuity and stability.

A principal characteristic of the cybernetic framework is the capacity for *self-regulation*—"a control loop whereby system components may be modified on the basis of information inputs regarding performance and the comparison of performance with a criterion value."[9] While most integrated computer systems are already programmed to undertake these functions, computers can only act based on the nature and type of information inputs programmed into their memory. And they are also pre-programmed to initiate specific actions when specific conditions fall below or above expected values or indices. Yet that would not be enough to deal with the increasing complexity of governance in the modern state, simply because "adequate knowledge of any system requires both structural-functional analysis and behavioral analysis."[10] Although "systems theory is frequently identified with cybernetics and control theory, this assumption is partly incorrect."[11] "Cybernetics, as the theory of control mechanisms in technology and nature is founded on the concepts of information and feedback, and is but a part of a general theory of systems; but cybernetic systems are a special case of systems showing self-regulation."[12] It tries to "show that mechanisms of a feedback nature are the base of teleological or purposeful behavior in man-made machines as well as in living organisms, and in social systems."[13]

Cybernetics has profound implications for the analysis of social systems, the prevailing institutions, as well as the behavioral properties of the processes that make the social system functional. The view of individuals and societies as complex self-regulating systems, interacting among themselves within complex environments should prove conducive to a more holistic approach to the social and behavioral sciences, and for the political sphere, as a forum for the resolution, or at least, the mitigation of the problems of competing value orientations.[14] From the perspective of systems analysis, it is also constitutive in the sense that it integrates all three components of general systems: the biological system (human beings), the mechanical system (technology, computers), and the social system (man in society, states and its institutions). It is therefore a model of governance as well as a framework for adaptation. It is a framework that lends itself to the capacity of a democratic society to understand, confront, and resolve very complex problems of social organization in such a way as to retain traditional freedoms and consultative political institutions while moving into evolving patterns of economic and social relations in which we realize that our relationship to the machine has become quasi symbiotic as well as enduring.[15]

As has been evident, "cybernetics is one of a few ancient systems terms, having been used in the context of steering a government by Plato in the context of his *kybernetics*, as the art of government in the social sciences by Ampére,[16] and by Karl Deutsch in his book *The Nerves of Government*."[17] On the other hand, and while "Clark Maxwell[18] used the word to describe feedback in mechanical governors; Norbert Wiener[19] extended the idea to incorporate both control and communication in animal and machine";[20] and also John Steinbruner's application of cybernetic model in the context of decision making.[21] It is quite an intriguing idea to introduce the notion of system control and coordination into the art of governance but in such a way that the role of the human factor is limited, or at best confined to specific functions within a broader network of interactions. In the same way that states and governments must maintain functional interrelationships (such as between constitutions, laws, or edicts and the actual practice of governance) in order to exist; still yet, such a consideration must be prefaced by the fact that "public problems, issues, policies, and programs should be considered and evaluated as interdependent components of a total system."[22]

In other considerations, the state is a dynamic gestalt (an organized whole that is perceived as more than the sum of its parts) in which there is an evolving tension between the whole and sub-systemic elements shaping and reshaping each other over time. While this tension or friction is necessary for continuity, it can also be a source of decay as a result of the system's inability to generate new input sources to rectify anomalies in its operational routine. At the same time, we must also consider the destabilizing effects of *change* and the *rate of change* in social systems, and its ability to adapt to those changes consistent with an existing capacity to absorb the implications they produce—and still maintain the stable state necessary for continuity. The rate of change in social systems can oftentimes be sudden and quite dramatic, and this creates not only uncertainty but also unexpected deviations from recognized patterns thereby introducing additional tension and flux into a system that is generally seen as unpredictable. For Kenneth Boulding, the "greatest source of change in social systems is the process of human learning in terms of both the development of new knowledge and know-how that the human race never had before, and also the spread of old knowledge around to new minds."[23] And for the fact that the cybernetic framework "diminishes the distinction that is often made between living and non-living systems (man and machine), it can be effectively applied in the analysis of biological systems as well as social systems as inanimate systems."[24]

As a control and communication system, "cybernetics also suggests that *steering* or governing is one of the most significant processes in the world, and that a study of steering in self-steering machines, in biological organisms, in human minds, and in societies will increase our understanding of problems in all these fields."[25] In the same way that we can program computers directly to stimulate behavior and to recognize specific pattern orientations and to address deviations from those patterns (a controlling function), the cybernetic analogy has also been used as a way of looking at the central nervous system,[26] or in the application of what Walter Pitts and Warren McCulloch[27] called *neural nets*. The neural net represents "an artificial design of a nervous system in such a way that several elements can be connected according to certain well-defined rules; but in which the output must either contain an impulse (catalyst) or not at any instant time (with sequencing or temporal coordinates attached to them)."[28] Although a biological analogy, the functioning of neural nets is in some ways akin to the functioning of social systems or government. The distribution of functions or activities, though directed to specific purposes, also follow a time-ordered sequencing of events (some serving as inputs or catalyst and others serving as outputs, which also serve as further inputs to other systemic elements, etc.), in such a way that the various distribution of functions among subsystem elements become routinized as well as follow specific pattern orientations directed at serving a specified goal or objective.

CYBERNETICS AND SYSTEMS THEORY

To view the state as a "cybernetic system is also to emphasize the importance of the operations, control, and policy centers, and the flows among them."[29] It places great emphasis on the operational level of the social system or organization—the level at which the production processes of the system are carried out, and it is by analyzing these technical flows—*inputs, throughputs, and outputs*—that we are able to understand the system.[30] While the "policy center sets the goals for the system—an activity that occurs in response to demands from the environment,"[31] the *interaction* among system elements are designed to follow specific pattern orientations such that the outcome of the system itself becomes more predictable. In cybernetics, "a system is generally described as a *black box* whereby the whole of a system's generative mechanisms are lumped into a single transfer function; and this acts on an *input* to produce an *output*,"[32] essentially in the same way that we view the Eastonian black box and its application to the analysis of political systems. But to ensure that the output is monitored so that a system may attain homeostatic conditions (in which critical elements or activities remain within acceptable limits); the output of the *transfer function* is brought back into its input where the difference between the desired and actual levels is identified."[33] This is one of the primary functions and contribution of the feedback loop in overall system maintenance—to provide signals about non-conforming or unexpected deviations from predicted norms.

Pattern Recognition and Feedback Loops

Using the Eastonian model as a template, one finds that the current one-dimensional analysis of the feedback loop underestimates much of the dynamics of the process, and its role in any functional analysis of applied systems frameworks. I am also of the view that the type of feedback sought, particularly for social systems conforms more to *negative feedback* (associated with seeking defined objectives via control parameters) as opposed to *positive feedback* (contained replication and growth or uncontained and unstable growth), which may lead to structural changes or death.[34] In dealing with the affairs of the state, there are specific goals or objectives that define the nature of public policy. There are also rules and regulations that govern the ways and means by which these policies are implemented, and of course, the normative expectation that they would achieve a particular public good. Negative feedback is therefore relevant in understanding how far and under what circumstances events do not meet expectations or when they overshoot the design parameters within which they must operate in order to sustain an *autopoietic* state. "Central to the concept of *autopoiesis* is the idea that the different elements of the system interact in such a way as to produce and re-produce the elements of the system; and that is to say that through its elements the system reproduces itself. A living cell, for example, reproduces its own elements, like proteins, lipids etc.; they are not just imported from outside."[35]

The logic of *autopoiesis* is also applicable to aspects of cybernetic systems (such as a thermostat) and has implications for the maintenance of steady states (flux equilibrium), particularly in social systems (i.e., a state). The idea of a *steady state* is one in which the particular configuration of parts and relationships reinforce a self-maintaining and repairing system—in which energies are continually used to maintain the relationship of the parts and keep them from collapsing in decay or atrophy.[36] While the feedback loop is considered a central element in the cybernetic system, yet it cannot be assumed to follow an ordered control system without multiple recursions that influence other activities within the whole system, similar to the "neuro-cybernetic structure and process found in man or living organisms."[37] When considered in light of the fact that because "each part is connected to the others in specific ways, all changes in one part affects the others";[38] hence the system itself can change as a result of oscillations and variations within and between the parts that make up the whole. The *steady state* itself is not spared, but is only sustained as a result of the balance of tensions between and within the parts of the system. And for this, there is a certain level of uncertainty and indeterminacy regarding the long-term viability of a steady state. Hence, it can only exist in a form of suspended animation so long as the balance of tensions does not overly sway outside of established parameters from one extreme to the other.

Because "any change made anywhere will eventually itself be changed by the consequences it triggers,"[39] we must also remain mindful of the fact that as a result of "the magnitude of the changes at each variable, the tightness of the couplings among variables, the number of times the feedback loop is activated, and the effects of exogenous variables, increasing amounts of instability could be introduced."[40] In such a case, isolated areas (subsystems) can appear that have only minor or even linear causal dependence of one part on the others—a term described as *mechanization* or *progressive* segregation.[41] In order words, gradual or dramatic changes can create new substructures that may redefine the original functional relationships and interactions that led to the creation of those substructures—even if their presence does not in a tangible way advance the primary objective of system durability. But then and while this is only one extreme of what is possible in the range from a completely connected system to isolated parts; it remains nonetheless, an inherent problem of the phenomenon of the feedback loop. There are reasons for that.

The Feedback Loop as a Subsystem

The notion of a feedback system is grounded in the fact that there are no absolutes in nature, and when dealing with systems of all types, errors do and can occur. It is therefore important for the survival of the system itself, to device a means for detecting, preempting, or adapting to these error signals if and when they occur. In the sense that "cybernetics includes the concept of *negative feedback* (that part of the output which is fed back into the system as a controlling input) as a central feature; it is from this concept, that the idea of adaptive systems and selectively reinforced systems (which modify their behavior in light of changing environments) are derived."[42] By "feedback or, as it is often called, a *servomechanism*—is meant a communication network that produces action in response to an input information, and includes the results of its own action in the new information by which it modifies its subsequent behavior."[43] In this regard, its "contribution to modern *control engineering* is a more sophisticated concept than the simple mechanical notion of equilibrium; and it promises to be a more powerful tool in the social sciences than the traditional equilibrium analysis."[44]

The notion of equilibrium seeks a certain level of stabilization in the processes that undergird the system, but it tells us very little about the internal dynamics of the processes that sustain the equilibrium, the degree of friction and tension among system elements, nor do we have any complete knowledge of existing or contingent weak spots that could unravel the equilibrium state itself. Knowing the single parts and processes of a system in its finest detail, while necessary is, however, insufficient to explain their organization or predict in the absolute sense of the term, the nature of their relationships with relevant parts of the system that matter. To the extent that the political system functions to produce responses in ways that often trump conventional wisdom and predictions; we must also remain mindful of the fact that "the way we think things should work comes from our conscious, conventional mind; but the way things actually work comes from somewhere else."[45] Feedback loops provide a circular logic but one that is reactive to whatever output emerges from the multiple interactions within the system as well as the larger environment within which it is embedded. In the sense that the product of the feedback loop can either be positive or negative in terms of its overall implication for the functioning of the whole system, this very fact seems to blur the nature of *cause*-and-*effect* relationships that dictate whether the feedback information is positive or negative. Traditionally, information derived from a series of feedback loops are oftentimes routine hence more predictable, than when such information pertain to unusual and complex events for which there are limited experience, hence greater uncertainty.

But a cursory review of the literature on general systems theory as well as the *input-throughput-outpu*t principle upon which the theory is anchored, points to a limited understanding of what goes on inside the feedback loop, and how it can, in and of itself, represent the Achilles heel of all systems modeling. Because "the cybernetic model places great emphasis on the operational level of the system—the level at which the production (functional) processes of the system are carried out; hence the analysis of these technical flows is vital to an understanding of the system and how the control and policy centers impact the input-throughput-output flows."[46] And when applied to social systems (states or governments), the feedback loop may be the very phenomenon that erodes the functionality of the system thus undermining its ability in the maintenance of homeostasis or stable states. This is the blind spot as well as the missing link in the effort to understand why some systems (or policies) endure and function much better over time, and while others do not. There are five reasons why this may be the case. I argue that the feedback loop:

- Is a subsystem within a larger system
- Is a replication of the whole system
- Creates ambiguity between cause-and-effect relationships
- May misrepresent output effects

- Can result from political compromise that does not address the actual issues introduced into the political system.

Against this background, what I want to do here is to sketch out two broad conceptual categories grounded in the competing notions of conformity and nonconformity, of disintegration and integration—all driven by the centripetal forces released from the internal friction inherent in feedback loops. As a rule, "all systems are governed by dynamic interaction of their components; and later on fixed arrangements and conditions of constraint are established which render the system and its parts more efficient, but also gradually diminish and eventually abolish its *equipotentiality*."[47] To address this functional anomaly, "monitoring environmental feedback on the system's past performance is an important mechanism of adaptation for any open system; hence discrepancies from policy or program standards are the occasion for corrective actions as prescribed by the policy objectives or goals."[48] And this is made possible by establishing mechanisms of a feedback nature that act as a servomechanism–"automatic device used to correct the performance of a mechanism by means of an error-sensing feedback, and in which the feedback and error-correction signals control the mechanical position."[49]

The feedback loop is a reactive phenomenon that activates based on the nature and severity (or degree of deviation) of the output from desired system objectives. That is, the feedback loop is a second-order effect that can only be initiated after a particular output has been experienced; and for better or for worse, such an output may have a deleterious effect on whole system operations, particularly in circumstances where signals from the feedback loop may already be too late for error correction or for the system survival itself. But the missing link in this analysis is that the feedback loop is not an end in itself, but is anchored on a secondary reaction in terms of cause-and-effect relationships. That is, the cause or the catalyst (energy) that initiates the feedback process is based on the nature of the output of the system as a whole. "In a broad sense, feedback may denote that some of the output energy of a system is returned to it as input; and to the extent that the behavior of an object is controlled by the margin of error at which the object stands at a given time with reference to a relatively specific goal, feedback is *negative*—that is, the signals from the goal are used to restrict outputs which would otherwise go beyond the goal."[50]

But it should also be understood that "any network whose operating rules can be modified by feedback processes is subject to internal conflict between its established working preferences and the impact of new information."[51] In this regard, "the judgment of a feedback loop's importance may often be purely arbitrary."[52] At each stage of the feedback loop, there are critical checkpoints or areas of tension that, in unexpected ways, may reshape the information conveyed through the feedback loop. In most cases, such information when conveyed as a new source of input into the system can create conditions that make it more difficult to accurately deal with the original issue in question. By relying on what type of information is fed back to the input stage, it makes it possible to introduce even more errors that could undermine the well-functioning of the system as a whole. For the fact that "the emergence of a feature in a system is unpredictable from any system description that can be given before that emergence,"[53] we are therefore left with a situation of greater complexity in the analysis of prevailing causal linkages to expected or unexpected outcomes.

The feedback loop is a distinct phenomenon with a logic of its own from the system as a whole, although it has a symbiotic relationship with it. Because "systems within other systems can have autonomy and freedom of decision";[54] it is possible to make the case that the internal logic that drives the feedback loop is different from the logic that drives the system as a whole. While the *output* of the system serves as an *inpu*t to the feedback loop, the output of the feedback loop serves as an input back into the system. On a practical level, this would mean that "information concerning the performance of a decision system is returned to it and may serve to negate, oppose, or reverse its current action if that action has been leading the system away from its goal";[55] or it could amplify such action if the information seems to contribute positively to the ends for which the system seeks. But ironically, the *throughput* of the feedback loop (the mechanism by which information is processed within the loop) is not only dependent on the output of the whole system, but also depends on environmental factors that exist or emanate outside the system. This very fact, in fundamental ways introduces more complexity and tension in the reliability of the feedback loop to offer accurate information and error detection.

Because the feedback process is partially locked in with aspects of the environment that surrounds it, increasing turbulence or complexity within the environment can generate different and unexpected outcomes that are fed back into the system operations as an input. There are two reason for this: First, "the goal situation sought in the feedback process is outside, not inside the goal seeking system; and second, to the extent that the feedback loop and the system itself is not isolated from the environment, its functioning depends upon a constant stream of information from the environment, as well as upon a constant steam of information concerning its own performance."[56] What these may mean is that there are multiple undetectable sources of *input* into the feedback process such that its capacity and probability of detecting all potential error signals is diminished. The same problem may persist overtime despite the best effort to address that which may seem most obvious as a central source of deviation or uncontrollable oscillations. "Because a system can often respond to feedback in a variety of ways, it can transcend fixed cycles of reciprocal cause and effects to achieve flexible adaptability; hence feedback messages operate in two directions with opposing consequences for the system."[57] "*Positive feedback* encourages the system to continue or increase its present activities because they are producing intended consequences or leading to desired goals; *negative feedback*, on the other hand, tells the system to cease or alter its activities because they are producing unintended consequences or not leading to desired goals."[58]

While "both types of feedback are vital for adequate system functioning, but an excess of either type can eventually destroy a system through unchecked rapid growth or stagnation."[59] And this was one of the reasons that Mancur Olson in his *Rapid Growth as a Destabilizing Force*[60] pointed to rapid economic growth as a major force leading toward revolution and instability. For him, "economic growth, like political reform, can awaken a people to the possibilities of further improvement, and thereby generate additional discontent."[61] To the extent that "the economic, social, and political systems are interrelated parts of a single society, and if one part changes quickly, there must also be instability in other parts of society."[62] What all this means is that achieving a stable state between system components is equally a function of the degree of balance a system can maintain between the *push-pull* of positive and negative feedbacks, and between order and disorder generated by the magnitude of friction between internal and external elements. On a practical level, the feedback loop provides a cumulative assessment of the recursive sets of interactions between system elements. It enables functional outputs to be compared to overall system goals in such a way that appropriate remedies and adaptations could be made when and if possible in a timely and responsive manner. It also suggests that in functional analysis, we must take account of the cyclical nature of relations between particular actions and the specific functions to which they are designed for. In other words, there is a certain level of reciprocity from *action* to *function* and then back to *action*. Functions, even when they may seem to have been accomplished, are not ends in themselves, rather they are still part of a continuing dynamic in the *action-function cycle* sustained by a form of homeostatic equilibrium. It is only when this equilibrium falls apart or is not enduring, that functions fail simply because the existing *process maintenance function* has itself failed.

THE CYBERNETICS OF POLITICAL SYSTEMS

In ontological and functional terms, the state is form of organization. It is also a social system, hence must conform to the same principles that govern the performance of open systems. It requires specific needs that must be met in order for it to survive or to do that for which it was created. As an open system, the state is capable of receiving input from its environment, processing that input, and releasing its output onto the environment. It is capable of self-maintenance in line with the basic principles that undergird general systems theory (a term that encompasses biological, mechanical, and social systems). In the sense that the parts or units that make up the system exhibit a high level of interdependence among them, it is equally important to point out that "the connections and interdependencies within a system component are apt to be tighter and of greater density than those between system components."[63] From an administrative point of view, the relationship between units within a department is denser than between another department, or when considered in light of the relationship between system elements *within* a state, or that *between* states.

But the connecting link between states and among system components is the process of communication and information exchange. As a science of control and communication, cybernetics "tries to unify different fields of research and different engineering cultures under the universal term of information processing."[64] By utilizing several analogies between information processing machines and the functioning of society, we are thus able to assess the information, and the communication and control channels that make particular social organizations functional.[65] As has been alluded to earlier, general systems theory not only addresses cybernetics as an information processing and control mechanism, it also shows how politics is fundamental to it.[66] "Politics used power and power processes to shape structures, manipulate information, and influence the way that people behave";[67] but its main objective has always been the maintenance of order and predictability in terms of political outcomes. To the extent that "a cybernetic definition of politics is grounded in a biological and functional perspective and is related, ultimately, to the biological problem of survival and reproduction in, and for, organized societies; politics in these terms can be viewed as a biological phenomenon that has played a functionally significant role in the evolutionary processes of complex social systems."[68]

Because "every viable system has a sub-system responsible for preserving the whole, and for maintaining the system's essential organizing characteristics over time";[69] this is why we must think in terms of the dynamic tension between elements of systems in mutual interaction, and how these reinforce existing stable states or the draw-down effects of the forces of inertia.[70] However, since all or most of the systems components have a degree of autonomy, it is possible for the system to survive even when some of its sub-systems are establishing a pathological hegemony.[71] In the sense that "the ordering process harbors purposeful virtual images that promote operational structure,"[72] my interest lies in social systems (states and governmental processes) that have some degree of rational/mechanical ordering that could overcome the tendency toward disorder, atrophy, or ossification. "Cybernetics is concerned with understanding the dynamics of social system functioning, on the levels of both social ordering—via control processes—and cultural ordering—via communication processes."[73] Cybernetic science therefore offers a crucial pathway within which to develop this framework while drawing implications for governance systems and how they operate.

As an organized whole made up of several competing or conciliatory components, and to maintain a steady state, the ratio of the friction generated by the interaction of system components must be equal or less than the sum of the systems adaptive capacity. When this is not the case, systems (social or political) could either fail or gravitate toward a state flux and disorder. Being "an organized whole therefore is not enough for a system to persist in time."[74] And for complex dynamic systems (such as a state or an organization), "anything that contributes to keeping the normality of the system functioning is functional to the system."[75] I believe I have illustratively made this very point in chapter 1. It is important that "some criteria of functional normality be operationally embedded in the system, to allow for the compensation of eventual perturbations among the system's organizational or structural elements."[76] For political systems such as the state, this is why we have laws, rules and procedures, regulatory capacity, sanctions and punishment as inbuilt mechanisms of political governance and social control. But ironically, for most states the way politics is played oftentimes casts a dark shadow over the functional authority of the political system itself; hence it is important to emphasis the role of the human agency and the idiosyncrasies that may contribute to systemic conflict and instability.

What if a State Can Function Like a Thermostat?

In the following section, I sketch a few epistemological propositions or hypothesis built around the functionality of the thermostat, drawing from its cybernetic and servo-mechanistic qualities as a control and communications regulator. I do not use this analogy as a way of explaining the state per se, but I use it as an illustrative proposition that illuminates the potential of self-regulatory capacity to our understanding of the processes of state action or its imagination. Some scholars have argued that the thermostat is a closed system, but I beg to differ. The thermostat is not a closed system as has generally been construed; it is not closed-off to the environment and, in fact, needs such exposure in order to function. It does not generate its own input or catalyst nor does it offer a direct output. In fact, its output is useless for its operations, because it does not result directly in any change in the surrounding temperature. It is the responsibility of the "heater" or the "air conditioner" to effect changes in the surrounding temperature based only on the signal or communication it receives from the thermostat. As a matter of fact, the relationship between the "heater" and the "thermostat" is one of input-output sequence in which change in the outside temperature (input) is detected by the thermostat (signal detection); the thermostat is then activated and processes the information according to its operational principles (throughput), and then sends a communication or signal (output) to the heater or air conditioner. The output (communication) from the thermostat becomes an input that activates the heater or air conditioning system which through its own operational principles (throughput) produces its own heat or cool air (output) that changes the variable in question (the external temperature).

The thermostat is only a processing or control center, receiving input and generating output in the form of information signals to the air conditioner or the heater to do their job. In fact, the thermostat is akin to a brain that controls the central nervous system, even though the biological analogy pertains to living systems. Without any detection of temperature change in the external or surrounding environment (which serves as the *input*, *energy*, or *catalyst*), the thermostat will not be activated nor would it send any communication or signals to the heater or air conditioner. Although the technical principles that guide the thermostat are different from that of a heater or an air-conditioning system, the relationship is functionally symbiotic—with the thermostat serving as the *central nervous system* or regulator. But even at that, oftentimes, the thermostat has to be physically *switched on* by the external intervention of humans before it could perform any of its function. Hence, it defies logic to construe the thermostat as a closed system when, in fact, it cannot activate itself based solely on any existing internal blueprints or programs that it may contain. It requires an external force or energy (change in the external temperature) to do that.

As a system that embodies the tendency toward self-regulation, a characteristic feature of the thermostat is the principle of negative feedback. Taking the case of a simple thermostat controlling a heater, we find that as the system (heater) moves away from its target condition, the negative feedback loop cuts in to induce the system back to equilibrium.[77] To the extent that the thermostat is a control system as well as bridging mechanism (an intermediary or blocker) between environmental factors and the heater or air-conditioning system, and while I agree that it functions at Boulding's level 3 (*Cybernetic systems*), but I am also of the view that it can function at level 6 (*Internal-image systems*) or at level 4 (*Open systems*), as provided below:[78]

- Level 3: *Cybernetic systems*: Systems capable of self-regulation in terms of some externally prescribed target or criterion
- Level 6: *Internal-image systems*: Systems capable of a detailed awareness

of the environment in which information is received and organized into an image or knowledge structure of the environment as a whole

- Level 4: *Open systems*: Systems capable of self-maintenance based on a throughput of resources from their environment.
- Level 8: *Social systems*: Multicephalous systems (social organizations) comprising actors functioning at level 7 (symbol-processing systems) who share a common social order and culture.

For the fact that "each higher-level system incorporates basic features of those below it; Boulding argues that it is also possible to analyze a social organization (a *state* in this context) as a *framework* (level 1), a *clockwork* (level 2), a *cybernetic system*, and so on up to *social systems* (level 8)—the level that captures the most complex, the higher-level, processes occurring in organizations."[79]

By dispelling the seemingly conventional notion of the thermostat as a closed system, the case is made that conceived in functional terms; the thermostat is actually an *open system* with aspects of the environment partially included in its operations. In order for the thermostat to perform its function, this partial-inclusion is essential and unavoidable. The thermostat cannot be construed in isolation from the environment that surrounds it. "The greater the degree of openness and the more the system is dependent on and influenced by its environment, the less vulnerable it is to entropy or eventual decay due to loss of vital resources."[80] The environment is an integral part of the functional architecture of the thermostat without which it cannot be activated. Conceived as an open system, it becomes more plausible to use it as a working model in the illustration of how states and governments could function better; and how error signals, deviations, and/or operational distortions could be mitigated or corrected in a timely manner. In the sense that we have used the cybernetic model to explain the principles governing social systems (*state and government*); and since it also follows cybernetic principles, the thermostat offers a useful analogy in explaining how states and governments could be made more adaptive and functional.

In this regard, figures 4.1(a)[81] and (b) provide an interesting pathway or heuristic on how we can conceptualize various aspects of state governance and functions. In figure 4.1(a), it is "the task of the control center to monitor the outputs, comparing their quality and/or quantity with standards as set forth in the *public policy*; but discrepancies create conditions for corrective actions as prescribed by the *program*."[82] This is the specific role of feedback (a) as the first of two checkpoints needed to address performance errors before they infect other system components. As the *primary loop*, feedback (a) is recursive, routine, and self-referential and occurs continuously at the operational level and is concerned with the sequence and timing of ongoing

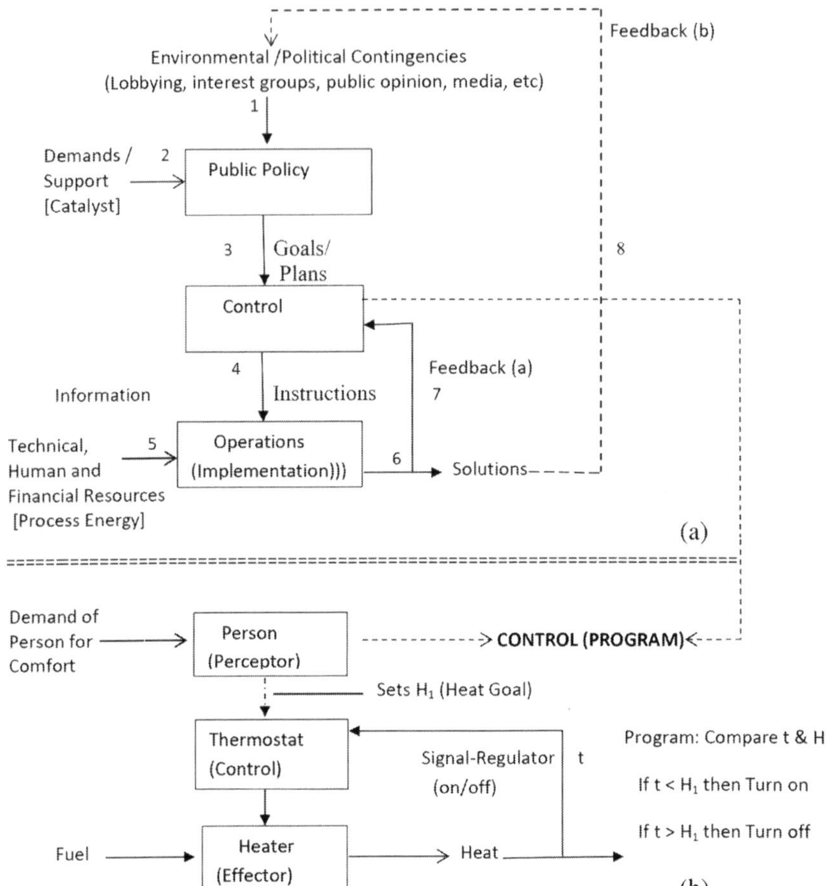

Figure 4.1 (a) Abstract Model of a Cybernetic System; (b) Illustration of a Cybernetic System: The Thermostat and the Heater. *Source*: (a) Modified by author based on Swinth (1974: figure 2.4, p. 23); (b) Modified by author based on Swinth (1974: figure 2.1, p. 18).

activities. The second feedback loop (Feedback 'b') is the *secondary loop* and is responsible for a holistic and system-wide scanning and assessment.

It demonstrates the possibility that reactions to the systems outputs by those outside the system (the public), may lead the policy or program to be revised in terms of goal and method of implementation.[83] For a state or a governance mechanism in "such double feedback systems, the primary loop (Feedback 'a') handles disturbances in 'degree,' applying existing decision rules, while the secondary loop (Feedback 'b') handles disturbances in 'kind,' determining whether it is necessary to redefine the rules controlling the operating levels."[84] Functionally, the thermostat is actually not a closed-up system since it will, of necessity, require human beings and/or other environmental variables to either initiate or complete the loop.

As illustrated in figure 4.1(a), to view a *state* as a cybernetic system is "to emphasize the importance of the operations, control, and policy centers, and the flows among them; and while the policy center sets the goal for the system, this activity occurs in response to demands, preferences, and support from the environment, that is, from the people (Flows 1 and 2)."[85] In the same vein, "the setting of goals is based on information presented to the *policy center* in terms of problems and issues (Flow 3), the policy center transmits goals or performance standards to the control center (Flow 4); and the control center (thermostatic analogy) applies its programs to the operational or implementation level"[86] where technical, financial, and human resource skills are applied in the transformation of the information into finished products or services (Flow 5). Feedback loops (a) and (b), more or less, provide a double check on the structure and variations within system components; the first (Flow 7) monitoring and adjusting ongoing activities on a routine or regular basis; while the latter (Flow 8) monitors the interactional effect between all system components and environment variables or contingencies that may have implications for the smooth functioning of the system. If feedback (a) is not able to capture and adjust to observed deviations and anomalies, then a second opportunity to do so does exist with feedback (b). To this effect, the system (be it the *state* or its institutions) is more likely to remain functional despite prevailing environmental turbulence and uncertainties.

The Thermostatic Analogy

As illustrated by Scott and Davis, the thermostat operates on the basis of functional relationship between interrelated parts, but this follows the same sequence consistent with the general principles governing all systems, in which inputs are converted into outputs. In other words, "the heater produces changes in temperatures detected by the thermostat; the thermostat controls a switch on the heater turning it on or off based on information provided by comparing the actual and desired temperatures."[87] Because the thermostat contains "the *program*—imprinted information that guides subsequent behaviour"[88] or "exercises control through information processing and decision-making—it is capable of self-regulation."[89] But what is missing from the conceptualization presented above is that it does not offer the clearest picture or justification of how the thermostat can interact with its surrounding environment, the sources of its input, and in what ways it produces its output. How then can the thermostat receive input and produce output, yet still be construed as a closed system?

Please note that I have presented this discussion of the thermostat based on figure 4.1(b) which is an expanded illustration of subsystem 4 (*Control "Program"*) in figure 4.1(a). Although a "person is capable of altering the system by reprogramming it, and by changing the desired temperature level, that person is not a basic component of the cybernetic system."[90] Admittedly, that person cannot be excluded as part of the functional linkage between the external *input* sources that dictate the type of information tendered into the thermostat's programming (without which it could not be activated), and the consequent information or communication it transmits to the heater or air conditioner. A thermostat's operative and/or technical closure should not imply a closed system model; it only implies a closure on the level of the internal operations of the system as a regulator in that no other technical operations (like the turning of a wheel) can enter nor leave the system. This mis-conceptualization or epistemological anomaly has already been addressed in this chapter in the sense that we view the thermostat as an open system, for the simple fact that it cannot act solely based on the *program* or imprinted signals that are embedded within it. It requires external *energy* in order to do so; and its output only comes indirectly through the transmission of information to a different mechanical system (heater or air conditioner) that produces either heat or cold air. The thermostat can produce neither hot or cold air, but acts only as a *regulator* that transmits information (directly or through feedback mechanisms) to another entity that does so.

In their *Every Good Regulator of a System Must Be a Model of that System*,[91] Conant and Ashby were concerned about the optimal method of feedback control. Drawing on two feedback arrangements they termed as "*error controlled*" and "*cause-controlled*," they see the former (i.e., a household thermostat) as intrinsically imperfect. "The thermostat has to wait until the environment drives the living room temperature away from its desired setting (after things have gone wrong) before it can go to work to correct the deviation. Error control, in this regard, never quite gets it right: some errors always remain (deviations from the optimal) even though they might be much reduced by the feedback mechanism."[92] On the other hand, they suggest a more perfect solution that is, a *cause-controlled* regulator that does not need to wait for something to go wrong before it acts. In such a case, "a *cause-controlled* thermostat (for example) would monitor the conditions outside a building, predict what those conditions are to the interior temperature, and take steps in advance to counter that—by turning down the heat as soon as the sun comes out. For the simple fact that in *cause-control*, all traces of environmental fluctuations might be blocked from affecting the controlled system; room temperature might never fluctuate at all,"[93] hence making the thermostat functionally useless. What is therefore gained from this epistemological insight is that "the minimal condition for optimal cause control is that the regulator should contain a model of the regulated system—that is, the regulator has to *know* how changes in the environment will affect the system it regulates if it is to predict and cancel the effects of those changes; and the model is precisely that *knowledge*."[94]

While control and stable states is at the core, it is equally important to note that "cybernetic systems result in behavior that is *goal-directed*, and not merely *goal-oriented*; since it is the deviations from the goal-state itself that direct the behavior of the system, rather than some pre-determined internal mechanism that aims blindly."[95] As a social system, states can *unlearn* old habits as they *re-learn* new ways of doing things as well as new processes and their potential or actual effects on political and administrative outcomes. But in the case of double-loop learning,[96] the values, strategies, and assumptions that govern administrative action are changed to create a more efficient environment. It involves a drastic rethink of the existing operational norms so that adverse consequences can be avoided, or at best, mitigated in the future. Argyris and Schon[97] point out that in situations where double-loop learning is insufficient to dealing with the more deeper cultural and process issues or where the status quo seems more resilient to change or to novel ideas, then *deuterolearning*—learning about improving the learning system itself (*learning to learn*) including the structural and behavioral components which determine how learning takes place, becomes more expedient.

HOMEOSTASIS AND THE ENTROPIC PROCESS: CONTINUITY AND DISCONTINUITY

A key distinction between systems is the role of the entropic process—energy that cannot be turned into work. "All systems spontaneously move toward a state of increasing entropy—a random arrangement of their elements, dissolution of their differentiated structures, or a state of maximum disorder."[98] "Open systems, because they are capable of importing energy (inputs) from their environment, can experience *negative* entropy—that is, by acquiring inputs of greater complexity than their outputs, open systems restore their energy, repair breakdowns in their organization, and may improve their structures and routines."[99] "It was an American, Walter B. Cannon, who first explicitly formulated the principle of homeostasis that lays emphasis on the feedback nature of our bodily organizations";[100] but its application goes beyond its importance to the functioning of the human body. Hence, "in order to extend the concept of homeostasis to matters external to the body, the nervous system can be considered as part of the control apparatus by which the body differentiates itself from its surroundings and by which it carries out its entropy-reducing process."[101] The ultimate aim therefore is one of maintaining a stable state as well as the survival of the individual and of the species despite short- and long-term environmental perturbations.[102]

Its relevance to cybernetic science revolves around the emphasis on the sensory power of a *servo-system* (in this case a *central nervous system*) to detect changes in the environment and to convey information signals that seek to return current performance or operations to a homeostatic state or equilibrium condition. For instance, "if the body heats up to some extent as a result of physical activity, then the increased temperature releases sweat from various ducts which have the effect of cooling the body—a critical feature of the feedback mechanism."[103] To this effect, the reaction to the draw-down effects of negative entropy oftentimes is reflected as involuntary reflexes induced by pre-programmed actions or *clockworks*—simple dynamic systems with predetermined motions[104] (Boulding's level 2). But then, and while the above may seem like a straightforward and less painful illustration, it harbors an inherent paradox that could, in and of itself, be a source of instability. "Many homeostatic effects are simply consequences of corrective changes produced by the deviations themselves, and some of these effects, often depend on triggered reactions, leading to interventions by some subsystems in the activities of others."[105] In other words, even when existing system states achieve homeostatic adaptation by correcting for *transient deviations* detected through the feedback loop, yet we are still not able to make the critical connection that explains the cause and effect relationships that drive variations among and within subsystem elements, within the feedback loop, and the system as a whole.

As a way of resisting negative entropy, open systems seek to acquire more input (energy) from the environment either to correct for errors or to repair breakdowns in the various functions that drive the system. Oftentimes it is a reflex reaction among systems to "fight back" against the entropic forces of retrogression so as to maintain their own survival; and this illustration is quite relevant when considered in terms of social systems (a *state*) and the various actions it initiates for its own survival. States or governmental systems are always in a state of flux, swinging (even if mildly) from one dimension to the other; but the ultimate aim is to prevent each of these swings from reaching a critical mass that could cause major failures or even death in the functioning of the state itself. For example, when a particular state is experiencing budget shot-fall in terms of revenues, it does not wait until it goes bankrupt; but to arrest its prospective decline and stoppage in administrative functions, the state either cuts back on its spending or goes to the bank or other financial institutions to borrow money. It borrows money (as an input or energy) so as to restore the well-being of the various functional activities critical to its own survival.

But unfortunately, the way the construct of entropy has been treated in the literature as a one-dimensional thermodynamic process masks a lot more detail and information needed to understand its true nature and inner workings. The rest of this chapter will attempt to illuminate the complexity of the entropic process and how, from a general systems perspective, its presence in the functioning of all systems is, more or less, naturally determined. The point is that even when a system's operation is restored to a stable state by escaping from the inertial pull of negative entropy, this does not bring the entropic process to an end. It simply continues, but at a much slower pace as its manifestations pick up strength and are magnified over time. The entropic process is an essential feature of all systems. It is a process of continuous degradation and a gradual decline into disorder that oftentimes leads to chaos, disorganization, and randomness.[106] Within all seemingly well-ordered systems, there is always an inherent disorder waiting to manifest. The postulation made here is akin to the central premise of nonlinear systems rationality which stresses that "some disequilibrium must be present in a 'healthy' system or else the system will become rigid and ultimately collapse completely rather than adapt and evolve."[107] There is always a certain level of incremental degradation, that if left unchecked or uninterrupted (depending on the type and characteristics of the system—mechanical, biological, or social), will eventually attain critical mass thereby ushering in the process of decay, atrophy or dissolution.

Because it often exists in a latent status even when its manifestations are not so obvious; and to the extent that the friction from the interaction of subsystem elements oftentimes leads to the breakdown of the whole system, this *interactive effect* can also be a continuous source of negative entropy. Because "any act of production involves a potential that is *used up* in the course of the production process, the *entropic process* of the *using up* of potential is almost universal in all systems."[108] The interactive effect (friction) requires the use and production of energy, and once the energy has been exhausted, it would need to be replenished—as a means of arresting the draw-down effects of negative entropy. As indicated earlier, dealing with the onset of negative entropy is a temporary adaptive process that may result in a temporary stabilizing effect, but it cannot eliminate the entropic process itself. For social systems, the entropic process emanates from three central sources—*behavioral*, *structural*, and *inertial* sources:

Behavioral Sources

Reduced to its barest minimum, social systems are made up of individuals, each with his or her own thought processes, preferences, and interests. While it is a known fact that not all individuals share the same personal values, even when everyone seems to be working toward the same collective objective. Over time, these subjective differences would come to represent central problems that oftentimes afflict social systems in negative ways. When individual interests and preferences conflict with the larger goal of the social system, it would begin to undermine the relational and functional integrity of the system; and to the extent that this seeks to weaken or hinder existing operations, the human agency and his oftentimes idiosyncratic behavior can reinforce the entropic process. The most important reason why we seek law and order, obedience to authority, and respect for each person's freedom is that it enables *state* and *society* to function in an ordered and responsible manner.

While we expect everyone to obey the law and to follow the rules of appropriate behavior in the larger society; but invariably, not everyone does so. There are those who are disposed to violating the law—committing crimes, stealing, drug dealing and addiction, human trafficking, driving above the speed limit, drunk driving, and so on. But what this does is that it undermines the smooth functioning of political and social institutions as well as undercut the existing value system that binds citizens to each other within the same political estate. Criminality and all the other violations mentioned above contribute little or nothing to the public good or the greater welfare of society, rather it tears down at the value system in ways that can only be detrimental to the existence of a well-ordered society. It would eventually lead to social and cultural decay if not authoritatively and effectively addressed. Criminality and all other socially deviant behaviors (i.e., '*wicked problems*' such as drug abuse, teenage pregnancy, acts of terrorism, homelessness, urban gang culture, and more)—in which no acceptable definition of the problem exists and in which solutions to them require the balancing of a variety of values rather than the predominance of any one value[109] are thus, in and of themselves, elements of the entropic process—they lead to social decay and retrogression.

Structural Sources

The way political and social institutions are arranged and the systems of accountability could make them dysfunctional. When political systems are designed in such a way that they offer specific advantages and opportunities to some and not to others; they become, in and of themselves, breeding grounds for sociopolitical discontent and acrimony. The stratification of society into classes (upper, middle, and lower) implies a de facto, if not implicit, acceptance of inequality as a natural feature of modern society. And when these divisions pit one class against the other, the blue-collar versus white collar, the wealthy versus the poor, the educated versus the uneducated, the urban versus the rural, the liberal versus the conservative, secularity versus non-secularity, they usually generate policy and political differences that are oftentimes intractable. When these differences shape public opinion and the evolving character of political discourse, the cumulative effect could create conditions where the political system and the prevailing culture begin to unravel at the seams. It could either result in a Hobbesian state of war-of-all-against-all or an Orwellian state characterized by endless intrigues and malfeasance. In the sense that the entropic process gravitates toward chaos and disorder, the structural features of the state and the distribution of political opportunity could be a source of perpetual instability and functional decline.

Inertial Sources

Instability within social systems (i.e., a state) can arise from objective sources, or from contradictions that result from system operations. In some situations, the system can overwork itself in such a way that it ends up reinforcing the same disorder it seeks to prevent. For social systems, inertial forces remain the great unknown. It is a process that could be said to operate at Boulding's level 9 (*Transcendental systems* composed of the *absolutes* and the *inescapable unknowables*).[110] Because their cause and effects are relatively unknown until they become evident, the consequences of inertia are magnified as a result of increasing uncertainty and the fact that it could occur at anytime from anywhere. When a social system (i.e., a state) operates under conditions of increasing uncertainty, it expends unnecessary energy or resources trying to mitigate or adapt to what may or may not happen; hence policy or program outcomes become less predictable. And when the probability of an outcome can swing in either direction (integration or disintegration), the chances of the system experiencing the drawn-down effects of the entropic process becomes more possible and profound. But even when all system operations are at their normal pace and seem to be working well, yet it does not preclude the fact that the entropic process is continuously at work. It would only take a matter of time to reach the critical mass that would seek the system's eventual decline or destruction.

COMPLEXITY AND REQUISITE VARIETY

The idea of requisite variety is based on the premise that for a system to survive as well as function well in achieving its objective, it must match its own internal complexity (sophistication) with an equivalent level of complexity imposed or forced upon it by the prevailing external environment. It is only by "incorporating required variety into internal controls can a system deal with the variety and challenge posed by its environment."[111] This principle was first formulated by the English cybernetician W. Ross Ashby[112] "who suggests that the internal diversity of any self-regulating system must match the variety and complexity of its environment if it is to deal with the challenges posed by that environment."[113] In his *An Introduction to Cybernetics*, Ashby views the *homeostat* as a regulator (or blocker)—in the sense that it stops some environmental disturbance from having its full impact on some essential variable.[114] Hence "it stands to reason that to be an effective blocker one must have at least as much flexibility as that which is to be blocked; otherwise one of the environment's dodges and feints (unpredictabilities and surprises) will get straight past the regulator and upset the essential variable."[115]

In practice, the logic of this principle can be built into the framework of political systems "around multifunctional units that collectively possess the requisite skills and abilities and where each individual member is as generalized as possible, creating a pattern of overlapping skills and knowledge bases in the overall unit or subsystem."[116] This enhances the ability of the overall system to deal with variations (sudden and unexpected changes) in the operational environment. As individuals or units discover new innovative approaches for dealing with their own local issues and problems; this also serves as an additional resource for innovation within the broader system—as the variety and innovation experienced is shared and used as a resource for future learning.[117] Because the principle of requisite variety "is particularly important in designing control systems or for the management of internal and external boundaries,"[118] it has "important implications for practical situations. For the fact that the variety of perturbations (disturbances) a system can potentially be confronted with is unlimited, we should always try to maximize its internal variety (diversity), so as to be optimally prepared for any foreseeable or unforeseeable contingency."[119]

Although "social systems include a mixture of both cooperative and conflicting interactions, as well as amical and hostile interactions; the alternating conditions of war and peace represent extreme ratios of these combinations whose parameters"[120] often swing between chaos (disorder) and normalcy (order). As a result, a cybernetic model of governance can help us in exercising objective control over the social system and its natural environment, thus offering "prudent and regularized intervention upon the body politic at the proper time and place."[121] A major functional benefit is that a state or governmental system would need to operate in a holistic and integrated way, developing additional internal variety and redundancy, as well as evolutionary or adaptive capacities that snow-ball throughout the whole system. And for the fact that "we are dealing with complex, dynamic, and nonlinear systems, it is not only necessary to understand how the *input-throughput-output* process works, but to possess sufficient know-how to predict or manipulate its positive and negative feedback loops over an extended period of time."[122]

Considered as a subsystem of the whole system, the feedback loop harbours an intrinsic paradox; it contains both elements of progression and retrogression, continuity and decay, and may, in fact, mask a greater degree of dysfunctional anomalies that reinforces the entropic process. In chapter 5, I first describe what is meant by "institutions." Secondly, I demonstrate how different types of institutional structures develop different and oftentimes competing sets of institutional effects. I also discuss the role of political culture in embedding belief systems as well as pattern orientations toward political objects and among members of the political system; and the role of state dirigisme in economic and growth policies.

NOTES

1. Porter, Arthur. 1969. *Cybernetics Simplified.* London: The English Universities Press Limited, vii.
2. Dechert, Charles R. 1966. "The Development of Cybernetics." In *The Social Impact of Cybernetics*, edited by Charles R. Dechert, 11–37. Notre Dame, IN: University of Notre Dame Press, 12.
3. Porter, Arthur. 1969. *Cybernetics Simplified.* London: The English Universities Press Limited, vii.
4. Dechert, Charles R. 1966. "The Development of Cybernetics." In *The Social Impact of Cybernetics*, edited by Charles R. Dechert, 11–37, 12.
5. Dechert, Charles R. 1966. "The Development of Cybernetics." In *The Social Impact of Cybernetics*, edited by Charles R. Dechert, 11–37, 12.
6. Triclot, Mathieu.2006.Norbert Wiener's Politics and the History of Cybernetics. The Global and the Local: The History of Scienceand the Cultural Integration of Europe. Proceedings of the 2nd ICESHS, edited by M. Kokowski, Krakow, Poland, September 6-9. https://halshs.archives-ouvertes.fr/halshs-00514062/document. Accessed on March 25, 2018.
7. Dechert, Charles R. 1966. "The Development of Cybernetics." In *The Social Impact of Cybernetics*, edited by Charles R. Dechert, 11–37, 27.
8. Dechert, Charles R. 1966. "The Development of Cybernetics." In *The Social Impact of Cybernetics*, edited by Charles R. Dechert, 11–37, 28.
9. Dechert, Charles R. 1966. "The Development of Cybernetics." In *The Social Impact of Cybernetics*, edited by Charles R. Dechert, 11–37, 14.
10. Dechert, Charles R. 1966. "The Development of Cybernetics." In *The Social Impact of Cybernetics*, edited by Charles R. Dechert, 11–37, 15.
11. Bertalanffy, Ludwig Von. 1968. *General Systems Theory: Foundations, Development, Applications.* New York: George Braziller, 17. See also Anatol Rapoport 1956. *General Systems.* Washington, D.C.: Society for General Systems Research.
12. Bertalanffy, Ludwig Von. 1968. *General Systems Theory: Foundations, Development, Applications*, 17.

13. Bertalanffy, Ludwig Von. 1968. *General Systems Theory: Foundations, Development, Applications*, 44.

14. Dechert, Charles R. 1966. "The Development of Cybernetics." In *The Social Impact of Cybernetics*, edited by Charles R. Dechert, 11–37, 34–35.

15. Dechert, Charles R. 1966. "The Development of Cybernetics." In *The Social Impact of Cybernetics*, edited by Charles R. Dechert, 11–37, 35.

16. Ampére, A.M. 1884. *Essay on the Philosophy of the Sciences*. Trans. Paris, France.

17. Deutsch, Karl W. 1963. *The Nerves of Government*. New York: Free Press.

18. Maxwell, J. Clark. 1864. *Proceedings of the Royal Society* 13. London.

19. Wiener, Norbert. 1948. *Cybernetics*. Cambridge, MA: MIT Press.

20. Flood, Robert L. and Ewart R. Carson. 1988. *Dealing with Complexity: An Introduction to the Theory and Application of Systems Science*. New York: Plenum Press, 96.

21. Steinbruner, John. *The Cybernetic Theory of Decision*. Princeton, NJ: Princeton University Press.

22. Manning, E. C. 1967. *Political Realignment: A Challenge to Thoughtful Canadians*. Toronto/Montreal, Canada: McClelland & Steward Ltd. See also Ludwig von Bertalanffy. 1968. *General Systems Theory: Foundations, Development, Applications*. New York: George Braziller, 4.

23. Boulding, Kenneth E. 1985. *The World as a Total System*. Beverly Hill, CA: Sage Publications, 83.

24. George, F. H. 1965. *Cybernetics and Biology*. San Francisco, CA: W. H. Freeman & Co., 1–2.

25. Deutsch, Karl W. 1966. *The Nerves of Government: Models of Political Communication and Control*. New York: The Free Press, 77-78.

26. George, F. H. 1965. *Cybernetics and Biology*. San Francisco, CA: W. H. Freeman & Co., 42.

27. Pitts, Walter and Warren McCulloch. 1943. "A Logical Calcula of the Ideas Imminent in Nervous Activity." *Bull, Math, Biophys* 5: 115–133.

28. George, F. H. 1965. *Cybernetics and Biology*. San Francisco, CA: W. H. Freeman & Co., 36–37.

29. Swinth, Robert L. 1974. *Organizational Systems for Management: Designing, Planning and Implementation*. Columbus, OH: Grid. See also Scott, W. Richard and Gerald F. Davis. 2007. *Organizations and Organizing: Rational, Natural, and Open System Perspectives*. Upper Saddle River, NJ: Pearson-Prentice Hall, 91.

30. Scott, W. Richard and Gerald F. Davis. 2007. *Organizations and Organizing: Rational, Natural, and Open System Perspectives*, 93.

31. Scott, W. Richard and Gerald F. Davis. 2007. *Organizations and Organizing: Rational, Natural, and Open System Perspectives*, 91.

32. Flood, Robert L. and Ewart R. Carson. 1988. *Dealing with Complexity: An Introduction to the Theory and Application of Systems Science*. New York: Plenum Press, 12.

33. Flood, Robert L. and Ewart R. Carson. 1988. *Dealing with Complexity: An Introduction to the Theory and Application of Systems Science*, 12.

34. Flood, Robert L. and Ewart R. Carson. 1988. *Dealing with Complexity: An Introduction to the Theory and Application of Systems Science*, 12.

35. Seidl, David. 2004. Luhmann's Theory of Autopoietic Social Systems, No. 2004-2. Munich Business School, Germany. "The theory of autopoiesis was developed by the two Chilean cognitive biologists Humberto Maturana and Francisco Varela in the sixties and early seventies. They were trying to answer the question: What is life? Or: What distinguishes the living from the non-living? Their answer was: A living system reproduces itself. This self-reproduction they referred to as autopoiesis."

https://www.zfog.bwl.uni-muenchen.de/files/mitarbeiter/paper2004_2.pdf. Accessed on June 18, 2018, 2–3.

36. Laszlo, Ervin. 1972. *The Systems View of the World: The Natural Philosophy of the New Developments in the Societies*. New York: George Braziller, 37.

37. Flood, Robert L. and Ewart R. Carson. 1988. *Dealing with Complexity: An Introduction to the Theory and Application of Systems Science*, 95.

38. Drack, Manfred. 2015. Ludwig von Bertalanffy's Organismic View on the Theory of Evolution. *Journal of Experimental Zoology (B) Molecular and Development Evolution* 324, no. 2: 77–90. http://www.ncbi.nim.nih.gov/pmc/articles/PMC4657461/, 5. Accessed on March 28, 2018.

39. Weick, Karl E. 1979. *The Social Psychology of Organizing*. New York: McGraw-Hill, Inc., 77.

40. Weick, Karl E. 1979. *The Social Psychology of Organizing*, 76.

41. Drack, Manfred. 2015. Ludwig von Bertalanffy's Organismic View on the Theory of Evolution. *Journal of Experimental Zoology (B) Molecular and Development Evolution* 324, no. 2: 77–90. http://www.ncbi.nim.nih.gov/pmc/articles/PMC4657461/, 5–6. Accessed on March 28, 2018.

42. George, F. H. 1965. *Cybernetics and Biology*. San Francisco, CA: W. H. Freeman & Co, 2.

43. Deutsch, Karl W. 1966. *The Nerves of Government: Models of Political Communication and Control*. New York: The Free Press, 88.

44. Deutsch, Karl W. 1966. *The Nerves of Government: Models of Political Communication and Control*, 89.

45. https://politicsofsoul.org/tag/cybernetics. Accessed on June 1, 2018, 1.

46. Scott, W. Richard and Gerald F. Davis. 2007. *Organizations and Organizing: Rational, Natural, and Open System Perspectives*, 93.

47. Bertalanffy, Ludwig Von. 1968. *General Systems Theory: Foundations, Development, Applications*, 44.

See also https://en.wikipedia.org/wiki/Equipotentiality: "*Equipotentiality* refers to a psychological theory in both neuropsychology and behaviorism. Karl Spencer Lashley defined equipotentiality as "The apparent capacity of any intact part of a functional brain to carry out… the [memory] functions which are lost by the destruction of [other parts]." In other words, the brain can co-opt other areas to take over the role of the damaged part. Equipotentiality is subject to the other term Lashley coined, the law of *mass action*. The law of mass action says that the efficiency of any complex function of the brain is reduced proportionately to how much damage the brain as a whole has sustained, but not to the damage of any particular area of the brain. In this context when we use brain we are referring to the cortex." Accessed on June 21, 2018.

48. Scott, W. Richard and Gerald F. Davis. 2007. *Organizations and Organizing: Rational, Natural, and Open System Perspectives*, 92.

49. https://www.britannica.com/technology/servomechanism. Accessed on June 21, 2018.

50. Deutsch, Karl W. 1966. *The Nerves of Government: Models of Political Communication and Control*, 88.

51. Deutsch, Karl W. 1966. *The Nerves of Government: Models of Political Communication and Control*, 95.

52. Weick, Karl E. 1979. *The Social Psychology of Organizing*, 75.

53. Costa, Antonio Carlos Da Rocha., Jose Mauro Volkmer De Castillo., and Dalcidio Morales Claudio. 1995. "Toward a Constructive Notion of Functionality." *Cybernetics and Systems: An International Journal* 26: 443–480, 453.

54. Laszlo, Ervin. 1972. *The Systems View of the World: The Natural Philosophy of the New Developments in the Societies*. New York: George Braziller, 51.

55. Deutsch, Karl W. 1966. *The Nerves of Government: Models of Political Communication and Control*, 192.

56. Deutsch, Karl W. 1966. *The Nerves of Government: Models of Political Communication and Control*, 186–187.

57. Olsen Marvin E. 1978. *The Process of Social Organization: Power in Social Systems*. New York: Holt, Rinehart and Winston, 24.

58. Olsen Marvin E. 1978. *The Process of Social Organization: Power in Social Systems*, 24.

59. Olsen Marvin E. 1978. *The Process of Social Organization: Power in Social Systems*, 24.

60. Olson, Mancur. 1977. "Rapid Growth as a Destabilizing Force." In *Comparative Politics: Notes and Readings*, 5th ed., edited by Roy C. Macridis and Bernard E. Brown, 437–452. Homewood, IL: The Dorsey Press, 438.

61. Olson, Mancur. 1977. "Rapid Growth as a Destabilizing Force," 437–452, 447.

62. Olson, Mancur. 1977. "Rapid Growth as a Destabilizing Force," 437–452, 441.

63. Scott, W. Richard and Gerald F. Davis. 2007. *Organizations and Organizing: Rational, Natural, and Open System Perspectives*, 98.

64. Triclot, Mathieu. 2006. Norbert Wiener's Politics and the History of Cybernetics. The Global and the Local: The History of Science and the Cultural Integration of Europe. Proceedings of the 2nd ICESHS, edited by M. Kokowski, Krakow, Poland, September 6–9, 763. https://halshs.archives-ouvertes.fr/halshs-00514062/document. Accessed on March 25, 2018.

65. Triclot, Mathieu. 2006. Norbert Wiener's Politics and the History of Cybernetics. The Global and the Local: The History of Scienceand the Cultural Integration of Europe, 765.

66. Yolles, Maurice. 2003. "The Political Cybernetics of Organizations." *Kybernetics* 32, nos. 9/10: 1253–1282.

67. Yolles, Maurice. 2003. "The Political Cybernetics of Organizations," 1253–1282, 1253.

68. *Synergy, Cybernetics, and the Evolution of Politics*. http://complex systems.org/publications/the-evolution-of-politics. Accessed on April 15, 2018.

69. https://politicsofsoul.org/tag/cybernetics. Accessed on December 4, 2017.

70. Bertalanffy, Ludwig Von. 1968. *General Systems Theory: Foundations, Development, Applications*, 45.

71. https://politicsofsoul.org/tag/cybernetics. Accessed on June 1, 2018, 2.

72. Yolles, Maurice. 2003. "The Political Cybernetics of Organizations," 1253–1282, 1256.

73. Olsen Marvin E. 1978. *The Process of Social Organization: Power in Social Systems*, 22.

74. Costa, Antonio Carlos Da Rocha, Jose Mauro Volkmer De Castillo, and Dalcidio Morales Claudio. 1995. "Toward a Constructive Notion of Functionality." *Cybernetics and Systems: An International Journal* 26: 443–480, 448.

75. Costa, Antonio Carlos Da Rocha, Jose Mauro Volkmer De Castillo, and Dalcidio Morales Claudio 1995. "Toward a Constructive Notion of Functionality." *Cybernetics and Systems: An International Journal* 26: 443–480, 445.

76. Costa, Antonio Carlos Da Rocha, Jose Mauro Volkmer De Castillo, and Dalcidio Morales Claudio 1995. "Toward a Constructive Notion of Functionality," 443–480, 448.

77. Little, Daniel 1991. *Varieties of Social Explanation: An Introduction to the Philosophy of Social Science*. Boulder, CO: Westview Press, 93.

78. Boulding, Kenneth E. 1956. "General Systems Theory: The Skeleton of Science." *Management Science* 2: 197–208, 200–207.See also W. Richard Scott and Gerald F. Davis. 2007. *Organizations and Organizing: Rational, Natural, and Open System Perspectives*, 89.

79. Scott, W. Richard. 2007. *Organizations and Organizing: Rational, Natural, and Open System Perspectives*, 89.

80. Olsen Marvin E. 1978. *The Process of Social Organization: Power in Social Systems*. New York: Holt, Rinehart and Winston, 23.

81. Swinth, Robert L. 1974. *Organizational Systems for Management: Designing, Planning, and Implementation*. Columbus, OH: Grid. See also: Scott, W. Richard. 2007. *Organizations and Organizing: Rational, Natural, and Open System Perspectives*. Upper Saddle River, NJ: Pearson-Prentice Hall, 91–92.

82. Scott, W. Richard. 2007. *Organizations and Organizing: Rational, Natural, and Open System Perspectives*, 92.

83. Scott, W. Richard. 2007. *Organizations and Organizing: Rational, Natural, and Open System Perspectives*, 92.

84. Ashby, W. Ross.1952. *A Design for a Brain*. New York: John Wiley. See also Scott, W. Richard. 2007. *Organizations and Organizing: Rational, Natural, and Open System Perspectives*, 92.

85. Swinth, Robert L. 1974. *Organizational Systems for Management: Designing, Planning, and Implementation.* See also Scott, W. Richard. 2007. *Organizations and Organizing: Rational, Natural, and Open System Perspectives*, 91.

86. Scott, W. Richard and Gerald F. Davis. 2007. *Organizations and Organizing: Rational, Natural, and Open System Perspectives*, 92.

87. Scott, W. Richard and Gerald F. Davis. 2007. *Organizations and Organizing: Rational, Natural, and Open System Perspectives*, 90.

88. Beninger, James R. 1986. *The Control Revolution: Technological and Economics Origins of the Information Society.* Cambridge, MA: Harvard University Press, 39.

89. Scott, W. Richard and Gerald F. Davis. 2007. *Organizations and Organizing: Rational, Natural, and Open System Perspectives*, 90.

90. Scott, W. Richard and Gerald F. Davis. 2007. *Organizations and Organizing: Rational, Natural, and Open System Perspectives*, 91.

91. Conant, R. C., and W. R. Ashby. 1970. "Every Good Regulator of a System Must Be A Model of That System," *International Journal of Systems Science* 1: 89–97.

92. Pickering, Andrew. 2010. *The Cybernetic Brain: Sketches of Another Future.* Chicago, IL: The University of Chicago Press, 150.

93. Pickering, Andrew. 2010. *The Cybernetic Brain: Sketches of Another Future*, 151.

94. Pickering, Andrew. 2010. *The Cybernetic Brain: Sketches of Another Future*, 151.

95. Buckley, Walter. 1967. *Sociology and Modern Systems Theory.* Upper Saddle River, NJ: Prentice-Hall. See also W. Richard Scott. 2007. *Organizations and Organizing: Rational, Natural, and Open System Perspectives*, 92–93.

96. Argyris, Chris. 1982. *Reasoning, Learning and Action: Individual and Organizational.* San Francisco, CA:

97. Argyris, Chris and Donald Schon. 1996. Organizational learning II: *Theory, method and Practice.* Reading, MA: Addison Wesley. See also Kalu N. Kalu. 2017. *Technology, Culture, and Public Policy: Critical Lessons from Finland.* New York: Routledge, 59 (Excerpted).

98. Scott, W. Richard and Gerald F. Davis. 2007. *Organizations and Organizing: Rational, Natural, and Open System Perspectives*, 96.

99. Scott, W. Richard and Gerald F. Davis. 2007. *Organizations and Organizing: Rational, Natural, and Open System Perspectives*, 96.

100. George, F. H. 1959. *Automation Cybernetics and Society.* New York: Philosophical Library, 175.

101. Young, John F. *Cybernetics.* London: Iliffe Books Limited, 49.

102. Young, John F. *Cybernetics*, 49.

103. George, F. H. 1959. *Automation Cybernetics and Society*, 176.

104. Scott, W. Richard and Gerald F. Davis. 2007. *Organizations and Organizing: Rational, Natural, and Open System Perspectives*, 89.

105. Rapoport, Anatol. 1986. *General Systems Theory: Essential Concepts & Applications.* Cambridge, MA: Abacus Press, 98.

106. https://www.merriam-webster.com/dictionary/entropy. Accessed on June 30, 2018.
107. Van Wart, Montgomery. 1998. *Changing Public Sector Values*. New York: Garland Publishing, Inc., 206.
108. Boulding, Kenneth E. 1985. *The World as a Total System*. Beverly Hills, CA: Sage Publications, 16.
109. Rosenbloom, David H. and Howard E. McCurdy. 2006. *Revisiting Waldo's Administrative State: Constancy and Change in Public Administration*. Washington D. C: Georgetown University Press.
110. Scott, W. Richard and Gerald F. Davis. 2007. *Organizations and Organizing: Rational, Natural, and Open System Perspectives*, 89.
111. Morgan, Gareth. 2006. *Images of Organization*. Thousand Oaks, CA: Sage Publications, 41.
112. Ashby, W. Ross. 1952. *Design for a Brain*. New York: John Wiley. See also W. Ross Ashby. 1960. *An Introduction to Cybernetics*. London: Chapman & Hall.
113. Morgan, Gareth. 2006. *Images of Organizations*. Thousand Oaks, CA: Sage Publications, 108–109.
114. Ashby, Ross. 2010. "Psychiatry, Synthetic Brains, and Cybernetics." In *The Cybernetic Brain*, edited by Andrew Pickering, 91–170. Chicago, IL: The University of Chicago Press, 149.
115. Pickering, Andrew. 2010. *The Cybernetic Brain: Sketches of Another Future*. Chicago, IL: The University of Chicago Press, 149.
116. Morgan, Gareth. 2006. *Images of Organizations*, 109.
117. Morgan, Gareth. 2006. *Images of Organizations*, 110.
118. Morgan, Gareth. 2006. *Images of Organization*, 42.
119. http://pespmc1.vub.ac.be/REQVAR.html, Accessed on February 12, 2017.
120. Arnopoulos, P. 1993. "Dialectics, Politics, and Cybernetics: The Sociophysics of Complex Systems." *Cyberntica* (XXXVI, 4): 345–353, 348.
121. Arnopoulos, P. 1993. "Dialectics, Politics, and Cybernetics: The Sociophysics of Complex Systems," 345–353, 351.
122. Arnopoulos, P. 1993. "Dialectics, Politics, and Cybernetics: The Sociophysics of Complex Systems," 345–353, 350.

Chapter 5

How Institutions Shape Political Action

What I want to do in this chapter is to explore the fact that social action is, more or less, a function of the institutional underpinnings associated with membership of a particular political society. This premise goes beyond the specific role of political structures such as bureaucracies or parliamentary systems, but draws from the fact that while "political institutions themselves are partly shaped by a country's cleavages and conflicts, once political arrangements become institutionalized they habitually acquire a force of their own."[1] In the sense that social action is reflected in various activities or functions, and when the functions become regularized, they create a structure that in itself turns back to regulate the very activities or functions needed to sustain it. Over time as these repeated cycles of events take on a life of their own, the relationship between function and structure becomes permanently embedded in the institutional mores that shape individual or collective action. For example, social action is different within different regime types as a result of the "microinstitutional features that differentiate them"[2] (democracy, theocracy, socialism, communism, or totalitarian) as well as economic types (free-market, mixed-economy, or centralized planning systems).

Because regime types and economic systems are institutions, they have regulatory power that enables them to structure how people think, act, or behave, both individually as well as collectively. For some political systems such as free-market liberal democracies, the institutional architecture seems to have worked quite well for majority of its citizens; while for nondemocratic totalitarian regimes, the citizens are not comparatively as free as one would expect under democratic regimes. To the extent that "political institutions define the framework within which political life takes place,"[3] the structure of the institutions within nondemocratic regimes seriously restrains or even circumscribes the bounds and character of individual and collective self-expression. Free-market systems encourage private property and individual wealth creation, while centralized economy reinforces the supremacy of the state in the context of public ownership of property as well as all factors of production. While free-market capitalist systems reinforce the Lockean notion of the labor theory of value and its corollary in private property, the centralized planning model relies on the quintessential Marxist mantra of *to each according to his needs and desires*. The point is that because all political regimes and their institutions are not alike (even those that may seem alike may also be different in several respects), it invariably suggests that the ways and means by which citizens respond or react to political objects, symbols, and the laws would be different. In fact, their collective notion of the meaning of freedom, liberty, citizenship, and the public good would also be different.

Additionally, while the meaning and essence of equality, freedom, and due process may be similar in countries such as the United States, Great Britain, or Canada, the meaning, practice, and interpretation of these terms are certainly different for North Korea, Venezuela, Iran, or the Comoro Islands. As a result some political regimes or governments are *functional* (i.e., they work well to serve the interests of their citizens) while others are *dysfunctional* (they undermine or even prejudice the interests of their citizens). Because "functions are abstractions, not concrete entities; the first task of any political analysis would therefore be to identify the structures or aspects of the structures that have something to do with the performance of the functions."[4] It is equally important to note that there is no uniformly ordered path through which all states evolve, and I am certainly not suggesting that. There are some states that are emergent, develop in specific times and context, and emerge following a disorderly trajectory in which competing social forces have battled each other for years. I am reminded of states like Pakistan that emerged following a tensed partition from India, East Timor from Indonesia, Russia and Ukraine that emerged from the Soviet Union, South Sudan from Sudan, Kosovo from Greater Serbia, or even Serbia itself that emerged from the disintegration of Yugoslavia. Nonetheless my baseline argument and without making any normative judgment about which one is better than the other, is that every political system aims for the maintenance of a stable system and for its survival, although they may differ in how they seek and/or achieve these existential objectives. While democratic-political systems rely on the power of the people and the Constitution as guides to state action, and totalitarian systems rely on the power of the leader and the state; theocratic regimes, on the other hand, rely very much on the tenets of their religious doctrine as a guide to state and civic action. Because states have different ways of seeking and appreciating similar objectives, yet still, the idea of *functional equivalents* does not address the issue of why most states generally have different outcomes than the others. Rather, they only reflect "qualitative notions that disclose little detailed structure behind them."[5]

There are also many other criteria by which we analyze countries in relation to others. This includes differences in economic development, industrialization, human capital development, structural power, and the extent of income inequality. We can study countries individually (unit level of analysis) or as part of other countries in the international system (system level of analysis). But whichever approach we use, it is based on finding ways to understanding the similarities and differences between countries. It is also important to know why some countries are well developed, and others are not; why some countries are wealthy, and the rest are poor; why some countries are democratic, and others are totalitarian; why some countries are secular, and others are non-secular (theocratic), why some countries respect or grant due process to their citizens, and others do not. Suffice it then to say that a great majority of these differences (absent of the ever-present human failures and desires), are due to differences in structural design (regime types such as democracy, authoritarianism, parliamentary systems, federalism, republicanism, socialism, bureaucratic-authoritarianism, theocracy, etc.) and deference to different political objects, symbols, cultures, and institutions (different socialization processes, the nature of political power and how it is distributed or used in various countries).

INSTITUTIONS: DEFINING CHARACTERISTICS

In its application to the regulation of the behavior of state actors in the context of interdependence, Robert Keohane defines institutions[6] as the "persistent and connected set of rules that prescribe behavioral roles, constrain activities, and shape expectations."[7] While this definition is closer to that of Douglass North who views institutions as "rules, norms and other humanly devised constraints that structure political, social, and economic interaction";[8] they both seek to emphasis the role of property rights, markets forces, contracts, opportunities and incentives as some of the driving forces in the evolution of institutions and in the institutionalizing process itself. This, however, differs somewhat from Elinor Ostrom's emphasis on methodological individualism (the analysis of social phenomena through seeing the motivations and actions of individual agents)[9] to demonstrate how social actors can in different contexts and under unique conditions develop the mechanisms and incentives (rules and norms) that enables them to cooperate and also mitigate some of the central issues (free-rider problem, defection, trust) that arise in matters of common ownership or in access and usage of a common pool resource. She defines institutions as the shared decisions and behaviors that regulate otherwise rational, but egoistical actions of individuals who seek to maximize their own benefits.[10]

While specific institutions can be defined in the first instance in terms of rules, it should be recognized that their effects are also embedded in practices.[11] Because "institutions favor a habit-driven behavior, stability, and resistance to change; they can also be altered deliberately to change practices so as to avert a potential trauma or to prevent the reoccurrence of an earlier one."[12] The idea of "practice" in this case refers to the manner of individual and administrative behavior toward citizens and other agencies of government within a nested setting (the state)—in the same way that the rules of any game shape the behavior and expectations of the participants toward one another. Institutions, therefore, are normative patterns that can, in fact, be differentiated relative to the situational exigencies and structural subdivisions of the social or political system.[13] Institutions help to maintain consistency and predictability in the behavior of community or social actors, but even when performance fails to meet expectations, they provide a natural basis in the search for new solutions.

Institutional durability and legitimacy is enhanced the more an institution is widely integrated into a larger social order in such a way that changes in one institution will necessitate reciprocal changes in others. Because they embody "social patterns that, when chronically reproduced, institutions owe their survival to relatively self-activating social processes,"[14] the average citizen must thus come to accept the necessity and importance of critical institutions. Though collective action dilemmas generally lead to the creation of institutions to solve them, institutions, on the other hand, provide the means by which cooperation dividends are captured and sustained. Because "new norms and principles incorporate a sense of interdependent practices, roles and expectations that oftentimes differ from their original institutional setting, they encourage new behaviors that seek to compensate for the disappointing performance associated with the first set."[15] By shaping change to make it more consistent with existing procedures and practices, institutions maintain stability in the face of pressure to change. Institutions provide integrative norms and sanctions that affect the ways in which individuals and groups become activated within and outside established rules of appropriate behavior, the level of trust among citizens and leaders, the common aspirations, belief systems, traditions and norms of a political community. And by obeying the rules that govern the existence of these institutions, individuals, invariably, give it legitimacy.

Common Properties and a Reconceptualization

However, my concept of institutions goes beyond what could be suggested in the contemporary interpretation. I generally include ordinary and routine individual behaviors repeated overtime in such a way that they fit nicely into the prevailing social convention. As a framework for guiding action most institutions are malleable as well as adaptive, hence they offer new frames for accommodating changes in the collective needs and expectations of a society. In my own view, institutions can be anything that has a regulatory or self-inducing authority, in the sense that people have come to accept and understand their individual obligations to affirm its legitimacy and to abide by such institutional rules and devices. By *rules* are "meant the routines, procedures, conventions, roles, strategies, organizational forms, and technologies around which political activity is constructed."[16] It matters little whether they are "imposed or enforced by direct coercion and political and organizational authority, or is part of a code of appropriate behavior that is learned and internalized through socialization or education,"[17] rules establish behavioral patterns that are habit-forming.

In other words, we do not individually create the rules that govern social behavior, rather rules emanate as collectively intentioned sets of practices that are repeated over time in such a way that they attain the status of a normative order. We do not necessarily create rules to govern us, rather rules evolve as part of our collective social experience and they contain structures or modes of action patterns that turns around to regulate our behavior in specific situations. I am always amazed when I come across the now common usage in the literature such as: "What is an institution? Do institutions matter? But the irony is that this is already a moot question, and those who have persisted in this fallacy have not been able to answer them. Of course, institutions do matter simply because they are everywhere in social life. Even those who are asking these questions are only able to do so being induced essentially by prevailing institutional effects. And it does not matter whether those effects are discrete, contextual, objective, subjective, or normative. Any phenomenon that instructs, informs, or shape conformity to existing social, economic, and political roles is an institution. This is based on the recognition that there are institutions that come in the form of norms, customs, conventions, or simply taken-for-granted practices that have endured overtime to the extent that they have become part of the ongoing framework of collective experience and identity.

Institutions, therefore, do not have to be physical or observable entities; but they are also cognitive (norms, values, beliefs, culture, social facts, public opinion) or noncognitive (rules and procedures, laws, agencies, instructions, time, and symbols). An institution is cognitive in the sense that by embedding itself in our schema (unconscious thought process), it is able to induce unconscious reflexes within us that corresponds to and shape specific responses to an external stimulus. Institutions can also be noncognitive to the extent that they exist in the form of symbols, instructions, illustrations or commands that shape our understanding and reactions toward particular political and social objects including the government and fellow citizens. But to be able do this, I will attribute several properties to the concept of institutions:

- Institutions confer rights and obligations
- Impose structure and conformity in the behavior of actors
- Contains self-inducing qualities (such as norms, values, culture, social facts)
- Are legitimized not only through the recognition and collective obedience of social actors (humans), but also through enforcement and affirmation by the state
- Are malleable as the structure of social relations, norms, and laws change

Functional institutions carry a specific deontology in the sense that they embody a series of obligations and expectations that have been recognized and/or accepted within a social structure, akin to what John Searle refers to as *collective intentionality*. Institutions give structure, context, and character to the outward responses we give to our daily experiences. While "differentiated roles can and do develop in localized contexts as repetitive patterns of action gradually become habitualized and objectified, it is also important to recognize the operation of the wider institutional frameworks that provide prefabricated organizing models and scripts for continuous action."[18] Hence, it is through obedience to authority as reflected in the institutions that the functional requirements of society are sustained; and by enabling people or policy makers to find areas in which complementary roles can bridge differences in ultimate goals (sustainability of the system) while at the same time facilitating integration across them, a "stable state" is achieved.

While these will be discussed in latter sections of this chapter, I am also of the view that no matter the best laid plans both in terms of organization and execution; effective institutions are, more often than not, dependent on the effectiveness of the individuals who have to perform the various activities critical to making the institutions effective. By recognizing the role of institutions in the governance of the state, we are also recognizing the central role of the human agency—without which institutions cannot function or act, all on their own. The law is an ordering device but it would require individuals to obey it. To the extent the law ends up shaping individual behavior in such a way that he or she conforms to an acceptable social convention, the very act of obedience, when continuously repeated over time takes on a life of its own hence becomes a regulatory institution. This is what I refer to as the *structure of order* (a concept that would be further explored in chapter 6).

POLITICAL CULTURE AS A NORMATIVE SCHEME

As a shared experience as well as a guiding norm, political culture[19] is a form of institution. Because it is something that people have come to accept and live by, it is also a regulatory device. While it may transcend aspects of state behavior and practices, it also draws upon the economic, cultural, regional, and partisan differences within the society. As political and social values change over time, and while they may help to produce and shape the political culture, they are also reproduced by it. Even when there are unique subcultural elements that make up the political culture, these are oftentimes muted for the simple fact that they are seen as constitutive of a much larger construct that could be used to study and understand the behavioral or attitudinal components of a state and its people. These attitudinal components are generally malleable and can drive the political system in positive or negative directions. In the end, the reciprocal effect may produce unintended consequences that serve to undermine existing system states and its institutions.

Generally, political culture is defined as set of widely shared beliefs, values, and norms concerning the relationship of citizens to the government and to one another. It is a "set of attitudes and sentiments which give order and meaning to a political process and which provide the underlying assumptions and rules that govern behavior in the political system; but also is expected to dictate the generally accepted scope or limits of political power and the boundaries between the public and private spheres of life"[20] To the extent that a country's political culture is "historically-based, involves widely-shared beliefs, feelings and values about the nature of political system,"[21] all of which can serve as a link between citizens and the government and to each other; it therefore goes to say that an understanding of "the political culture and the processes of institutionalization is crucial to the operation of any political system."[22] Instead of talking about geopolitical or cultural differences, we can talk about their uniqueness but in such a way that they highlight cross-cutting cleavages that could be drawn upon to build bridges and to advance the course of political integration as a shared obligation of citizenship.

Among the "major dimensions of political culture are included a sense of national identity, attitudes one holds toward one's fellow citizens, attitudes about governmental performance, and knowledge and attitudes about the political decision-making processes."[23] But on the general premise that the "political culture of a nation is the particular distribution of patterns of orientation toward political objects among the members of the nation; we also need to have some way of systematically tapping individual orientations toward political objects."[24] Gabriel Almond and Sidney Verba[25] provide a classification system indicating three types of orientations—the internalized aspects of objects and relationships:

- Cognitive orientation—knowledge of and belief about the political system, its roles and the incumbents of these roles, its inputs, and its outputs.
- Affective orientation—feelings about the political system, its roles, personnel, and performance.
- Evaluational orientation—the judgments and opinions about political objects that typically involve the combination of value standards and criteria with information and feelings.

On the premise that basic attitudes are, more often than not, products of the subjective civic culture—beliefs, feelings, and values that significantly influence political behavior—and to the extent that these draw upon different socialization processes typical in multiethnic societies, individuals are therefore bound to create different cognitive maps that orient them toward each other as well as the political system. Where this aggregation is institutionalized, it rather unfortunately, becomes a most convenient way for evaluating the political system and its operations even in the face of contradictory evidence. As the institutionalization process endures over time, and as it morphs into different political attitudes or ideologies—the divergent views or nature of political thinking that people develop about how government should work and how it actually works—often lead to political paralysis or outright hostilities and conflict. All cultural orientations, therefore, draw upon the knowledge and belief people have toward the political community in which they reside, the constitutional and political system it provides, and the government officials who comprise its political leadership.

Political culture does not reveal itself by itself, but it requires people to think and reflect upon it, and then act on it at specific moments in time and space. It is constitutive in the sense that while shared culture reflects "a body of definitions, premises, statements, postulated, presumptions, propositions, and perceptions about the nature of the universe and man's place in it";[26] norms, on the other hand, "are oriented to patterns for action"[27] (how to behave in specific situations and under what conditions). In the abstract sense of the term, norms provide a priori rationalization and justification for later action. And because "constitutive rules operate at a deeper level of reality creation, involving the devising of categories and the construction of typification processes"[28] by which "concrete and subjectively unique experiences are ongoingly subsumed under general orders of meaning that are both objectively and subjectively real";[29] "institutions, therefore, are an external constraint when they are internalized."[30]

What all these suggest is that political culture is not only an "out there" kind of abstraction; it *informs* us at the same time and in the same way as we *validate* it. And to the extent that the political culture helps to shape institutions, institutions therefore harbor a cultural-cognitive component. They harbor "the shared conceptions that constitute the nature of social reality that create the frames through which meaning is made and social action undertaken."[31] On the premise that the extant political culture has enormous influence in the shaping of belief systems among members of a political community, the shared experience and beliefs can go a long way in bridging competing cleavages and disagreements before they manifest into overt conflict. And because the people have come to understand them and their centrality to the well-being of the political system, enduring political cultures (such as the high value Americans place on the issue of *freedom* and *private property*) are not only habit-forming, they have also become permanent fixtures in the cognitive schema and the unconscious reflexes that drive social action.

Religion and Ecclesiastical Politics

For centuries, the moral ethos of religious doctrine has always been a factor in shaping particular orthodox belief systems in social life. One of the critical factors of any civilization is its religious beliefs. In some political cultures, religious beliefs are interwoven with native traditions and mores to sustain an integrative and monolithic structure within which culture and religion are transformed into a unique identity (as is also the case in theocracies). Examples abound such as the Irish and Catholicism, the polytheism of the Aztecs, the Malays and Islam, the Indians and Hinduism, and the Japanese and Taoism. While Oriental belief systems in general were often influenced by the ethic of Buddhism, Taoism, and Confucianism, various parts of the now Middle East saw the Islamic religion as the gateway to their salvation, hence puritan adherence to the doctrine ensured that the ultimate objective of Godly ascent was attained. But in the Occidental world, it was the works of Max Weber that brought into sharper focus and, I might say, extended the debate on the role of religious doctrine in the monumental advance of industrial development and western civilization above all other competing civilizations throughout the ages.

Weber's seminal contribution to the sociology of religion was his essay on the *Protestant Ethic and the Spirit of Capitalism* in which he saw Protestantism as providing adequate motivation for the acquisitive activity, the norms of asceticism (savings), and wealth creation in a system of market relationships which we characterize as capitalism.[32] The normative obligation which he refers to as a "calling" was therefore not only inspired by obedience to God's Divine mandate but also to the development of certain basic attitudes or orientations toward worldly activity and man's relationship to each other.[33] Because it shapes individual belief systems and also guides him toward particular behaviors and orientations, religion is a form of institution. As has been the case in "the connection of the spirit of modern economic life with the rational ethics of ascetic Protestantism, the magical and religious forces and the ethical ideas of duty based upon them, have always been among the most important formative influences on conduct."[34] Like ideology, religious beliefs and practices have also crept into the arena of political beliefs as well as specific patterns of orientation toward political objects, symbols, and public policies. For theocratic states like Saudi Arabia or Iran, religious doctrinaire provides inspiration and directive in all forms of political action, an orthodox-traditionalist doctrine that even permeates and regulates the private lives of individual citizens.

But for most secular western democracies, religion is one of a few remaining indicators that seems to influence political attitudes and voting behavior. Individuals with conservative orientations on issues like abortion rights, gun control, or capital punishment tend to associate with or vote for the party that carries their own individual preferences on these policy issues. And for most people, religious belief is a matter of faith and calling; hence is the primary filter through which they engage in social and political action. Although what has been witnessed in many advanced western democracies is an increasing orientation toward the secularization of political life, this phenomenon is not because people have decided to abandon any kind of belief in a Divine omnipresence, or any belief at all. Yes, most still have beliefs while some do not, but it has become disaggregated in the sense that the existence of such beliefs now seem to draw inspiration from multiple and even arcane sources that compete and even contradict each other. This is partly as a result of rising sociopolitical discontent, mistrust of governments, the increasing population of weary and frustrated youth so unsure of what the future holds for them, and the relentless allure of the Internet and all its hidden trappings, movies, hard music, drugs and alcoholism that seem to suggest a novel and more rewarding way of life. While all these social phenomena have become bottled up into what is now interpreted in various western societies as the new progressivism; yet progressivism does not represent any specific and concrete epistemology or ideology other than the ideology of change. But then what is the change and in what form should it take? The inability to answer this question has led to an increasing level of moral relativism in which people have become more comfortable in making up their own choices and justifications (no matter how it appeals to common sense and interest) on important matters of public or democratic discourse.

As a result of the decreasing level of shared ethos about the nature of government and its relationship to the political society and to the citizens, we now have a situation where people disagree on issues based more on differences in ideology as opposed to differences on the actual facts of the matter. As a construct, ideology reflects the views or nature of shared political thinking people develop about how government should work, how it actually works, and its relationship to the people. In contemporary liberal societies, the rise in political tensions tied to ideological conflicts is seen as one way of extracting democratic accountability for policy makers, but also as a means of engaging each other in the broader arena of public discourse. From the rise of the counter-culture and the radical dissent of the 1960s, right wing versus left wing advocacy groups, the debate over the ability of the free-market system and the current social welfarism of advanced industrial democracies; there still remain the ideological divide on how best the government can use available resources to address contemporary issues of inequality, the economy, and quality of life.

The essential point made here is that ideological differences, even where they offer divergent policy premises, influence people's attitude toward the government and to each other. It goes a long way to dictate the political choices they make, the political orientations they prefer, and the public policies they advocate and support. Because conservatives, liberals, libertarians and anarchists are less likely to agree on the same policy choices (at least most of the time), the political choices they make and the intensity with which they seek specific outcomes would be different, if not conflictual. The same situation is also, for all practical purposes, applicable to differences in partisan orientations or political party affiliation. Parties differ on the types of programs or policies they support and they seek to build a following or popular support for those issues. In this regard, partisanship becomes an organizing symbol as well as an institutional reference point for individual or group action. And like ideology, it continues to be one of many other sources of political disagreement and dissent. And oftentimes, this situation can endure over time.

THE INSTITUTIONAL FOUNDATIONS OF PUBLIC OPINION AND TIME

Even when not present or physically felt, there are certain phenomena that constrain or influence individual behavior, by channeling it toward particular orientations or objectives. Public opinion and time can be considered as *institutional artifacts*; though not naturally present or observable, they are able to shape social action through their activation of the cognitive processes that guide individual behavior as well as social action. Noticeably, I have tended to use the term *artifact* more liberally in the sense that it can mean a lot of different things at the same time. But my reference to *artifacts* in the context of this work is based on "something characteristic of or resulting from a particular human institution, period, trend, or individual; or as a product of artificial character due usually to extraneous agency (such as humans)."[35] Public opinion and time (though to a lesser extent) are products of the human agency; but at the same time have a controlling influence on what humans do and how and when they do it. Because they help us navigate social and political relations within specified parameters, *public opinion* and *time* are also regulatory devices. In the following sections, I will attempt to sketch out a few propositions that will provide further illumination to the logic of the argument as set forth.

Public Opinion as Latent Function

It is oftentimes easy to articulate the notion of public opinion without giving much credence to what it is and why it seems to resonate so well in matters of democratic policy making. Because policy makers rely on public opinion as a legitimizing force regarding specific policy choices or as a means by which the will of the majority is sampled regarding an issue; we have come to developed a rather naive understanding about public opinion. It is much more than that. Here I offer an alternative hypothesis that sees public opinion as a form of political institution, in the sense that it can affect the processes that shape political behavior, political outcomes, and public policy. It has a fluid and organic structure that sets the boundaries for individual and collective choice-making as well as serve as a regulatory device that shapes dispositions toward particular political symbols, issues, and objectives. Although it has been defined in various ways, I am more given to the definition of public opinion as the aggregate of individual opinions on a particular issue or policy. But opinion expressed in such a way that while it can be stable and endure over time; does not, in itself, preclude the fact that it can equally be temporary and fleeting only to be changed in the course of *time*. Expressions of public opinion can still be used to legitimize public policies or particular expressions of public interest, even after the fact (latent function).

Digging much deeper into what public opinion is requires a broader understanding of the ontological roots that inform the phenomenon, but such an inquiry cannot go beyond the fact that it is a form of human experience shaped by an individual's self-interest, self-awareness, and idiosyncrasies, as well as contextual factors that have overtime shaped individual history and experience. Why do people express one opinion over another, oftentimes without any consideration of existing empirical or factual evidence? Why do most people stick to their own opinions even in the presence of more credible and competing evidence? It is the resiliency of public opinion and its influence on the human character that makes it a lucrative political tool in public policymaking—particularly when sourced through opinion surveys or polls. Pollsters oftentimes resist suggestions that their 'objective science' of measuring opinions influences political outcomes; but by virtue of empirical evidence, the fact remains that the ubiquitous application of polls in democratic politics affect the decisions citizens make—including how to vote, and who to vote for?[36] "If the public thinks something is important, political leaders will usually respond in the direction of public interest; hence opinion polls clearly matter in setting the national policy agenda—because it helps shape which topics political leaders pay attention to."[37] And by "responding to public opinion in the media and through interaction with citizens who have requests, complaints, arguments, suggestions, ideas, and new perspectives,"[38] legislators engage in the act of policy making.

But public opinion, with all its virtues so to say, also harbors an intrinsic paradox as a double-edged sword that can oftentimes lead to failed public policies. It is somewhat undemocratic due to its overwhelming reliance on majority or popular opinion on an issue. But empirical evidence over the years has shown that just because a majority opts for a particular issue position does not ipso facto mean that the majority is right in the absolute or in any other sense of the term. The point is that majority opinion can be wrong most of the time in the same way that minority opinion can. For example in 2013, approximately 73 percent of Americans expressed the opinion that supports the use of force to overthrow Saddam Hussein in Iraq; similar views were also expressed in the months prior to the overthrow of Muammar Gaddafi in Libya. But then look at where we are now with respect to the chaos and anarchy that continues to bedevil these two countries even after many years from the initial punch. While there is no reasonable end in sight and in light of the hornet's nest that has been unleashed, it is now a universally acknowledged fact that the decision to overthrow Hussein and Gaddafi in the forceful manner and at the time they were done was an egregious mistake. If you conduct the same public opinion poll today, it is quite likely that you will get less than 1 percent of those approving to reaffirm their earlier opinion. Even those at the helm of US foreign and defense policy making during that time now openly acknowledge that they made a strategic mistake by removing these (though discredited) leaders.

There is also another intrinsic value that qualifies public opinion as a cognitive construct as well as an institution. When people express an opinion on an issue either as individuals or part of a collectivity, the power of public opinion is not based on the fact that it has been expressed; rather its relevance is in terms of the fact that it is able to change or affirm people's judgment, evaluation, and support for a particular point of view. Because a majority seems to favor a particular view more than the others, it means that public opinion can, in and of itself, provide its own justification. It helps individuals not only to affirm the rightness of their own beliefs, values, or point of view, it also enables them to reconcile the cognitive tension that we normally experience when we are faced with the dilemma about the rightness or wrongness of a particular choice. Invariably, because a majority of people have already expressed a particular opinion, we then (almost automatically) assume that they "must" be right. Hence we are more inclined to concede our own long-held views on the issue in deference to the majority opinion. Because it helps to sway our independent judgment, the power of public opinion as an institution and as a regulatory device is not an "out there" that is external to the individual. It is an integral part of what drives human behavior.

Public opinion, therefore, is not about what people make of it, but it is more about what people make of what they hear and how they react to it. To secure increased legitimacy for their actions, political and administrative leaders have generally been receptive to the idea of public opinion, or citizen engagement in governance through public meetings, focus groups, opinion surveys, and other channels of public input into the decision-making process.[39] But to the extent that the role of the average citizen is quite limited when it comes to the decision-making process about specific policies, it becomes a problem as to who would be responsible for the effects or outcome of a policy. Would it be the citizens or the administrative officials who implemented the policy? If so, how much responsibility should each party bear for the policy outcome? Hence, the key problem of public opinion is, first, it dilutes the onus of administrative responsibility; and secondly, it offers, by default, a seemingly innocuous avenue for legitimizing potential administrative incompetency.

All said, it is also important to ask an enduring and profound question: Do most people who express an opinion on an issue actually understand the issues or actually know what they want? Because "increased specialization and professionalization of pursuits within the arena of government has tended towards an elitist rather than a pluralist form of decision making";[40] the average citizen lacks "inside" knowledge of how most bureaucracies work, the internal challenges they face, or the political imperatives they have to secure. On average, they have only a generic understanding of how government ought to function in the dynamic world of domestic and international politics. They suffer from information asymmetry. Limited information means that critical issues would not be adequately (or democratically) deliberated upon; expressed opinions and or participation would be superficial and decision-making haphazard at best. Certainly involving citizens (by way of public opinion) in every decision raises important questions: How do you assure that an appropriate level of expertise is incorporated into the decision process? How can we be sure that the most complete and practical knowledge is brought to bear on the problems of the state? While the "essential condition of democracy is that all citizens have an equal opportunity to exert influence through political activity if they chose to do so; decisions are still controlled by the greatest number (majority) expressing their preferences in favor of a particular alternative."[41] And this makes it more imperative that "as more government processes open up to citizen input and public opinion, the need for citizen education and the need to provide citizens with the highest quality of information becomes more profound."[42]

Time as Unconscious Reflection

Though it might seem like an abstraction, time as a construct does not have body and texture but through its transcendence is able to impose its dictates on human behavior and social action. Because it forces itself upon us, sometimes without overt compulsion; and because it compels us to choose the "when" and "how" we do certain things, time is a regulatory device. Because its impact is experienced or brought to life through the ways and means by which individuals respond to social phenomena or events, community affairs, political objects and symbols, and other factors of social life, time is an enduring institution. "Social science analysis of the transition from agrarian to industrial society began with a clear-cut dichotomy between the modern and the traditional";[43] between "people who see time as a linear progression and are likely to be more time conscious than those who see time as a repeating cycle."[44] In "many human situations the most easily identifiable property of objects or events is the *time* subscripts associated with them";[45] although this easily observed condition often represents a complex set of individual, social, and organizational practices and expectations.[46] For the fact that "different norms, beliefs, and attitudes to time can combine to create all kinds of contradictions and dysfunctions";[47] time is a central element in any analysis of social action.

The value of time does not derive from itself, but only from how it shapes human conduct and in the structuring of social relations such that a sense of order and sequence is maintained in the exercise of individual or social action. And because it harbors qualities such as extension, durability, and temporality, time cannot be imagined but can only be reflected in the lived experience of the social world of human beings. In the same way that nature regulates the occurrence of day and night, autumn, winter, and spring based on immutable laws that are beyond human; worldly time itself, is embedded in the very essence through which humans react to and address critical issues of society, state, and government. In all political societies, every social action is a response to time (durability), is extended (occurs hourly, daily, monthly, or yearly), and has temporality (has both the qualities of past, present, and the future). To the extent that all human action takes place in the context of intrinsic but unavoidable time domains, and as Eric Voegelin points out, "time is the everlasting and moving likeness of eternity."[48]

Time drives individual and social action by stipulating in advance the where, when, and duration of what humans do. It does not have body, and it lacks structure; but it embeds itself in our consciousness without our consent, and dictates the sense of urgency and precision within which we are forced to handle the various necessities of life that surround us. In all social relations, there is a time for everything—a time to go to work, a time to eat, a time for elections, a time for a meeting, a time to marry, a time to give birth, a time for dinner, a time to sleep, and a time to wake up in the morning. Invariably, and by necessity, these are regulated by an abstract notion (of time) that, though not inherent in the various activities as stipulated, has become a central element of human consciousness and action. Time manages to regulate and control human affairs not only by imposing itself on us, but by creating a sense of a *timeless order* constructed as a natural and integral part of what humans do. And that is why people always say "I need more time; there is not enough time," "please give me more time." But unbeknownst to them, nobody can give anybody more time, because time is what it is and functions according to its own logic despite human needs. Rather than giving someone more time (which is impossible), individuals always adjust what they are doing or what they intend to do in response to the internalized consciousness that we have come to know as *time*.

Like most other normative institutions, time does not have corporeality or causal texture; but it embodies a *utility function* that has remained an inescapable fact of human and social life. It is an objective feature of the world that relentlessly casts its gaze on us as a constant reminder of the temporal imperatives necessary for the sustainability of our social system. It is also a subjective feature of the world by unceasingly embedding itself in our daily routines, customs, and practices. The only thing that links today with yesterday and today with tomorrow is time. The former represents the history, but the latter the future of time. Time is a phenomenon that must manifest itself in all aspects of our material transactions in both nature and in the social world of human experience; hence is embedded in both the history and future of the human condition. Because it helps to organize and coordinate the sequencing of human action without actually being part of that action, *time* is thus a regulatory institution. And to the extent that it is inseparable from all social action, the institutional and structural effects of time are everywhere.

In the following sections, I will illustrate the role of political structure in shaping different sets of political order (regime types) over time, as well as the obligations it imposes on individuals and groups as social actors. I do this in such a way that we can see not only existing similarities between regimes types, but also the distinctive differences that inform different sets of political preferences and political outcomes. All regime types may be alike when considered in terms of *functional equivalents* (the essential obligations of a state, such as security, law, and order), but some are unalike when it comes to matters governing political participation, electoral practices, civil liberties, economic opportunity, political and religious tolerance.

REGIME TYPES: POLITICAL STRUCTURE AND POLITICAL ORDER

The idea of regime type reflects, on the one hand, the way the institutions of the political system are arranged and, on the other, the mechanisms and processes through which citizens make demands or express their interests to the political system (such as voting, plebiscites, demonstrations, lobbying, campaigns, etc.). This is very important because it will determine the extent to which we can say that a political regime is developed or not developed. Political development represents the emergence of more extensive capabilities in the political system (rule of law, multiparty system, free and fair competitive elections, independent judiciary, free press), in the sense that political structures and processes become more specialized and effective in maintaining internal operations and responding to environmental demands. Over time, as they exhibit higher levels of sophistication and complexity in terms of legal authority and specialization, they are able to develop extensive capabilities to respond to the demands of the people and the political system in a coherent and sustained manner.

Placed on a continuum, the scale of human values may be inexhaustible since they have the tendency to change over time. The greater the need for organization and conformity to address the various scale of values, it would seem that there is also a greater danger of conflict between values and the political responsibility necessary to reconcile them.[49] Coincidentally, that is why "although different societies may emphasize different traits and values, each has to select those qualities and institutions that will fit its pattern of values, or at least not counteract it."[50] In this regard, political regimes and types matter a lot. Regime types offer different kinds of freedoms and liberties to their citizens, but they are also illustrative in terms of how people get elected into public office. In some countries it is by popular elections (such as the United States, Canada, and much of Western Europe), and in others it is either by a one-party electoral mandate, or by a forceful usurpation of political authority by an individual, a clique, or an oligarchy (e.g., Saddam Hussein (Iraq), Ghaddafi (Libya), Assad (Syria), Kim Jong-un (North Korea), or Hugo Chavez/Nicolas Maduro (Venezuela)). But in some cases, there are countries that fall in the middle; that is, they act and seem democratic, but then are more likely to engage in practices that do not support broadly accepted democratic norms. We call these *illiberal regimes* (countries like the Philippines, Thailand, Nicaragua, Panama, Mexico, Russia, Iran, and others have oftentimes been construed as *illiberal regimes*).

As has already been alluded to, political institutions reflect the various tools, mechanisms and approaches that allow a country to engage as well as implement various activities critical to governance. Although these institutions may perform similar functions, they do so in different ways consistent with the central tenets, ideology, or underlying philosophical principles of the political regime. The nature of the political regime (democratic, authoritarian, theocratic, etc.) will determine (to an extent) the character and the structure of the prevailing political institutions. For example, although the formal institutional structure of the American government was established by way of the Constitution which was ratified in 1789, the actual distribution of power and influence among the various branches of government (Articles 1, 2, and 3), between levels and within the individual branches of government—all follow established procedural mechanisms based on the law and authority of the state. If one goes to a country like China, Russia, or even Mexico, the nature and pattern of these institutional relationships would be quite different to a noticeable extent. For example, the central feature of the Chinese regime is the single-party system, and decision-making rests effectively with a small group of top officers of the Communist Party of China within the Politburo.[51] This institutional feature ensures top-down control of public policy, political control of forms of expression, and public and private enterprise. But the distinction with Russia is not as starkly different. Russia is "a semi-presidential system in which the president and the prime minister both have considerable powers."[52] But with somewhat weak institutions and checks and balances between the executive and the legislature (the Duma) presidential personality oftentimes reigns supreme and overshadows most other aspects of state governance. "The president can even veto no-confidence votes in the legislature, and though these may be subject to legislative override by the Duma";[53] but still, it makes one to wonder how often and to what extent this particular provision has been successful in contemporary Russian realpolitik.

Illustratively, the separation and division of powers among American political institutions (the Executive, Legislative, and Judiciary), the fluid nature of the party system, the design and processes of election, the role of the Supreme Court, and the nature of Congressional representation (bicameralism), and their geopolitical jurisdictions (districts and states)—provide a functional portrait of the nature and relationships between American political institutions. Although "constitutional norms (and the practices influenced by these norms) may vary in the extent to which authority is partitioned among and within such major institutions as the executive, legislature, judiciary, and the bureaucracy";[54] the extra-governmental institutions have over time become indispensable actors in the context of American democracy as well as in many other countries. In a conditional way and because they also play crucial political roles, one should also consider including the news media, interest groups, civil society, and other nongovernmental organizations as political institutions.

Whether a state's institutional framework is of the presidential type (United States) or the parliamentary (United Kingdom) or is Unitarian such as theocratic states like Saudi Arabia or Iran, they are nonetheless, to be seen equally as functional models of governing institutions. "Political institutions have practical and symbolic value both as a collective decision-making mechanism, and as having well-defined procedures for undertaking governmental action"[55] consistent with the specific norms and philosophy of governance that distinguishes one state from the other. An illustrative example would be the state of Iran,[56] which after having emerged from years of monarchical rule (The Qajar Dynasty, 1795–1925) and the later Pahlavi Dynasty, became an Islamic Republic in 1979 following the Iranian Revolution. The current Iranian regime has elected features of a republic interlaced with institutions of Muslim clerics, with the Supreme Leader as the preeminent cleric and figure in national politics. The country has a popularly elected president that governs with the cabinet; and a parliament known as the *Majlis* which is designed to exert some check on presidential power. But as part of the institutional structure, there is also the Guardian Council made up of twelve religious clerics with the power to approve or reject candidates for presidency, parliament, and for ministerial positions. The Guardian Council can also veto legislation made by the Majlis if they are seen to be contrary to Islamic law or the Constitution. In light of the intermittent political crisis and protests that have characterized Iranian politics in recent years, it is not too difficult to discern the inherent difficulty in any attempt to marry a somewhat Western-styled republican government with a dogmatic theocratic rule.

In the following sections, I will try to provide additional emphasis to support most of the points made above regarding political institutions. But in doing so, I am careful to point out that all political action are rarely value-neutral; they serve either narrow or broader interests that are generally circumscribed within the context-specifics of one regime type or the other. And this has been the case with regime types that could be characterized as democratic, authoritarian, or totalitarian. But what makes this a bit more complex is the fact that we have a situation where the logical structure of political action is simultaneously locked in with an overarching ontological structure constitutive of the state, government, and ideology in such a way that all three become inseparable, and none without the other. This can apply to all regime types, but in fundamentally different ways.

Of Democratic States

Democratic regimes are political systems with extensive political, economic, and social pluralism. They offer many opportunities for citizens to participate in the political and economic systems (directly or indirectly) as they chose, but consistent with established rules of appropriate conduct and behavior that does not hinder the participation of others as well as the stability of the political system itself. The key tenets consists of the fundamental political equality of all individuals in the political process; guaranteed individual freedoms, multiparty competition, constitutional guarantees of fundamental civil liberties, and in-built systems of checks and balances. The idea of a multiparty system means that there is the existence of free competition for political power among autonomous groups arising spontaneously out of society[57] (such as political parties). "The electoral process, therefore, is the main instrument through which most citizens in a democracy participate and exercise their influence."[58] While a party may win an election into public office, yet it must remain accountable to the entire electorate or people. And so what you see in democratic regimes[59] (such as the United States) is an institutionalized organization of power within the framework of a constitutional order (the US Constitution), and the allocation of responsibilities and rights (the various articles of the US Constitution) to the various institutions of government. These rights and responsibilities confer status functions on the government and its various agencies.

I should also point out that there are a few other ideological variants associated with the idea of democracy; but it is more or less a matter of extremes, or how far one wishes to seek the expression of the liberties granted under democratic rule. "Different democratic countries vary a great deal not only in the structure and processes of *organizational pluralism* but also in the shape and importance of the problem of democratic pluralism itself."[60] "Like social structures generally, organizational pluralism influences both the ways in which individuals and groups perceive their interests and also how much they can actually gain from cooperation and conflict."[61] There is the issue of *democratic liberalism*—an idea that favors a limited state role in society and economic activity; and emphasizes a high degree of personal freedom over social equality. There is also *social democracy*—an ideal which supports private property and markets but believes that the state has a strong role to play in regulating the economy and providing benefits to the public; it seeks to balance freedom and equality by emphasizing various redistributive policies often associated with the welfare state.[62] Countries that are often construed as *social democracies* include Canada, Great Britain, many of the Nordic countries of Europe (Finland, Sweden, Norway, and Denmark).

It has been argued elsewhere that the notion of democracy, in and of itself, cannot be a cure-all for all the social problems affecting most countries of the world. Rather, the amenability of democracy as a political ideal rests squarely on the contextual and sociocultural characteristics within which it is introduced. It also depends on the distributive dividends it offers to each of the contending parties. For liberal democratic states such as the United States, it has also been noted that "legislators serve as little more than rubber stamps for the edicts of government ministers, bureaucrats, or policy-drafting committees."[63] And even when it is necessary to ask questions, the public seems quite disinterested to know why. It is obvious that in a representative democracy where citizens elect people to represent their collective interests and to serve different constituencies, the reelection opportunities of those representatives depends on how much and how frequently they "bring home the bacon" to their respective constituencies.

Despite the fact that "democratic responsibility refers both to a process of deliberation (giving reasons for policies of government) and to a process of accountability to the electorate";[64] elected officials often become captive tools or "sell out" in the hands of an interlocking directorate often referred to as the 'iron triangle.' Even though most democracies may be seen as "open governments" in which the people's right to know is supreme, but the real fact is that the people get only a marginal slice of available information, and only if the policy maker or the bureaucrat deems it of political benefit. They are, more or less, forced to enter into legislative or political contracts that often end up harming the very ideal of representative democracy, and in fact, democracy itself. Hence, "beyond what legislators can do in structuring the legislative process, the constitutional structure of government, including the rules governing their re-elections";[65] yet institutional structures are the basis for the existence of competition and compromise in policy making and the nature and timeliness of the information available to constituencies in their collective choice making.

Instead of fostering constructive competition, institutional features that increase the likelihood of divided control increases the likelihood that ambition and partisanship will be pitted against each other, while the real public interest is straddled in the middle.[66] But this is not a coincidence; rather it is an artifactual relic of the democratic ethos. "Democratic governments are by their very definition committed to the permanent acceptance of disagreements and inconsistencies. It is not seen as a flaw that rival political parties have different sets of values and different fundamental beliefs."[67] Good public policy therefore derives from the eventual assimilation of conflicting values, beliefs, and interests through exhaustive and competing deliberations. The notion of freedom has remained a common parlance used in conjunction with the ideal of democracy; but few also note that unrestrained freedom can itself be a destabilizing force that could undermine the very liberty it seeks to preserve. The paradox of democratic freedom is that while unrestrained liberty often leads to chaos, complete uniformity in thought and action deprives the individual of any liberty worthy of the name.[68]

For contemporary democratic politics, the twenty-first century has seen normally sane political discourse or disagreements turn into riots, violence, and caustic recriminations without end. In many of them, opposing groups do not talk to each other; rather they talk past each other. Judicial rulings and majoritarian outcomes are no more held sacrosanct or accepted as a fait accompli. As we continue to redefine and reorient the traditional values that have helped us to sustain social order and integration; respect for authority and law and order have become (for most people) part of the "problem" as opposed to the solution. And much of these developments underlie every state's attempt to restore order by restricting the expression of specific liberties in the face of declining acquiescence to institutional authority in western democracies.

As much as we may desire it, unrestrained freedom, particularly, in the Rousseaunian tradition often generates a contradiction that is opposed to the stability of the very institutions needed for its validation. It is often the case that "when political systems are placed under severe strain, we tend to see much more clearly what they are made of and what they are capable of."[69] Just as "nobody can fly in the face of convention by walking naked in the street, nor use his or her personal freedom for instigating the overthrow of the social order";[70] the "solution for those who desire a free society that *functions* is a balance between the two opposing poles of individual liberty and organization of society, diversity and uniformity, that would achieve integration through unity on fundamental principles and yet permit the greatest degree of difference on all others."[71] Furthermore, and because there are basic institutional requirements that are more amenable to specific types of governmental systems as well as other hybrid forms, it is important that we focus on existing institutional durability and performance and use that as a focal point in deciding what model of government would be more adaptable to the cultural and political demands in a specific geopolitical context.

The irony of democracy is that while it makes it possible for issues and policies to be contested, genuine victory is only possible if all actors agree to abide by the rules of the game. But where fundamental institutions are lacking or where they are easily changed or renegotiated, it becomes very difficult to establish a durable foundation upon which these rules of the game can be adjudicated and/or legitimized. Furthermore, the level of openness and permissiveness that liberalization entails oftentimes generates its own contradiction. "Political liberalization has the tendency to resurface critical issues of poverty, resource distribution, property rights, and power relations as the cornerstone of political contestation. When broad political interests diverge and become factionalized, they present continued breeding grounds for factional conflict and political dissent."[72] To the extent that functional roles and activities reinforce the durability and efficacy of the social and political system, they also at the same time become enduring institutions.

Of Authoritarian States

Authoritarianism is a political system with limited political, economic, and social pluralism. In some cases, most authoritarian regimes are in some kind of transition toward a more broadened form of political participation. On a broader level, "authoritarianism is a catch-all name for political regimes that are either nondemocratic or are in a transitional phase but not yet fully democratized; examples would include: autocracy, tyranny, satrapy, dictatorship, absolutism, bonapartism, despotism, military rule, oligarchy, junta, theocracy, and even outright gangsterism."[73] While many states, even democratic ones may use authoritarian devices such as declaring a state of emergency, or Marshall Law as a temporary means to restore law and order in periods of civil strife and disobedience;[74] authoritarianism becomes more pronounced when it is reflected in every activity and directive of the state to the extent that it becomes an institutionalized form of political conduct by which the outside world would come to know it. Prominent examples are Libya under Gadhafi, Iraq under Saddam Hussein, Italy under Mussolini, Nazi Germany under Hitler; Argentina under Peron, Somoza of Nicaragua, Jean Bedel Bokassa of Central African Republic, and Spain under Franco, to name but a few.

Authoritarian regimes have developed in countries where there is a highly unbalanced relationship between the state and society. In some cases, the state and its agencies overpower the rest of society by playing a dominant role in the economy, in employment, or in organizing and controlling other societal activities and associations, including religious ones."[75] The state tends to incorporate existing institutions and turns them into willing instruments of its predatory rule. While "the ruling elite may refuse to compromise and share power, they invariably impose authoritarian solutions to remain in power."[76] In this way, "authoritarian regimes manipulate and determine the organization of interest, the organization of consent, and the organization of rights"[77]—in the sense of making individuals, groups and associations march in lock-step for the validation of the authoritarian state and its dogma. "As a result, *civil society*[78] remains unorganized, many are jailed or tortured, and social forces or voices of opposition are brutalized into submission to the will of the ruling authoritarian elite."[79] The general features of authoritarian regimes are:[80]

- The organization of command—concentration of power in the hands of a limited political elite.
- They seek to generate some basic instruments of support by emphasizing decisional swiftness, efficacy, and civic order; by rewarding supporters of

the regime and excluding others; and seek to incorporate various socially autonomous groups (through threats and the creation of incentives) to join and or support the regime in power.

- Most authoritarian regimes are *tyrannical*;[81] and in most cases evolve as a result of military rule and overthrow of elected civilian governments. In other cases, a ruling oligarchy could simply deploy tyrannical measures to scuttle the opposition and to remain in power.

Nonetheless, authoritarian regimes also have its variants such as *traditional authoritarianism*—based on hereditary monarchy[82] (Bahrain, Morocco, Kuwait, Oman, Saudi Arabia, Jordan, United Arab Emirates); and *military authoritarianism*—as was the case in the military regimes of Libya under Gadhafi, Iraq under Saddam Hussein, or Uganda under Idi Amin. There is also another subcategory known as *theocratic authoritarianism*—which seeks strict conformity to religious-based rule (oftentimes founded on extreme fundamentalist beliefs). "So far, all the modern examples of this have been cases of Islamic rule, particularly in states like Afghanistan under the Taliban, Iran under the revolutionary clerics, North Yemen, and the Sudan."[83] Saudi Arabia under Wahhabism can, to an extent, also fit into this profile. But a key structural distinction in all of these is that they oftentimes "involve either an autonomous military running the country outright, or a bureaucratic-authoritarian regime (including civilian bureaucrats) in which the military continues to exercise so much control and oversight that the regime cannot be called democratic."[84]

Of Totalitarian States

Totalitarian regimes[85] share many of the characteristics common to all authoritarian regimes: *political power* is concentrated and the command structure is not subject to the limitations and restraints such as exists in democratic systems; the *leadership* manipulates and controls public consent—using police and other instruments of coercion to ensure compliance. It controls the various *media of communication* to limit demands; it *dominates and controls* the configuration of interests; and it pays little attention to individual rights, since few guarantees are extended to the individual, who remains at the mercy of the ruling elite. In totalitarian regimes, "the state penetrates and virtually absorbs most societal forces; and new institutions are created in order to bring all social groupings under the unchallengeable control of the ruling elite."[86] Through the use of ideologies (no matter how barren and unsophisticated), totalitarian regimes engage in the process of political mobilization and indoctrination as a way of securing popular consent and allegiance to the tenets of the regime and its philosophy about social life, education, culture, politics, power and authority. In this regard, "the totalitarian ideology is comprehensive in nature, and its proponents claim singular authority for it, to the exclusion of all other belief systems."[87] Totalitarianism, therefore, is a combination of totalist ideology[88] as a norm, and the monopoly of power to ensure that it is enshrined in the politics of the state (even if by force).

Thomas Hobbes' argument for the establishment of order and security under the control of the state has been viewed as providing the intellectual origins of authoritarianism, and to an extent totalitarianism (though oftentimes misconstrued). While some totalitarian regimes may employ the language of democracy, frequently using variations of such concepts as the "sovereignty of the people," the "representatives of the people," "individual rights," and so on, and may even have many of the institutional and structural representations of democracy, they invariably, use these to facilitate an unlimited acquisition and exercise of political power. Characteristically, totalitarian regimes[89] are *monopolistic* (they seek involvement and control over all spheres of social and political life); *one-dimensional*—in terms of seeking political conformity (they do not allow alternative ideologies); *vertically oriented*—extensive dominance of political discourse by the political elite; *exclusive*—of those who are not members of the party or organizing ideal, but are also *integrative*—they seek to *i*ntegrate all segments of society into the ideological and partisan framework of the regime. Examples include the Soviet Union under Josef Stalin; Italy under Mussolini; Nazi Germany under Hitler, Iraq under Saddam Hussein's Baath Party; North Korea under Kim Jong Un or his father Kim Jong-il before him. The "legitimacy" of the totalitarian state requires a coercive apparatus as well as a submissive public; although the primary goal is one of order and control. And by designing the structure of social relations to advance this onerous objective, the regime is able to maintain total control of the ways and means by which people become engaged in social and political action.

POLITICAL ECONOMY AND POLITICAL ACTION

Political Economy is the relationship between the economy and the state in the interactive process of production. The state can affect the economy in many ways—such as through *macroeconomic policy* (raising or reducing taxes, providing grants to local and municipal authorities, regulating interest rates, inflation, and unemployment, as well as policies that encourage consumer *demand* for goods and services); and *microeconomic policy* (granting of subsidies to private sector businesses, liberal loans, price supports, and anti-trust regulation). In addition to particular political ideologies, countries also have specific economic systems or models under which goods and services are produced and distributed, and the relative price mechanisms that undergird supply and demand. Different economic systems have different approaches to *macroeconomic policy* (policies used for the overall management of the economy—such as interest rates, monetary and fiscal policies, as well as different tax regimes); and *microeconomic policy* (policies geared toward the regulation of economic activities in the private sector—to preserve competition, prevent price-fixing, collusion, prevent creation of artificial barriers to market entry, and other anti-trust violations).

States play various roles in the management of economic policy. In liberal free-market regimes such as the United States, the role of the government in the economy has been the key to growth and employment as well as an effective adjustment mechanism for addressing relative market failures. At the supranational level, states also play critical roles in economic growth and development, particularly when they come together under the banner of a single institutional framework. In this case, I am reminded of the two Bretton Woods institutions (the World Bank and the IMF) that were created in 1944 to help rebuild the shattered postwar global economy and to promote international economic cooperation—a new postwar economic order based on the notions of consensual decision-making and cooperation in the realm of trade and economic relations.[90] Ironically, the Bretton Woods institutions ended up (beyond their original founding mission) being the central lender to the new post-independent states of the Southern countries following the end of colonial rule.

There was also the European Recovery Program (Foreign Assistance Act 1948), otherwise known as the Marshall Plan (June 3, 1948), under which the United States provided food and reconstruction aid to prevent mass starvation in major areas of the European war theater. The plan had two major objectives: "to prevent the spread of communism in Western Europe and to stabilize the international order in a way favorable to the development of political democracy and free-market economies."[91] In fact, the Marshall Plan, as an institutional framework, became the economic arm of the United States' *policy of containment* against the global spread of communism—a foreign policy posture that lasted for more than 40 years after the end of World War II and may still be the case today. Although it was created mainly for European postwar reconstruction, the Marshall Plan also contributed in various ways to the reconstruction of Japan following its unconditional defeat in 1945. But still, the political import was not lost of both donors and benefactors that the plan was a means to build a new world made safe for democracy. Evidence points to the fact that "the real lesson of the Marshall Plan is that the rule of law, property rights, the various facilities offered by the free market system, and an entrepreneurial culture were what was necessary for economic success and institutional development."[92] Hence, the ensuing interdependent relationships between free-market economies would deepen to the extent that all member countries would seek peace and stability rather than conflict and war.

Free-Market Economy

This is an economic system in which private economic actors are quite free from state constraints, and the state engages in only the most limited efforts to shift resources among private actors. The basic assumption is that there is no need for any state intervention in the market system (laissez-faire) because the market (itself) would be able to self-adjust to bring supply, demand, and price toward equilibrium. And to the extent that there is an *invisible hand* at work (the reaction of consumers to changes in price and supply); this will also influence the *demand* for goods and services—which will ultimately drive all the three elements (supply, demand, and price) toward equilibrium or a state of balance. The philosophical underpinning of the market system (capitalism) and the principle of laissez-faire (government stay away) is attributed to the work of Adam Smith, particularly his book the *Wealth of Nations*, published in 1776 (the same year of the American Declaration of Independence). Ironically, and although Smith had cautioned against its literal interpretation, the laissez-faire ideal did not save the United States from the Great Depression of the 1930s, but it took government intervention and the presidential activism of Franklin D. Roosevelt to institute practical measures that led to economic recovery.

Today, the stability of Germany's economic growth and current account surplus reflects a mix of competing values and regulatory pressures cast on the operation of the market system. As bargaining institutions help to secure wage restraint; employers see it as an economic incentive for continued employment while union members see it as a reasonable trade-off for job security.[93] In typical Keynesian economics, it is hoped that as wages gradually pick up over time, they would help to shift demand away from exports toward consumption, thereby creating additional growth and employment for the domestic economy. The same applies to Japan, a country considered among the world's most technologically advanced producers of motor vehicles, electronic equipment, machine tools, ships, steel, and nonferrous metals.[94] With a focus on niche manufacturing and economies of scale already achieved in the household sector (such as electronics and appliances), the country's economy has also excelled both in the scale and types of technology and innovation brought to bear on the production and consumption of export and domestic goods. For Germany and Japan, the structure of the market and the specialized institutional structures that drive them, have served both countries well.

Mixed Economy

The greatest challenge for the state in a mixed-economy concerns the difficulties of striking a proper balance between competition and control, between a free-market and a planned economy, and between private profit and the sharing of society's resources. But then, real-world economies are so immensely complex and dynamic that the search for such a balance is always continuous and in some cases impossible. But what is missing in the mixed-economy model is the absence of a total embrace of the Marxist logic that the "key to any society is its mode of production or specific combination of socioeconomic forces of production and class relations of property ownership and surplus appropriation."[95] Rather what we see is an attempt to construct an economic model that recognizes the productive capacity of industrial societies as well as the need to address the technical and human costs (spill-over effects) associated with all forms of social and economic organization. Socialism, in this regard, attempts a complex balance between *state involvement* and *private control*. Some major productive resources are owned or controlled by the *state*, and the state actively intervenes in the economy; but most production decisions are private, and the value of goods and services are established primarily by supply and demand.

While the policies in a socialist state attempt to reduce inequalities significantly, they do not aim for total economic equality. In comparison to capitalism, a *socialist state* seeks to redistribute societal resources toward those citizens who are less advantaged economically. That is, the socialist state is substantially more involved in economic planning, regulation, and even ownership of productive means than would a state under a purely market economy or capitalism. In more specific terms, the *mixed economy* (socialist) model involves:

- Considerable private ownership and control of productive resources (land, labor, capital).
- Profit maximization and competition
- State's role in regulating the free-market, providing guidance and incentives for production decisions, and redistributing some money and goods to the less advantaged individuals in society.

Mixed-economy models are most evident in the Scandinavian states, the Benelux countries, and major European countries like Germany and France. Canada and Great Britain can also to an extent be considered as "mixed-economy" models. Sweden and Denmark are typical examples of what are known as "democratic socialist states" (or social *market* systems), because they blend *socialist economics* with *democratic politics*. In these countries, there is also a higher level of taxation, revenue reallocation in the form of *transfer-payments* or subsidized goods and services (health care, housing, education) to the citizens. The state is also more active in protecting individuals from the economic activities of private firms (such as price fixing, collusion, unsafe working conditions, and environmental degradation). In some countries, the state retains ownership and control of major productive sectors (such as energy, health, and transportation) that have strategic importance for the production and distribution of goods and services. Today, although one could be tempted to put Vietnam as a centrally planned economy, but the free-market dynamics on the ground, at least at this point, pretty much suggests otherwise.

Centralized-Planned Command Economy

In centralized or planned economies, "autonomy in the direction of organized productive units is greatly reduced, and in the extreme case, completely eliminated."[96] In this regard, "all economic action, so far as it is carried through, is oriented to rules which enjoin certain modes of action and forbid others, and which also establish a system of rewards and punishment."[97] A communist *command*-and-*control economy* holds the notion that the state must control all factors of production (land, labor, and capital). The state must guide the utilization of all the major factors of production by means of a *centralized planning*, as well as set the price in all productive exchanges—so that the production and distribution of goods serves the best interests of the entire population. Although it is primarily an economic system linked to the *command economy*, communism emphasizes an ideological commitment to economic and social equality among all its citizens; although there are several cases of disconnect between theory and practice. While some countries have historically embraced this model including China, North Korea, Cuba, and Vietnam; but it should also be pointed out that the end of the Cold War in 1991 essentially brought to the forc the fallacy of the communist economic ideal and exposed the widening gulf between theory, practice, and rhetoric. *Today* and as a result of their growing market economies and the economic resurgence of the middle class, it would be very difficult (and in fact inaccurate) to categorize China and Vietnam as wholly *command*-and-*control* economies.

MACROECONOMIC INSTITUTIONS AND THE DIRIGISTE STATE

Although it is considered a regulatory institution, historical experience points to a simple truism that there is no absolute free-market system in the practical sense of the term.[98] The philosophical debate between Keynesianism and classical laissez-faire economics notwithstanding, suggests that both ideals, more often than not, have been complementary as opposed to being mutually exclusive. While Keynesianism focuses on the demand side of the macroeconomic spectrum as a necessity for growth and development, classical laissez-faire economics view growth as a function of supply and independent market adjustments that result from consumer choices in response to supply and demand. Hence, the sensitivity of the market to dramatic shifts away from the equilibrium will generally create automatic adjustments that would drive price, supply, and demand back toward equilibrium. But where such is not the case, we are told to put the onus on the regulatory and restrictive policies of government, particularly in those situations where the actions of government seem to stifle economic incentives for investment in the private sector—the main engine for capitalist economic growth.

Although "the role of government has traditionally been defined with *market failures*; its interventions have been targeted specifically to overcome the failures of the market economy to take sufficient care of important social tasks such as education, public safety, and infrastructure."[99] But "with complex and dynamic policy problems that involve numerous private, civil, and public sector actors; systemic coordination is unlikely to take place entirely through the market mechanism."[100] During much of the Great Depression in the United States which began on October 29, 1920, the free-market system was not able to alone make the necessary adjustments needed to bring the economy back to a state of equilibrium. The American stock market which had been performing well for almost a decade crashed, plunging the country into its most severe economic downturn yet. Speculators lost their money, banks failed, the nation's money supply diminished, an estimated $30 billion dollars in stock holdings evaporated, and companies went bankrupt and began to fire their workers in droves.[101] It did not end there. World-wide GDP fell by 15 percent, while "personal wealth, tax revenues, profit and prices dropped and international trade fell by more than 50%."[102] Furthermore, "unemployment in the United States rose by 25% and in some countries by as high as 35%."[103]

In response to the economic crisis, President Franklin D. Roosevelt who took office in 1933 acted swiftly to stabilize the economy and provide jobs and relief to the suffering citizens. Over the next eight years, the government instituted a series of experimental projects and programs that aimed to restore some measure of dignity and prosperity to many Americans.[104] This culminated in his New Deal program (1933–1938) which saw the creation of a motley of growth and employment related programs that included the Emergency Banking Act, the Agricultural Adjustment Act, the National Industry Recovery Act, the Home Owners' Loan Act, the Tennessee Valley Authority, the Federal Deposit Insurance Act, the Federal Housing Authority, the Wagner Act, the Social Security Act, and many more. "From 1933 until 1941,

President Roosevelt's programs did more than adjust interest rates, grant farm subsidies, or create short-term back-to-work programs."[105] It also created new political coalitions that lent further support to his recovery initiatives, hence their broader receptivity within the American electorate. It was the height of presidential activism yet unparalleled in US government administration, but one that ran counter to the core tenets of classical free-market liberalism. The Japanese bombing of Pearl Harbor on December 7, 1941, forced the United States' entry into World War II, but ironically the war effort and related expenditures helped to stimulate the American economy and speed up the recovery efforts that eventually ended the Great Depression.

Yet many instances of state dirigisme abound in the formative or later stages of the economic development of most countries. These actions range from deliberate interventionist measures such as direct grants of liberal loans to domestic businesses, quota systems, manipulating existing tariff structures; or by instituting meandering bureaucratic bottlenecks as a way of protecting domestic industries from external competition. Dirigisme was introduced in France following World War II to promote industrialization and protect against foreign competition, and it was subsequently mimicked in East Asia. It took the form of indicative planning, which entailed government credit policies and subsidies, developing new technologies, and the regulation of employment overseen by a special planning commission, the *Commissariat au Plan*.[106] It built an elite university for public administration the *École National d'Administration*, to train future state planners. The government also embarked on ambitious projects, encouraging the formation of national champions in large industry groups, such as the transportation system. In their policies toward the Stability and Growth Pact (SGP) which is part of the European economic governance system, the French government successfully influenced the reshaping of the fiscal policy architecture, loosening domestic economic constraints, and thus introduced a more dirigiste interventionism in the interpretation and implementation of the Pact.[107]

Just as France had done, "state authorities in Japan also pursued dirigiste or neo-mercantilist policies prioritizing selected sectors for rapid development and recruiting technocrats from the nation's elite schools for positions as planners in the state administration."[108] Through the organs of the Ministry of Trade and Industry (MITI), the country was able to offer liberal loans and engage in several protectionist measures to protect domestic manufacturing. By reinforcing the corporate culture of *keiretsu* (economic group), it ensured that domestic companies can pull their resources together to create a controlling influence and dominance in a market segment or industrial sector. This also enables each major *keiretsu* to be capable of controlling nearly every step of the economic chain in a variety of industrial, resource and service sectors including banks and other financial and lending institutions. In like manner,

South Korea sought to promote its own national economic group, the *chaebol*—providing long-term subsidized credit to various industrial groups, as well as putting artificial export barriers to protect domestic industries.

As China integrates its hitherto command-and-control economy to become a major player in the international political economy, it has also learned to embrace dirigiste practices to its advantage. It forces countries to become heavily indebted to it, so that it can use that a subtle leverage to maintain de facto control over the debtor country's economic policy and oftentimes its politics. It also manipulates its currency by artificially devaluating it relative to the dollar, thus making her export goods cheaper in both international and domestic markets. This induces an artificial rise in the value of a comparative currency relative to the *yuan*, hence using the consequent high price of competing export products as a surrogate for protectionism and as an artificial barrier that limits how much of it is sold or purchased in China. Using the power of the Central Bank (The People's Bank of China), its monetary policy oftentimes is meant to prop up its slowing economy through a mix of targeted but unconventional liquidity and lending facilities.[109] "Since 1978, China has shown both flexibility and unwieldly resolve in its continued pursuit of wealth and power; but she also knows that there are now things she wants from far beyond her borders—ideas as well as markets, raw materials and investments."[110] Hence must integrate strategically into the mainstream of international capital if the ideal of state dirigisme and market dominance is to succeed and endure.

For China, such integration has not come without political costs and questions raised about its commitment to a free-market economy, even if on a de facto level. The summer of 2015 saw a free-fall of China's stock market and the sudden decapitation of the hitherto earning capacity of its investment shares and stocks. As a series of investment portfolios drained within a matter of days, potential investors balked and those who already had much committed in China's fledgling capital market began to seek the next exit out. Seeing what portends for the economy and the political hegemony of the Communist party, Chinese government officials led by the People's Bank of China "cut interest rates, increased the amount of money banks can lend out and pumped funds into the stock market—measures meant to boost domestic demand."[111] Also by artificially devaluing the Chinese currency (*yuan*), "authorities turned into a controversial growth-boosting tactic"[112] to the effect that a devalued *yuan* would make Chinese products cheaper and more competitive in the export market. This gave an unfair advantage to Chinese export products, particularly when placed against American products or western products.

For China, currency manipulation has always been a favorable macroeconomic policy tool as well as an adjustment mechanism for propping up the country's exports. By arbitrarily pumping money into the economy, the

People's Bank of China ensures that there will be enough liquidity in the economy to sustain business and private borrowing at an interest rate that does not dry up productivity or increase unemployment. This kind of loose-money policy would encourage growth, stabilize employment, and make Chinese products artificially more competitive in the global market. This came but to the chagrin of other competitors like the United States, South Korea, and Japan. In the usual diplomatic parlance, Chinese government officials deflect evident criticisms by arguing that its actions were consistent with its objective of seeking a more market-determined exchange rate regime that would properly reposition the country as it integrates into the free-market system.

None the less, amid recent developments in trade relations between the United States and China, it would seem that China's enduring trade brinksmanship may have caught up with it following the 2016 election of Donald Trump as president of the United States. Trump has variously accused China of unfair trade practices that range from currency manipulation, creation of artificial barriers to market entry for American firms and products into the Chinese market, theft of intellectual property, and of "government's pressure on foreign companies to transfer technology to local partners in China."[113] The result is a growing trade deficit that favors China but harms the United States. In response, Trump raised the tariff on selected Chinese products (including steel and aluminum imports) up to the tune of $34 billion in new levies (and also hiking the tariff on auto imports from the European Union countries to the tune of 25 percent) for which China and the Europeans also retaliated against the United States with their own tariff measures covering an array of products and imports from the United States. If the hard-nosed approach results in the saving of American manufacturing jobs and reduced unemployment, it would mean that more workers would have the additional disposable income to spend on goods and services which, invariably, would also spur more productivity, growth, and consumer demand.

But to a lesser extent than China, the same kind of state-led economic activism can equally be said of a resurgent Russia under Vladimir Putin. Amid a slew of wrenching economic sanctions from the West against Russia following its foreign policy forays into other countries' internal or territorial affairs (particularly Ukraine), Russia embarked on a series of measures to protect its domestic oil-driven export economy and to soften the ever-growing pains of economic stagnation. This situation was magnified by the plunge in oil prices from an average of almost $110 a barrel in the first half of 2014 to below $60 dollars a barrel in July 2015. More than two-thirds of the country's export economy comes from energy, hence the consequent decline in the value of the *rouble* relative to the dollar and the rising indebtedness of several Russian businesses, almost forced the country to the precipice of economic collapse.

In response, Vladimir Putin's push-back strategy involved a series of dirigiste inward-looking options set to withstand the economic ripple effects of the sanctions. "While the falling *rouble* made some export industries like farming more competitive, Putin's other import-blocking counter-sanctions against the West allowed Russia to maintain a sizeable trade surplus,"[114] as well as domestic industrial productivity to a level where the unemployment rate and industrial productivity could still be manageable at least in the short-term.

But to the extent that "Russian defences could still be tested by any one of a succession of possibilities—a continuous fall in oil price, a failed debt rescheduling plan by Russian firms that could drive them to imminent bankruptcy, and the possibility of more Western sanctions";[115] there is little to say that other extra-free market approaches could not be put in place to stem further economic crisis. This situation is made even more profound by the simple fact that "when economies are on an unsustainable course, international finance often acts as a fast-forward button, pushing countries over the edge more quickly than politicians or investors expect."[116] The case of Finland should also be of note here. Although relatively different from that of Russia, China, South Korea, or the United States, it nonetheless, underscores a similar refrain regarding the centrality of state dirigisme in macroeconomic policy or in making critical adjustments necessary to contain decline and stagnation.

Furthermore, it reinforces an enduring role for collectively organized economic actors in labor markets and technology policy in such a way that in Finland, collaborative technology policies and scientific research actively facilitated the rapid redistribution of resources to an emerging information, communications, and technology (ICT) industry.[117] Instead of relying primarily on the reallocation of resource inputs through the free-market system, "institutionalized commitments between firms, banks, employer associations, trade unions, and state agencies created public goods on the supply-side of the economic spectrum."[118] The consequent growth in employment generated enough disposal income to create the conditions necessary for economic stability by striking a balance between production and consumption. As Douglas North would argue, change in the economic structure came not only as a result of the on-going tension between gains from specialization and the cost arising from specialization;[119] but also from the fact that the development of institutional constraints created new patterns of loyalty and common interests that reinforced the emergent economic performance and order.

I continue this discussion in chapter 6 where I focus on explaining sets of behavioral frameworks that act as regulatory devices either in the form of social facts, heuristics, organizing, or as cognitive maps that direct as well as constrain individual or social action in specific situations. I also discuss in greater detail, my notion of structured or induced order (earlier introduced in chapter 1) as utilized in this work. Finally, I draw upon the role of artificial intelligence, neural networks, and servomechanisms to reinforce the argument that such self-regulatory capabilities can, in fundamental ways, be interfaced with human action to offer the kind of monitoring, controlling, and stabilizing effects necessary for government and society to function effectively.

NOTES

1. Dahl, Robert A. 1982. *Dilemmas of Pluralist Democracy: Autonomy vs. Control*. New Haven, CT: Yale University Press, 65.
2. Macintyre, Andrew. 2003. *The Power of Institutions: Political Architecture and Governance*. Ithaca, NY: Cornell University Press, 163.
3. March, James G., and Johan P. Olsen. 1989. *Rediscovering Institutions: The Organizational Basis of Politics*. New York: The Free Press, 18.
4. Eckstein, Harry. 1977. "Authority Patterns." In *Comparative Politics: Notes and Readings,* 5th ed., edited by Roy C. Macridis and Bernard E. Brown, 271–299. Homewood, IL. The Dorsey Press, 276.
5. Deutsch, Karl W. 1966. *The Nerves of Government: Models of Political Communication and Control*. New York: The Free Press, 36.
6. This paragraph was partly excerpted from Kalu N. Kalu. 2011. "Institution-Building, Not Nation-Building: A Structural-Functional Model." *International Review of Administrative Sciences* 77, no. 1: 119–137, 124.
7. Keohane, Robert. 1988. "International Institutions: Two Research Programs." *International Studies Quarterly* 32 (December): 386.
8. North, Douglass C. 1991. "Institutions." *The Journal of Economic Perspectives* 5, no. 1: 97–112, 97.
9. Forsyth, Tim., and Craig Johnson. 2014. "Elinor Ostrom's Legacy: Governing the Commons and the Rational Choice Controversy." *Development and Change* 45, no. 5: 1093–1110, 1095.
10. Ostrom, Elinor. 1982. "Beyond Positivism: An Introduction to this Volume." In *Strategies of Political Inquiry*, edited by Elinor Ostrom, 11–28. Beverly Hills, CA: Sage.
11. Keohane, Robert. 1988. "International Institutions: Two Research Programs." *International Studies Quarterly* 32 (December).
12. Haas, Ernst B. 1990. *When Knowledge is Power: Three Models of Change in International Organizations*. Berkeley, CA: University of California Press, 173.
13. Parsons, Talcott. 1960. *Structure and Process in Modern Societies*. Glencoe, IL: The Free Press, 171.
14. Jepperson, R. L. 1991. "Institutions, Institutional Effects, and Institutionalization." In the *New Institutionalism in Organizational Analysis*, edited by W. W. Powell and Paul J. DiMaggio, 143–163. Chicago, IL: University of Chicago Press, 145.
15. Haas, Ernst B. 1990. *When Knowledge is Power: Three Models of Change in International Organizations*. Berkeley, CA: University of California Press, 174.
16. March, James G., and Johan P. Olsen. 1989. *Rediscovering Institutions: The Organizational Basis of Politics*. New York: The Free Press, 22.

17. March, James G., and Johan P. Olsen. 1989. *Rediscovering Institutions: The Organizational Basis of Politics*. New York: The Free Press, 22.

18. Scott, W. Richard. 2001. *Institutions and Organizations*, 2nd ed., Thousand Oaks, CA: Sage Publications, 58. See also Erving Goffman. 1974. *Frame Analysis*. Cambridge, MA: Harvard University Press; and Erving Goffman. 1983. "The Interaction Order." *American Sociological Review* 48: 1–17.

19. The section titled "Political Culture as a Normative Scheme" is based on a revised and updated excerpt from an earlier work titled Kalu N. Kalu. 2018. *Political Culture, Change, and Security Policy in Nigeria*. New York: Routledge Publishers, 28–30.

20. http://www.encyclopedia.com/topic/Political_culture.aspx. "Political Culture." International Encyclopedia of the Social Sciences, 2008. Accessed on February 14, 2016, 1.

21. http://study.com/academy/lesson/political-culture-definition-theory-types-examples.html. Accessed on August 10, 2017.

22. Alesina, Alberto, and Paolo Giuliano. 2015. "Culture and Institutions." *Journal of Economic Literature* 53, no. 4: 898–944, 920.

23. Mahler, Gregory S. 2013. *Principles of Comparative Politics*. Upper Saddle River, NJ: Pearson, 16.

24. Almond, Gabriel A. and Sidney Verba. 1963. *The Civic Culture: Political Attitudes and Democracy in Five Nat*ions. Princeton, NJ: Princeton University Press, 15.

25. Almond, Gabriel A. and Sidney Verba. 1963. *The Civic Culture: Political Attitudes and Democracy in Five Nations*, 15.

26. Schneider, David. 1976. "Notes Toward A Theory of Culture." In *Meaning in Anthropology*, edited by Keith M. Basso and Henry L. Silby, 197–220. Albuquerque, NM: University of New Mexico Press, 202–203.

27. Schneider, David. 1976. "Notes Toward A Theory of Culture," 197–220, 202–203.

28. Scott, W. Richard. 2014. *Institutions and Organizations: Ideas, Interests, and Identities*, 4th ed., Los Angeles, CA: Sage Publications, 77.

29. Berger, Peter L., and Thomas Luckmann. 1967. *The Social Construction of Reality*. New York: Doubleday Anchor, 39. See also W. Richard Scott. 2014. *Institutions and Organizations: Ideas, Interests, and Identities*, 77.

30. Wendt, Alexander. 1999. *Social Theory of International Politics*. New York: Cambridge University Press, 358.

31. Scott, W. Richard. 2014. *Institutions and Organizations: Ideas, Interests, and Identities*, 67.

32. Weber, Max. 1947. *The Theory of Social and Economic Organization* .Translated by A. M. Henderson and Talcott Parsons. New York: The Free Press, 78.

33. Weber, Max. 1947. *The Theory of Social and Economic Organization*, 79.

34. Weber, Max. 1958. *The Protestant Ethic and the Spirit of Capitalism*. New York: Charles Scribner's Sons, 27.

35. https://www.merriam-webster.com/dictionary/artifact. Accessed on July 27, 2018.

36. Morone, James A., and Rogan Kersh. 2018. *By the People: Debating American Government*, 3rd ed., New York: Oxford University Press, 211.

37. Morone, James A., and Rogan Kersh. 2018. *By the People: Debating American Government*, 3rd ed., 217.

38. Dickovick, J. Tyler, and Jonathan Eastwood. 2016. *Comparative Politics: Integrating Theories, Methods, and Cases*, 2nd ed., New York: Oxford University Press, 202.

39. See Kalu N. Kalu. 2017. *Citizenship: Identity, Institutions, and the Postmodern Challenge*. New York: Routledge, 85–86.

40. Fagence, M. 1977. *Citizen Participation in Planning*. New York: Pergamon Press, 331.

41. Rosenbaum, N. N. 1978. "Citizen Participation and Democratic Theory." In *Participation in American*, eds., edited by S. Langston, 43–54. Toronto, Canada: D. C. Heath & Co., 44.

42. Simonsen, W., and M. D. Robbins. 2000. *Citizen Participation in Resource Allocation*. Boulder, CO: Westview Press, 11.

43. Huntington, Samuel P. 1977. "Postindustrial Politics: How Benign?" In *Comparative Politics: Notes and Readings*, 5th ed., Roy C. Macridis and Bernard E. Brown, 501–516, 515. Homewood, IL: The Dorsey Press.

44. Gannon, Martin J. 2004. *Understanding Global Cultures: Metaphorical Journeys Through 28 Nations, Clusters of Nations, and Continents*. Thousand Oaks, CA: Sage Publications, 424.

45. March, James, and Johan Olsen. 1986. "Garbage Can Models of Decision Making in Organizations." In *Ambiguity and Command: Organizational Perspectives on Military Decision Making*, edited by James March and Roger Weissinger-Baylon. Marshfield, MA: Pitman, 17. See also Scott Sigmund Gartner. 1997. *Strategic Assessment in War*. New Haven, CT: Yale University Press, 47.

46. Scott Sigmund Gartner. 1997. *Strategic Assessment in War*. New Haven, CT: Yale University Press, 47.

47. Morgan, Gareth. 2006. *Images of Organization*. Thousand Oaks, CA: Sage Publications, 133.

48. Voegelin, Eric. 1957. *Plato and Aristotle*. Baton Rouge, LA: Louisiana State University Press, 199.

49. Heimann, Eduard. 1938. *Communism, Fascism, or Democracy*? New York: W. W. Norton & Co., 37.

50. Heimann, Eduard. 1938. *Communism, Fascism, or Democracy*? 36–37.

51. Dickovick, J. Tyler. 2019. *Comparative Politics: Integrating Theories, Methods, and Cases*, 3rd ed., New York: Oxford University Press, 418.

52. Dickovick, J. Tyler. 2019. *Comparative Politics: Integrating Theories, Methods, and Cases*, 535.

53. Dickovick, J. Tyler. 2019. *Comparative Politics: Integrating Theories, Methods, and Cases*, 535.

54. Dahl, Robert A. 1982. *Dilemmas of Pluralist Democracy: Autonomy vs. Control*. New Haven, CT: Yale University Press, 65.

55. Holcombe, Randall G. 1997. "A Theory of the Theory of Public Goods." *Review of Austrian Economics* 10, no. 1: 1–22, 16.

56. Dickovick, J. Tyler. 2019. *Comparative Politics: Integrating Theories, Methods, and Cases*, 476.

57. Macridis, Roy C. and Steven L. Burg. 1991. *Introduction to Comparative Politics: Regimes and Change*. New York: Longman, 21.

58. Macridis, Roy C. and Steven L. Burg. 1991. *Introduction to Comparative Politics: Regimes and Change,* 53.

59. Macridis, Roy C. and Steven L. Burg. 1991. *Introduction to Comparative Politics: Regimes and Change*, 22–24.

60. Dahl, Robert A. 1982. *Dilemmas of Pluralist Democracy: Autonomy vs. Control*. New Haven, CT: Yale University Press, 75.

61. Dahl, Robert A. 1982. *Dilemmas of Pluralist Democracy: Autonomy vs. Control*, 77.

62. See Roy C. Macridis and Steven L. Burg. 1991. *Introduction to Comparative Politics: Regimes and Change*. New York: Longman, 110: "The ***welfare state*** is the major instrument for ensuring social and economic rights in a country. This includes the complex of state organizations and the public agencies that provide services and payments that support the well-being of the population. Although originally conceived of as privileges, the various forms of publicly funded support characteristic of the modern welfare state have come to be understood as social and economic rights and "entitlements." But they benefit not only the poor and underprivileged but also the middle class and even the upper middle class and income levels."

63. Lupia, Arthur, and Mathew W. McCubbins. 1995. "Who Controls? Information and the Structure of Legislative Decision Making." In *Positive Theories of Congressional Institutions*," edited by Kenneth A. Shepsle and Barry R. Weingast, 201–233. Ann Arbor, MI: The University of Michigan Press, 201.

64. Thompson, Dennis F. 2005. *Restoring Responsibility: Ethics in Government, Business, and Healthcare*. Cambridge, UK: Cambridge University Press, 51.

65. Lupia, Arthur, and Mathew W. McCubbins. 1995. "Who Controls? Information and the Structure of Legislative Decision Making," 201–233, 210.

66. Lupia, Arthur, and Mathew W. McCubbins. 1995."Who Controls? Information and the Structure of Legislative Decision Making." In *Positive Theories of Congressional Institutions*, edited by Kenneth A. Shepsle and Barry R. Weingast, 201–233. Ann Arbor, MI: The University of Michigan Press, 211.

67. Searle, John R. 2010. *Making the Social World: The Structure of Human Civilization*. Oxford, UK: Oxford University Press, 162.

68. Heimann, Eduard. 1938. *Communism, Fascism, or Democracy*? New York: W. W. Norton & Co., 57–58.

69. Macintyre, Andrew. 2003. *The Power of Institutions: Political Architecture and Governance*. Ithaca, NY: Cornell University Press, 3.

70. Heimann, Eduard. 1938. *Communism, Fascism, or Democracy*? 56.

71. Heimann, Eduard. 1938. *Communism, Fascism, or Democracy*? 58.

72. Kalu, Kalu N. 2008. *State Power, Autarchy, and Political Conquest in Nigerian Federalism*. Lanham, MD: Lexington Books, 201.

73. Macridis, Roy C. and Steven L. Burg. 1991. *Introduction to Comparative Politics: Regimes and Change*. New York: Longman, 17.

74. Macridis, Roy C. and Steven L. Burg. 1991. *Introduction to Comparative Politics: Regimes and Change*, 119.

75. Macridis, Roy C. and Steven L. Burg. 1991. *Introduction to Comparative Politics: Regimes and Change*, 121.

76. Macridis, Roy C. and Steven L. Burg. 1991. *Introduction to Comparative Politics: Regimes and Change*, 119.

77. Macridis, Roy C. and Steven L. Burg. 1991. *Introduction to Comparative Politics: Regimes and Change*, 17.

78. **Civil Society** refers to the arena of the political system where self-organizing groups, movements, and individuals, relatively autonomous from the state, attempt to articulate values, create associations and solidarities, and advance their own interests. Civil society can include various social movements such as women's groups, neighborhood associations, religious groups, trade unions, journalists, the media, business groups, labor unions, environmental groups, or even student unions/groups. A *civil society* allows individuals and groups to collectively influence the government in power without actually being part of it or being directly involved in the governance process itself.

79. Macridis, Roy C. and Steven L. Burg. 1991. *Introduction to Comparative Politics: Regimes and Change*, 121.

80. Macridis, Roy C. and Steven L. Burg. 1991. *Introduction to Comparative Politics: Regimes and Change*, 122–124.

81. When *tyrants* seize political power; they seek to wield it personally and absolutely. Because most *tyrannies* are intensely personal, they are rarely amenable to institutionalization or conformity to the prevailing norms of civil governance. The marching order for all tyrannies is—*command* and *control*, and by controlling the means of coercion, tyranny represents the most "successful" and most extreme form of *authoritarianism*. In it, power has no restraints, can be exercised arbitrarily, subordinates every interest and every individual, and is based on intimidation and fear; while allowing no political freedoms or civil rights (Macridis and Burg 1991, 126–127).

82. Siaroff, Alan. 2005. *Comparing Political Regimes: A Thematic Introduction to Comparative Politics*. Toronto, Canada: Broadview Press, 217.

83. Siaroff, Alan. 2005. *Comparing Political Regimes: A Thematic Introduction to Comparative Politics*, 220.

84. Siaroff, Alan. 2005. *Comparing Political Regimes: A Thematic Introduction to Comparative Politics*, 219–220.

85. Macridis, Roy C. and Steven L. Burg. 1991. *Introduction to Comparative Politics: Regimes and Change*, 147–152.

86. Macridis, Roy C. and Steven L. Burg. 1991. *Introduction to Comparative Politics: Regimes and Change*, 148.

87. Macridis, Roy C. and Steven L. Burg. 1991. *Introduction to Comparative Politics: Regimes and Change*, 149.

88. Macridis, Roy C. and Steven L. Burg. 1991. *Introduction to Comparative Politics: Regimes and Change*, 151–152.

89. Macridis, Roy C. and Steven L. Burg. 1991. *Introduction to Comparative Politics: Regimes and Change*, 152–153.

90. http://www.brettonwoodsproject.org/2005/08/art-320747/. Accessed on July 29, 2018

91. https://www.loc.gov/exhibits/marshall/marsh-overview.html. Accessed on July 29, 2018.

92. Dempsey, Gary. 2001. The Folly of Nation-Building in Afghanistan. The Cato Institute. http://www.cato.org/pub_display.php?pub_id=3870, 1–2.

93. The Economist. 2017. "Vorsprung durch Angst." *The Economist* 424, no. 9048 (July 8): 18–20, 20.

94. The CIA World Factbook, "Japan," https://www.cia.gov/library/publications/the-world-factbook/geos/ja.html. Accessed on February 25, 2019.

95. Skocpol, Theda. 1979. *States and Social Revolutions: A Comparative Analysis of France, Russia, and China*. Cambridge, UK: Cambridge University Press, 7.

96. Weber, Max. 1947. *The Theory of Social and Economic Organization*. Translated by A. M. Henderson and Talcott Parsons. New York: The Free Press, 214.

97. Weber, Max. 1947. *The Theory of Social and Economic Organization*, 213.

98. The section titled "Macroeconomic Institutions and the Dirigiste State" is a revised and updated version of an earlier work excerpted from Kalu N. Kalu. 2017. *Technology, Culture, and Public Policy: Critical Lessons from Finland*. New York: Routledge, 30–34.

99. Hamalainen, Timo. 2013. *Building Blocks for a New Socioeconomic Model*. Helsinki, Finland: SITRA, Version 10, 10.

100. Hamalainen, Timo. 2013. Building blocks for a new socioeconomic model, 10.

101. http://www.history.com/topics/new-deal, 1–7. Accessed on July 3, 2015.

102. Frank, Robert H., and Ben S. Bernanke. 2007. *Principles of Macroeconomics*, 3rd ed. Boston, MA: McGraw-Hill, 98.

103. Frank, Robert H., and Ben S. Bernanke. 2007. *Principles of Macroeconomics*, 3rd ed., 98.

104. http://www.history.com/topics/new-deal, 1–7. Accessed on July 3, 2015.

105. http://www.history.com/topics/new-deal, 6. Accessed on July 3, 2015.

106. Encyclopedia Britannica.http://www.britannica.com/topic/dirigisme, 1. Accessed on July 3, 2015.

107. Clift, Ben. 2006. "The New Political Economy of Dirigisme: French Macroeconomic Policy, Unrepentant Sinning and the Stability and Growth Pact." *British Journal of Politics and International Relations* 8, no. 3: 388–409.

108. Encyclopedia Britannica. http://www.britannica.com/topic/dirigisme, 1. Accessed on July 3, 2015.

109. The Economist, The People's Bank of China, November 22, 2014, 14.

110. The Economist, "What China wants," August 23, 2014, 48.

111. Hilsenrath, Jon and Brian Blackstone. 2015. "Cheaper Currency has Global Impact." *The Wall Street Journal*, August 12, p. A1.

112. Hilsenrath, Jon and Brian Blackstone. 2015. "Cheaper Currency has Global Impact," p. A1.

113. The Wall Street Journal, Thursday July 26, 2018, p. A6.

114. The Economist, "Russia's wounded economy," November 22, 2014, 9.

115. The Economist, "Russia's wounded economy," November 22, 2014, 9.

116. The Economist, "Russia's wounded economy," November 22, 2014, 9.

117. Ornston, Darius. 2006. "Reorganizing Adjustment: Finland's Emergence as High Tech Leader." *West European Politics* 29, no. 4: 784–801, 784.

118. Ornston, Darius. 2006. "Reorganizing Adjustment: Finland's Emergence as High Tech Leader," 785.

119. North, Douglass C. 1981. *Structure and Change in Economic History*. New York: W. W. Norton & Co., 209.

Chapter 6

Behavioral Paradigms in Politics and Institutions

The notion of order and stability has always been at the center of most discussions of general systems. This is most profound in situations where a series of actions results in a functional structure characterized by reciprocal relationships directed toward a specific goal. These actions are reflected in individual behaviors, the existing value system, or in specific schemas or scripts permanently embedded in the cognitive structures that shape human responses to the physical objects around them. Why do most drivers stop at red traffic lights? Why do they drive off when the light changes to green? Why do people stand in a queue when they could simply go in front of everybody? Why do most people pay their taxes on time even when they could do otherwise without immediate repercussions? Part of the answer is that most people have come to appreciate the prevailing social institutions, conventions, and civic rules of appropriate behavior; or they have learned that it is simply the proper way to behave in an organized and civilized society.

Either way, individuals are able to process incoming information and then react to it based on a structured or induced order or through cognitively embedded schema or scripts that tells them to behave one way or the other under certain conditions. These *action scripts* are already well-known but can only be activated at moments when the occasion evokes them; the individual expends little or no energy thinking about the situation, or worrying about the ramifications. People just act based simply on involuntary reflexes that point their reactions to the situation in the right and expected direction. The premise that I want to illustrate here is that of a governance system without hierarchy or formalized institutional structures but one driven by a structured order, social and political conventions, culture, customs, tradition or what Emile Durkheim calls *social facts*. In other words, this would be akin to the maintenance of order and stability in the sense that prevailing institutional structures are taken for granted, hence have become locked into our unconscious reflexes. They have become part of the self-organizing frameworks around which a series of functions could be activated. Illustrative of this very fact can be adduced from John Searle's premise that although "institutional structures enable us to do all sorts of things that we could not do without those structures, but this enabling function can be performed only if it is (at least in part) constituted by a *deontic system*—a system of desire-independent reasons for action."[1] In other words, we have a condition where institutional structures impose their dictates on us whether we consent to it or not, and certainly with little or no contemplation or rationalization regarding what we are about to do. We simply do it because we have to do it even though we may not have thought about it before we did it. Sometimes, we may not even recollect that we have done it, so life goes on without further ado.

When individuals in a social system (a *state*) abide by the rules and regulations that sustain the system, it not only makes the system functional, but it also validates it as a legitimately organized framework for collective action. Laws are made, but its utility as a regulatory device requires that people obey them; but when this is not the case all of the time, then it becomes one among many other factors that could undermine the well-functioning of the system. So the issue is how to inculcate into the mind of the average citizen that doing things one way and not the other is essential for maintaining order and stability within the *state* as a social system. It is "about how people might begin to understand the world around them and communicate this as knowledge to fellow human beings"[2] in such a way that everyone becomes both a teacher and a leaner to and from everyone else. It is a view that sees "human beings and their experiences partly as products of their environment, or one in which they are, more or less, conditioned by their external circumstances"[3] and interactions with similarly-situated others. To the extent that every element in a society renders a contribution to its integration or disintegration and change;[4] I have always believed that if everyone were to be *Mother Theresa*, then there would be no need for laws or regulations in human society. And because there has only been one Mother Theresa, it therefore becomes imperative to develop a structured order in which specific behaviors serve as patterned responses toward specific ends.

COGNITIVE AND NONCOGNITIVE CATEGORIES

Consistent with what we already know about the functionalist explanation in social science in terms of the importance of understanding order, equilibrium and stability in society and the way in which these can be maintained;[5] it is equally important that we situate this discussion within the broader context of two mutually reinforcing categories: the cognitive (subjective) and non-cognitive (objective) categories.

The Cognitive

The notion of cognition draws from the fact that human actions are driven essentially by thought processes; and so when we talk about *social cognition*, we are simply making reference to individual cognitive processes which when collectively expressed becomes the basis for social action and learning. Although some individual actions may seem to be driven by emotion, instinct, or even hysteria, but these are still, for better or for worse, preceded by cognitive processes that offer the rationalizations we oftentimes use to justify what we do as humans. My focus therefore is not necessarily on actions driven by emotion and/or hysteria, but on those actions that are preceded by some form of cognitive considerations. Applied to the analysis of social systems, one can therefore see that the cognitive category (to the extent that it applies to thinking individuals) contains an implicit *subjective* dimension as well as an explicit *objective* dimension (to the extent that it applies to the collective thought processes of members of the social system or society). As a subjective dimension, individual cognition "seeks explanation within the realm of individual consciousness and subjectivity, within the frame of reference of the participant as opposed to the observer of the action; while *social cognition* on the other hand, insofar as it is recognized to have any existence outside the consciousness of any single individual, is simply a network of assumptions and intersubjectively shared meanings"[6] (beliefs, norms, culture) among members of the social system.

In this regard, social cognition represents a collective notion of how members of a society make sense of their world and the common experiences that define that world. When they have a common understanding and shared values about *what should be and in what ways it should be*, they are therefore more likely to behave in ways that validate as well as legitimize such practices, customs, or conventions. As they become conformists to the value system that engender stability, order, and continuity of the social system (state or society), individual members serve a reciprocal role as *regulators* on the one hand, and as the *regulated*, on the other. They are consciously and unconsciously involved in the creation and validation of the same norms of appropriate behavior necessary for their mutual coexistence and survival.

The Noncognitive

The non-cognitive category represents various structural and objective factors that shape and influence individual behavior and responses toward various social and political objects. This could be in the form of laws, statutory regulations, standard operating procedures, signs and symbols, or simply by following the formal rules and procedures required to function in a civilized society. An illustrative example would be such things as posted speed limits, road signs, and weather alerts, signs warning motorists about "ice on the bridge" or "slow down—men at work." The general expectation is that once people come upon each of these designations, they would naturally respond in the expected manner as dictated. When *most* people comply with these stipulations, a sense of social order and safety is maintained in the collective interest of all. It is also equally possible (as has generally been the case) that when some people are confronted with the above situation and as they process the suddenness of the information coming to them, they sometimes allow their own independent judgment and the likely *utility function* to decide whether or not to comply. They ponder about how much precious time it would cost them if they complied by the speed limit or if they should slow down before crossing the possibly *iced* bridge. But by ignoring the applicable road convention and warning signs, by endangering his or her own safety and that of others, the driver helps to contribute to social disorder.

Administrative systems and the rules and procedures that govern bureaucratic institutions and their relationship to the public are governed by formal protocols and technical details that dictate how particular issues are addressed, who addresses them, and what the likely outcome would be. In any formal encounter between bureaucrat and citizen, there are formal rules of reciprocity and conduct that determine how specific requests are followed up and how the outcome is reported back to the citizen. The essence of all this is that order and stability is maintained in the sequence of events that follow as soon as a citizen makes a formal contact with any public agency. The average citizen will behave differently in the post office and in the police department, for the simple reason that each of these institutions place different sets of procedural demands on the citizens (institutional effects), thereby regulating their behaviors in different ways.

The structure of work, in fundamental ways, induces on employees a form of administrative and social learning. It enables activities to become regularized into routines, that over time become practices and such practices eventually become norms that define organizational cultures. Routines or the regularity within which work is done reinforce existing standard operating procedures, and also make organizational outcomes less complex and more predictable. Because individuals have come to accept that certain things ought be done in certain ways, and by becoming used to the way certain things are done, they also invariably, legitimize it. Hence they are not likely to seek less predictable alternatives just for the sake of doing so. Because they present a sense of order, sequence, and continuity, "routines help to avoid conflicts, they provide codes of meaning that facilitate interpretation of ambiguous worlds; they constrain bargaining within comprehensible terms and enforce agreements, and they help mitigate the unpredictability created by open structures and processes by regulating the access of participants, problems, and solutions to choice opportunities."[7] In the sense that they provide structure, context, and directive that guide organizational or social action, routines are regulatory devices.

In the same vein, the *cultural* and *socioeconomic* stratification of society is also a crucial factor in shaping civic attitudes and responses to political issues and demands. To the extent that specific norms and the meanings attached to them "reside in social institutions, individuals none the less, play roles that are given to them as a result of their location upon the social map."[8] Because some individual actions of members of social systems can be explained in terms of their position in the network of functional relationships, they often act or behave according to their relative rankings or offices in relation to others. The restraining power of social and administrative structures therefore constrains (regulates) and limits the boundaries and scope within which individuals can act or express alternative dispositions that could upset or undermine the way things are seen or understood by the larger society. As order and continuity is maintained, the social system threads along as if nothing ever happened.

Reification and Heuristics as Cognitive Maps

The constructs of state and government do not have physical bodies, and they do not exist apart from the individuals that inhabit them. In order words, when I look for a state or government, I do not find them; except that what I see are individuals engaged in a series of activities and functional relationships all directed toward the achievement of the same goal of *order* and *stability* in society. Drawing from the Weickean notion of organizations as *organizing*, it is equally possible, at least as a hypothesis, to construe the idea of government as *organizing*—since the state, government, and organizations are social systems, but also share some comparable attributes. Organizing therefore reflects the "repetitive, reciprocal, and contingent behaviors that develop and are maintained between two or more actors"[9] as a means of "helping them reduce equivocality (doubt) or the information uncertainty they face in their lives."[10] As a process, "organizing is directed toward the establishment of a workable level of certainty"[11] and, to an extent, predictability in the activities that lead to the attainment of organizational (or social) objectives.

In his *The Social Psychology of Organizing*,[12] the famed organizational psychologist Karl Weick saw the idea of organizations as an illusory mind game. His argument was that:[13]

> *Most "things" in organizations are actually relationships, variables tied together in systematic fashion. Events, therefore, depend on the strength of these ties, the direction of influence, the time it takes for information in the form of differences to move around circuits. The word organization is a noun, and it is also a myth; hence if you look for an organization you won't find it. What you will find is that there are events, linked together, that transpire within concrete walls and these sequences, their pathways, and their timing are the forms we erroneously make into substances when we talk about an organization. Events inside organizations and organisms are locked into causal circuits that extend beyond their artificial boundaries.*

Weick's concept of *organizations* as *organizing* has heuristic utility and can be utilized as a useful analogy in the functional analysis of *states* and *governments* as social systems, or even as organizations. Based on the oftentimes "dynamic and intangible nature of *structure*, and the need to avoid *reification* and oversimplification, the idea of organizing is also an attempt to present systems theory in processual terms."[14] Interlocked behaviors through organizing leads to the creation of a collective structure and the development of means-convergence. As "a heuristic device the dynamic essence of individual interactions and sense-making within organizations (states or social systems) can be maintained as events are conceptualized in terms of an open field of continuous action."[15] As communal sense making gives rise to a repertory of repeated routines and patterns of interaction, the various interactions themselves constitute the process of organizing.[16]

To the extent that we can view *organizing* as a "category of thought which we describe as objectivism (consisting of *behaviourism* and *abstracted empiricism*),"[17] it can thus make a genuine contribution to social systems theory—the way we understand the various functional relationships and interactions within society and political systems broadly construed. But translating this logic into the framework of state governance also raises a profound question: How do individuals, each with their own individualistic thought patterns and preferences find "shared meanings" so that a reasonable degree of understanding and action is possible? How do their idiosyncratic thoughts result into some form of shared aggregate that is useful for concerted and purposeful action? The answer suggests that after a time, individuals within a group or an organization tend to think alike, at least to some degree. They achieve what the cognitive school of organizational analysis calls *cognitive consensuality*. Consensuality in this regard, does not necessarily imply perfect agreement, nor does it imply that individuals have conducted a formalized process of reaching a consensus. It merely implies that, whatever the process—conscious or unconscious, deliberate or not—individuals have achieved a certain similarity in the way they process and evaluate information. They have developed and attached meanings to shared experiences, plus an understanding of specific scripts or schemas devoted to enacting dynamic patterns of behavior and knowledge of expected sequences of events that guides one's behavior so that it is appropriate for given situations.

Cognitive consensuality (the shared aggregate of values, beliefs, understanding, and cycles of interlocked behavior) thus becomes the *cognitive map* (sets of causal beliefs or assertions) by which individual and collective action is directed toward the attainment of the objectives or ends critical to overall system functioning and survivability. This is akin to what Durkheim[18] refers to as the "*conscience collective*" or a form of 'organic solidarity' arising from the interdependence of parts and driven by a normative system of values, beliefs, and sentiments.[19] Because "maps can help to structure the territory sufficiently so that someone can initiate activity in that territory—activity that may introduce order";[20] cognitive maps consist of the concepts and relations an individual uses to understand organizational or institutional conditions as well as the appropriate ways to react to them. As a social system, the *state* must be seen not as a stand-alone corporeal entity with a life of its own distinct from the people who inhabit it in both time and space; rather it must be seen as a constitutive body made up of individuals in their functional relationships with each another. As a heuristic, *organizing* therefore provides a frame of reference within which we can understand the *state* and all its trappings (like all other organizations) as nothing but a reified abstraction of the various activities that takes place within it; or "as a fuzzy set in which no element is singularly essential but which tend to cohere in homeostatic clusters."[21]

BEHAVIORAL FRAMEWORKS AS REGULATORY DEVICES

In what ways do shared understandings create frameworks of interlocking knowledge that enable individuals to act, and requiring no justification on their part, in ways that always seem to hold up to acceptable social conventions and to existing norms of appropriate behavior? It is quite difficult to discern the series of motives and rationalizations that inform individual dispositions toward each other, to the prevailing institutions, and to political objects and symbols. In the absence of any absolute criteria, I argue however that there are objective and subjective factors that often dictate what we do, how we do it, and under what circumstances we do it. Sometimes some of these guiding principles are within the ambit of human control, but in others they are not. Although I am more concerned and interested in the latter, it is equally important to note that where people have come to appreciate certain norms and practices and as these take on a life of their own, they become the basis for social interaction and action. I am interested in those things or phenomena that induce individuals to act reflexively in the right direction, without any overt or explicit compulsion to do so. It is a kind of self-directedness that is situated and reinforced at the unconscious or subconscious level. Even though consciousness exists in human minds, but human minds are able to share each other's consciousness through language and communication.

Reminiscent of Rousseau's *General Will*, people develop common awareness, meaning, and interpretations of their relationship to one another and within a social system in which "the structure of preferences and capabilities alone often generate multiple equilibria."[22] And each of these can swing toward order or disorder at any particular moment in time. This is not surprising in the sense that "social institutions and practices, as well as the beliefs and desires of the members of particular social groups, are continually in a state of flux and evolution which will always seem to appear indeterminate."[23] But as in game theory, this unpredictable situation could be solved by "the development of common knowledge, by defining 'salient outcomes' or 'focal points' around which individual expectations can converge (rules, regulations, SOPs, customs, tradition, culture, etc.), and by reducing transaction costs and uncertainty, thereby enabling individuals (actors) to coordinate their strategies around a single equilibrium"[24] (the maintenance of order and stability). Individuals governed under the tenets of the *General Will* see it as a self-reinforcing *social contract* in which they and similarly-situated others have agreed to abide by specific norms of social and political behavior. And by obeying those common norms, one obeys the *will* of the others as he also ascribes to his own *will* at the same time; on the simple recognition that self-interest and the common interest have now become inseparable. Should one therefore willfully violate the norms and rules of which he was instrumental in the making? That is the question.

If we utilize the "law of averages" in analyzing any distribution of benefits within a particular social system, it is possible to surmise that individuals will generally adhere to those principles that bring some good to them and to others in the same community; but in situations where the advantages gained by some crosses out that of others thereby increasing the other's disadvantage; those who are disadvantaged by the new 'equilibrium' are more likely to seek unconventional or alternative measures to limit their own disadvantage or to undermine the advantage of the other. But where normative principles of justice and equity are applied in the distribution of social goods and political opportunity, a consistent adherence to those principles would reflect a continuous validation of the basic assumptions and norms that undergird them; and by validating these norms every inch of the way, the act, in and of itself, becomes a regulatory device for the maintenance of social order.

But how do people and under what conditions are they more likely to accept the same basic assumptions as everyone else in the political community? And to what extent could these assumptions be said to be the *cause* of a person's action in specific circumstances to which the assumptions could apply? As an example, let us for the sake argument assume that the assumptions are premised on the basis of the fact that 'what is good for all is also good for the self;' but even at that, it could be argued that "the kind of knowledge one has of one's own reasons in acting one way or the other is not compatible with the existence of a causal relation between reason and action."[25] And because a person knows (ought to know) his own intention in acting infallibly; *reason* so construed cannot be the cause of the actions that it seeks to rationalize.[26] It is also true that in trying to understand a person and his actions, we must also weigh against one another all the basic assumptions that seem to justify his actions, to see to what extent they "accord with our theory of how beliefs and attitudes are formed and changed under the influence of experience and/or reflections."[27] The following section discusses four objective factors that help to modulate individual behavior and responses to political objects and symbols, in ways that also advance system stability and order: *social facts, culture, social capital, and active citizenship.*

Social Facts

Central to Durkheim's proposition was the idea that *social facts* exist outside of men's consciousness and has the capacity to restrain them in their everyday activities. To the extent that "the stability and ordered nature of the natural world was viewed as characterizing the world of human affairs, the epistemological basis of *social facts* was to understand the nature of this regulated order."[28] In various ways, the crystallized consciousness of the public reflects *social facts*—"which exist only in the individual consciousness and throught."[29] Social facts consist of relevant laws, norms, and social conventions that shape individual action—"his ways of acting, thinking, and feeling, and though external to the individual, are endowed with power of coercion of which they control him."[30] Because "meanings are given to men by their society, shared orientations become institutionalized and are experienced by later generations as social facts"[31] Men are thus, "constrained by social facts which determine their actions and their consciousness."[32] But the most important thing to note here is that an individual "does not need to know the rules of the institution to follow them in order to conform to them; rather, he is simply disposed to behave in a certain way under specific circumstances because he has acquired those unconscious dispositions and capacities in a way that is sensitive to the rule structure of the prevailing institution."[33] John

Searle refers to this as someone having acquired a set of background habits, skills, dispositions that unconsciously shape behavior and conformity.

When individuals act in support of the public interest, such action also helps to recreate the same condition under which independent action and freedom is denied. The power that generates the impulse to conform does not come from within but from without, and is premised on a common interpretation of social meanings by individuals. Such interpretation "involves clarifying the field of concepts that constitute a social practice and provides for shared values and sense of community."[34] This is so because one cannot turn back upon oneself, thus becoming self-conscious, other than by imaginatively assuming the perspective of the other through the public.[35] For George Mead,[36] this self-dialogical process is constitutive of reflective thought and decision making; because it explains how self-hood can both integrate an individual into a community, affording them a sense of belonging, and also give rise to reflective and argumentative agency[37]—in which "particular constellations of meaning are only sustained by continual reaffirmation in everyday actions."[38] This particular notion is also consistent with Weber's argument that while "social action may be oriented by the actors to a belief (*Vorstellung*) in the existence of a legitimate order; it may at the same time derive from a rational belief in the absolute validity of the order as an expression of ultimate values, whether they be moral, aesthetic, or of any other type."[39] The average individual wants to be law-abiding and wants to be seen as doing so; but ultimately individuals act one way or the other, based on how they are able to resolve the tension generated by a series of reactionary impulses that exist within particular social or environmental contexts.

To make an illustrative point about the regulatory power of social facts, let us consider two situations that may look similar but none the less pose different sets of constraints on the individual. A person drives up to a red light on a four lane traffic that has other drivers on opposite sides of the road. The person suddenly stops at the red light and remained patient enough until the light turns green and he drives off. As the person looked around, there was no cop around, and for all practical purposes, he could possibly have driven across the red light without any penalty or complaint from any one. While almost every driver confronts the same type of situation or a daily basis; why did the driver in this case stop before and not cross the red light? A second situation also presents itself to the same driver, but this time it was at night and he was driving on a lonely rural road and suddenly came upon a red light at a four way crossing. It was evident that there was no cop around and there was no other traffic on either side of the roads. Yet, the driver stopped and waited patiently for the green light to turn on before proceeding. While both accounts suggest that the driver has internalized the socially acceptable norm of obeying traffic regulations, but it is an obedience that has a causal property outside of the driver. Why do some people still maintain obedience to the rules of the game even when they know that they could violate it without cost or sanction?

In both cases, it is obedience reinforced by *social facts*; but in the first situation in particular, it is also an obedience reinforced by the driver's attempt to avoid *shame*—a shame imposed upon him by drivers on the other side of the road as well as those behind and in front of him. Shame in this context, might suggestively seem as an absurdity, but it is a phenomenon that has an effect. The sense of self-guilt and the certain condemnation and frowning by the other drivers (in the abstract sense) and the horror of having been seen and singled out (in the imaginative sense) for this omission is the *dread* that restrains the driver from willfully crossing the red light while others wait for the green light.

A very interesting corollary to the situation the driver finds himself is akin to what the French existentialist Jean Paul Sartre[40] illustrated in his narrative of "*The Look*" in the *Encounter with the Other*. In it, Sartre explains a situation where an individual makes an awkward or vulgar gesture, but only to discover with shock that someone else had also seen him. The sudden realization of the vulgarity of the act elicits shame; but it is a shame that is not reflective on me (the individual), but rather is reflective of the presence of another in my isolated consciousness. As the *Other* becomes an indispensable mediator between *myself* and *me*, I am only ashamed of myself as I appear to the *Other*. But my appearance is a "mode of consciousness which seem (even while remaining strictly in for-itself) to point to a radically different type of ontological structure which happens to be mine. I am thus, only concerned about myself, and yet this concern for-myself reveals to me a being which is *my* being without being-for-me."[41] For the fact that that *being* can only be what the *Other* makes of me, the individual experiences we have with others may reveal a lot more about us and who we are. This is the inner consciousness reflected in and born out of the tension between what others see and think about you; and what you want them to see and think about you. Because the individual is both the cause and effect of this tension, its resolution becomes a crucial pathway through which he is able to reveal himself to the world outside of himself—but this time in his own way as a rule follower, but not as one who breaks it.

Culture

In all human societies, cultures emerge from people's struggles to manage uncertainties and create some degree of order in social life. In the American context as in many other countries, it transcends many symbols of the national heritage and world view: the communitarian ideals of interdependent individualism, the rustic competitive spirit of western frontier adventurism, the extended ethno-linguistic system that has remained the locus of economic activity and identification, and a liberated market economy founded on the laissez-faire model. "When we observe a culture, whether in an organization or in society at large, we are observing an evolved form of social practice that has been influenced by many complex interactions between people, events, situations, actions, history, and general circumstance."[42] In this context, cultures provide people with accepted ways of expressing and affirming their beliefs, values, and norms—by providing them with procedural repertoires or forms that members of a community use to express the substance as well as make sense of their respective worlds.[43]

Cultural forms imbue actions and other activities with meanings; they enable people to communicate and celebrate their ideas in many different ways. "The role of ideas in shaping behavior has a long intellectual pedigree, and during the 19th century was largely coded under the concept of ideology."[44] As a collective phenomenon, our cultural responses to daily experiences falls into two categories: *ideologies*—shared, emotionally charged belief systems; and *forms*—observable entities, including actions through which members of a community express, affirm, and communicate the substance of their culture to one another. Cultures cannot be produced by individuals acting alone; rather, they originate and endure as individuals interact with one another. "It is structured in terms of patternings of meaning which, when stable, imply in turn generalized complexes of constitutive symbolisms that give an action system its primary sense of direction, and which must be treated as independent of any particular system of social interaction."[45] Belonging to a culture involves believing what others believe and doing as they do.

In turbulent times, culture helps a people to manage their anxieties and disagreements and to channel their individual emotions and resistance in such a way that it does not fundamentally undermine the socially established order for achieving deliberative consensus. Though it may seem inherently symbolic, cultures are historically based; hence a particular culture will be based in the unique history of a particular group of people coping with a unique sets of physical, social, political, and economic circumstances. Once individuals in a cultural group come to share some set of beliefs, ideas and practices, these eventually take on a life of their own—thus creating "the possibilities of their preservation over time, and of their diffusion from one personality or social system into another."[46] But while cultures create continuity and persist across generations of members, they are not static, but dynamic. Cultures continually change, and adapt, more or less as a result of changes in the larger political and social environment of which they are a part.[47] Externally induced cultural changes are oftentimes subtle and incremental, while internally driven cultural changes are somewhat more dramatic. Because a dramatic shift away from the *status quo* is more likely to be noticed, it often generates increased and emotion-laden resistance.

In the same way they provide causal models for explaining and legitimating collective and individual behaviors, cultures are also ideologies. Because most ideologies explain and justify existing social systems in ways that make them seem natural, logically compelling, and morally acceptable; cultures that endure require committed citizens as moral agents in the pursuit of the collective interest. The durability of specific cultures allow for the creation of a stable social order, continuity, collective identity, commitment, and the management of uncertainties. Because "it impressed itself on us not necessarily by force but through repeated obedience to the collective consciousness of the public, it thus becomes a guiding norm for individual action and reasoning in particular situations."[48] To the extent that shared culture "circumscribe institutional processes while at the same time being maintained and created by these institutional processes,"[49] it can help to bridge philosophical and idiosyncratic differences among community members.

However, it is also quite possible, and in fact, true that in some multi-ethnic societies, ethno-linguistic and historical cleavages as a result of ethnic, religious, or language distinctions have made it quite difficult or almost impossible to bridge cultural differences. Because ethno-driven communal cleavages have a tendency to complicate or even undermine the give-and-take necessary for mutual accommodation, this has been postulated as one of many reasons that often leads to civil wars and ultimately institutional decay and failure. Because this phenomenon is often accentuated by the structure of government and the nature of political competition, cultural and religious differences, more or less, become the criteria for the distribution of political opportunities. As ethno-cultural differences becomes the organizing symbol in the development of political parties or the framework upon which competing groups vie for political power; the integrative potentials or the socially binding qualities of culture may be lost. A critical factor that has wrecked many communities has been the lack of a unifying and facilitative social culture, deep communal cleavages, lack of mutual trust, and opportunistic tendencies based on absolute self-interest. This is not because culture itself cannot bring people together or help to accommodate each other in the context of shared values; rather it is because those values have already been made more resilient and impenetrable as a result of the different sociological foundations that informed their origins.

Social Capital

Social capital is viewed as the internal social and cultural coherence of a society, the norms and values that govern interactions among people and the institutions under which they live. It is oftentimes seen as the glue that holds societies together without which there can be no progress or human well-being. It refers to our relations with one another, on the assumption that the more we connect with other people, the more we trust them, and vice versa. The concept of social capital is also consistent with the virtues of democracy. In practice, democracy requires a sense of affinity between the citizens that surpasses other loyalties. But because this is frequently lacking in many countries and communities, deep seated cleavages developed along parochial lines have the tendency to create an increasingly intransigent social culture where compromises and accommodation between and within groups are almost impossible to attain.

Active Citizenship

While it is structurally anchored on the state system, the central value of citizenship lies in the practical role it plays in the service of community in terms of welfare, security, and cultural harmony.[50] But unfortunately, it requires the kind of civic virtue that may not be readily available among citizens of most societies. The premise advanced here is one of viewing citizenship as a shared identity, set apart from many other unique sets of identity feelings, and to recognize and respect the norms and values that give it life and legitimacy. Because the primary responsibility of the virtuous citizen is to ascertain the 'truth' about the moral nature of individual behavior, to assimilate that truth to one's self (one's goodness), and then cast it in terms of one's civic life (the goodness of the society);[51] recognizing the role of citizenship and the individual temperament needed to consent to its obligations is, in and of itself, an ordering device that reinforces the durability and efficacy of the social system.

Citizenship is one among many identities an individual will feel. While it is distinguished by being necessary for moral maturity, and by its potential to moderate the divisiveness of other identity feelings—gender, religion, race, class and nation—it helps to reinforce specific attitudes and behaviors expected of citizens.[52] Seen in this light, citizenship can thus be construed as a habit, a behavior, and an attitude which when collectively expressed by members of the community, helps to secure the public good. When this habit acquires enduring value and becomes embedded in the very idealism that drives individual and collective action, it is then that shared ownership in the project of the community becomes possible. When citizenship in this regard is connected to a communally held value premise, it thus becomes, in and of itself, an *ordering device* that defines the scope and boundaries of what is or is not permissible in the larger community. As long as people abide by responsible and acceptable conduct in the exercise of their daily activities, they would in turn, validate the same principles that undergird their collective notion of citizenship and statesmanship. Citizenship, therefore, becomes an enduring institution.

Because "a major activity of institutions is educating individuals into knowledgeable citizens,"[53] they also mitigate the chances of personalizing cultural issues into political conflicts. A knowledgeable citizen is one who is familiar with the rules of appropriate behavior and with the moral and intellectual virtues of the community, and who thus knows the institutional reasons for behaviors, and can justify them by reference to the requirements of a larger order.[54] Because citizenship transcends both the universality of rights and the pragmatism of individual obligation, it on the one hand, implies the recognition of a universal principle, and on the other, a form of social contract between the community and the individual. In the end, one finds that it may be those little things that hold the fabric of society together that oftentimes are instrumental to the eventual success and durability of the state and the well-being of its citizens.

THE NOTION OF STRUCTURED OR INDUCED ORDER

The concept of structured or induced order captures the idea that specific social structures, institutions, and design systems do, in fact, create individual or collective responses that not only reinforce the legitimate order; but also affirm the nature of social relations and existing norms of reciprocity within communities. As action systems evolve into routines and practices, they help to shape the structural frame of reference for consequent actions that are followed or imitated by others. Although Weber denotes three elements of action in terms of *brauchen* (usage or need), *interessenlage* (interest), and legitimate order (the orientation of action to the existence of an order as an accepted norm);[55] he also makes the point that "the stability of regularities of action based on interests lies in the fact that any actor who does not consider the interests of others in his action thereby calls forth their resistance, which becomes an obstacle to the attainment of his own ends."[56] In most cases, it is the self-sanctioning by individuals that reinforces their inclination to conform to the established normative or legal order. And this is done partly either because they see everyone doing it, or they have been conditioned to it as a result of a series of prior repetitive actions.

There are a series of observations that could be brought to bear on the above illustration, but first, we must establish the end for which social action is generally directed. There are ends such as to safeguard public safety or public health, support for law and order, grant of equal freedom for others, paying ones taxes so that the state would have the financial and material resources to provide for needed public goods and services. But whatever are the specific ends being sought, it is a fact that if people do not comply as required, it would disrupt the process by which such ends are sought. It is common knowledge that if individuals are left specifically to their own devices, and while some may comply; there are certainly others who would not but will find ways to circumvent or violate the established norms of appropriate behavior. Such is the case that where individual interests or preferences conflict with collective ones, they produce collective action dilemmas that makes coordination much more difficult.[57] It is therefore imperative that "institutional solutions to these dilemmas create sanctioned norms that guide people to behave in specific ways to increase social order."[58] And that is why the state or governing authorities must find ways to induce in people a habit of conformity to prevailing norms, not necessarily by force, but by creating a structure of involuntary compliance, even when one does not necessarily intend to do so.

The concept of structured or induced order includes such pattern-governed behaviors that are essential for sustaining existing social frameworks in such a way that norms are enforced and conflicts between individual and collective rationality are reconciled in the greater interest of maintaining social order. It also seeks to illustrate how rule-governed structures of human institutions play causal roles in the way individuals develop sets of dispositions (consciously or unconsciously) that are sensitive to existing rule structures that govern social action. As Durkheim points out, "there can be no society which does not feel the need of upholding and reaffirming at regular intervals, the collective sentiments and the collective ideas which make its unity and its personality."[59] It is also well understood that because state authorities are not and will not be everywhere to check on everyone's compliance to existing rules of appropriate behavior; it would thus be problematic to leave compliance to the whims and caprices of individuals. That is one of the reasons why we have laws and other regulatory measures as tools for securing compliance or conformity to the prevailing norms. Because "people rationally calculate the costs and benefits of breaking the law, they are more likely to abide by it if sanctions are sufficiently severe; whereas they tend to break the law if sanctions for doing so are mild."[60] And this may be one reason why Elinor Ostrom had cautioned that focusing on norms and other-regarding preferences would not be enough for individuals to overcome the kind of social dilemmas that arise in situations of this nature; but instead she argues that "rules are needed to back up these norms or counteract dangerously escalating negative reciprocity."[61]

But even in situations where some people may have the belief that they can get away scot-free from not obeying the law despite the prevailing rules of acceptable behavior; oftentimes they may still be persuaded otherwise either by their own self-discipline or as a result of personal fidelity to the existing social mores and conventions. Obedience therefore is a matter of compliance to the prevailing authority as well as the generally accepted social values.

Because "values are not the only forces at work in an actual, ongoing situation; they are but one narrow band of causes in the total spectrum of forces impinging on a person."[62] Values are effective in inducing behavior when people have come to internalize and accept them as leading to some public good; but yet "the form and shape of society and the way it is developing have much to do with whether such values are sustained over time or not."[63] Often, compliance or "conformity is an overlay that makes obedience easier, quicker, and sudden because the obedience of others is evident around us—hence conformity becomes an autonomous act of going along with the crowd, without the added impetus of orders."[64] And this is evident where micro-level action is induced by macro-level effects in such a way that specific behaviors or patterned responses are activated whenever the same situation presents itself.

In their work titled *Conformity, Obedience, Disobedience: The Power of the Situation*, Bocchiaro and Zamperini reinforced the importance of "conformism and obedience as essential elements in maintaining social order."[65] But they also point out that in certain contexts, while "simple situational factors may be more powerful than personality traits in shaping human behavior; the same situational factors can also be manipulated to stimulate people to act in a positive way; that is, virtually anyone, independently of his or her personality structure, can overcome social pressures toward conformity and obedience."[66] In all forms of governance, whether in the public or private sectors, we have developed physical and normative structures (standard operating procedures, etc) to guide individual behavior toward desired ends. Even in private lives, the role of the family structure, schools, churches, and institutions have become agents that promote teaching of the rules of obedience, conformity, and authority.[67]

At the same time, people make choices whether or not to adhere to that which is widely held by similarly-situated others as the correct thing to do because it serves the broader collective interest. But in other cases, people simply act based on their unconscious reflexes knowing fully well and prior to their action that it would certainly (or at least) lead to a desirable end. An illustrative example would be the garbage collection or waste recycling containers or bins so prevalent in a certain Nordic country that I am familiar with. The garbage containers are appropriately labeled according to the type of materials and biohazards that could be disposed into them. There are usually separate containers for paper (paperi), cardboard (kartonki), mixed waste (sekajäte), biowaste (biojäte), metal (metallic), glass (lasi), and glass packaging (lasi pakkaukset). It is evident that by virtue of the structural design and placement of the waste recycle containers, they will certainly have schedule-induced or schedule-controlled behavioral effects on members of the immediate community that use them. In this case, induced behavior involves all intentional actions that are, on the one hand, relevant for the realization of a fundamental objective (garbage disposal or public health), and on the other hand, directly or indirectly triggered or motivated by the existing regulatory conventions and the social rule system.[68] Because the "social rule system does not only encompass formal legal rules but also social values and informal norms, it also stimulates and restricts social behavior by means of sanctioning and control."[69] And this is where cognition also plays a critical role in enabling an action; because the simple *thought* of these restrictions and controls, are in themselves, quite sufficient to channel individual behavior in the proper direction.

The relevance of the induced-behavior analogy is that the same method can be used to design institutions and/or dictate how individuals should behave under specific conditions for the sake of public order, safety, and welfare. Individuals can be forced to change their behaviors simply by changing the environment and existing structural designs in ways that will motivate them to change; as well as offers them more incentives to follow the rules.[70] That is the main reason why we have road signs, speed limits, turn signals, weather alert systems, parking designations, work zones, travel rest areas, and signs in public buildings and facilities pointing to one direction or the other and providing related information as guide to people. Can anyone imagine what would happen to existing social and political order or society as a whole if none of these instructional devices were in existence?

ELEMENTS OF STRUCTURED OR INDUCED ORDER

The notion of structured or induced order as utilized in this case is akin to the way people demonstrate affinity for their respective religions. In the same way as religious behavior, induced order "resembles instinctual behavior that is, more often than not, responsive to antecedents in the apparent absence of reinforcement."[71] For the simple fact that "behavior may arise in the context of exposure to response-independent schedules of reinforcement, such behavior and its persistence are induced (emergent) in the sense that they are part of a complex response that was not specifically shaped into existence."[72] Using the garbage containers in a metaphorical sense, I illustrate three qualities or elements (*structure, communication, and sanction*) that can help to reinforce the social rule system—"out of which functional behavior may arise."[73] It impresses and reinforces it on individuals to develop the habit of sorting and separating out their domestic or household garbage in the privacy of their homes and to dispose them off in the designated or labeled containers.

Structure

For the most part, structure induces a system of order or behavior modification that could lead to the regularization of specific forms of habit. Which then raises some profound questions: Will everyone obey the speed limit if there were no road signs to that effect; will drivers heed the hand signal of the policeman directing them to follow an alternative exit; will drivers willfully slow down if there were no signs depicting "ice on the bridge"? What about the bank? Will customers rush the counter if there were no designated lines or if there were no "take-a-number" dispensers in the facility? The same applies to the post office, the grocery store, the movie theaters, or even the local restaurant. What we find are structurally encoded messages that inform, educate, as well as direct. While these may come in the form of (sign posts, signals, customs, pathways, tunnels, garbage containers, or even goal posts), they initiate a series of specific action sets that are repeated and followed on each occasion or episode. And by this, we create functional routines that over time, take on a life of their own and become habit-forming.

By "erasing the distinctions between ends, means, and conditions of rational action, we make actual action a process only of adaptation to given conditions and predictions of their future state"—that is, such actions are more likely to be repeated again so many times because they lead to good and socially acceptable outcomes. Because we know that most waste recycling trucks pick up the garbage in the morning hours, we self-program ourselves to have the garbage dropped off (in plastic bags) at the collection point some hours or minutes ahead of time. But where there are stationary garbage containers, we would have already sorted the waste in their respective categories (plastic, paper, metal, biowaste, etc), and then drop each of them into their designated containers at any time of our choosing. This process is followed methodically both at home (by sorting the various categories of waste in advance), and outside the home (by dropping each bag into their designated containers); as opposed to dropping all of them (unsorted) into a single garbage container. As this process becomes routinized, the evolving structure of activities takes the form of a social rule, practice, or convention that must be adhered to for the greater good and health of the community.

Communication

The value of communication lies in its ability to convey specific sets of information critical to inducing appropriate behavior or to provide information about expectations. The information provided on the garbage containers (similar to what we have on handicapped parking signposts) are generally in clear language and bold words that could not have been mistaken for any other thing else. To the extent that they help to dissuade aberrant behavior, the labels on the garbage containers as well as handicapped parking signposts are functional. Because, they help to script individual behaviors in ways that channel them toward desired objectives, "emerging patterns of communication eventually become institutionalized forms of communication in the social system";[74] thereby offering communicative alternatives beyond the issuance of direct orders or enforcement.

Communication has become a central element in the governance of modern societies, such that everywhere we look, it is all around us. From newspapers and journals, bill boards, posters, and the Internet, we receive one form of information or the other. However, the effectiveness of communication is dependent on the how it is adapted to new challenges and new visions of how our current society and the society of the future would evolve. As society changes in fundamental ways, so should the means by which we communicate governments' intentions and motives regarding maintenance of the political and social order. Political institutions, even of totalitarian types, also need effective communication channels to shape and influence the behavior of their citizens in expected ways. Cultures, values, and prevailing social mores are often transmitted through structurally encoded communication channels from generation to generation.

Sanction

Beyond the public health issue illustrated above, people are more likely to put their household wastes in plastic bags and to drop them off at the proper designated places; out of fear that to do otherwise would invoke some sanction or punishment from the authorities, or that it would make their neighbors unhappy and unappreciative. A "social structure or practice is often sustained through a set of powers of enforcement and retaliation conferred on various agents within a state or social system."[75] As a result, individuals can become self-induced to engage in the appropriate behavior. The intent to impose sanctions is simply to convey the implication of treating applicable rules and conventions as binding. Sanctions, in and of themselves, are not necessarily meant to be punitive or retributive; they are meant to deter or to reorient individual actions from deviating from the existing rules of the game. Because "action must always be thought of as involving a state of tension between two different orders of elements (the normative and the conditional); it also involves a process of alteration of the conditional elements in the direction of conformity with norms."[76] But that was not the case in the following illustrative example.

A former student of mine once came to me and was distraught that she had been issued a ticket to pay a fine of $150 dollars for packing in a handicapped parking space. I asked her why she had parked in a handicapped space and whether she had seen the designated sign including the sum of $150 dollar stipulated as the penalty for infraction. She told me that she saw the sign and read the wordings indicated on it, but for whatever reason, still went ahead and parked in the space. Even though all the information needed to induce appropriate behavior on the part of the student were there (the signpost, the written words, the penalty, and the handicapped symbol), why then did she not conform? To her dismay and without giving so much of a comfort, I simply told her to pay the fine as reflected on the ticket. The student's action was induced by a preference for a conditional choice that issued in the wrong direction (parking in an unauthorized space), even though an alternative condition for conformity was still available (by choosing not to pack in the space). It was a situation where the student rolled the dice hoping not to be ticketed, but by chance, the dice unfortunately hit a $150 penalty. In the end, one would hope that the heftiness of the fine would most assuredly condition or induce a more appropriate behavior in the future. In the same way that laws and regulations elicit compliance; sanctions also can lead to behavioral modifications of the kind that leads to conformity and obedience.

Our administrative systems represent no more than clusters of communication and informational exchanges between functional departments or units, individuals, and groups. To this end, functional structures and the requisite communication designs can be used to induce conformity and obedience as well as reinforce specific types of behavioral patterns, values, and normative orientations over time. Because much of what we do in today's evolving human society requires us to transform a whole lot of information into usable formats, we have found ourselves in a situation where much of what we do or need, would be more difficult and, in most cases, unattainable without an ongoing synchronization between man and machine. I will attempt to illuminate this facet of our discussion in the following sections.

OF ARTIFICIAL INTELLIGENCE, NEURAL NETWORKS, AND SERVOMECHANISMS

It is an inescapable fact of contemporary history that the fate of man and, in fact, human society has become integrally tied to the ubiquity of technology and machines and, to a degree has become an essential part of life itself. The functioning of human society, the control and analysis of daily accumulation of information, and the continuous growth in technological applications and innovation suggests a world in which its original, pristine, and natural state is now irrecoverable. Today's human needs require increasing levels of analytical capability and precision to solve complex problems both at the individual and social or organizational levels of analyses. In chapter 4 and previous sections of this book, I offered a series of illustrations for the maintenance of stable states using the same operational methods as neural networks (the central nervous system) or servomechanisms that function in the same way as cybernetic systems or thermostat. While the central nervous system is controlled through brain signals, servomechanisms require imprinted and structured programs. The notion of artificial intelligence suggests a situation where machines take on (or are made to take on) a central role in analyzing and solving specific human problems.

In the sense that these machines would be 'self-conscious' and by using various list-structured data base of language or commands to generate new knowledge (a sequence of motor commands) in ongoing applications as well as in decision making; I suggest that machines capable of generating artificial intelligence are operating at Boulding's level 7, that is, *symbol-processing systems*[77]—systems which possess self-consciousness and so are capable of using language (such as humans). On a functional level, cybernetic systems and servo-systems are forms of artificial intelligence but they act only in confined technical fields. But contemporary developments in computerization, software, and new methodologies in data analytics seem to have upped the ante such that when we now talk about artificial intelligence, we would be talking about machines that are primed to take over decision making, forecasting, and the predictive capacity critical to solving human problems.

The Industrial Revolution was "the revolution of the power-driven passive machine; when machines were shown to be capable of performing complex muscular acts with a speed and efficiency that no human being could match."[78] From the development of the steam engine by James Watt in 1765, Arkwright's invention of the water frame in 1769, and Faraday's invention of the dynamo in 1831; or the universal Turing machine as developed by Alan Turing,[79] the future of civilizations and of man's adaptation to the machines he has created have now attained the level where they (the machines) would now decide whether man lives on this earth or whether he becomes extinct without them. This rather awkward situation was not lost on Hannah Arendt confessional statement that "the human condition comprehends more than the conditions under which life has been given to man; but men, instead, are conditioned beings because everything they come in contact with turns immediately into a condition of their existence."[80] Because "the impact of the world's reality upon human existence is felt and received as a conditioning force; Arendt therefore concludes that whatever enters the human world of its own accord or is drawn into it by human effort becomes part of the human condition."[81]

Most discussions of artificial intelligence revolve around the increasing power and sophistication of standalone computers or computers built into other machines (large computer mainframes) or mechanical systems (such as robots) as the brain or central nervous system. Through imprinting, the computer or rather the software is programmed "in the early stages of the system's lifetime, to learn to identify certain patterns of sensation, or correspondence with internal concepts,"[82] and then make decisions to address deviations from the norm, or to facilitate actions that meet performance expectations. The attraction of artificial intelligence is not only about the ability of machines to engage in complex repetitive tasks yet still achieve a high degree of precision in result. But it is more about the ability "to tackle practical problems that would otherwise defeat us by their complexity—i.e., coordinating the traffic around an airport, stabilizing the flows of money between banks, normalizing the composition of the blood in a patient";[83] and monitoring the temperature fluctuations in a nuclear plant reactor—a situation where things must work right as planned and in which there is zero tolerance for error of any kind.

Today, "machines are constructed for a variety of different purposes, such as solving mathematical equations, making deductive inferences,"[84] adding up numbers at a high level of computational power, classifying information into patterns where they could be recognized and matched to specific outcomes, testing and experimentation. As a result of dramatic advances in next generation technology and in 3-D printing processes, we now have shoes engineered to boost performance; elevators that move no only up and down but also sideways; airborne drones that undertake mapmaking designs and search-and-rescue operations; electric cars that offer more than 200 miles of driving distance on a single charge; *Forward*—a clinic that redefines preventive care by preempting medical issues; facial recognition machines; and mugs that heat your coffee just right.[85] Artificial intelligence has also found its way into the revolution in military affairs (RMAs) in terms of increasing application in laser-guided munitions, agile fighter aircrafts; and the new celebrated "Israeli Defense Forces *Merkava Mark 4 Barak* main battle tank—the first tank to have a smart mission computer that will manage the tank's tasks using artificial intelligence, updated sensors, and voice recognition (VR) capabilities to help reduce team member's workload and to more accurately locate and strike targets."[86]

In consideration of the fact that cyberneticians have always believed that machines can be made to perform actions as organisms perform them, that is organisms are essentially constructible; F. H. George proclaimed that "there is no reason, in principle, why we should not ourselves construct human beings."[87] Although the reference above is not that human beings could be constructed literarily, the supposition here is that machines could be made to think and act like humans in certain respects. Of course there are certain things that humans do (such as the expression of sensual feelings or emotions or the reproduction of similar kinds), but machines can and do operate at a higher level of abstraction, precision, and analytical capability than humans. There is also a point that has received little attention in matters concerning individual behavior or idiosyncrasies that could undermine system stability and overall functioning. When offended or facing any sort of displeasure, humans can change their moods and reaction driven by changes in their emotional states and/or experiences. Humans can cheat, connive, or demonstrate a level of malice, selfishness, and indifference that could undermine existing stable states and long-term system survival. On the premise that they could oftentimes be 'temperamental' (refuse to function) as a result of failure in one or more of the parts that make up a machine; machines generally do not carry the emotional 'baggage' and the often selfish biases that have been lot of humans.

Computers operate basically on the initial information that has been programmed into them; hence this makes the output more *objective* than individual decisions or actions, which can oftentimes, be filtered through self-interest, bias, or opportunistic advantage. Research and new knowledge in biology and psychology have enabled us to have a more nuanced understanding of the stability characteristics of social systems, what makes humans cling together in terms of specific behavioral norms or beliefs, and what factors are more likely to lead to dissension among them. To the extent that we are able to program these factors into the memory that drives say, a servo-system, we can improve our chances of eliminating lags as well as increasing the probability of optimum performance.[88]

Although there are already in existence, "self-controlling machines that can stimulate many of the activities of human operators";[89] there are also, in particular, servo-systems that can copy almost any human operation, such as man's handwriting, and pattern recognition functions. This still leaves the field of automation and artificial intelligence wide open for all sorts of machine designs.[90] I make reference to the development of "the *conditional probability machine*—a machine whose strategy is not wholly fixed in advance, but one with an in-built capacity for collecting and classifying information about the external world and acting in accordance with that information, on the basis of frequency and recency of occurrence of events."[91] It is a fact that "we humans can solve many problematic tasks once we are given the correct answer a couple of times; but to learn largely independently, we need plenty of real-life observations (raw data), and a handful of correct examples (labelled data) and perhaps some corrections."[92] While "it may take several decades before the intelligence of machines surpasses that of human beings; but things like 'digital co-workers' that utilize a simpler form of artificial intelligence is almost around the corner."[93]

In other words, governance processes and program implementation could be left to machines with the computational and adaptive capacities and sophisticated algorithms necessary to maintain desired stable states. Through "systems of negative feedback, the machines engage in error detection and error correction automatically in such a way that movements beyond specified limits in one direction initiate movements in the opposite direction to maintain a desired course of action."[94] The point is that when a "continuous process of information exchange is created between a system and its environment, allowing the system to monitor changes and initiate appropriate responses; it can thus be assumed that the system is operating in an intelligent and self-regulating manner."[95] While it has been argued by some that the learning abilities of a system is limited in that the system can maintain only the course of action determined by the operating norms or standards guiding it; but this argument falls apart and is rejected for the simple reason that by the very act of engaging in error detection and error correction, systems generate new knowledge as well as capabilities that creates novel pathways for dealing with unforeseen and emergent problems. And through this, systems also engage in new learning as well as "self-questioning activities that influence the standards that guide their detailed operations."[96]

The question has also been asked whether, in fact, machines (as inanimate objects) can learn which, by virtue of the act itself, involves some kind of cognitive capacity. In very fundamental ways, this question is already being answered. We already have available certain machines that are able to recognize repeated patterns, to classify the patterns into frameworks or building blocks of action, and to generate probabilities regarding how the process of pattern recognition would unfold in the future. In situations where there are limited or incomplete information to make determined predictions, machines can also generate approximations within acceptable margins of error. Not only can machines learn or function in part as *mechanical* brains or central nervous systems that coordinate a series of activities toward a specific goal; machines can also teach people as well as correct them in their habitual errors or mistake-making. A good example would be the computerized test that one takes in order to obtain a driving learner's permit. The computer or machine generates a series of questions, makes a determination between the correct and wrong answer choices, and then provides the correct answer depending on whether the wrong answer choice was made. The whole process involves not only *learning* (because the machine has mastered the difference between the right and wrong answer choices) but is also able to *teach* (in the sense that it is able to direct the test taker to what the correct answer choice should be).

While it may be true that the computer or machine is able to process information or issue commands or corrections based on the information that were already programed into it; but then the computer uses the logic of its own-in-built algorithms and calculative power to repackage and reproduce the information based on received signals. This process involves information retention (mechanical 'cognition' or memory) on the one hand, and information reproduction ('cognitive' analysis), on the other. Yes, although these are processes that are generally associated with humans, but the mechanism by which a machine can simulate this kind of biological behavior has been illustrated in the earlier works of A. M. Uttley[97] and Frank H. George,[98] and to an extent, Stafford Beer.[99] Today, "intelligent machines are offering new insights, reinventing how work is done, as well as creating significantly untapped potentials in reimagining business processes from the ground up as self-improving procedures that can sense, comprehend, act and learn—all in real time."[100] It is believed that "this exponential leap will also unlock entirely new roles and new ways for humans and machines to work together in delivering profound results across industries, the economy, and society as a whole."[101]

Within the political system as well as the administrative state, intelligent machines have helped in data analysis, information classification, and socio-economic audits that go into decision making, policymaking, program evaluation, development of new skill sets, human resources and staffing programs, and in making service delivery more effective. Artificial intelligence does not necessarily eliminate human input into the production process; rather it enhances human capabilities that make them more employable and productive. Governments can provide what we can call low entropy carriers such as rules, laws, morality, and the Constitution; but artificial intelligence provides us with higher entropy carriers although with higher levels of uncertainty, unpredictability, and creativity.[102]

THE SHAPE OF THINGS TO COME

In his widely acclaimed book titled *The Shape of Things to Come*,[103] H. G. Wells talked about the Treaty of Versailles (1648), and the extent to which the following years were punctuated by long periods of war and peace; casting its spell on what could be the tipping edge of a future world that is possible but yet imagined. While his account was anchored on history, politics, and melodramatic abstractions, yet it should not be lost on the reader that the speed by which technology has transformed the modern state and human society as a whole suggests that it would be unavoidable to discuss the future of mankind without articulating how technology and science, broadly construed, would shape it. There is little doubt that technology and automation has brought about dramatic changes to human society and life itself; it has also brought about efficiency in the work process, and improvements in health and human welfare.[104] The natural state of mankind, to the extent that it ever existed, has become morphed into an artificially constructed system such that the possibility of reversing to its original and pristine nature has been lost for good. Human society and the ecosystem that surrounds it has become, to an extent, a captive audience.

History reveals that technological futurism is largely unchanging over time, while the present vision of the future continue to display a startling,[105] and unselfconscious world of automatism, linearity, and precision. Amid many other automatic control devices, "we now have vast storage systems with data-processing arrangements that are capable of storing millions of facts and figures, any of which may be made available in a matter of seconds; computer control of production units and other automatic operations; and ongoing research to improve existing methods of measurement, storage capacity, and input-output systems of every kind.[106] The quest to achieve greater efficiency and precision in the production process has ironically spawned its own Achilles heel—the replacement of humans with robots or machines and created a situation where human skills would not be able to match the new standard set by the machines, no matter how hard we try. Although "engineers have been able to produce servo-systems and automatic control systems in general at a very high level of efficiency";[107] but what we will need for the future are machines that have deductive and inductive capabilities (to analyze, predict, and communicate social phenomena based on imprinted as well as self-generated information) so that the level of predictive power can generate higher levels of probabilities and accuracy in dealing with the flux, uncertainty, and indeterminacy that is characteristic of the behavior of social actors (humans) and social systems (states or organizations).

Amid increasing tension between the need to control and our wish to preserve our values, the heightened prominence of technology in society makes the interrelated task of profiting from its opportunities and containing its dangers a major intellectual and political challenge of our time.[108] While it remains rather unclear where technologies of the future would take human society, but if the past can be used as prologue, the future seems pregnant with many possibilities. How these possibilities eventually shake out are relatively unknown, but nonetheless, are partly predictable at this time. There is a complementary relationship between a strong technological foundation and economic growth; both are critical in laying a solid foundation for future prosperity and social well-being.

Technology has continued to push beyond the boundaries in the development of new solutions in areas as diverse as "digital content, e-commerce, e-learning, financial management, Internet connectivity, neural networks, smart cards, spatial information systems, and in nurturing new mobile applications and services."[109] The perennial focus on a healthier future, aging, and quality of life issues has continued to engender advanced and cutting-edge research and development in the field of biosciences and biotechnology—from genetic profiling, biochemical analysis and drug targeting, research into vaccines and immunotherapeutics. "Advances made in areas such as enzymes and drug discovery are opening up new possibilities for more efficient industrial processes, diagnostic systems, and safer and more efficient therapies for various chronic diseases."[110] The ongoing universal campaign on life-style changes, physical fitness, food and nutrition are also part of a broader policy regime geared toward advancing quality of life as well as preventive medicine. But this effort has not stopped in the areas of health care or bioscience; it essentially covers all other areas that can contribute in fundamental ways to improvements in human and social well-being.

Governing the Future: Predictions and Possibilities

Today, we witness the resulting convergence of three elements: politics, economy, and technology. Everyone is learning from everyone and everywhere because new and advanced technologies have broken down the walls of distance. The building of the computer in 1946 and the consequent birth of the Internet and the World Wide Web years latter has led to new possibilities, new horizons, and new ways of life. In response to global challenges, we stand to be inundated with exotic, and even romantic technological solutions ranging from smart health care, smart city solutions, smart old-age support, advanced data analytics, to predictive decision support systems. Technology is continuously being pushed onto almost everything about life and the human society we live in. No one or community has been spared. "In America, facial recognition technology is used by churches to track worshipper's attendance; in Britain, by retailers to spot past shoplifters; in China, to verify the identities of ride-hailing drivers; and by law enforcement agencies to track criminals."[111] And there is no doubt that "the ability to record, store, and analyze images of faces cheaply, quickly and on a vast scale promises one day to bring about fundamental changes to notions of privacy, fairness and trust."[112]

The world of organizations and businesses continue to witness dramatic shifts from traditional hierarchical arrangements to lateral or horizontal formations. We are now at the end of automation but witnessing the beginning of Industrialization 4.0 (the new Industrial Revolution)—the idea of intelligent machines communicating and interacting alongside with intelligent production. It is a "new industrial concept where all machines are connected through Internet-based system solutions, and can communicate with each other and make decisions."[113] By integrating new technologies into products and processes, the new Industrial revolution takes automation and smart connectivity to a much higher level. It is now the new normal in which intelligent robots in smart factories have become the major drivers of the digital economy in which "factories can become almost completely autonomous in the future—thereby changing the demands and professional skills of current and future workforce."[114] As revolutionary as it seems to be, Industrialization 4.0 will demand new processes and skill sets in dealing with robots manufacturing other robots as well as the complexity of goods in charge of their own production.

Mobility patterns will be enhanced by the ability to reconfigure communication and technical linkages. What has generally been known is that "as innovation widens across populations, it tends to prompt the emergence of new sub-populations and niches which then confront each other in new ecosystems of competition and domination."[115] Hence the evolving *knowledge economy* will necessitate increasing volatility and restructuring of social and economic relations both in terms of distribution and consumption patterns and in the emergence of novel organizational architectures. Colonization of futuristic technological fields whether at the micro (market-led) or macro (state-led) levels will depend on the distinctive institutional, technological and political path dependencies involved in its own socio-economic development considered in light of their abrasion against those of the international system.[116] Hence, as creative innovations become diffused and taken up across the wider society; they are more likely to abrade against larger cross-currents of social and economic change, further tipping them in new and uncertain directions.[117]

In the end, the challenge and promise of artificial intelligence hinges essentially on two things, both imaginative and equally profound. Human evolution or adaptation of the species has been in motion even before Charles Darwin's observations of the Galápagos Islands, and the consequent development of his theory of biological evolution and natural selection; but what is different this time is the seemingly inescapable symbiotic relationship between man and machine. As machines increasingly take over hitherto human functions either as standalone fixtures or in combination with human input, it is possible to suggest that artificial intelligence may, in fact, represent the last stage of human evolution—a process that could result in a more complex world being governed by *automatons*.

In chapter 7, I focus on the role of law and jurisprudence in the maintenance of social order and conformity. I begin with an extended discussion of Greco-Roman law and mechanisms of legal practice. Construed in the context of justice, deterrence, and order, the law is seen as central institution in the evolution and character of social life. I also discuss the issue of moral arbitrariness in legal arguments that oftentimes dictate the outcome of judicial rulings; and the implications of majority rule and due process in the evolving nexus between law, justice, and political order.

NOTES

1. Searle, John R. 2010. *Making the Social World: The Structure of Human Civilization*. New York: Oxford University Press, 141.
2. Burrell, Gibson and Gareth Morgan. 1979. *Sociological Paradigms and Organizational Analysis*. Aldershot, UK: Ashgate, 1.

3. Burrell, Gibson and Gareth Morgan. 1979. *Sociological Paradigms and Organizational Analysis*, 2.

4. Dahrendorf, R. 1959. *Class and Class Conflict in Industrial Society*. London: Routledge and Kegan Paul, 160–162.

5. Burrell, Gibson and Gareth Morgan. 1979. *Sociological Paradigms and Organizational Analysis*, 26.

6. Burrell, Gibson and Gareth Morgan. 1979. *Sociological Paradigms and Organizational Analysis*, 28.

7. March, James G., and Johan P. Olsen. 1989. *Rediscovering Institutions: The Organizational Basis of Politics*. New York: The Free Press, 24.

8. Burrell, Gibson and Gareth Morgan. 1979. *Sociological Paradigms and Organizational Analysis: Elements of the Sociology of Corporate Life*. Aldershot, UK: Ashgate, 98.

9. Weick, Karl E. 1969. *The Social Psychology of Organizing*, 1st ed. Reading, MA: Addison-Wesley, 91.

10. Kreps, Gary L. 1986. *Organizational Communication: Theory and Practice*. New York: Longman, 11.

11. Weick, Karl E. 1969. *The Social Psychology of Organizing*, 40.

12. See also Scott, Richard W., and Gerald F. Davis. 2007. *Organizations and Organizing: Rational, Natural, and Open Systems*. Upper Saddle River, NJ: Pearson-Prentice Hall, 104–106.

13. Weick, Karl E. 1979. *The Social Psychology of Organizing*, 2nd ed. New York: McGraw-Hill, 8.

14. Burrell, Gibson and Gareth Morgan. 1979. *Sociological Paradigms and Organizational Analysis: Elements of the Sociology of Corporate Life*, 160.

15. Burrell, Gibson and Gareth Morgan. 1979. *Sociological Paradigms and Organizational Analysis: Elements of the Sociology of Corporate Life*, 160.

16. Scott, Richard W., and Gerald F. Davis. 2007. *Organizations and Organizing: Rational, Natural, and Open Systems*, 105.

17. Burrell, Gibson and Gareth Morgan. 1979. *Sociological Paradigms and Organizational Analysis*, 49.

18. Durkheim, Emile. 1938. *The Rules of Sociological Method*. Glencoe, IL: Free Press, 148.

19. Burrell, Gibson and Gareth Morgan. 1979. *Sociological Paradigms and Organizational Analysis*, 45.

20. Weick, Karl E. 1979. "Cognitive Processes in Organizatioins." *Research in Organizational Behavior* 1: 44–74, 46.

21. Wendt, Alexander. 1999. *Social Theory of International Politics*. New York: Cambridge University Press, 02.

22. Wendt, Alexander. 1999. *Social Theory of International Politics*, 167.

23. Fay, Brian. 1994. "General Laws and Explaining Human Behavior." In *Readings in the Philosophy of Social Science*, edited by Michael Martin and Lee C. McIntyre, 91–110. Cambridge, MA: The MIT Press, 103.

24. Wendt, Alexander. 1999. *Social Theory of International Politics*, 167.

25. Davidson, Donald. 1994. "Actions, Reason, and Causes." In *Readings in the Philosophy of Social Science*, edited by Michael Martin and Lee C. McIntyre, 675–686. Cambridge, MA: MIT Press, 684.

26. Davidson, Donald. 1994. "Actions, Reason, and Causes," 675–686, 684.

27. Follesdal, Dagfin. 1994. "The Status of Rationality Assumptions in Interpretation and in the Explanation of Action." In *Readings in the Philosophy of Social Science*, edited by Michael Martin and Lee C. McIntyre, 299–310. Cambridge, MA: MIT Press, 307.

28. Burrell, Gibson and Gareth Morgan. 1979. *Sociological Paradigms and Organizational Analysis*, 26–27.

29. Durkheim, Emile. 1994. "Social Facts." In *Readings in the Philosophy of Social Science*, edited by Michael Martin and Lee C. McIntyre, 433–440. Cambridge, MA: MIT Press, 434.

30. Durkheim, Emile. 1994. "Social Facts," 433–440, 434.

31. Burrell, Gibson and Gareth Morgan. 1979. *Sociological Paradigms and Organizational Analysis*, 198.

32. Burrell, Gibson and Gareth Morgan. 1979. *Sociological Paradigms and Organizational Analysis*, 198.

33. Searle, John R. 1995. *The Construction of Social Reality*. New York: The Free Press, 44.

34. Martin, Michael. 1994. "Taylor on Interpretation and the Sciences of Man." In *Readings in the Philosophy of Social Science*, edited by Michael Martin and Lee C. McIntyre, 259–279. Cambridge, MA: MIT Press, 258.

35. Mead, George Herbert. 1967. *Mind, Self, and Society from the Standpoint of a Social Behaviorist* (edited with an Introduction by Charles W. Morris). Chicago, IL: University of Chicago Press.

36. Mead, George Herbert. 1967. *Mind, Self, and Society from the Standpoint of a Social Behaviorist* (edited with an Introduction by Charles W. Morris). Chicago, IL: University of Chicago Press.

37. Crossley, N. 2001. "Citizenship, Intersubjectivity and the Lifeworld". In *Culture and Citizenship*, edited by N. Stevenson, 33–46. Thousand Oaks, CA: Sage Publications, 36.

38. Burrell, Gibson and Gareth Morgan. 1979. *Sociological Paradigms and Organizational Analysis*, 199. See also D. Silverman. 1970. *The Theory of Organizations*. London: Heinemann.

39. Weber, Max. 1968. *On Charisma and Institution Building*, 11.

40. This paragraph is a revised and updated excerpt from an earlier work by the author titled Kalu N. Kalu. 2017. *Citizenship: Identity, Institutions and the Postmodern Challenge*, 14.

41. Sartre, Jean-Paul. 1965. *The Philosophy of Jean-Paul Sartre* (Edited and Introduced by R. D. Cumming). New York: Vintage Books, 188–189.

42. Morgan, Gareth. 2006. *Images of Organization*, 146.

43. Trice, Harrison M., and Janice M. Beyer. 1993. *The Cultures of Work Organizations*. Upper Saddle River, NJ: Prentice Hall, Inc.

44. Scott, W. R. 2014. *Institutions and Organizations: Ideas, Interests, and Identities*, 150.

45. Parsons, Talcott. 1977. *Social Systems and the Evolution of Action Theory*, 178.

46. Parsons, Talcott. 1977. *Social Systems and the Evolution of Action Theory*, 178.

47. Trice, Harrison M., and Janice M. Beyer. 1993. *The Cultures of Work Organizations*

48. See Kalu N. Kalu. 2017. *Citizenship: Identity, Institutions and the Postmodern Challenge*, 75.

49. Turner, Jonathan H. 1972. *Patterns of Social Organization: A Survey of Social Institutions*. New York: McGraw-Hill, Inc, 13.

50. This paragraph is a revised and updated excerpt from an earlier work by the author titled Kalu N. Kalu. 2017. *Citizenship: Identity, Institutions and the Postmodern Challenge*, 76–79.

51. Hart, David K. 1984. "The Virtuous Citizen, the Honorable Bureaucrat as Public Administrator." *Public Administration Review* 44 (Special Issue): 111–120, 14.

52. Gilbert, R. 1992. "Citizenship, Education and Postmodernity." *British Journal of Sociology of Education* 13(1): 51–68, 2.

53. March, James G., and Johan P. Olsen. 1989. *Rediscovering Institutions: The Organizational Basis of Politics*, 161.

54. MacIntyre, Alasdair. 1988. *Whose Justice? Which Rationality?* Notre Dame, IN: University of Notre Dame Press.

55. Parsons, Talcott. 1949. *The Structure of Social Action: A Study in Social Theory with Special Reference to a Group of Recent European Writers*, 650. See also Max Weber. 1922. *Wirtschaft und Gesellschaft (Economy and Society)*. Tubingen: Verlag Von J. C.B. Mohr, 5.

56. Parsons, Talcott. 1949. *The Structure of Social Action: A Study in Social Theory with Special Reference to a Group of Recent European Writers*, 699.

57. Tuomela, Raimo. 2013. *Social Ontology: Collective Intentionality and Group Agents*. New York: Oxford University Press, 23.

58. Tuomela, Raimo. 2013. *Social Ontology: Collective Intentionality and Group Agents*, 224.

59. Durkheim, Emile. 1912/1961. *The Elementary Forms of Religious Life*. New York: Collier Books, 74–475. See also Scott, W. Richard. 2014. *Institutions and Organizations: Ideas, Interests, and Identities*, 13–14.

60. Tyran, Jean-Robert., and Lars P. Feld. 2001. Why People Obey the Law: Experimental Evidence from the Provision of Public Goods. File:///C:/Users/kkalu/Downloads/Why_do_people_Obey-the-Law.pdf. Accessed on October 17, 2018, 1. See also G. S. Becker. 1968. "Crime and Punishment: An Economic Approach." *Journal of Political Economy* 76: 169–217.

61. Ostrom, Elinor. 2005. *Understanding Institutional Diversity*. Princeton, NJ: Princeton University Press, 120–121.

62. http://www.psicosocial.net/grupo-accion-comunitaria/centro-de-documentacion-gac/psicologia-y-tecnicas-de-control-social/operaciones-psicologicas/627-obedience-to-authority-an-experimental-view/file. Accessed on October 18, 2018.

63. http://www.psicosocial.net/grupo-accion-comunitaria/centro-de-documentacion-gac/psicologia-y-tecnicas-de-control-social/operaciones-psicologicas/627-obedience-to-authority-an-experimental-view/file. Accessed on October 18, 2018.

64. Hamilton, Lee V., and Joseph Sanders. 1995. "Crimes of Obedience and Conformity in the Workplace: Surveys of Americans, Russians, and Japanese." *Journal of Social Issues* 51(3): 67–88, 81–82.

65. Bocchiaro, Piero, and Adriano Zamperini. 2012. "Conformity, Obedience, Disobedience: The Power of the Situation." In *Psychology: Selected Papers*, edited by Gina Rossi, 275–294. Rijeka, Croatia: InTech Europe, 290.

66. Bocchiaro, Piero, and Adriano Zamperini. 2012. "Conformity, Obedience, Disobedience: The Power of the Situation," 275–294, 290.

67. Bocchiaro, Piero, and Adriano Zamperini. 2012. "Conformity, Obedience, Disobedience: The Power of the Situation," 275–294, 282.

68. Wiechmann, Thorsten. 2007. Induced versus Autonomous Behavior in Regional Development: A Process Model for Regional Strategy Formation. Association of European Schools of Planning, 1–13, 7. See also https://docplayer.net/48524581-Induced-versus-autonomous-behaviour-in-regional-development-a-process-model-for-regional-strategy-formation.html. Accessed on October 19, 2018.

69. Wiechmann, Thorsten. 2007. Induced versus Autonomous Behavior in Regional Development: A Process Model for Regional Strategy Formation. Association of European Schools of Planning, 1–13, 7. See also https://docplayer.net/48524581-Induced-versus-autonomous-behaviour-in-regional-development-a-process-model-for-regional-strategy-formation.html. Accessed on October 19, 2018.

70. Morin, Amy. 2018. What is Behavior Modification? Use Behavior Modification Strategies to get your Child to Follow the Rules. https://www.verywellfamily.com/what-is-behavior-modification-1094788. Accessed on October 15, 2018.

71. Strand, Paul S. 2009. "Religion as Schedule-Induced Behavior,"191–204, 198.

72. Strand, Paul S. 2009. "Religion as Schedule-Induced Behavior,"191–204, 198.

73. Strand, Paul S. 2009. "Religion as Schedule-Induced Behavior,"191–204, 191.

74. Hirokawa, Randy Y. 2005. *Introduction to Theories of Human Communication*. University of Hawaii, Hilo.

75. Little, Daniel. 1991. *Varieties of Social Explanation: An Introduction to the Philosophy of Social Science*. Boulder, CO: Westview Press, 104.

76. Parsons, Talcott. 1949. *The Structure of Social Action: A Study in Social Theory with Special Reference to a Group of Recent European Writers*, 732.

77. Scott, Richard W., and Gerald F. Davis. 2007. *Organizations and Organizing: Rational, Natural, and Open Systems*, 89.

78. George, F. H. 1959. *Automation, Cybernetics, and Society*. New York: Philosophical Library, 32–33.

79. George, F. H. 1959. *Automation, Cybernetics, and Society*, 32–33.

80. Arendt, Hannah. 1958. *The Human Condition*. Chicago, IL: The University of Chicago Press, 9.

81. Arendt, Hannah. 1958. *The Human Condition*, 9.

82. Jacobs, Walter. 1972. "How a Bug's Mind Works." In *Cybernetics, Artificial Intelligence, and Ecology: Proceedings of the Fourth Annual Symposium of the American Society for Cybernetics*, edited by Herbert W. Robinson and Douglas E. Knight, 95–125, 119.

83. Ashby, W. Ross. 1972. "Setting Goals in Cybernetic Systems," 33–44, 33.

84. George, F. H. 1959. *Automation, Cybernetics, and Society*, 24.

85. Time. 2017. The Best Invention of 2017: For the Future, for Life, for Good, for Play. *Time* 190(22-23), November 27–December 4, 69–93.

86. https://defence-blog.com/army/israel-reveals-details-next-generation-merkava-main-battle-tank.html. Accessed on July 22, 2018.

87. George, F. H. 1959. *Automation, Cybernetics, and Society*, 46.

88. George, F. H. 1959. *Automation, Cybernetics, and Society*, 122.

89. George, F. H. 1959. *Automation, Cybernetics, and Society*, 122.

90. George, F. H. 1959. *Automation, Cybernetics, and Society*, 122–123.

91. George, F. H. 1959. *Automation, Cybernetics, and Society*, 168.

92. Statement credited to Harri Valpola. 2018. Researching the Third Wave of AI. *This is Finland* 2018–2019, 11.

93. Koslenlaakso, Leena. 2018. Making the Most of AI. *This is Finland* 2018–2019, 6.

94. Morgan, Gareth. 2006. *Images of Organization*, 82.

95. Morgan, Gareth. 2006. *Images of Organization*, 83.

96. Morgan, Gareth. 2006. *Images of Organization*, 84.

97. Uttley, A. M. 1954. "The Classification of Signals in the Nervous System." *Neurophysio* 6: 479–494.

98. George, Frank H. 1958. "Probabilistic Machines." *Automation Progress* 3(1):

99. Beer, Stafford. 1956. A Technical Consideration of the Cybernetic Analogue for Planning and Programming. *Process Control and Automation* 3(8 and 9). See also Stafford Beer. 1959. *Cybernetics and Management.* New York: John Wiley & Sons, Inc.

100. Daugherty, Paul R., and H. James Wilson. 2018. *Human + Machine: Reimagining Work in the Age of Artificial Intelligence*. Cambridge, MA: Harvard Business Review Press.

101. https://www.accenture.com/us-en/insight-process-reimagined. Accessed on July 19, 2018.

102. Statement paraphrased from Dr. George Gilder, "Life, Liberty, and Levin," *Fox News Network*, November 24, 2018, 9.30 pm CST.

103. Wells, H. G. 1936. *The Shape of Things to Come*. New York: The Macmillan Company, 17–108.

104. The materials in the sections titled "The Shape of Things to Come" and "Of Futurisms and New Directions" were updated and expanded based on excerpt from Kalu N. Kalu, *Technology, Culture, and Public Policy: Critical Lessons from Finland.* New York: Routledge Publishers, 2017, 64–66.

105. Edgerton, David. 2009. "The Shock of the Old." In *Technology and the Future*, ed. Albert H. Teich, 63–73. Boston, MA: Wadsworth, 67.

106. George, F. H. 1959. *Automation, Cybernetics, and Society*, 130.

107. George, F. H. 1959. *Automation, Cybernetics, and Society*, 130.

108. Mesthene, Emmanuel G. 2009. "The Role of Technology in Society." In *Technology and the Future*, edited by Albert H. Teich, 77–86. Boston, MA: Wadsworth, 80–81.

109. High Technology Finland. 2003. Communications and information. *High Technology Finland.* Helsinki, Finland: High Technology Finland, 32.

110. Herring, Peter. 2003. Inspired by ideas. *High Technology Finland* 2003. Helsinki, Finland: High Technology Finland, 11–12.

111. The Economist. 2017. Nowhere to Hide. *TheEconomist* 424(9057), September 9, p. 11.

112. The Economist. 2017. Nowhere to Hide. *TheEconomist* 424(9057), September 9, p. 11.

113. https://www.ltu.se/org/ets/Smarta-fabriker-staller-nya-krav-pa-arbetet-1.177938?l=en. Accessed on September 25, 2018.

114. https://www.ltu.se/org/ets/Smarta-fabriker-staller-nya-krav-pa-arbetet-1.177938?l=en. Accessed on September 25, 2018.

115. Room, Graham. 2011. *Complexity, Institutions, and Public Policy: Agile Decision-making in a Turbulent World*, 279.

116. Room, Graham. 2011. *Complexity, Institutions, and Public Policy: Agile Decision-making in a Turbulent World*, 283.

117. Room, Graham. 2011. *Complexity, Institutions, and Public Policy: Agile Decision-making in a Turbulent World*, 308.

Chapter 7

Law, Justice, and Jurisprudence

Every society or political system, at least in modern times, needs a set of rules, standards, norms, and organizing symbols for the regulation of social and political actions. It is to establish a sense of order, procedure, and justice that *laws* have become a central feature of all human societies. In his book *The Penguin History of Greece*, A. R. Burn narrates an encounter between Pericles and his ward Alkibiades in which the later asked Pericles to explain to him what *Law* is? Pericles explained that "all enactments are laws, which the people in parliament has approved and published, laying down what shall be done or not done."[1] But when pushed further by the seemingly inquisitive interrogator, Pericles reinforced his earlier response by stating that "everything the government of the city, after deliberation, publishes, as to what is to be done, is called law."[2] But pushed further, Pericles reluctantly made an exception to laws made by tyrants pointing to the fact that "everything which one forces another to do without his consent, whether by public enactment or otherwise, is an exercise of arbitrary power, rather than law."[3]

In recognition, Plato had also voiced similar opinion on the premise that because "incidents of human life are of such an infinite variety that the just and equitable can never be formulated in general rules or laws; it is therefore the test of the truly wise statesman as a lawgiver to make laws which come as near as possible to true justice and equity, but because of inevitable imperfections, he may still on occasion deviate from his own laws, without necessarily violating the tenets of true justice and equitableness."[4] The above premise is suggestive of the fact that the law was seen as an instrument of the state, to be adjusted and reformulated to serve specific objectives but with an overriding interest in maintaining justice and equity in its application to social and political life. Because the law was seen as an exercise of public right (publici juris) in the sense of extending justice and equity to all, the state was also seen as the guarantor of those rights or as a custos morum (guardian of morals) that helps to sustain the civic virtue and general welfare of the polis. Accepting the fact that "the rule of law is present even in deviant constitutions, except for the most extreme forms such as tyranny, extreme oligarchy (dynasty), and even extreme democracy;"[5] Aristotle was also of the view that since the laws derive from the constitution (and not the other way round), and in states where the laws do not rule, there is no constitution. "Law is as important a moral force in public life as religion used to be in earlier societies; but moral guarantees alone cannot be the object of the law or its facilitation."[6] To the extent that the law is meant to seek and pursue objective justice, it is in this regard that it could be used (in its unbiased application) to secure equality of outcomes.

Although there may be exceptions in the way the law is made and applied in most societies, I am more interested in the normative basis for all laws despite the obvious misapplication in some political regimes. I will focus on the essential premise that the purpose of law is to seek due process and justice on the one hand, but on the other, it is meant to secure deterrence and obedience as well as punishment for infractions inimical to the existing social order. Although it comes in many gradations and to the extent it serves as a regulatory device, we can consider traditional institutions, customs, ceremonies, and belief systems of tribal and primitive societies as forms of law. But in modern societies and political systems, the corpus juris has always been seen to evolve not only with changing times and social values, but also with the modernizing trend induced by technological development and advancements in education and learning. In this regard, I will like to draw from the development of law and society in classical Greek and Roman civilizations, and how these over time saw their eventual manifestations in contemporary modern societies; albeit, in different variations and applications.

GRECO-ROMAN JURISPRUDENCE

In the same way that the development of the new states of Renaissance Italy and the ancient Greek city-states or polis could be considered a work of art in terms of political governance; it was also a period characterized by "an increasingly conscious analysis of problems, the sudden liberation from tradition, and also the containment of anarchy within new, simple forms and types which basically were reinterpretations of ancestral forces."[7] In other words, Greek and Roman law drew immensely from extant belief systems, traditions, myths and legends that provided the framework from which the law (as institution) was embedded into the political and social life of the state. As it became obvious that the polis may have crystallized very rapidly and spontaneously in many localities and as way of creating tighter communal bonds and to prevent change from descending into chaos, the law became a means for imposing political order on a rapidly evolving society.[8] As "the *polis* began to improve the existing public judicial and deliberative machinery and efforts were made to secure the basic rights of citizens, written codes of justice began to appear by the middle of the seventh century; abuse of privilege was also checked by the ever latent threat to turn back to personal leadership if justice or traditional rights (*eunomia*) were undermined or denied."[9]

As a framework for order, the law offered guidance to the political character of the polis, commerce and trade, cultural and religious relations, war and peace, as well as issues of family, lineage and patrimony. By anchoring traditional practices and belief systems in legal precepts, the polis at the same time assured continuity and predictability in the way the practices endure now and in the future. And because the sense of community and family was based on the experience of common practices, the Greek and Roman civilizations were able to secure for themselves, that which made them noble citizens worthy of admiration by foreigners and others who are not related to them by either blood or culture. For Athens, in particular, it should also be noted just as in its modern applications (particularly in democratic polities), that "punishment (*timoria*) expended by virtue of the law was seen as an expression of the communal will and was applied impartially to all members of the citizen body irrespective of status, power, or prestige."[10] It differed from tribal vengeance in that its orientation was prospective, not retrospective—but with the ultimate aim of not inflicting harm in retribution for past wrongdoing.[11] The law therefore was established for two main reasons: "to deter everyone from doing anything wrong, and to punish wrongdoers to the edification of others."[12] And because they dispensed 'impartial' justice through the law, "the courts became the supreme embodiment of people power and the ultimate guardians of the constitution—in the sense that when the people (*demos*) cast the votes used to reach verdicts in the law courts, they invariably, also become masters of the state (*politeia*).[13]

In the hope that proper education will direct individual behavior toward the right and communally accepted course of action; virtue and sensibility to justice was expected to guide the conscience of lawgivers as well as those who deliver judgment. The law was relevant in all aspects of human endeavor ranging from patrimony, marriage, children, the nature of witness, exchange of money or currency, inheritance, property, and the security and protection of orphans.[14] In the beginning, "the law in the Greek city states (particularly Athens) was what the king made of it; and his judgments were the visible emanation of the wisdom implanted in him by Zeus, the king of the Gods."[15] But eventually the advent of written law brought about substantive changes in the administration of justice, by distributing functions which had originally been united in the person of the king. Even though the juror system, however, made little distinction between political and nonpolitical issues; but other considerations such as "the litigant's past services to the state, the amount he had paid out in taxes or other forms of public outlay, were all allowed their weight, as were the tears of the defendant's children and much else."[16] It was such that what a charitable critic might call *equity* had more force in an Athenian court than the strict letter of the law, and the notion of equity had a highly political flavor.[17]

And for all intents and purposes, the ancient Greeks viewed the law of the state as the source of all standards of human life premised on the collective virtue of the citizens[18]—a situation that also saw political involvement as the highest form of virtue. Even when "the decision of a particular matter has to be made, presumably by a judge instead of the legislator (an elected representative); but then the judge would still have to reproduce the solution the legislator would have given had he known the circumstances."[19] Hence, judges should not make or dictate the laws; they should only speak out what the law says. For Aristotle, prudence, while evidently not considered as scientific knowledge for it concerns that which is done in action; it is only for those with experience and insight into the particularity of the circumstances in each area who should judge the particular works correctly.[20] This point was also echoed by Cicero in support of "the concept of general rules (*legeslegum*) which govern legislation, the conception that we obey the law in order to be free, and the conception that the judge ought to be merely the mouth through whom the law speaks."[21]

As was evident in the "course of the seventeenth century when the influence of Latin writers largely replaced the direct influence of the Greeks in the development of civil law";[22] the tradition derived from the Roman Republic (particularly the Laws of the Twelve Tables)—which was said to have been drawn up in conscious imitation of Solon's laws, became the foundation of its liberty which also had much influence on Western civilization and political morality.[23] While "priority was given to liberty over equality; but liberty in this regard (not to be confused with license), signifies doing what the law permits in accord with one's social status."[24] In fact, "no other author shows more clearly that during the classical period of Roman law it was fully understood that there is no conflict between law and freedom and that freedom is dependent upon certain attributes of the law—its generality and certainty, and the restrictions it places on the discretion of authority." Although much of these was lost and replaced by economic freedom during the Justinian era; but yet the spirit of the law of free Rome was passed on to later generations mainly through the works of historians and orators such as Marcus Tullius Cicero.

Cicero's writings[25] had enormous influence on the philosophical education of Rome and much of European civilization in the areas of law, logic, oratory, citizenship, and republican politics. Besides his civil defense of individuals in legal matters, he wrote and delivered speeches against political authoritarianism and the rise of dictatorship and misgovernment in republican Rome. Among these were *The Verrine Orations* delivered against Gaius Verres, governor of the province of Sicily, the *In Catilinam*—a political tirade delivered against Lucius Sergius Catilina following what became known as the Catilinarian conspiracy to overthrow the Roman republic, and the *Philippics* against Marc Antony and the Triumvirate. There were also philosophical treatises such as the *Tusculan Disputations* and his *Letters to Atticus*. His three books which exercised enormous influence on the development of contemporary western moral and political thought were *De re publica* (On the Commonwealth)—an assemblage of people associated with one another by agreement on law and community of interest; and *De legibus* (On the Laws) as well as *De officiis* (on Duties)—his work on political morality and the republic. Collectively, and besides providing us with critical information and understanding of the period as well as the framework of Roman politics, society, and citizenship, these works have endured and remain influential in shaping contemporary political thinking, jurisprudence, and freedom under the law.

For Cicero, although we are obliged to obey the laws, but then laws are not imposed on us by nature (with the exception of *natural laws*) or by our innate sense of justice; rather they are imposed by the *fear* of being penalized.[26] But where such fear does not exist or where the penalty could possibly be reduced or bargained away in the courts, obedience to the laws ceteris paribus may bring not justice, but injustice to those who fall victim as a result of others' refusal to abide by the prescriptions of the law. This was the case in republican Rome to which Cicero mounted a fearless defense not only for the preservation of the juridical state but also against the usurpation of political authority and the negation of the laws that held the republic together. Because the law was seen as a divine gift from God, they also drew upon the resilience of ancient Roman customs and beliefs which must be passed on from generation to generation. Because there was no written constitution in the formal way we have in most modern states, the consequence of breaking the law was therefore seen as a negation or as a threat to the customs and traditions of Roman society—particularly in matters of voting, marriage, commerce, descent, inheritance, and in civil political discourse.

LAW AND FUNCTIONALISM: EFFICACY AND THE LIMIT OF DETERRENCE

On the premise that because of differences in the character of human societies and in regimes types, the contemporary world has come to settle on a kind of judicial relativism, despite the over-arching influence of natural or universal laws that potentially apply to all of humanity. The notion of the right, the just, due process, and the obligatory originates with the idea of law and does not precede it;[27] but either way, laws are formulated and directed toward specific ends—that of order, predictability, certainty, obedience, sanctions and, to an extent, deterrence. But in what ways do laws preserve social order? In Thomas Aquinas' *Summa Theologica*, "human enactment or positive law was understood in terms of its connection with eternal law, natural law, or revealed law. Law, as such, was seen as an ordinance of reason, made, promulgated, and enforced for the common good by the community's ruler."[28] While "its commands are summons to duty and its prohibitions declare that nothing wrongful must be done; but the commands and prohibitions are only effective where good men are concerned, while neither would have any effect on men who are bad."[29] Because obedience to the law grants it credibility and effect; it would still take individual will to determine whether the law is obeyed or not. Therefore the *law*, ipso facto could not be construed as deterrence in the absolute sense of the term. While it could serve as deterrence for some, there are many who are not deterred by it.

In his *The Spirit of the Laws*, Baron de Montesquieu defined the law as "the necessary relations deriving from the nature of things." In other words, "laws emerge as a form of blind necessity and reasoned choice, rather than governance rationally aimed at some good."[30] "Laws are relations; they exist objectively and by necessity, govern the actions of all things—of God on the world, of bodies on each other, and in all other human endeavors."[31] But because "law, in general, is human reason in so far as it governs all the peoples of the earth";[32] Montesquieu argues that "the political and civil laws of each nation ought only to be the particular cases in which this human reason is applied."[33] While not disputing the fact that "the laws are very closely related to the way that various peoples procure their subsistence,"[34] he was also in agreement that there are universal principles that apply in laws governing the administration of the republic, crime against nature, commerce, and the condition of women in various governments.

The law is a mechanism for regulating human behavior in society as well as imposing sanctions in the face of behaviors that deviate from desirable patterns. One of the key reasons for the emergence of civil political society was to avoid the characteristic anarchy of a Hobbesian state of war-of-all-against-all; hence to prevent individuals from sticking pretty much to their own selfish devices to the exclusion of others, certain rules of conduct and coexistence had to be imposed on the civic order for mutual self-preservation. "Politics, like economic life, depends on human cooperation, based on coordinated expectations";[35] but the coordination of human efforts toward the attainment of some goal or goals can be greatly accelerated or facilitated by recourse to the existing law.[36] Human actors are always engaged in a form of exchange between or across multiple dyads or interactions, and oftentimes such interactions generate their own dysfunctional effects or conflict situations. By "specifying how existing values, beliefs, customs, and traditions are to be realized in day-to-day interaction among actors";[37] the law serves as a formal and informal control mechanism that "facilitates coordination by increasing conformity and hence the predictability of social action."[38] Yes, legal or statutory stipulations embed normative structures among social actors by their integration into everyday practices, which in a recursive way also becomes the basis for the institutionalization of the same legal stipulations that initiated the normative structure. The mere fact that a law exists somewhere (when it is not applicable or referenced in a particular case); that, alone can have a controlling or *normalizing* effect on human behavior in their adherence to the existing social order. In Searlean terms, the law also has deontic power.

As a framework for the allocation and enforcement of basic rights, the preservation of basic moral and social values, as well as adjudication in matters pertaining to group interests and conflict resolution, the law derives its efficacy through statutes, precedents, and customs. Because laws provide the legal basis for funding and implementation of public polices, they are also relied upon as a basis for investigation or explaining why certain policies worked or did not work in the way that was expected. In order words, the role of a law does not end simply by authorizing a specific policy, program, or regulation; rather its "consequences often feed back into the system and become part of the explanation of why the system is as it is."[39] When the state uses coercion in the enforcement of public order and conformity, it does that "only under restraints that come with the legal institutionalization of authority"[40]—by way of the law. The law can also be used as legal justification for whatever it is the state wants to do; and even in the face of competing disagreement, once a law is passed to that effect, the policy often becomes a fait accompli.

In contemporary societies (and I will also assume the same for the political systems that existed during the classical period), not all laws have universal appeal or approval. There have always been disagreements over whether a law is just or unjust, desirable or not, or can foster justice or deny it. Empirical evidence has shown that the mere existence of a law cannot prevent people from violating it, or from committing crime. And even if they are evidently guilty of the crime, the law itself can also be used to set them free to the evident consternation of those who may have been harmed by the offence. We rely on the law to establish a sense of order and to regulate behavioral patterns in society, but we also look upon the law to grant justice and due process. In most familiar cases, while the law may achieve the first, it may fall short achieving the later. In fact, by appealing to procedural and technical shortcomings involved in a case, the law can be used to confer innocence on the guilty—all the more raising the perennial issue of whether the law can, in all circumstances, be relied upon to achieve *justice for all.* The United States offers many examples of situations whereby on the basis of mere technicality or violation of judicial procedures both in the collection of evidence and in the granting of due process or equal treatment under the law (all of which are constitutional guarantees), the obviously guilty are able to defraud the system by getting away scot-free.

The very idea of *innocent until proven guilty* does not necessarily work in favor of the victim, but actually helps the defendant to string out the judicial proceedings as well as impose the burden of proof on the plaintiff more than the defendant. One of the other reasons why the law often cannot be used to extract justice is that individuals who may be on trial for allegedly having committed a crime rarely admit that they did it. In fact, they (almost) always plead "*not guilty*," even though by all indications and empirical evidence, they are as guilty as guilty can be. But what should we make of this sort of hypocrisy and bad faith? Why should the law be used as legal cover for lying or for cheating the norms of justice? Nonetheless, the most universal explanation has always been that while we need to grant *due process* to all, there is also that other seemingly normative axiom of "*innocent until proven guilty*" that must be recognized. And because judicial rulings can oftentimes generate incompatible courses of action that undermine the true meaning of justice, the irony in all of this is that such a situation rarely grants due process to the victim or the aggrieved nor does the right claim of "*innocent until proven guilty*" apply to him or her.

What I am stating here is that while the law is necessary for the establishment of public order and conformity, it also harbors within it, elements that can often be used to enshrine disorder, cheating, and bad faith. The Achilles heel of the law resides in the fact that while it cannot prevent some people from committing crimes, it only becomes evident in a case, more or less, as an after-the-fact or as a reaction to a crime that has already been committed. There are restrictions and regulations against illegal acquisition and/or ownership of guns, yet people acquire guns illegally; there are restrictions and regulations on the illegal manufacturing and distribution of contraband drugs, yet people still engage in this practice; there are laws that seek to prevent people in the exercise of their official responsibilities from discriminating against other people, yet people do discriminate; and then there are laws and warnings of enormous penalties waiting for those who would think of cheating on their taxes, but still many people cheat on their taxes.

And there are reasons for all of this. First, many people have already convinced themselves that the chances of their being caught are minimal or possibly unlikely; others feel that even if they are caught, the balance of gain weighs in their favor even if they have to go jail for a limited period of time; while others simply take a gamble or throw the dice and leave the outcome to fate and Providence. Or perhaps, it is a function of human nature, that while some may want to live upright and law-abiding lives, others are simply evil in their moral wiring and simply lack the common decency to do and think about that which is always right. These are the sort of things that undermine the deterrence capacity of the law, thereby making it less functional than would otherwise be the case if people had chosen to abide by its precepts. Other cases of the breakdown of law and order "grow out of the failure, or loss of moral plausibility and of the implicit theory of a just social order that comes with any institution";[41] and that is why regulatory institutions such as the law are often ineffective because of a shortage of the moral resources and loyalties that are needed for their support.[42]

LAWYERS AND JUDGES: JURISPRUDENCE WITH A NARRATIVE

The framework of the American judicial system is based on English law, which was itself a product of the Roman Empire.[43] In addition to being a *positive law system* (man-made law) that is based on natural law concepts (Divine or moral law), the English colonists also introduced *common law* principles to the United States which eventually formed the foundation of the legal system.[44] They were of the view "that all positive law derives its validity from some rules that have not in this sense been made by men but which can be *found* and that these rules provide both the criterion for the justice of positive law and the ground for men's obedience to it."[45] But "as government developed on both the federal and state levels, much of the common law was codified and replaced with constitutions and statutes; although common law still serves an important function in the overall legal system."[46]

In practice, judicial rulings in the United States are built on the principle of stare decisis (judicial precedent) and due process. While the first is derived from the fact that there is need to maintain consistency in the interpretation and application of the law, the latter derives from constitutional protections offered in the 5th and 14th Amendments of the US Constitution. "The due process clauses of the 5th and 14th Amendments were the only ones in the Constitution that mentioned property; but during the next 50 years after passage, they thus became the foundation on which the court built a body of law concerning not only individual liberties but government control of economic life, including the use of police power and of taxation."[47] It is partly for this reason that whatever dictate ensues from the law is rarely challenged but taken as a given, hence justifying the use of force in its enforcement. And in the midst of ambiguity and/or conflict in the law, we rely on the courts to interpret or provide judicial guidance on the same laws for which they are also mandated to enforce.

I have made some references to the legal system of the United States partly because it is the one I am most familiar with, but also one which is relatively unique both in the politicization of the nomination for justices to the Supreme court and in the power of the court to overrule specific actions of the legislature and the executive by means of judicial review. Although judicial rulings are supposed to be objective and value-neutral, but this is only in theory to the extent that the practical facts do not bear this out. Judges and lawyers harbor their own judicial philosophies or political beliefs to the extent that it makes it difficult to clearly separate where politics and the law diverge. The boundary between politics and law, between justice and political authority is blurred when judges overrule executive authority over specific matters of foreign policy, immigration, and budgetary and spending authority of the executive; even when it is the case that politics, law, and justice oftentimes serve competing but different ends. Some justices or judges are considered judicial activists who seek judicial interpretations outside of the tenets of the Constitution as a way embracing emerging values and new aspirations in the larger society; while others fall under the caption of judicial restraint otherwise known as *textualists* who prefer judicial or constitutional interpretation based on the original intent or the strict construction of the Founding fathers in the crafting of the Constitution. Because competing judicial interpretations do not seem to be value-neutral, they therefore could not be effectively used as a means of guaranteeing both justice and due process.

It is also true that "every person accused of a serious crime is entitled to a lawyer and the lawyer has an ethical obligation to provide a defense against criminal charges no matter what the crime, be it rape, child molestation, or serial murder."[48] While this could be an example of extending due process to the defendant or the accused; but ironically, the plaintiff receives little or no constitutional guarantees that the defendant would be found guilty if, in fact, he committed the crime or violation as alleged. While the fate and optimism of the plaintiff hangs in the balance, the defendant seems, more or less, privileged to exhaust all judicial procedures, arguments, and excuses granted under the law in his or her defense. But then this still begs a much larger question about judicial ethics and the role of lawyers in undermining it, either for economic or political reasons or both:[49] Are defense attorneys obligated to do everything the law will allow to win an acquittal or avoid a financial judgment against their client? Or, if the evidence seems clear that the defendant is guilty, should they temper their defense strategy to ensure that justice is done? The American Bar Association (ABA) rules specify how the lawyer as advocate is expected to behave in all situations. The ABA Rule 3.4 states that "lawyers shall not alter, destroy, conceal, or obstruct another party's access to evidence; falsify evidence or counsel witnesses to testify falsely; disobey court rules; make frivolous discovery requests during pre-trial; or make irrelevant or personal opinion statement at trial."[50]

Unfortunately, for most lawyers, a sizeable proportion of them are not actually concerned about justice per se; rather they are concerned about winning the case at all costs, not only because of the positive publicity it brings (now that we have media court trials), but also the opportunity it affords to attract new and more lucrative customers and the economic benefits that come with it. Instead of seeking objective truth and justice, we now have lawyers who, more often than not, lie, cheat, and obfuscate their way to victory. But it is a hollow victory and not one grounded in justice or due process. Instead of using legal reasoning to make judicial arguments, many of today's lawyers use political reasoning to make arguments that reflect their personal biases and political suasions. To win a case, most lawyers purposefully take steps to conceal non-exculpatory evidence, obfuscate by drawing upon frivolities and non-pertinent analogies and precedents, and by undermining the very laws upon which they base their arguments, they end up giving the legal system a bad name.

While the specialized knowledge that enables lawyers to seek *justice* may be put to other uses as well; there is no doubt that as long as there is the monetary incentive, lawyers oftentimes create problems (where none should exist) to advance their own economic interests.[51] And "even when they believe their clients committed horrible crimes, criminal lawyers seek their acquittal; as they try to help their clients reduce or escape legal culpability for the injuries they caused."[52] By promoting or defending immoral and illegal acts, lawyers deliberately or by default compound the immorality,[53] and by so doing secure neither justice nor security for society at large. Although the United States has an adversarial justice system and certainly lawyers are permitted to mount vigorous advocacy for their clients within the scope of the law; but still yet, it does not remove the fact that when a lawyer defends criminality, he or she is, in fact, defending injustice, even if the moral of their arguments is founded on procedural due process.

Invariably, the American state and the civic life within it has not escaped what is now regarded as the politicization of the judicial system, particularly on highly contentious issues that can only be *resolved* by the Supreme Court. To this effect, and in a "nation so politically divided, people of different ideological and social persuasions are coming to view the court less as an interpreter of the law than as an activist imposer of moral and political outcomes."[54] Tribal politics, gender politics, and media politics have all combined to produce a new dynamic where judicial rulings and interpretations are, more or less, now shaped by or high-jacked by what goes on outside of the hallowed chambers of the US Supreme Court. This particular occurrence has been confounded by a "series of major judicial decision in the past several decades that have given partisans on both sides of the political divide something to dislike about the court—from abortion rights to campaign finance to health care."[55] Even though there is no such explicit right granted in the US Constitution (unless a clever lawyer can make a credible argument that such a right could be implied by recourse to the ambiguous provisions of the 9th Amendment), the Supreme Court, nonetheless, "granted a 'right to privacy' that made abortion legal nationwide. Since then, the court has legalized sodomy, same-sex marriage, expanded gun rights, and allowed unlimited corporate spending on elections."[56]

As a result of the increasing political divide, the Supreme Court, by default to an extent, is now in a position to make public policy on various highly contentious issues by judicial imposition and enforcement. Values and practices that are opposed by a great majority of the people are being rammed down their throats whether they like it or not, and without much debate or consideration for their views. While this continues to erode the legislative authority of Congress, it also undermines the Constitutional principle of *advice* and *consent*, as well as the supposedly nonpartisan role traditionally expected of the judicial system. In an era "when politics determines the ordinary issues of life—jobs, retirement, health care, education, housing, lifestyle choices, and more—and the political battles over those end up in the courts; the debate about judicial nominations also becomes overly combative and those who fear losing the battle often resort to desperate means."[57] Because most judicial rulings from the courts have become quite dictatorial, they confer neither justice nor due process in the absolute sense of the term.

Trial by Jury: Procedural versus Substantive Justice

There is also this other instrument of the legal system known as *trial by jury* (as granted in the 6th and 7th Amendments of the US Constitution). "The American legal culture is filled with myths, in the sense that some of what happens or is experienced in the larger society (such as movies that extoll *crime scene investigation*) adds greater judicial burden on the prosecution because jurors now expect high-tech forensic science and they are disappointed when the prosecution fails to deliver, with the consequence that jurors acquit more defendants even when they may, in fact, be guilty."[58] Because jurors are chosen from the communities or societies in which they live, they have also been socialized into the political culture of those communities. Their thinking and cognitive biases are shaped by widely held views within their respective communities as well as their own personal experiences and ideological preferences. Often jurors experience "cognitive difficulties and motivational distortions that undermine"[59] or seriously affect their sense of judgment, fairness, and the temperament necessary to reach a conclusion that culminates in justice as the final outcome of their deliberations. While maintaining "the opinion that the judge should be guided by the general principles and goals of the existing law (to the extent that it embodies the constitutional and legislative intent), yet Aristotle, though grudgingly accepting the contribution of the judge in filling out gaps in the law, did not hide his evident mistrust toward the *juror-judge* as was entrenched in the Platonic *corpus juris*."[60] Hence he offers, in the opening chapter of the *Rhetoric* a profound repudiation of how personal circumstances could bias fair and equitable judgment:[61]

> First of all, therefore, it is proper that laws, properly enacted, should themselves define the issue of all cases as far as possible, and leave as little as possible to the discretion of the judges; in the first place, because it is easier to find one or a few men of good sense, capable of forming laws and properly pronouncing judgements than a large number; secondly, legislation is the result of long consideration, whereas judgments are delivered on the spur of the moment, so that it is difficult for the judges properly to decide questions of justice or expediency. But what is most important of all is that the judgement of the legislator does not apply to a particular case, but is universal and applies to the future, whereas the members of the public assembly and the *dicast* (juror) have to decide present and definite issues, and in their case love, hate, or personal interest is often involved, so that they are no longer capable of discerning the truth adequately, their judgement being obscured by their own pleasure or pain. (Georgiadis 1987)

The point is that while the recourse to *trial by jury* may grant procedural justice in cases where it applies, it does not always grant substantive justice in terms of judicial outcome. While it may satisfy one judicial requirement (the processes by which substantive rights and due process are granted), it oftentimes sacrifices the other (the rights, duties, and obligations granted in the law). There are many reasons for this, and one of them is the evident ambiguity in the justification for the use of jurors in cases for which most of them may not be equipped to handle the complexities of the matter. The argument that a *jury of your peers* stands to make better judgment that secures due process and justice does not square well with the facts of the matter. The problem arises in the random selection of jurors and in the attempt to democratize the judicial process in the false hope that a randomly selected juror pool would be more amenable to securing justice than those who are actually better trained in the letters and intricacies of the law.

While most jurors are not trained in the law, some may not be as educated and discerning as the others, some may hold extreme as opposed to balanced opinions on the issue of the case, and the personal or individual characteristics and experiences of a juror may, as is unavoidably the case, filter into his or her judgments about a case—a judgment which often satisfies personal sentiments and preferences, than a judgment that leads to objective justice. Within the average juror pool, there is a competing mix of contradictions and power plays that end up in the end, sacrificing justice and due process. No matter how much we try, we cannot absolutely separate a juror from his or her sentiment; jurors bring a lot of baggage and unavoidable idiosyncrasies into the judicial system, and that is why some recalcitrant jurors may refuse to convict even in the face of overwhelming evidence. We have witnessed many cases where jurors actually fell in love with a criminal defendant, and for them, this love affair (so to say) will trump every other consideration of fairness, or even justice itself. Most jury pools suffer from information asymmetry, they may lack background knowledge about the legal imperatives of the case for which they have been assigned, they are not trained in the process of isolating critical or peripheral evidence, their decision premises or boundaries of judgment are already circumscribed by the presiding judge; hence jurors may not be able to think outside the box they have been locked in. It may also be a function of the fact that the average citizen is lacking in the basic forms of civic education and socialization, hence they are not able to properly articulate how their decision is shaped by or may influence current and future life in the broader civic society.

In today's jury system, one is often unsure whether the process is an exercise in public relations, political paternalism, or a reflection of how much democratic politics and majority rule has infected the judicial system. "The transformation of political issues into legal disputes furnished judges with the opportunity to influence the course of public policy; judges have sometimes been more than willing to seize the opportunities presented to them."[62] In a recent case concerning the Trump administration's policy on illegal immigration, the judge in his objection asked the administration to show *legal reasoning* for its policy on the issue (restraining illegal immigration); but on the simple premise that the people illegally crossing the border are not American citizens and yet have broken existing US law on cross-border entry, the judge is asking the administration to provide "legal reasoning" to justify its policy against an act of "illegality" (unauthorized entry into the country). Ironically, the judge was holding the administration *par delictum* (equally at fault) as the illegal immigrant who broke the law; even as the Constitution grants the president the foreign policy power over who enters or does not enter the country. And more of this abounds every day.

MORAL ARBITRARINESS AND THE LAW

The moral basis of *justice* has gone through various conceptualizations that it would be apt to ask a simple question—*whose* justice? There are variations of justice as fairness, as virtue, as lawfulness, as due process, or as giving each person his or her due—the last part also invoking the idea of positive or negative justice. And this also begs the question as to *which* justice would be applicable in specific situations and in what form? Part of the reason why people disagree so often about justice, particularly among liberal societies, is that we assess it based on what it results in (the outcome) as opposed to what it stands for. For those on the losing end of a judicial trial, it would not be justice but injustice; but for those on the winning side, it would certainly be justice. Because "the origin and nature of justice lies between what is most desirable, to do wrong and avoid punishment, and what is most undesirable, to suffer wrong without being able to get redress; justice, therefore, lies between these two and is accepted not as being good in itself, but as having a relative value."[63] Nonetheless justice, to the extent that it is anchored on virtue and practical wisdom, is necessary for the full realization of human nature.[64]

In *The Republic*, Plato depicts a scene in which Glaucon and Socrates were engaged in dialogue concerning the meaning of justice. The account offered deviates from any consideration of moral equivalency, but is founded on the illustration that when each of the three classes (businessmen, auxiliaries, and guardians) perform the social duties assigned to them consistent with their natural qualities, and if in the end this arrangement contributes to the excellence of the city (state), then this can be construed as justice. Justice therefore is embodied in a man's inward self, concern and interest in seeing that a harmonious whole is achieved when each and every one performs and minds their own business without intervening in that of others. Hence justice is produced by establishing in the mind a similar natural relation of control and subordination among its constituent parts.[65] Justice is therefore a matter of proper arrangement of social and political functions in the city in such a way that everyone is assigned to responsibilities for which their nature (or natural gifts) permits. Anything to the contrary would be injustice and thus would be harmful to the welfare of the city.

Although "the *Republic* teaches about politics by examining the nature of justice, which appears to be the goal of political life; and by showing that the full realization of justice is impossible in politics, the *Republic* also circumscribes and defines the limitations of politics."[66] The *Laws*, therefore, can only show how the man of reason can work with and within the pious traditionalism that dominates most political life.[67] On the premise that we should "reject the argument that good men naturally follow the true, authentic path of justice and not merely what is thought to be just";[68] but to the extent that "justice is conformity to written laws and national customs (and if everything is to be tested by the standard of relative utility), then anyone who thinks it will be profitable to him will, if he is able, disregard and violate the laws."[69] As Aristotle points out in the *Nicomachean Ethics*—"an act of injustice is different from what is unjust, and an act of justice from what is just."[70] It is often difficult to separate the dual nature of justice (its substantive and procedural qualities) from each other since, in most cases, both qualities could be applicable under the same circumstance.

Yet, if we accept the fact that justice stands for distinguishing the difference between right and wrong, and applying reward or sanctions accordingly (in terms of what Aristotle calls *rectificatory justice*), we must also have a common agreement concerning those things that ought to be construed as right or wrong. In the more realistic absence of that, justice is therefore reduced to its *relativeness* depending on which side of the divide the bone of contention weighs more heavily. For Aristotle, the value of justice is premised on its distributive quality as well as in its expression and effect on the *other*. Justice therefore is a form of complete virtue in relation to another. It is the virtue that the just person expresses in just actions and decisions. But justice is also a matter of giving each person his due in the sense that "equality for the people involved in an enterprise will be the same as for the things involved; since the relation between the people will be the same as the relation between the things involved."[71] But when the people involved are not equals, then they should receive unequal shares; because justice demands that equals receive equal shares and unequals receive unequal shares. In this regard, proportional equality would be consistent with the aim of justice. But above all, Aristotle considers justice as a teleological movement toward the mean; because it concerns an intermediate condition, while injustice concerns the extremes.[72] But since it would be difficult to know when an individual act has reached or crossed the mean, the contention is that the most just of individual acts would be those guided by *temperance* or the "principle of the golden mean"—a mid-range between two extremes.

From the liberal point of view, the key tenets of justice should be expected to satisfy a set of basic assumptions premised on the concept of rights, equality, and the application of the rule of law in such a way that it is the same, particularly in all cases that are similar. One of the major purveyors of liberal justice is John Rawls whose conception of justice takes as its starting point the argument that "*the most reasonable principles of justice are those that everyone would accept and agree to from a fair position*"—a fair position in this regard being that of "a rational agent situated behind a veil of ignorance such that he does not know what place in society he will occupy."[73] From the vantage point of being in the *original position* of equality, such a person would be indifferent and would have no prior knowledge of his class, position in life, would be unaware of any risk involved, or possible benefits that may derive from making particular choices concerning any distribution of goods in the social order. "They do not know how the various alternatives will affect their own particular case and they are obliged to evaluate principles solely on the basis of general considerations."[74] And such a distribution must meet the standard of two principles of justice:[75]

- First principle—Each person is to have an equal right to the most extensive total system of equal basic liberties compatible with a similar system of liberty for all, and,
- Second principle—Social and economic inequalities are to be arranged so that they are both (a) the greatest benefit of the least advantaged, consistent with the just savings principle, and (b) attached to offices and positions open to all under conditions of fair equality of opportunity.

For Rawls, justice requires that all "social primary goods—liberty and opportunity, income and wealth, and the bases of self-respect—are to be distributed equally unless an unequal distribution of any or all of these goods is to the advantage of the least favored."[76] Even though Rawls' "theory is concerned with the basic structure of society, and the way it allocates rights, duties, wealth, power and opportunities; but underlying the 'veil of ignorance' is a moral argument whose main idea is that the distribution of income and opportunity should not be based on factors that are *arbitrary*."[77] It is also premised on that fact that "we must somehow nullify the effects of specific contingencies which put men at odds and tempt them to exploit social and natural circumstances to their own advantage."[78] In a fair distribution of social goods, although Rawls grants primacy to justice over efficiency, but one can equally argue that the two terms are inseparable since they reinforce each other; because a distribution that is fairly done could also be construed as having been done efficiently, hence would be considered just as long as each person got his or her fair share and is satisfied by it.

Many critiques[79] of the Rawlsian concept of the "veil of ignorance" point out that a *rational* agent would not necessarily be expected to operate from behind a veil from which he knows nothing about the issue he would be dealing with. On the other hand, Rawls' conception of the principle of equality based on needs, particularly of the "worst off" sector of the community in respect of income, wealth, or other goods, as well as the efficacy of the "difference principle" in all situations, seems inconsistent with the free-market ideals of the liberal capitalist economy. While the free-market economy is premised on the competitive spirit and effort of individuals and businesses, free choice with respect to market entry and exit, and the role of the invisible hand in the regulation of supply and demand, Rawls' argument would need a proactive government intervention instead of the market to redistribute basic social and economic goods.

Since the market alone, may not be able to provide a fair distribution to the fullest extent and degree that Rawls would prefer, in what areas and to what extent should the political action of government be used to justify moral arbitrariness? Perhaps, this would be applicable where existing opportunities are unequal, or where initial starting points in life are skewed in favor of one and not the other. But then this still begs the question as to whether an individual's adverse economic situation, for which the cause may be unknown or could be traced directly to the individual himself, would also evoke specific moral questions and responsibilities placed on others or the public. Are all economic and social inequalities a result of someone's moral deficiency thereby raising issues of culpability and restitution? In all, there should be a general understanding that justice cannot construct or create its own meaning; rather justice derives from the cultivation of the soul in such a way that every thought or action is directed to some good. For the simple fact that any "idea of justice supposes a rule of conduct and a sentiment which ought to sanction the rule,"[80] justice requires the exercise of moral identity and moral obligation in dealing with matters within the private or public spheres. "Moral identity has to do with how people understand themselves as moral, such as when a person who considers himself truthful always feels the pressure to engage in truth-saying as a way of validating his self-concept";[81] and as a result, moral identity functions as a self-regulatory mechanism that motivates moral action.[82]

In my own view, the most thorough explication of the idea of moral obligation is the account provided by Panaetius as illustrated by Cicero in *On Duties* III. By answering three basic questions, Panaetius argues that an individual should be able to make a choice or judgment that point in the right and just action:[83]

- Is a thing morally right or wrong?
- Is it advantageous or disadvantageous?
- If apparent right and apparent advantage clash, what is to be the basis for our choice between them?

Of the three questions, the third might seem to be the most difficult to answer, since according to some people, "advantage can never conflict with right, for the fact that everything which is morally right is advantageous, and there can be no advantage in anything which is not right."[84] But I argue that it is conceivable for right to be in conflict with advantage—*in the distribution of the advantage*. The question that ought to be asked is: Who benefits most from the advantage and who benefits least? At whose expense was the advantage achieved, and at what cost? In this regard, right can certainly conflict with advantage when the source of the advantage is at the expense of others. Rawls would certainly argue that such a right does not make if the advantage was obtained at the expense of the least-advantaged in society; and Aristotle would equally raise the concern as to whose well-being does the *advantage* serve—that of the individual or the polis?

The Case Against Majority Rule

Justice as virtue, fairness, or due process is indivisible and its meaning cannot be rightfully adjudicated by recourse to mathematical numbers.[85] That, in itself, would be a negation such that in the search for justice, we only end up undermining it. In liberal democracies, the most pluralistic basis for making political choices and decisions is by the principle of majority rule. But as a mechanism for choice-making, it does not necessarily yield its conclusions based on the best logic or facts, rather it seeks the determination of specific choices by relying on the largest number that may, in fact, have little or no bearing on the substance and accuracy of reasoning that belies the facts. The concept of majority rule does not offer the ideal choice for making most judicial decisions; hence the question arises whether it can justly be used for all choice arbitration in democratic politics? For instance, in a multiethnic society, majority rule has a curious way of making democracy undemocratic. As illustrated elsewhere,[86] if one of the major ethnic groups has a majority, then it would be able to dominate the government (especially the legislature) on an almost permanent basis as long as it does not allow its votes to split between two or more parties. Majority interests would, more often than not, trump minority or collective interests.

In his rather loose defense of majority rule, Rawls argues that "the fundamental criterion for judging any procedure is the justice of its likely outcome";[87] hence "if the various sectors of society have reasonable confidence in one another and share a common conception of justice, the rule by bare majorities may succeed fairly well."[88] But where this "underlying agreement is lacking, the majority principle becomes more difficult to justify."[89] The above Rawlsian pseudo-justification is too "thin" and does not provide sufficient grounding for the majority rule principle and therefore should be rejected for the following reasons. First, we may not be able to know the *likely* justice of the outcome a priorily until the outcome has occurred, and by then it may already be too late. Secondly, for the simple reason that liberal democracies encourage diversity and difference of opinions, the various sectors of society that Rawls talks about may not have reasonable confidence in one another nor do they share the same conception of justice all the time. In fact, the raison d'etre of liberal democratic states is the opportunity to differ and to have competing ideas about government and society. The mere fact that "different persons are situated differently will assure that some differences of power and knowledge persist, allowing agreements, even voluntary ones, to be influenced by factors arbitrary from a moral point of view."[90]

Thirdly, even if all members of society share the same views about justice (and they rarely do), still yet, the sharing of similar views has no bearing on what the outcome of justice would be. In fact, any abridgment of justice would become even more noticeable in circumstances whether all members of society share similar points of view regarding its scope and meaning.

But the use of the principle of majority rule to adjudicate specific political or moral questions may end up reinforcing not justice for all, but injustice for some. Numbers alone do not in the absolute sense justify a superiority of logic and reason nor does it constitute a demonstration of truth or evidence of reality for choosing one choice over another. Taken collectively, a majority is simply a group of individuals who have opinions and most often interests contrary to other individuals whom one calls the minority.[91] But does that in any way suggest that the majority has a command on knowledge and virtue than the minority? While lamenting the inauspicious role of majority rule in American democracy, the French diplomat Alexis de Tocqueville[92] points out that its moral claim is based essentially "on the idea that there is more enlightenment and wisdom in many men who are brought together than in one alone, more enlightenment and wisdom in the number than in the choice of legislators; hence the interest of the greatest number must be preferred to those of the minority." But in doing so, we end up enshrining a practice that, more often than not, leads to abuse of power thereby undermining the very tradition of representative democracy. This is evidenced by the fact that "once a majority has formed on a question, there are virtually no obstacles which can stop, or even slow down its march and allow it the time to listen to the complaints of those it crushes in passing; and the consequences of this are disastrous and dangerous for the future."[93] "Liberty thus, is in danger when this power finds no obstacle before it which can check its march and give it the time to moderate itself on its own."[94]

We can take two instances in American politics where the principle of majority rule only ends up making a lot of people angry and frustrated, even as they accept their fate with resigned indignation. The Electoral College vote is a procedural mechanism for electing the president of the United States, whereby in a winner-take-all contest, the winner of the majority of the popular vote in each state, takes all the Electoral College votes for that state. And this even when the winning candidate is a percentage or two more than the candidate that lost. How fair it is that after all the campaigns and expenditure of effort, time, and money; yet one does not secure a single Electoral College vote even if the losing candidate got 49 percent of the vote? For many states with millions of voters, scoring 49 percent support of the eligible voters is a lot of people not to be rewarded for. The irony in all of this is that there is no way, even if remotely, to determine whether the 51 percent that voted for the winning candidate understood the issues or are more intuitively knowledgeable than the 49 percent that voted for the other candidate. And this also applies to the winning candidate, even though the criterion for the winner-take-all is premised on the majority vote.

We can also look at the nature of voting in the US Senate where out of 100 members, a 51/49 vote would grant judgment to the policy preference or point of view of the 51. Beside the fact that 49 out of 100 is a lot of people with equally important opinions and ideas to be so easily dismissed or even seen as hopelessly defeated. In a representative democracy, do the opinions and policy preferences of the 49 Senators matter, and if so, to what extent can these be accommodated in the logic of majority rule? How do we know that the majority (51) is right and the minority (49) is wrong? While it can be argued for the sake of argument that a minority or a single Senator can hold up a debate (filibuster) on the Senate floor on an issue that he or she does not support; but then this tactic is rarely used and, in most cases, is considered a nuisance factor. Although it can also be ended by invoking a cloture or 60 votes (a majority) of members of the Senate; but then how does this method reflect the interest of justice as due process?

Although "justice is ordinarily regarded as an attribute of outcomes, whereas democracy is ordinarily regarded as an attribute of process; it can be the case that a seemingly impartial process often yields an outcome that is itself partial, giving everything to one part of the community and nothing to others."[95] And this point is equally reinforced by Keith Dowding[96] to the effect that "democratic procedures and just social outcomes are not the same thing." He argues that given the "competitive nature of democracy and the fact that most, if not all, political issues concern the distribution of scarce resources, unjust distributions (under the same theory of justice) are likely to be the norm rather than the exception."[97] As in the case of majority tyranny over the minority, and invariably so, majority rule is no less democratic for its being tyrannical; it is simply less just."[98] In his *Dilemmas of Pluralist Democracy*, Robert Dahl also proffers a cautionary note stating that "if a body of citizens were to deprive any citizen of any fundamental right necessary to the democratic process, then by its own action it would violate the criteria of the democratic process."[99] Therefore and if we accept the unvarnished premise that "the function of the political realm is to render service to individual interests and purposes, to protect citizens in the exercise of their rights, and to leave them unhindered in the pursuit of whatever individual and collective interests and purposes they might have";[100] it is debatable and even contestable to assume that the majority rule principle can be used as a feasible platform to validate and secure the full extent of these rights and interests.

Similarly, we are also confronted with the *utilitarian* argument in favor of the *greatest good of the greatest number* which, in itself, implies the aggregation of utility. But how do we accurately and without conjecture, measure every *good*, particularly those that could fall under the category of relative pleasure, benefit, leisure, comfort and the likes? And by what other criteria do we establish the *greatest* good, other than by using numbers (more people) in this regard? But do numbers alone confer entitlement to a *good* and what is the qualitative or normative relationship between a number (a numeric value) and a specific good? To what extent do mere numbers alone justify any moral compass used in the distribution or redistribution of specific public goods? For John Dewey, answers to these questions are a forgone conclusion because "institutional designs are always partial, contestable, and experimental."[101] And this problem is more magnified in the sense that most "egalitarian debates are largely about what is to be equalized and maximized—utility, welfare, resources, opportunities, capabilities, and power—but all too often say little about the institutions which are to deliver the goods."[102]

But the point remains that the "greatest good of the greatest number" is only possible if it leaves a victim in its wake; that is, by creating a *lesser* good for the *lesser* number. While impartiality is a necessary condition of both democracy and justice, it is not a sufficient condition.[103] The demands are much higher, and majority rule has been used to unnecessarily simplify it. But to grant more benefits and opportunity to "some people for no more reason than that they have more votes is ordinarily substantively unjust."[104] For the same reason that "arguments for principles of justice are supposed to deliver the institutions that are thought to follow from those principles; socially just institutions must also take into account the incentives they create for people in order to shape a society in accord with their justificatory principles."[105]

As forms of decision making and choice, the principles of majority rule and utilitarianism are economic means of resolving social and political issues for which people disagree or for which alternative methods of distribution or conflict resolution may be difficult to find. While both approaches normally end up simplifying what, in fact, are hard choices, still "economy should never be used as justification for actions which threaten the common good; and neither should the application of the 'greatest good of the greatest number' be allowed to jeopardize the constitutional guarantees of a minority."[106] "For this reason justice denies that the loss of freedom for some is made right by a greater good shared by others."[107] And to the same effect, De Tocqueville argues that the seeming "omnipotence of the majority, and the rapid and absolute manner in which its desires are complied with in the United States, not only makes the law unstable, it also exercises the same influence on the execution of the law and on the action of public administration."[108]

Ironically, while pluralist liberal democracies are supposed to entertain multiple and even divergent opinions on critical issues of public governance, but of what use will it be, if the views of some become public policy while the views of the few are of no accord? Of what use is the ideal of citizen engagement in public deliberation if at the end of the day, the vote of the many will trump the views of the few? It is on this very premise that "when a nation is divided between several great irreconcilable interests, the right of the majority is often refused acceptance because it becomes too difficult to submit to it."[109] The point is that to use the principle of majority rule to end further debate on a critical issue is very short-sighted for two main reasons. First, it is possible that continuous deliberation on an issue could yield better ideas and solutions based on individual intuitive abilities without being subjected to a vote count; and secondly, there may not be any empirical referent to suggest that majorities are always right. There is no empirical correlation between majority vote and the correctness of a choice. In the likely situation where such may seem to be the case, the outcome could be the result of random coincidences that neither the majority nor the minority could have controlled.

DUE PROCESS AND THE CONSTITUTION OF RIGHTS

The idea of due process implies that people should be treated the same way when they qualify under the same or similar conditions.[110] In the end, due process is a means of validating specific rights but is also a means of securing equal treatment and, invariably, justice. In addition to rule by precedent, judicial rulings in the United States are supposed to follow and secure due process for all. The right to due process is granted in the Fifth and Fourteenth Amendments of the US Constitution. There are two types of due process: Procedural due process grants procedural rights and justice. It seeks to answer to a basic question: Was he treated in the same way as the other person both of whom qualify for similar treatment under similar cases as applicable? The same rights, the same benefits and privileges and the same procedures of treatment that is applied to one must be applied to all under similar conditions. The other one is a substantive due process which "holds that government is barred from enforcing policies that are irrational, unfair, unreasonable, or unjust, even if such policies do not run counter to other specific constitutional prohibitions."[111] It also might ask the question whether one is able under the law to secure similar "quantity" of remedies sought in a case or whether one's share of benefits is seen as being fair and equitable. However, because of the overwhelmingly qualitative nature of due process, there may be situations where it may not be able to secure justice for all in the absolute sense of the term. Where some might claim that due process has been served, others might claim otherwise. And so, whose due process and whose justice should we claim to have been served? Because we rely on the courts to adjudicate issues of this nature, it will still require judicial opinions to make determinations on a case-by-case basis. But how and with what criterion is this determination made?

One role of the Supreme Court "is to keep peace between rival social groups adhering to rival and incompatible principles of justice by displaying a fairness which consists in even-handedness in its adjudication."[112] But how much fairness or even-handedness is displayed when the Supreme Court bases its judicial rulings on the majority vote of the Justices. There are nine Justices in the Supreme Court and five votes constitute a majority and four the minority. By this, due process and justice itself is thus reduced to numbers irrespective of the persuasiveness or superiority of the argument of the minority. When they use the principle of majority rule to make legal determinations, it becomes less of a judicial affirmation but is the equivalence of a political judgment. When they disagree on an issue, how are we to know with absolute certainty that the opinion of the majority has more substantive legal merit than that of the minority? When oftentimes the nine Justices review the same issue in the context of the same legal or constitutional provisions, but still come up with different interpretations and/or views, it could be more about inherent contradictions within such constitutional provision as opposed to lack of intuitive logic on the part of the Justices themselves. The "judgement about who is entitled to receive what service, who is to be accorded what treatment, or who is to be taxed at what rate creates legal categories that singles out this or that group for attention."[113] Therefore relying on the applicability of majority rule in the resolution of intractable judicial questions is a rather superficial way of resolving the differences within and between legal categories. Because we are not sure which side is correct except by recourse to a numeric vote that may have little to do with the actual substance of the case; judicial majority rule grants neither due process nor justice for all. And "as such, legal categories necessarily discriminate"[114]

On the June 26, 2015, ruling in *Obergefell v. Hodges*, the Justices in a 5-4 decision ruled in favor of same-sex marriage, and by implication determining such restriction as unconstitutional. Writing the majority judicial opinion in this case, Justice Anthony Kennedy invoked the due process and equal protection clauses of the Fourteenth Amendment. In the end, there was no unanimity on the part of the Justices, but the way they could resolve the deadlock was not based on the superiority or correctness of the arguments from each side. They had to resort to a political mechanism as opposed to a judicial logic. They had to vote and the resolution of the court was made by majority rule. For the fact that there is only one US Constitution, *due process* also demands that the Justices have the same understanding of *due process* as well as justice. If and when they disagree as to the meaning and the constitutional interpretation, then they are bound not to offer different judgments and adjudication in matters for which only the principle of *unanimity* can be said to secure justice and due process.

The above point can be drawn more succinctly from Thomas Hobbes' argument in the *Leviathan* stating that "when question is of the meaning of written laws, he is not the interpreter of them that writeth a commentary upon them; for commentaries are commonly more subject to cavil than the text, hence need other commentaries—and in this process, there will be no end of such interpretation."[115] But because the only way the Justices could get out of the dilemma was to apply the majority vote, the issue may still be unresolved since no side can claim that the logic of its own argument was superior to that of the other. Because a mere majority vote cannot decide that, the ruling can be seen as a political judgment in which ideology and judicial activism played central roles more than the logic and substance of the arguments. But then what type of due process and justice does the Fourteenth Amendment grant, and to whom? In addition to the *due process* provision, the equality (equal treatment under the law) clause states as follows: "No State shall - - - - - - deny to any person within its jurisdiction of the equal protection *of the laws.*" The key words in this clause are "*of the laws.*"

The rights granted by the Fourteenth Amendment are the rights of citizenship, due process, and equal treatment *under the law*. But it grants only procedural rights (the ways and means by which the law should be adjudicated or applied) and substantive rights (equal or similar sets of benefits or incentives) under or in lieu of an *existing or applicable law*. It does not and cannot be used to make law, but can only be used to enforce the law after such a law has already been made. It is therefore quite moot on what specific laws it should or not satisfy. It is not concerned about why a particular law was made; rather its relevance is about how a law has been implemented. But a separate law has to exist a priori before any claim under the equality clause of the Fourteenth Amendment can be granted or legitimized. For instance, in the same way that the equality clause of the Fourteenth Amendment must apply in the case of employment discrimination, but there is a law to which it could be referenced, and that is Title V11 of the Civil Rights Act of 1964; and it is the same with the Fair Housing Act of 1968. But then to which law does the ruling in the *Obergefell v. Hodges* apply, since there is yet to be any *existing law* legislated or passed by Congress that would satisfy the remedy being sought in this case? While *equal treatment under the law* is an acceptable judicial and political premise in the United States, it still begs the question in the *Obergefell v. Hodges* 2015: "Equal treatment under *which* law?"

It should be an issue for judicial pundits as to whether the Fourteenth Amendment by its own text and meaning can be used to make law or whether it can grant any specific right *sub silentio* (in silence) other than a right tied to an already existing law. It is for this very reason that Chief Justice Roberts wrote in his dissenting opinion in *Obergefell v. Hodges* same-sex marriage ruling stating thus "Do not celebrate the Constitution, it had nothing to do with it," pointing rather specifically that the remedy sought in this particular case cannot be found or obtained within the corpus juris of the Fourteenth Amendment. Justice Scalia joined by Justice Thomas added more scathing remarks to the effect that "the majority had strong-armed its personal values into the Constitution, executing a judicial putsch."[116] Although Justice Kennedy had written for the majority opinion citing constitutional grant of equal dignity, but neither the vote nor the opinions expressed has been able to rest continuing debate and disagreement on this issue.

Nonetheless, while the "multiplicity of fragmented concepts are used at one and the same time to express rival and incompatible social ideals and policies; they are also used to furnish us with a pluralist political rhetoric whose function is to conceal the depth of our conflicts."[117] It is the case that "in a just society, while the liberties of equal citizenship are taken as settled; the rights secured by justice are not subject to political bargaining or to the calculus of social interests."[118] And this is what the Supreme Court did in this particular case, by misreading into the Fourteenth Amendment, a right to which it does not and cannot guarantee, and a law that does not exist anywhere within its judicial horizon. In the end, it is equally important to point out that nothing in this argument suggests, let alone implies, any specific inclination for value judgment; but what the argument entails is about tasking the law and drawing out from it the specificity and meaning of its language. To the extent that "everything depends on the probable justice of the outcome, the test of constitutional arrangements is always the overall balance of justice."[119] Understood as such, "the intensity of desires or the strength of conviction on any particular issue should be irrelevant when questions of justice arise";[120] and this particular point applies to both majority and minority alike. Because justice as fairness is indivisible and must be seen as an end in itself; it is only the principle of unanimity, not majority rule that can secure justice for all including the minority. Where this is not tenable, the very idea of using the outcome of a numeric vote to make judicial determination runs afoul of the very intent and essence of justice. Justice itself becomes a victim of political judgment and mathematical reductionism rather than an outcome founded on exhaustive logic and substantive jurisprudence.

Laws are generally fraught with precedents that oftentimes run contrary to the precise meaning and intent for which they were designed. An example could be the Second Amendment to the US Constitution where an enduring debate still persists as to whether it confers individual or collective rights to bear arms—even though the text precisely indicates the right to bear arms in the context of a well-regulated militia. And this is why most judicial policy makings rarely escape political judgment, no matter how much we wish to avoid it. Democracy and justice are "compelling ideas, and many people wish to be associated with those organizations and institutions that provide for democracy and justice."[121] "Public institutions and organizations have the highest of purpose—the people's purpose; hence their job is to make the organized achievement of these purposes possible."[122] But where this balance weighs overwhelmingly in favor of the majority not by the persuasiveness or logic of the argument but simply by virtue of a numeric vote, then justice becomes untenable or is denied. Unfortunately, and despite all the best of intentions, the law can be used to serve two contradictory purposes—justice and injustice, both of which are essentially and fundamentally antithetical to each other.

In chapter 8, I discuss the role of reason in shaping political judgments by individual and state actors, and how history and experience offer a mirror through which political choices are made, particularly in matters of war and peace, nuclear proliferation and deterrence. The special case of North Korea's nuclear brinkmanship is also discussed as a classic example of how sovereign state interest rather than international norms is used as the basis for compliance or noncompliance to international obligations.

NOTES

1. Burn, A. R. 1965. *The Penguin History of Greece*. London: Penguin Books, 254.
2. Burn, A. R. 1965. *The Penguin History of Greece*, 254.
3. Burn, A. R. 1965. *The Penguin History of Greece*, 254.
4. Fritz, Kurt Von and Ernst Kapp. 1974. *Aristotle: Constitution of Athens and Related Texts*. New York: Hafner Press, 39.
5. Miller, Fred D. 1995. *Nature, Justice, and Rights in Aristotle's Politics*. Oxford: Clarendon Press, 82.
6. Raadschelders, Jos C. N. 2003. *Government: A Public Administration Perspective*. Armonk, NY: M. E. Sharpe, 126–128.
7. Starr, Chester G. 1961. *The Origins of Greek Civilization* (1100–650 BC). New York: W. W. Norton & Co., 342.
8. Starr, Chester G. 1961. *The Origins of Greek Civilization* (1100–650 BC), 342.
9. Starr, Chester G. 1961. *The Origins of Greek Civilization* (1100–650 BC), 342–343.
10. Herman, Gabriel. 2006. *Morality and Behavior in Democratic Athens: A Social History*. Cambridge, UK: Cambridge University Press, 96.
11. Herman, Gabriel. 2006. *Morality and Behavior in Democratic Athens: A Social History*, 196.
12. Herman, Gabriel. 2006. *Morality and Behavior in Democratic Athens: A Social History*, 196.

13. Herman, Gabriel. 2006. *Morality and Behavior in Democratic Athens: A Social History*, 136.

14. See the *The Laws of Plato*, particularly Book V, 112–135.

15. Andrewes, Antony. 1971. *The Greeks*. New York: Alfred A. Knopf, 176–177.

16. Andrewes, Antony. 1971. *The Greeks*, 190.

17. Andrewes, Antony. 1971. *The Greeks*, 190.

18. Plato. 1974. *The Republic*. Translated with an Introduction by Desmond Lee. 2nd ed. New York: Penguin Books, xxxii.

19. Georgiadis, Constantine. 1987. "Equitable and Equity in Aristotle." In *Justice, Law and Method in Plato and Aristotle*, edited by Spiro Panagiotou, 159–172, 163.

20. Georgiadis, Constantine. 1987. "Equitable and Equity in Aristotle." In *Justice, Law and Method in Plato and Aristotle*, edited by Spiro Panagiotou, 159–172, 163.

21. Hayek, F. A. 1960. *The Constitution of Liberty*. Chicago, IL: The University of Chicago Press, 166.

22. Hayek, F. A. 1960. *The Constitution of Liberty*, 166.

23. Hayek, F. A. 1960. *The Constitution of Liberty*, 166.

24. Wood, Neal. 1988. *Cicero's Social and Political Thought*. Berkeley, CA: University of California Press, 207.

25. This paragraph is excerpted from the author's earlier work titled Kalu N. Kalu. 2017. *Citizenship: Identity, Institutions, and the Postmodern Challenge*. New York: Routledge Publishers, 21.

26. Cicero. 1993. *On Government*. Translated by Michael Grant. London: Penguin Books, 179.

27. Strauss, Leo and Joseph Cropsey. 1972. "Montesquieu." In *History of Political Philosophy*, edited by Leo Strauss and Joseph Cropsey, 487–508. Chicago, IL: Rand McNally & Co., 489.

28. Strauss, Leo and Joseph Cropsey. 1972. "Montesquieu." In *History of Political Philosophy*, edited by Leo Strauss and Joseph Cropsey, 487–508, 488.

29. Cicero. 1993. *On Government*. Translated by Michael Grant. London: Penguin Books, 183.

30. Strauss, Leo and Joseph Cropsey. 1972. "Montesquieu." In *History of Political Philosophy*, edited by Leo Strauss and Joseph Cropsey, 487–508, 488.

31. Strauss, Leo and Joseph Cropsey. 1972. "Montesquieu." In *History of Political Philosophy*, edited by Leo Strauss and Joseph Cropsey, 487–508, 488.

32. Strauss, Leo and Joseph Cropsey. 1972. "Montesquieu." In *History of Political Philosophy*, edited by Leo Strauss and Joseph Cropsey, 487–508, 489–490. See also Montesquieu, *The Spirit of the Laws*. Translated and Edited by Anne M. Cohler, Basia Carolyn Miller, and Harold Samuel Stone. Cambridge, UK: Cambridge University Press.

33. Strauss, Leo and Joseph Cropsey. 1972. "Montesquieu." In *History of Political Philosophy*, edited by Leo Strauss and Joseph Cropsey, 487–508, 489–490. See also Montesquieu, *The Spirit of the Laws*. Translated and Edited by Anne M. Cohler, Basia Carolyn Miller, and Harold Samuel Stone. Cambridge, UK: Cambridge University Press.

34. Montesquieu. 1989. *The Spirit of the Laws*. Translated and edited by Anne M. Cohler, Basia Carolyn Miller, and Harold Samuel Stone. Cambridge: Cambridge University Press, 289.

35. Deutsch, Karl W.1966. *The Nerves of Government: Models of Political Communication and Control*. New York: The Free Press, 123.

36. Deutsch, Karl W.1966. *The Nerves of Government: Models of Political Communication and Control*, 123.

37. Luhman, Niklas. 1982. *The Differentiation of Society*. New York: Columbia University Press. See also Jonathan H. Turner. 2003. *Human Institutions: A Theory of Societal Evolution*. Lanham, MD: Rowman & Littlefield, 85.

38. Turner, Jonathan H. 2003. *Human Institutions: A Theory of Societal Evolution*, 84.

39. Luhman, N. 1987. Rechtssoziologie, Opladen: WestdeutscherVerlag. See also http://www.lawandmethod.nl/tijdschrift/lawandmethod/2015/04/lawandmethod-D-15-00001.pdf. Accessed on September 2, 2018.

40. Roermund, Berat van. 2015. Law and Functionalism: The Limited Function of Law. *ReM* 2015-04. http://www.lawandmethod.nl/tijdschrift/lawandmethod/2015/04/lawandmethod-D-15-00001.pdf. Accessed on September 2, 2018.

41. Offe, Claus. 2006. "Political Institutions and Social Power: Conceptual Explorations." In *Rethinking Political Institutions: The Art of the State*, edited by Ian Shapiro., Stephen Skowronek., and Daniel Galvin, 9–31, 19.

42. Offe, Claus. 2006. "Political Institutions and Social Power: Conceptual Explorations." In *Rethinking Political Institutions: The Art of the State*, 19.

43. Corley, Pamela, Artemus Ward, and Wendy L. Martinek. 2016. *American Judicial Process: Myth and Reality in Law and Courts*. New York: Routledge, 4.

44. Corley, Pamela, Artemus Ward, and Wendy L. Martinek. 2016. *American Judicial Process: Myth and Reality in Law and Courts*, 7.

45. Hayek, F. A. 1960. *The Constitution of Liberty*, 237.

46. Corley, Pamela, Artemus Ward, and Wendy L. Martinek. 2016. *American Judicial Process: Myth and Reality in Law and Courts*, 7.

47. Hayek, F. A. 1960. *The Constitution of Liberty*, 189.

48. Corley, Pamela, Artemus Ward, and Wendy L. Martinek. 2016. *American Judicial Process: Myth and Reality in Law and Courts*, 93.

49. Corley, Pamela, Artemus Ward, and Wendy L. Martinek. 2016. *American Judicial Process: Myth and Reality in Law and Courts*, 93.

50. Corley, Pamela, Artemus Ward, and Wendy L. Martinek. 2016. *American Judicial Process: Myth and Reality in Law and Courts*, 93. See also American Bar Association, "Model Rules of Professional Conduct," Rule 3.4.

51. Tarr, G. Alan. 2014. *Judicial Process and Judicial Policymaking*, 6th ed. Boston, MA: Wadsworth Cengage, 88.

52. Tarr, G. Alan. 2014. *Judicial Process and Judicial Policymaking*, 89.

53. Tarr, G. Alan. 2014. *Judicial Process and Judicial Policymaking*, 89.

54. Ball, Molly, and Tessa Berenson. 2018. The Cost to the Court. *Time* 192, no. 14 (September 30).

55. Ball, Molly, and Tessa Berenson. 2018. The Cost to the Court. *Time* 192, no. 14 (September 30).

56. Ball, Molly, and Tessa Berenson. 2018. The Cost to the Court. *Time* 192, no. 14 (September 31).
57. Pilon, Roger. 2018. When the Supreme Court is Everything. *Time* 192, no. 14 (September 32).
58. Corley, Pamela, Artemus Ward, and Wendy L. Martinek. 2016. *American Judicial Process: Myth and Reality in Law and Courts*, 1.
59. Jolls, Christine, Cass R. Sunstein, and Richard Thaler. 1998. "A Behavioral Approach to Law and Economics." *Stanford Law Review* 50, no. 5: 1471–1550, 1546.
60. Georgiadis, Constantine. 1987. "Equitable and Equity in Aristotle." In *Justice, Law and Method in Plato and Aristotle*, edited by Spiro Panagiotou, 159–172, 164.
61. Georgiadis, Constantine. 1987. "Equitable and Equity in Aristotle." In *Justice, Law and Method in Plato and Aristotle*, edited by Spiro Panagiotou, 159–172, 164. See also Aristotle, *Rhetoric* I, 1354a31-b11.
62. Tarr, G. Alan. 2014. *Judicial Process and Judicial Policymaking*, 6th ed. Boston, MA: Wadsworth Cengage, 13.
63. Plato. 1974. *The Republic*. Translated with an Introduction by Desmond Lee. 2nd ed. New York: Penguin Books, 42.
64. Miller, Fred D. 1995. *Nature, Justice, and Rights in Aristotle's Politics*. Oxford: Clarendon Pres, 67.
65. Plato. 1955. *The Republic*. New York: Penguin Books, 154.
66. Pangle, Thomas L. 1980. *The Laws of Plato*. Translated with Notes and Interpretive Essay by Thomas L. Pangle. New York: Basic Books, 377.
67. Pangle, Thomas L. 1980. *The Laws of Plato*, 377.
68. Cicero. 1993. *On Government*. Translated by Michael Grant. London: Penguin Books, 179.
69. Cicero. 1928. *De Re Publica and De Legibus*. With an English Translation by Clinton Walker Keyes. London: William Heinemann, 345.
70. Aristotle. 1985. Nicomachean Ethics (1135a10). Translated by Terence Irwin. Indianapolis, IN: Hackett Publishing Company.
71. Aristotle. 1985. Nicomachean Ethics, 123.
72. Aristotle. 1985. Nicomachean Ethics, 134.
73. Rawls, John. 1971. *A Theory of Justice*. Cambridge, MA: Harvard University Press, 136.
74. Rawls, John. 1971. *A Theory of Justice*, 136–137.
75. Rawls, John. 1971. *A Theory of Justice*, 302.
76. Rawls, John. 1971. *A Theory of Justice*, 303.
77. Sandel, Michael J. 2009. Justice: *What's the Right Thing to Do*? New York: Farrah, Straus and Giroux, 152–153.
78. Sandel, Michael J. 2007. *Justice: A Reader*, eds. New York: Oxford University Press, 219.
79. See Nozick, Robert. 1974. *Anarchy, State and Utopia*. New York: Basic Books; Michael J. Sandel. 1982. *Liberalism and the Limits of Justice*. New York: Cambridge University Press; Michael J. Sandel. 2007. *Justice: A Reader*. New York: Oxford University Press; and Michael J. Sandel. 2009. Justice: *What's the Right Thing to Do*? New York: Farrah, Straus and Giroux.

80. Mill, John Stuart. 2007. "Utilitarianism." In *Justice: A Reader*, ed. Michael J. Sandel, 14–47. New York: Oxford University Press, 41.

81. Clair, Judith A. 2015. "Procedural Injustice in the System of Peer Review and Scientific Misconduct." *Academy of Management Learning & Education* 14, no. 2: 159–172, 165.

82. See Aquino, K. and A. Reed. 2002. "The Self-Importance of Moral Identity." *Journal of Personality and Social Psychology* 83: 1423–1440; and Damon, W. and D. Hart. 1992. "Self-Understanding and Its Role in Social and Moral Development." In *Development Psychology: An Advanced Textbook*, 3rd ed., edited by M. H. Bornstein and E. Michael, 421–464. Hillsdale, NJ: Lawrence Erlbaum Associates Inc.

83. Cicero. 1960. *Selected Works*. Translated by Michael Grant. Harmondsworth, Middlesex, England: Penguin Books Limited, 161.

84. Cicero. 1960. *Selected Works*, 16–2163.

85. The section on "The Case Against Majority Rule" is a revised and updated excerpt from an earlier work by the author titled Kalu N. Kalu. 2017. *Citizenship: Identity, Institutions, and the Postmodern Challenge*. New York: Routledge Publishers, 41–48.

86. Kalu, Kalu N. 2008. *State Power, Autarchy, and Political Conquest in Nigerian Federalism*. Lanham, MD: Rowman & Littlefield Publishers, 188.

87. Rawls, John. 1971. *A Theory of Justice*, 230.

88. Rawls, John. 1971. *A Theory of Justice*, 231.

89. Rawls, John. 1971. *A Theory of Justice*, 231.

90. Sandel, Michael J. 1998. *Liberalism and the Limits if Justice*, 2nd ed. New York: Cambridge University Press, 114.

91. De Tocqueville, Alexis. 2000. *Democracy in America*. Translated and Annotated by Stephen D. Grant. Indianapolis, IN: Hackett Publishing Company, 106.

92. De Tocqueville, Alexis. 2000. *Democracy in America*, 103–104.

93. De Tocqueville, Alexis. 2000. *Democracy in America*, 104.

94. De Tocqueville, Alexis. 2000. *Democracy in America*, 108.

95. Goodin, Robert E. 2004. "Democracy, Justice, Impartiality." In *Justice and Democracy: Essays for Brian Barry*, edited by Keith Dowding, Robert E. Goodin, and Carole Pateman, 97–111. New York: Cambridge University Press, 98.

96. Dowding, Keith. 2004. "Are Democratic and Just Institutions the Same?" In *Justice and Democracy: Essays for Brian Barry*, 25.

97. Dowding, Keith. 2004. "Are Democratic and Just Institutions the Same?" In *Justice and Democracy: Essays for Brian Barry*, 25.

98. Goodin, Robert E. 2004. "Democracy, Justice, Impartiality." In *Justice and Democracy: Essays for Brian Barry*, 98.

99. Dahl, Robert A. 1982. *Dilemmas of Pluralist Democracy: Autonomy vs. Control*. New Haven, CT: Yale University Press, 49.

100. Oldfield, Adrian. 1998. "Citizenship and Community: Civic Republicanism and the Modern World." In *The Citizenship Debates: A Reader*, edited by Gershon-Shafir, 75–89. Minneapolis, MN: University of Minnesota Press, 76.

101. Caspary, William R. 2000. *Dewey on Democracy*. Ithaca, NY: Cornell University Press, 14.

102. Dowding, Keith. 2004. "Are Democratic and Just Institutions the Same?" In *Justice and Democracy: Essays for Brian Barry*, 9.

103. Goodin, Robert E. 2004. "Democracy, Justice, Impartiality." In *Justice and Democracy: Essays for Brian Barry*, 99.

104. Goodin, Robert E. 2004. "Democracy, Justice, Impartiality." In *Justice and Democracy: Essays for Brian Barry*, 99.

105. Dowding, Keith. 2004. "Are Democratic and Just Institutions the Same?" In *Justice and Democracy: Essays for Brian Barry*, 9–30.

106. Cooper, Terry. 1984. "Citizenship and Professionalism in Public Administration." *Public Administration Review* 44 (Special Issue): 143–149, 148.

107. Rawls, John. 2007. "Justice as Fairness." In *Justice: A Reader*, edited by Michael J. Sandel, 203–221. New York: Oxford University Press, 203.

108. De Tocqueville, Alexis. 2000. *Democracy in America*, 105.

109. De Tocqueville, Alexis. 2000.*Democracy in America*, 104.

110. The section "On Due Process and the Constitution of Rights" is a revised and updated excerpt from an earlier work by the author titled Kalu N. Kalu. 2017. *Citizenship: Identity, Institutions, and the Postmodern Challenge*. New York: Routledge Publishers, 48–52.

111. Stephens, Otis H. Jr., John M. Scheb II., and Colin Glennon. 2015. *American Constitutional Law Volume II: Civil Rights and Liberties*, 6th ed. Stamford, CT: Cengage Learning, 25.

112. MacIntyre, Alasdair. 1992. "Justice as Virtue." In *Communitarianism and Individualism*, edited by ShlomoAvineri and Avner de-Shalit, 51–64. New York: Oxford University Press, 62.

113. Ducat, Craig R. 2013. *Constitutional Interpretation*, 10th ed. Boston, MA: Wadsworth Cengage, 1142.

114. Ducat, Craig R. 2013. *Constitutional Interpretation*, 1142.

115. Hobbes, Thomas. 1994. *Leviathan*, edited by Edwin Curly based on the Latin edition of 1668. Indianapolis, IN: Hackett Publishing Company, Inc., 182.

116. Bravin, Jess. 2015. Ruling. *The Wall Street Journal*, Saturday/Sunday June 27–28, 2015, A6.

117. MacIntyre, Alasdair. 1992. "Justice as Virtue." In *Communitarianism and Individualism*, 2.

118. Rawls, John. 2007. "Justice as Fairness." In *Justice: A Reader*, 203.

119. Rawls, John. 1971. *A Theory of Justice*, 37.

120. Rawls, John. 1971. *A Theory of Justice*, 361.

121. Frederickson, H. George. 2000. "Can Bureaucracy Be Beautiful?" *Public Administration Review* 60, no. 1: 47–53, 52.

122. Frederickson, H. George. 2000. "Can Bureaucracy Be Beautiful?" *Public Administration Review*, 52.

Chapter 8

Political Reasoning and Political Judgment

Life in political society has always been one of contest between opposites, between virtue and vice, war and peace, right or wrong, and emotion versus reason. As Leo Straus points out "all political action is guided by some thought of better or worse; but the thought of better or worse implies thought of the good. The awareness of the good which guides our actions has the character of opinion; that is, it is no longer questioned but, on reflection, it proves to be questionable."[1] Because political judgment can either be the outcome of reason, emotion, opinion, or combinations of the above, how we resolve the tension between them often determines how best we are able to address competing issues of our modern society. And this should not be lost on the simple truism that the character of political knowledge and of the demands made on it has been profoundly affected by recent changes in the character of modern society where traditions that have endured for decades are now being replaced by seemingly novel and progressive ideas that have no basis either in history or in the value structures that have sustained contemporary civilization.[2] The good old days of acquiring political knowledge through reason, experience, and recourse to timeless history are "no longer sufficient because we now live in dynamic mass societies—in societies which are characterized by both immense complexity and rapid change."[3]

Constructions, assumptions, and argumentation serve important functions in the interpretations necessary for understanding how social and economic roles shape the reality of our human experience in a world of increasing uncertainty and flux. "Political processes are generally characterized by stability and incrementalism, but occasionally they produce large-scale departures from the past";[4] and this makes it all the more imperative that political judgment and action be preceded by introspective reflection anchored on reason, history, and experience as a first principle. While retrospective reflection enables us to look back at the implications of our political judgments, we should also remain mindful that the notion of *stasis* rarely applies to political systems, and even when it does, it is only temporary. And the "clearest explanation for this is that both marginal and large-scale policy changes comes from the interaction of multilevel political institutions and behavioral decision-making—a combination that creates interacting patterns of stability and flux."[5] And so the key question raised in this chapter is: In what ways do some of these create policy paradoxes that undermine the very solutions needed to solve them, and how do we live and govern in an increasingly restless world?

While many examples abound in this regard, let us just take the act of war between two or more adversaries, as an example. We should also note here that whatever may be the logic or conviction that leads countries to fight each other, the very act of going to war requires a political judgment. But it is a judgment that is either founded on reason, emotion, or a sense of retributive justice. "Judgments have a performative force: they constitute actions, actions are consequences of judgments—and to act means to implement a judgment."[6] For the fact that most states see their own involvement in war as justified because of the need to rectify a certain wrong; but reason poses a different question on whether the outcome of the war (victory or loss) and the potential cost associated with it would be enough to compensate for the wrong that was the basis for going to war in the first place? The uncertainty of war precludes an absolute answer to this because the destructiveness of the phenomenon always yields relative costs both to the victor and to the loser. Even when there is stalemate or a negotiated end to war, still yet both sides incur enormous costs. For the simple fact that the fundamental issues that led to the war are not readily resolved either by winning or losing, the lingering acrimony and effects can sway political judgment in ways that often lead to future or perpetual wars between states or communities.

The real point is that war as a means of conflict resolution (in the sense that a conflict "ends" once a victor emerges) does not necessarily resolve the issue of contention; it simply shifts it into another dimension in the continuum of social and political relations. The recorded history of what may have transpired or not during the war lingers on as a constant reminder of an injustice (depending on which side you are) that would need to be accounted for now or at a later point in time. We are constantly reminded of the banality of war ranging from the Peloponnesian war, the Crusades, the wars of the Ottoman Empire, the Thirty Year's War among the European powers, the Turkish pillage and plunder of the Armenians, World Wars I and II, the Korean wars, the Vietnam War, the Serbians versus the Kosovars, and others quite numerous to mention. While few of these have shown any clear benefits in absolute terms (except of course the Allied victory in World War II to end the scourge of Nazi Germany), several issues of contention and the memories from these wars continue to stoke expressions of anger and disapproval. So much is it that any mention of the name "Japan" in the same sentence along with "China and South Korea" in any historical account of World War II will immediately generate different reactions—all of which are founded upon different sets of histories, experiences, and memories of the war.

Although these wars have already "ended" (so to say), but yet, they still cast their gaze on contemporary interstate relations, shaping and redefining in very subtle and often introverted ways, the nature and character of our political judgment. Wars do not occur by themselves until man decides that they should; and in fighting wars, we always seem to provide one justification or the other. Justifications or what some may call rationalizations for going to war often come in the form of arguments for self-defense, to prevent aggression, to eliminate injustice, to end genocide, to restore order and peace to the system of interstate relations, or to prevent existing or potential harm. But then these seeming justifications for going to war are really not the *reasons* for going to war; rather they are political judgments that result from the *justifications* we have already made about going to war. Although reason and emotion can provide justifications for going to war, then and to the extent these justifications could be self-serving, they do not offer a normative basis for determining what is just or not. Political leaders often justify to themselves what is or is not just based on how historical or evolving events affect their own national security and survival. Political judgments derived from such *self-justifications* can generate new conflicts or reinforce existing ones that could undermine the functioning of the international system.

The literature in international relations is fraught with all kinds of examples as to why countries go to war with each other;[7] but the question rarely asked is in what ways would countries, in the absolute sense, guarantee that they would win a war? This question is relevant even if the two opposing forces are asymmetrically related both in firepower and in the resources needed to effectively prosecute a war. Certainly no country goes to war expecting to lose, or knowing fully well that it will lose. But still yet, they go to war against a more formidable adversary. Countries go to war, more or less, because they expect to win, or ceteris paribus, they can extract concessions or advantages that could suffice more than an outright loss. We have been told that political leaders, just like individuals, are rational actors; but in the same guise, states are also rational actors in the sense that their actions and preferences are based on individual decision-making. The notion that the outcome of a war is a fait accompli when a powerful state confronts a weaker adversary is not based on reason, but on the *assumption* or rule-of-thumb that it is always the case that a stronger state would "always" defeat a weaker opponent. If these were to be the case, then biblical David would not have been able to muster the courage to confront Goliath if he ever doubted his ability to slay him. For him, reason has become an article of faith and a conviction that must be redeemed even if the outcome were not known in advance.

It may be true that "reasons are causes to the extent that they provide motivation and energy for action," but it still does not tell us what makes for or constitutes *reason*. If reason is considered as something that is normatively good because it is assumed to result from an exercise based on rational logic, does that also make it just? Reason therefore requires a much more complex and deeper subjective exercise than the superficial rationalizations we often use to justify actions for which the outcome remains uncertain and highly unpredictable. As "a rational animal, man by nature possesses the power of self-control, the ability to regulate the passions, and the willpower to resist temptations. But in unsparingly succumbing to immoderate grief, anger, and violence to resolve competing issues of national interest, man abdicates the throne of reason and let passions overrule his reason."[8] Was it *reason* that led Hitler to invade Czechoslovakia on March 15, 1939, thereby initiating the process that led to World War II, and was it *reason* that led President George W. Bush to launch the invasion of Iraq in 2003? While the first ended very badly for the aggressor, the latter (the war in Iraq) is still ongoing and has since metamorphosed into something for which the end may not be forthcoming anytime soon. In both cases, the justifications given for going to war did not result in a better outcome, than if reason (rather than emotion or public opinion) had guided the political judgment.

While I do not make the claim about the unjustifiability of some wars, but to the contrary, I agree that some wars are quite justified. But the point made here is that although some wars have been fought for unreasonable excuses, the authorization as well as the concrete actions taken in the course of war is a function of political judgment. Therefore the justification for going to war (no matter how meritorious) must be set apart as a different moral category for going to war. As they say, you may start a war today, but you can never, in the absolute sense of the term, tell how or when it will end. It is on this basis that Robert Bates in his book *Prosperity and Violence*, and in what may seem as a sobering but cautionary note, points out that "civil wars entail not only the targeting and killing of enemies but also the destruction of the political structure and economic institutions within which they reside. Hence, when states collapse, warlords and criminals step in; and the order they provide assures neither security nor prosperity"[9]—the essential characteristics of development and the very institutional infrastructures necessary for the state to function effectively. It is therefore important to "defend reason against its potential abuse by those who do not understand the conditions of its effective functioning and continuous growth."[10]

REASON AND ARGUMENTATION: COMPETING EPISTEMOLOGY

Political decisions are not made in a vacuum and the policies that derive from them are not necessarily value-neutral. In the same way that political decisions can result from a bargaining process, compromise and/or accommodation, it can also be a result of unhealthy collusion, manipulations, and adversarial zero-sum games. In the end, no matter the structure of existing political institutions, checks and balances, or number of veto points that needs to be reconciled before any form of consensus; the individual or human agency remains a central actor in all political systems. While institutions may matter, there are other things that may matter even more, and at the core are individuals. Yes, it takes individuals to design institutions, and it also takes individuals to abide by the regulatory authority exercised by or through institutions. By so doing, individuals grant legitimacy to the role of institutions in regulating social behavior and action. But then it also takes individuals to undermine in fundamental ways the same institutions they have set up for social relations and for the governance of public affairs.

In addition to obeying the law, individuals also regularly break the law, overthrow duly elected governments, avoid paying their taxes, commit crimes against the state and against other individuals, undermine social conventions, and do whatever they can to undermine the established normative order. Because society cannot function effectively under this scenario, individual indiscretion and disloyalty create a collective burden for everyone—hence the necessity for law. What I want to do in the following sections is to sketch a few competing arguments and hypotheses about the nature of knowledge and how we (should) understand and apply it in the context of contemporary social and political institutions. Although I focus on three epistemological schemes (behavioralism, positivism and post-positivism, and postmodernism), my objective is not to argue in favor of one or the other, or to make a normative judgment in preference of one school of thought to the other. Rather my intention is to explore how the premise of each school allows us to advance the notion of reason (as a construct) in the various methods we use in social scientific analysis, and in understanding differences in political judgments over time.

Behavioralism

As one of the many research approaches used in political science (particularly in voting behavior and elections) as well as psychology, behavioralism[11] assumes that political institutions largely reflect underlying social forces and that the study of politics should begin with society, culture, and public opinion. While early behavioralists sought to use the methodology of the social sciences to establish cause and effect relationships; but later behavioralists (neo-behavioralism) embraced the notion of combining scientific or empirical methodology with the role of intuition (reason) in understanding political behavior and action. Though behavioral research yielded important insights into the political behavior of individuals (voting patterns and political preferences), it often explained little about actual governance or the understanding of public policy.

Because political behavior is shaped by basic attitudes that are, more often than not, "products of the subjective civic culture (beliefs, feelings, and values) within a political system; and to the extent that these draw upon different socialization processes within the broader society, individuals are therefore more prone to creating different cognitive maps that orient them toward each other as well as the political system."[12] They engage in what Karl Weick[13] calls the *selective imitation of interindividual variations*—in the sense that just as *groups* may imitate other groups, *members* within one group may imitate the actions of other members of that same group. Where this phenomenon is institutionalized, and as it morphs into different political attitudes or ideologies, it often leads to increased sociopolitical discontent, policy paralysis, or outright conflict.[14] Representative governments endeavor to take into consideration the reaction of the citizens to every major political judgment they make (i.e., the 2003 decision to go to war with Iraq), but when things do not work out the way it was speculated or intended, no amount of *mea culpa* could undo the damage brought about by a political judgment not guided by reason. More often political leaders are not guided by (or refuse to be guided by) the simple question: *what if*? That is, what if unfolding events do not turn out the way we have envisaged? But instead, most political judgments are guided by the prevailing winds of the moment, ego-boosting, and unguarded hubris—all of which help to blind us to an awareness of the constant presence of failure in all our individual or public undertakings.

While it may not be totally possible to make absolute judgment about what may, or may not happen in the future, but in most cases we can only speculate based on probabilities. But then, we should also, as part of our cognitive calculus, try to factor in the fact that we may not achieve our set objectives in the way we envision it. It is this kind of thinking that enables us to build into the framework of our actions, what I would call *shock absorbers*—to understand and/or mitigate potential setbacks or failures even before they occur. It is also a way to disabuse us from making the type of one-dimensional judgments in which "all opposition and contradictions are harmonized into a system wherein real conflict and contradictions are not really eliminated but made indivisible by a neutralizing rhetoric."[15] Because the environment in which political decisions and choices are made is also changing, individual and political judgments reinforced by the pervasiveness of technology, media, and changes in the structure of social relations often combine to produce actions that have limited or no foundation in history or precedents.

Positivism and Post-Positivism

The idea of knowledge and understanding (epistemology) and the nature of being (ontology) have been matters of central focus in the realm of philosophy of science. For both, the application of different methodological approaches in how we come to know the world or the various objects of interest and inquiry produces competing notions of *what is* or *is not*. Positivism represents the idea that empirical facts are enough to understand the truth about the object of inquiry or what we experience; hence we should use that as a basis for understanding the world so that we can best adapt to its challenges and opportunities. For positivists, "there is no room for metaphysical speculation, reason, or innate ideas."[16] Alternatively, post-positivism holds the premise that empirical observations, data, or numbers alone explain little in the sense that we can only impose our own meaning on them; and because numbers alone do not speak for themselves, we must also rely on our understanding of natural or universal principles (theory) and deductive reasoning in the scientific quest for truth concerning phenomena or objects of inquiry.

While it is often the case in positivist research (logical empiricism) that data are collected and only then subjected to interpretive comment or what Robert K. Merton calls post factum interpretations, this procedure in which observations are at hand and the interpretations are subsequently applied to the data has the logical structure of clinical inquiry, but not social scientific research.[17] And because "such post factum explanations (designed to 'explain' observations), differ in logical *function* from speciously similar procedures where the observational materials are utilized in order to derive fresh hypotheses to be confirmed by new observations; they remain only at the level of plausibility (low evidential value) rather than leading to compelling evidence (a high degree of confirmation or falsifiability)."[18] The social system in which most social science research takes place is not an environment that is in permanent stasis, but it is one characterized by complexity, flux, uncertainty, and turbulence. Social systems also harbor several elements that may lack body and texture (form), hence are practically unknown and unpredictable as to their nature and behavior. What this means is that making political decisions or judgment based exclusively on the observed data (what we see) or experience (what may have been) may preclude the fact that "alternative interpretations equally consistent with the observed data would not have been systematically explored and that inferences drawn from the interpretation also may not have been tested by competing or new observations."[19] We are told that although "falsification is a process of conjectures and refutations; hypotheses, propositions, or theories cannot be scientific unless there is the possibility of a contrary case."[20] "Pursuit of an interesting theory, even if inaccurate, can also be justified because the offshoots of the *thinking* (the things observed in the process of speculating), may themselves be more accurate."[21] It is by looking at a phenomenon or an event across all possible dimensions within which it could possibly manifest, that we begin to lay the foundation upon which reason replaces speculation as the premise for making political judgments.

And the reason why most people find a proposition interesting may not be because it tells them some truth they did not know already, but because it tells them some truth they thought they already knew was wrong.[22] It is not only important to know about *how* something or an event happened; it is equally relevant, even more so, to know *why* it happened the way it happened? While the first proposition can be deduced through observable facts tied to the event; the second proposition calls upon a broader knowledge base, ideas, experience, hunches, and basic intuition—the building blocks of reason. Like in war, all calculations and assumptions about potential victory must also be followed by an acknowledgment of a potential loss. Because states often engage in actions for which the ultimate outcome may be unpredictable in all possible manifestations; it is therefore by articulating both sides of the same coin, that we are able to direct all efforts to avoid a worst possible outcome.

Postmodernism: Uncertainty and Doubt

Postmodernism is a reactionary movement to the validity or "truthfulness" of the existence of universal principles.[23] While it maintains an antifoundational sentiment, it at the same time seeks a repudiation "of 'certainties' or universalizations in science, philosophy, religion, opinion, the arts, and morality."[24] By rejecting the "kinds of 'totalizing narratives' that claims to govern complex fields of social activity and social representation, the postmodernist rejects the possibility of knowing the past, because history is fragmented and relative."[25] It holds that because there are "no set of ultimate standards, hence all 'grand narratives' are suspect; and all traditions have to be seriously questioned and perhaps abandoned altogether."[26] Rather, social life operates on the logic of discontinuities, paradoxes, ironies, and differences. These, therefore must be appreciated, even celebrated if we are to be able to capture real truth in both form and content.

Reason is one *form* of a larger grand narrative that can be broken into various parts, because there are different currents or paths for developing the *will* to knowledge. Reason, therefore, is constitutive because it derives from the same *in itself* for which we can know its form only after it has escaped from *itself*. Considered as a process, values harbor an element of indeterminacy and non-permanency; but it depends on "how they are used, invoked, negotiated, and managed in dialogue between persons and in the individual's interaction with a situation."[27] Drawn from this premise, postmodernism has been "marked by the renunciation of foundational thought, of rules governing art, and of the ideological discourses relative to liberalism and Marxism."[28] Although liberalism and Marxism emphasize the structural role of social class and the mechanisms of production as foundational elements in state formation and social organization, postmodernists argue that "what has so far been taken as privileged discourse is merely a construction that conceals power and self-interest."[29] As we witness "disparate elements of contemporary social change give way to a range of labels, including postindustrialism, postmaterialism, post-Fordism, disorganized capitalism, and information society";[30] postmodernism has become the collective identification that captures the essence of these new developments.

Rather than searching for laws that guide action, "the postmodern theorist is committed to framing propositions that together constitute a working model tailored to an empirically verifiable situation";[31] that is tied to the reality of individual experience, sense-making, and interpretation. To the extent that life in the West is increasingly characterized by pervasive consumerism, informationalism, and distinctive "organizational forms, and by views of knowledge which dissolve history's grand narratives; the importance of postmodernism in the construction of *judgmen*t or citizenship lies not in the objective forms of media, technology, or information, but in how they are appropriated into new modes of experience and expression—how they shape identity."[32] Ironically, the postmodern emphasis on seeking different and alternate paths to self-expression seems to magnify the same thing that it wishes to avoid. It constitutes a diversification of social worlds each with its own codes of behavior, its scenes and economies, and pleasures; and for those who have access to them they do provide space in which to assert some choice and control over everyday life.[33] In Foucauldian terms, it helps to reinforce "identities and differences—elements of the self that constitute the civilization to which it is subject."[34]

Although this "anti-foundationalism rejects the notion that foundations to systems of thought and beliefs actually exist and are necessary for value judgments";[35] the postmodern culture of "anything goes" and the inclination to seek the truth by negating the very historical foundation upon which we form our own abstract notion of what the truth may be, reflects a quest for knowledge that is nether technical nor pragmatic but emancipatory. They seek continual novelty on the excuse that since "we are already caught within the infinite displacement of images; we should swim buoyantly in that flow rather than seeking firm ground."[36] Postmodernists deny the existence of a shared objective reality, and question the authenticity of that which has worked and worked well for ages. They seek change not necessarily because they have a better idea, but solely for the sake of change itself. Instead, they claim that different cultural groups live in different realities, hence a people's reality is only their *perception* or *interpretation* of the external world, and is not the world itself. Therefore, we are really creating truth as we interpret, but certainly not discovering it.[37]

This kind of blind skepticism has sought to confuse reason (rationality) with irrationality, and common sense with an unbridled ambivalence about how society and social systems evolve or have evolved overtime. It is by constructing words, symbols, and signs phrased in semantic esotericisms, that rational will formation becomes increasingly difficult when language loses its ability to communicate discrete real-world experiences.[38] "Worse, symbols interacting in hyperspace without benefit of mooring in work-a-day reality can only come back around to distort any reform of that reality."[39] Postmodern thinking has also opened up a Pandora's Box of skepticism and rejectionism with an end that is oftentimes illusory, but yet indeterminate. To seek the deconstruction of traditional institutions and structures that have withstood the test of time, simply for the thrill of a possible end that is neither here nor there, would seem to undermine the whole essence of objective rationality.

But like ideology, the postmodern argument seeks, ironically, "to unify and render manageable a social universe which because of the evident loss of worldliness has become increasingly chaotic and incomprehensible to its inhabitants";[40] and to the extent that it reflects the cognitive aspect of genuine worldliness, it hopes to offer a way for humans in their own respective selves to transform the chaotic and accidental into the patterned and explicable.[41] While the idea of universal rights and a repudiation of the state seem to have opened a loophole that fired much of the value deconstructionism engaged by postmodernists, predictions surrounding the demise of the state abound. Although, for the moment, the nation-state remains the primary vehicle in the enforcement of any universally defined rights, including matters dealing with international conventions."[42] Even if the postmodern deontological argument sounds plausible enough, its latent attempt to challenge the sovereign and regulatory authority of the state also implies a repudiation (or rather deconstruction) of the structural and normative basis of society without offering a more *functional* or replacement alternative.

As the rise of group-based claims further erode the sense of shared civic purpose and solidarity within liberal democracies,[43] the prospects of recovering traditional forms of identity in our postmodern condition could become more elusive. These accounts and others have shaped the tension underpinning the contemporary crisis in culture between seemingly extant traditionalism and an unsettled postmodern dogmatism, in the ideological "quest for total control, or rationalization of social and political life—and of history itself."[44] Fox and Miller[45] put it more succinctly to the effect that "postmodernism has come to represent the return and revenge of the different, the assertion of the random nonpattern and the unassimilable anomaly." In the continuing effort to "splice and tape cultural identities so that any reassuring sense of fixity or essence is subverted,"[46] the apparent postmodern skepticism regarding all forms of rationality brings us no comfort or closure in the sense that their own view (if any) about where the ultimate truth may lie is also in doubt. The result has been the rise of arcane cultures, romanticization of language, interpretive relativism as a new moral fabric, the rationalization of the profane, and the endless rupture of tradition to which the contemporary world is now exposed—most of which have little or no phenomenological grounding in history and in existing social practices.

POLITICAL REASONING AND INTERNATIONAL POLITICS: OF PRIDE AND PREJUDICE

The field of international politics has not been found wanting when it comes to explaining models of state behavior in the international system. Differences in the behavior of states are, in most cases, a function of the specific worldviews they have about the behavior of other states and how the internal system works or ought to work. Because we have managed to put each state into its own philosophical classification, we are thus able to make predictions about what type of political judgments it could make and under what conditions. Amid several explanatory theories of international relations and state behavior, there are the realist, idealist, or liberal institutionalist, structuralist, and constructivist explanations. While all these are fully elaborated in any text on international relations or world politics, my premise is simply to point out how they help to drive, one way or the other, the various choices states make in matters of their relations with other states or the international community.

Much of the above is tied intrinsically to how states chose to relate to other states and the frame of reference or assumptions that guide such relationships. The main argument of realism is that states relate to each other by seeking to project their own power or interests onto the international system. Notwithstanding the fact that "institutions call for the decentralized cooperation of individual sovereign states; but without any effective mechanism of command and control,"[47] states are more likely to act on their own with less regard as to how it affects the system as a whole. States do not trust each other; therefore they can never be sure about the intentions of other states and what this uncertainty may mean for their own survival. In this regard, the realist school views international politics as anarchic and one in which power projection and protection of national interest always reigns supreme. Even though "states may not be in a constant state of war with each other, they are still in a state of enduring security competition (which no amount of cooperation can eliminate), with the possibility of war always in the background."[48] But it should also be clarified that the "notion of *anarchy* as employed by realists has nothing to do with conflict or chaos; rather it is an ordering principle, which says that the international system comprises of independent political units or states that have no central authority above them"[49] And to safeguard their own security interests and increase their chances of survival, states operate in a self-help system—each on its own, and each according to its own desires.

But liberal institutionalists see it differently. By extending their "faith in human progress and the possibility of social harmony to the behavior of states, they argue that increasing the role of international institutions and other linkages between states could facilitate and promote cooperation, coordination, and nonviolent modes of conflict resolution."[50] The aim is to create a regime of rules that restrain state behavior as well as direct it in a cooperative direction. Though they acknowledge the fact that states are self-interested actors, they also believe that state interests could be made to yield to the collective interest that enhances overall system stability. For them, we can solve the relative-gains problem (where cooperation offers greater advantage for some states over other states) simply by putting in place a framework that enhances trust thereby making cheating more difficult. But since state interests can change or diverge over time, it has been difficult to eliminate the issue of trust and relative advantage in interstate relations. Liberal institutionalism accepts the notion of alliance structures between states, but then alliance structures can change in the same way identities and interests of states change over time. Alliance structures (formations) are temporary fixtures that are malleable and can change as the winds of fortune changes for each state. Because "it pays to be selfish in a self-help world, we now have a situation where todays alliance partner might be tomorrow's enemy, and today's enemy might be tomorrow's alliance partner."[51] Contemporary examples abound where Russia and Iran are cooperating with Syria in its war against the insurgency; United States and Israel cooperating with Saudi Arabia in its war against the Houthis in Yemen; and Israel cooperating with Sunni Arab Middle Eastern states to checkmate or even undermine Iran's nuclear ambitions and its geopolitical influence in Middle East politics and in the Arab world.

There is also the constructivist approach to the understanding of international relations. The theory is predicated on the assumption that ideas, beliefs, and historical experiences, shape state responses to the international system.

By rejecting realism's claim that state behavior is largely a function of the given structure of the external world and the material structure (anarchy) that defines it;[52] constructivism views international relations through the ideas, belief systems, norms, and experiences (including idiosyncrasies) that make it possible for state actors to construct different sets of realities about *what is* or *is not* in the nature of their relations to others in the international system. What "actors do in international relations, the interests they hold, and the structures within which they operate are defined by social norms and ideas rather than by objective or material conditions."[53]

Constructivism does not necessarily deny the existence of anarchy, it simply holds the view that there is no universal or specific material cause that leads to anarchy, but it is only states that can shape their own independent views of anarchy and how it may or may not influence their own behavior toward other states and the international community. Considering the way international politics is played even in such liberal institutionalist schemes like the United Nations where the votes in the General Assembly and the expression of veto power in the Security Council have generally mirrored how each state constructs its own views and opinions about important international issues—particularly on such issues as nuclear non-proliferation, the war in Syria, sanctions against Iran and North Korea, and in the use of force to resolve contentious international issues. For the simple fact that in the international system, agents or political actors can choose or modify their behaviors in response to potential advantages or disadvantages, but the constructivist argument is that "more is actually going on in the process of bargaining and choice-making than just the squaring of means to ends. Agents or political actors are also continuously instantiating and reproducing identities and narratives of who they are."[54] A conception of anarchy is therefore relative to each state's history, experience, domestic politics, and worldview; hence for Wendt, "anarchy is what states make of it."[55]

There was a time when the structure of the international system was characterized by bipolarity—the existence of two equivalent power structures that shaped the character of international politics throughout the post–World War II period (1945–1991). Because the United States and its western allies including NATO members were on one side of this bipolar divide, and the Soviet Union and its Warsaw Pact nations on the other, it was possible to maintain relative peace and stability of the international system. There were two reasons for this: the seeming existence of mutually assured destruction otherwise known as the MAD doctrine, and also the fact that each of the polar powers (the United States and the Soviet Union) was able to restrain the adventurism or excesses on the part of the members of their respective blocs, in such a way that the period in question became one of relative peace with no major conflicts between the United States and the Soviet Union—both of which have nuclear weapons and the first and second-strike capabilities to go with it.

The fall of the Berlin wall in 1989, the dissolution of the Soviet Union, and the end of the Cold War in 1991 changed all that. It threw the international system into a period of indeterminate flux and cautious optimism. It was a historic time when the global community needed answers about what was happening and how best to understand and explain the behavior of states amid the unfolding events. Although Francis Fukuyama's *End of History* and Samuel Huntington's *Clash of Civilization* theses heightened sudden interest in this debate, I am also inclined to include John Mearsheimer's *Why We Will Soon Miss the Cold War* as an extension or part of the debate. He begins the first paragraph of the article with a profound, yet prophetic statement: "*Peace, it is wonderful. I like it as much as the next man, and have no wish to be willfully gloomy at a moment when optimism about the future shape of the world abounds. Nevertheless my thesis in this essay is that we are likely soon to regret the passing of the Cold War.*"[56] Simply put, Mearsheimer bemoans the fact that the Cold War bipolar order that had maintained relative global peace for almost 50 years, would now give way to a multipolar (less regulated and chaotic) global order in which various states would now be at liberty to strike out on their own, particularly on such minor issues that could drag the two nuclear powers into a violent, more or less, nuclear confrontation. Just as between the major European powers that have fought destructive wars between them (1648–1945), untamed anarchy and a Hobbesian war-of-all against all might become the fate of the world in the absence of the bipolar regime of the Cold War.

While raising other concerns and ambivalence about the fate of nuclear proliferation and the democratic peace process in the post–Cold war era, Mearsheimer concludes that a complete end to the Cold War would create more problems than it would solve.[57] Yet he is not alone in his assessment of the emergent international order. Kenneth Waltz also argues that two *poles* will find it easier to cooperate in managing the world's common problems than will many;[58] the point being that "in a bipolar world, the important states are less likely to miscalculate their relative power position because there is less uncertainty about potential threats, and so are less likely to initiate wars by mistake."[59] The structure and "distribution of capabilities in a bipolar system encourages wariness and discourages irresponsibility; while in a multipolar world, relative power is hard to calculate because nobody can be quite sure who will side with whom in periods of conflict,"[60] or who will defect when the opportunity presents itself. But even if global events have not yet turned out completely the way Mearsheimer propositioned them, but there could be some evidence to partially vindicate his hypothesis.

Multipolarity may generate too many *conflict dyads* that could over time make it more difficult to manage or control. The international system is still evolving in such a way that new developments and orientations seem to create a more chaotic and complex world that could raise increasingly ominous prospects than what the Mearsheimer thesis could tell us. In the post–Cold War years, we have had more civil or intrastate wars than we did during the Cold War, new and more lethal weapon systems are being developed, terrorism and insurgency abound everywhere, rising narco and human trafficking, and unregulated immigration and transborder crimes; the nuclear nonproliferation regime is in flux because very few countries respect or abide by it, and the appetite to acquire nuclear weapons has become a fatal attraction for many states including totalitarian dictatorships of all kinds. Evidence suggests that "the highest nonproliferation priority today is to prevent non-state actors from acquiring nuclear weapons or nuclear technology."[61] In light of the fatal implications, a nuclear bomb smuggled into a country inside a ship or truck by non-state actors and detonated by surprise would leave no return address for a retaliatory strike or the warning signals that a missile has been launched from without.[62] Is the world of today more dangerous or more peaceful, than during the bipolar governance regime offered by the Cold war?

The Premise of War and Reason

In earlier sections of this chapter, I made specific reference to the issue of war and political reasoning. As one of the most visible avenues for the expression of political disagreements, war requires political reasoning and judgment both in its origination and its execution. From a realist perspective, the pursuit and maintenance of power is the ultimate quest of states in the international system; and war is one of the strategies that states employ in that endeavor. But then why do states seek power? The answer would depend on which variant of the realist perspective one finds most persuasive. While "Morgenthau argues that states strive to gain power because they have an innate desire for power; Waltz, on the other hand, maintains that the structure of the international system forces states to pursue power to enhance their prospects for survival"[63]—taking into consideration the anarchic nature of the international system. While Morgenthau justifies the quest for power from the perspective of *human nature realism* (that states are infused with the natural will or instinct to power just as human beings); Waltz argues that defensive realism (security and survival) makes it imperative for states to seek power.

To seek or to maintain power, states oftentimes go to war with each other. There are many reasons that states go to war with other states. However, it is not possible for outsiders to completely know why a particular state decides to go to war, simply because the motives and intentions are often quite different from the official statements presented as justifications for going to war. Some of the reasons given as to why states go to war range from the disposition of human nature to conflict, the character and personalities of political leaders, the structure and distribution of power in the international system, differences in political ideology, to deter aggression, false illusions of early victory, miscalculation of advantage, and misperception. States may even decide to go to war as a result of resentment, vindictiveness, envy, as retribution for past historical offences committed against them; or as Socrates would have it, "as a result of personal passions untampered by thoughtful objectives."[64] Decisions about war and predictions about their relative outcomes "result from complex calculations that depend on a variety of unknown and hard-to-determine factors (strategy, leadership, *esprit de corps*, capabilities, geography) and thus contain inherent uncertainty, noise, and chance."[65] In the choice-making game concerning matters of international relations and conflict, normative theorists often tell us that "rational decision makers are generally motivated by their values but constrained by their power."[66] They argue that because "rational actors do not make choices naively on the basis of their preferences alone; and that the array of individual values is modified by the realization that some courses of action, are more likely to succeed than others."[67] In the end, the most basic reality in choice making is the fact, as Daniel Little would argue, that the mechanisms that link cause and effect are typically grounded in the meaningful, intentional, behavior of individuals;[68] although I would argue that these mechanisms are similarly grounded in their irrational and unintentional behaviors.

War, generally, is always an expensive proposition and may involve prohibitive costs both to the winner and the loser. This also applies even in situations of stalemate. "Stalemates rarely seem solid to those with a strong stake in overcoming them; belligerents conjure up one set of military stratagems and schemes after another to gain the upper hand, or they hope for shifts in alliances or outside assistance to tilt the balance of power, or they gamble that their adversary will be the first to lose heart and crack."[69] Hence, stalemates are simply brief respites than can be broken at will. To the extent motives and intentions may provide the reason for going to war or for its continuation once it has started; the judgment for going to war is reflected in the overt decision made to justify going to war. It is the later that is more discernable, while the former is essentially less transparent. For the fact that a rational actor is one who applies reason (as opposed to emotion) in the political judgment to go to war; he or she is also capable of applying the same reasoning to avoid going to war, at least to the fullest extent possible. But above all, the point remains that motives and intentions we do not always know because they are hidden; and as a result, we may never know for certainty why states go to war, even when available evidence may nudge us in one direction or the other.

The prevailing notion of *jus ad bellum* offers a cautionary note for the justification to go to war. It professes what has become known as the *just war* principles—that is, "war should be fought only for a just cause—which in itself, has come to mean that initiating war is impermissible unless its purpose is to resist or reverse a terrible wrong."[70] Ironically, "how strong the presumption against war should be has been an issue of debate within the just war tradition, and the predominant views seem to have changed over time."[71] In war or in the preparation for war, states often disagree on the definition and parameters of what is *just* or not depending on which side of the debate they find themselves. But for many, the moral basis for initiating a war can only be credible if it supports the specific ends they seek.

We know that the ongoing war in Syria and Yemen (which began in the mid-2000s or even earlier) involves the role of the majors powers (United States and Russia), but it also involves other regional states such as Israel, Iran, Saudi Arabia, and others who may be offering one type of support or another, to one or the other of the belligerents. All of them have their rationalizations of why they support their side of the war. Russia sees Syria's Assad regime as a geopolitical ally and as fighting a *just cause* in self-defense as a result of internal and external aggression; the United States sees the Assad regime as a brutal one for which the Syrian opposition has a *just cause* to remove from power; while Iran sees Syria for strategic reason as part of its extended deterrence with Israel as the existential target. The Israelis, on the one hand, and for strategic reasons, see the Assad regime (albeit reluctantly) as a somewhat "stabilizing" force for politically expedient reasons (compared to the great unknown that may come if the opposition groups win), but on the other hand, does not want Syria to be used as a forward deployment base for the Iranian regime. For all practical reasons, it would seem that as these countries engage in a series of balancing behaviors, none of them can argue that its involvement in the Syrian war was not driven by a *just cause*.

It is not my objective to make the case that war should not be fought where and when necessary as the most expedient means for attaining justice and preventing the loss of lives. If humans have the intellectual capacity and the skills to transform the earth into a comfortable living space; they also ought to have the same capacity and skills to prevent its destruction. Because a war fought, even between unequal adversaries, also involves relative destruction of lives and property on both sides. I have always resisted the temptation to view its consequences in terms of cost-benefit analysis. The cost of war cannot be reduced to quantification alone, particularly in a situation where lives lost would be irreplaceable. Rather, the cost of war should be adjudged in terms of the value placed on the peace that could have been achieved in its place. If there was peace, lives would not be lost and society stands to gain more by the development that occur in times of peace as opposed to the destruction and violence that would result in the absence of peace.

Many reasons have been given as conditions for the use of force and the justification for doing so, including as a test of national will. But then, there is no need for each side to a conflict "to measure the power and will of the other relative to its own through the medium of war, if such an understanding can be achieved in another way."[72] What I want to do in the following sections is to flesh out some of these arguments while at the same time making the case that for whatever justification, use of force always results in the same outcome—destruction. War always seeks to destroy the same thing that it seeks to preserve. It presents the same security dilemma that countries face when they seek to acquire nuclear weapons because of the assumption that it makes them safe and secure by deterring attack from potential enemies. But from a security standpoint, it should make no difference. A country would not be any safer if it uses a nuclear weapon against another country that also has a nuclear deterrence, than if it never uses the nuclear weapon in the first place.

THE NUCLEAR REGIME: DETERRENCE, RATIONALITY, AND PROLIFERATION

There is a single most important reason why nuclear weapons are considered a non-conventional weapon system: it is rarely used, and countries dread using it. The theoretical association between nuclear weapons and its potential use is confounded by the notion of deterrence. Deterrence in this regard serves two strategic purposes: checkmating an enemy and also avoiding potential war. In other words, "deterrence is premised on the fact that an enemy will not strike if it knows the defender can defeat the attack or can inflict unacceptable damage in retaliation."[73] There is a divided opinion about whether deterrence works in fact; or whether deterrence essentially serves the same end that outright victory through conventional war could achieve. While much of the argument "is not that deterrence has been inappropriately rejected or embraced, it is that it is often muddled";[74] or in some situations may be the wrong strategic ploy for dealing with a serious issue in international politics. But my own contention is that deterrence is only effective if it can dissuade a potential adversary in *absolute* terms; and as such, deterrence works in contemporary international politics only on a *conditional* or *contingent* basis. States are deterred only if they choose to be deterred; and this situation holds in both symmetric and asymmetric nuclear dyads.

The governance structure that has traditionally been used to tame state behavior in the international system, particularly between the major global nuclear powers (the United States and the Soviet Union/Russia), has been the notion of mutually assured destruction (MAD Doctrine). This means that should either the United States or Russia decide to launch a preemptive nuclear strike on the other, either will face a devastating retaliatory strike and would, in fact, be committing suicide should it decide to strike first. Although the concept has now been broadened to include all other nuclear states, it still raises the question: "Do nuclear weapons embolden the states that possess them, leading to conflicts that would not have occurred in their absence?" Study by Bell and Miller point out that "rather than aggressing against more conveniently powerful states, there is evidence to show that states possessing nuclear weapons tend to initiate disputes against new and weak adversaries."[75] Because the MAD Doctrine does not remove the possibility that a state could use nuclear weapons against another, it does not offer absolute deterrence. It only offers contingent deterrence in the sense that states with nuclear weapons could still use it against another country if they have the will to do so. What is holding them back is not because they have been deterred in the absolute sense of the term, but they are only held back because they do not have the will or they have calculated that it would not be in their best interest to do so, at least for the moment. Nuclear deterrence holds not because states could not potentially attack each other with nuclear weapons, rather it is only because the practical reasoning that undergirds their choice and decision making informs otherwise.

With the number of nuclear weapons in the hands of a few states and many seeking to develop the capacity to build their own, the thought of a zero probability of nuclear war continues to diminish on a daily basis. India and Pakistan have fought several wars in the last few decades, even when it was obvious that each had nuclear weapons. In fact, Pakistan was willing to use its nuclear weapons as a last gasp to avoid imminent defeat by India. Although neither of the countries was deterred from fighting the other because it had nuclear weapons; they were only dissuaded from introducing nuclear weapons into the conflict because the political leaders were rational. But then, how does the concept of the MAD doctrine extend to North Korea, a country that has threatened to use nuclear weapons against its adversaries, including the United States and South Korea? While many pundits and analysts view the North Korean leader Kim Jong Un as an "irrational" actor, I see him otherwise. I see him as a rational actor for the simple reason that his political reasoning and judgments are driven by what he believes to be in the "best" interest of his country and regime. It is not a matter of whether or not we agree with such judgments, it is only that he has justified to himself that firing ballistic missiles across the Sea of Japan or threatening to annihilate the United States with an unimaginable nuclear Armageddon serves his strategic interest. Because he has already calculated and convinced, probably only himself, about what he stands to gain and what he may lose from engaging in such an action, he is a rational actor to the extent that he is sane enough to restrain himself within the limits of his own hubris and rhetoric. In the absence of a universal norm about what is rational or what is irrational, it would thus suggest a kind of normative relativism—in which one person's "rationality" could be another person's "irrationality," and vice versa.

Although it has never happened before between two nuclear adversaries, would it ever be possible that a state could be so obsessed that it decides to attack another with a nuclear salvo knowing fully well that it too would be annihilated in the process? Nobody ever imagined that 19 terrorists would hijack a plane and use that as a weapon of mass destruction on innocent citizens on that fateful day in September, but 9/11 happened. Since then, the world has become increasingly numb when extraordinary acts of violence or eventful *black swans* are visited on innocent people around the world. While we can say that certain acts or events are unimaginable, this premise is both false and ironic, because an event or act can only be unimaginable if it has already been imagined. Otherwise, how would we know that a thing that has never been imagined (thought of) is unimaginable? The point is, at least potentially, that a state could decide to go nuclear against its adversary, if only knowing too well that it too would also perish in the process, but is willing to take everyone with it. Even if there is a very low probability of this occurring, but if and when it does, such a state could therefore not be said to have been deterred by another country's nuclear deterrence. September 11, 2001 (9/11), was also of a very low probability and was even "unimagined" until it created a new world order where everything is now 'imaginable." Bottom line, the MAD doctrine provides neither deterrence nor security in the absolute sense of the term, and to the extent that there is always the probability that personal will, motive, or "irrationality" could preempt the use of nuclear weapons between two or more countries, then we are potentially already doomed. The contemporary world barely lives but it lives precariously only as the clock ticks by the minutes.

BRINKMANSHIP AND PROLIFERATION: THE NORTH KOREAN CONUNDRUM

There are two countries that are currently in the "eye of the storm" when it comes to the issue of nuclear proliferation: North Korea and Iran. The difference is that North Korea seems to have built the bomb, and Iran is still maneuvering to build one. But both countries are engaged in their nuclear programs in contravention of the nuclear nonproliferation treaty (NPT 1968) which they are presumably signatories. I will dwell on the North Korean case because the context in which its nuclear program evolved is one in which great power politics and ideology played a critical role. Beyond the strategic and military benefits, North Korea's main political judgment to build nuclear weapons arose out of its fear of being attacked by the United States (even if there is no basis for it), and perhaps of South Korea's fast-paced technological and security alliance with the United States. Hence the evolution of North Korea's nuclear program cannot be divulged from the history of the Korean War, the geostrategic issues of the Korean Peninsula, and in contemporary efforts at United States-North Korean nuclear diplomacy.

The Korean War began when North Korea attacked South Korea in 1950. As part of the United States' "policy of containment" against global communism, a United Nations multilateral force led by the United States was put up to defeat North Korea's aggression toward the South. The war ended in 1953, not by a full-fledged armistice, but by a tensed "cease-fire" that has since then been anchored on the US presence in the DMZ (de-militarized zone) and forward deployment bases in South Korea, Japan, and other areas of the South Pacific and the Korean Peninsula. But still yet, and due to its vehement authoritarian communist regime and behavior, North Korea remains a "pariah state" that has earned it the title as one of the three legs of the *axis of evil.* But of greatest concern to US national security and interest in the Korean Peninsula are North Korea's nuclear ambition, its continued development of ballistic missile capability, and the secrecy within North Korean society. As epitomized by North Korea, the point is that (at the barest minimum), nearly all military opponents whom the US forces are likely to meet on the future battlefield possess chemical and biological weapons and the means to deliver them, including ballistic missiles. Furthermore, the same adversaries continue to seek the acquisition of nuclear weapons which can be strategically married to other weapons of mass destruction (WMD) assets they already have.

Of greater political import is that a nuclear North Korea would dramatically change the strategic balance of power in the South Pacific and would seriously disrupt the political balancing act that has preserved the tensed peace between North and South Korea since the end of the Korean War. Currently, the US military has a decisive edge in conventional symmetrical warfare; but that is not necessarily what it will face in the future. As has been pointed out earlier, the DMZ reflects more or less an unsettled armistice between North Korea and South Korea. But even as the South reaches out to the North (with economic incentives—"carrots") in the hope of one day achieving a unified Korean federation; the North continues in its bellicose rhetoric and belligerency toward the South. Today, North Korea[76] has the third largest army in the world, with 1 million men/women in uniform, and third only to Russia and China. The combined US forces are about half that of North Korea. In addition, North Korea continues to maintain a menacing "forward deployment" of their forces with approximately two-thirds of the total based about 100 km from the South Korean border. If there were to be a breakout of hostilities, this therefore gives North Korea the advantage of over-running Seoul (capital of North Korea) in one massive push across the DMZ very early in the conflict. Note that Seoul is a few kilometers to the DMZ and has about the highest concentration of population in South Korea. In fact, Seoul stands to be turned into the first battlefield should a conflict develop between the two countries.

In 1989, North Korea suddenly started to off-load the "fuel rods" from the nuclear reactor at its Yongbyon nuclear plant.[77] This was against the advice of international inspectors and the IAEA (International Atomic Energy Agency). Between 1993 and 1994, North Korea sped up its processing of more "fuel rods" that could yield enough enriched plutonium for about six nuclear bombs; she kicked out IAEA inspectors, broke the seals on the equipment as she continued to move the "fuel rods" to more secret locations (perhaps underground plutonium enrichment facilities). This was a violation of the Nuclear Nonproliferation Treaty (NPT) which North Korea had signed. But North Korea rejected a return of the inspectors, and also argued that it would consider any economic sanctions imposed on it as "an act of war." As soon as it became evident that North Korea was seeking to start/or had started the process of plutonium enrichment, the United States considered using aerial bombardment to take out the nuclear sites at Yongbyon. As the United States considered the OPLAN 5027[78]—a strategic military plan for defeating North Korea—it was a choice between economic sanctions versus the military option. But a reprieve came in June 1994 when former president Jimmy Carter took a secret trip to North Korea and met with the leader Kim Il Sung. He informed the White House that the North Koreans were willing to negotiate an agreement with the United States on its (North Korea's) nuclear program. The United States accepted, and after a series of grueling negotiations, this led to the signing of what became known as the "Agreed Framework." The key provisions of the "Agreed Framework" were as follows:

- North Korea accepts freezing its current nuclear program and opening it up for IAEA inspections;
- It continues to maintain the "freeze" while at the same time taking steps to dismantle the nuclear facility at Yongbyon;
- On its part, the United States will provide North Korea with "fuel oil" as an energy substitute for the nuclear reactor at Yongbyon that would eventually be shut down;
- And South Korea, Japan, and the United States agreed to construct two power-generating reactors in North Korea that can only produce non-weapons grade plutonium, but a less dangerous type of fuel that would be sent abroad for reprocessing.

However, it became obvious very quickly that trusting North Korea to abide by its obligations in any agreement was like expecting a male chicken to lay an egg. The crisis exacerbated in 2003 when North Korea's current leader Kim Jong suddenly threw out the international inspectors from the Yongbyon nuclear facility, just as the United States was preoccupied and was getting ready to engage in the war with Iraq. He started to reprocess about 8000 "fuel rods" which intelligence officials agreed could allow North Korea to make more than six nuclear bombs. North Korea also unilaterally withdrew from the nonproliferation treaty (NPT) in 2003. To salvage what was left of the negotiations, the *Six-Party Talks* was then convened by China (with the blessing of the United States) to discuss the critical issues of North Korea's nuclear program. The member countries included the United States, China, Russia, Japan, North Korea, and South Korea. An agreement was reached in principle on February 13, 2007, calling for:

- North Korea's freeze of its nuclear program and Yongbyon
- Disabling all its nuclear facilities and programs
- Security guarantees for North Korea (that the United States would not attack or engage in acts of "aggression" toward it)
- Guarantees of economic aid for North Korea.

The North Koreans quickly gave the agreement a different interpretation and refused to follow through as it had originally agreed. Instead the North Koreans now sought a "one-on-one" bilateral talk with the United States, but at the same time invoked its "sovereign" right to develop its own nuclear program. The United States disagreed and also refused to hold bilateral talks with North Korea, unless it was within the context of the *six-party talks.* In July 2006, North Korea fired a series of missiles toward the Sea of Japan. Although the missiles did not achieve the required altitude or distance, it nonetheless raised further concerns of North Korea's nuclear ambition and the means to deliver its missiles. Some of these are the generic "Scud-type" missiles with a short intermediate range. But of equal concern is the *Taepodong* missiles that may have ranges between 3500 and 9300 miles. That is, some of these missiles may have the capability of reaching Alaska and the territories in the Western coast of the United States (if not further).

On October 8, 2006, North Korea announced to the world that it has successfully tested an underground nuclear explosion. Amid worldwide condemnation, the United States and U.N. Security Council swung into action regarding possible action against North Korea. Since the primary objective of the *six-party talks* has been to prevent North Korea from going nuclear, and if the evidence accurately points to the fact that it has detonated a bomb, then the options are limited. And the wild card in all this was Iran, still waiting on the sidelines to see how the United States (in particular) and the international community (in general) are able to handle this matter. The general threat assessment and issues raised by North Korea's nuclear brinkmanship further complicates the US nonproliferation initiative, and more importantly the balance of power and security in the South Pacific as well as the regional security. Among the concerns are that it would lead to:

- Increase or change in the military threat to South Korea, and US forces in South Korea and Japan.
- North Korea might sell some of the enriched plutonium to "rogue states" or terrorist groups to get desperately needed hard currency in light of its worsening economic situation.
- A nuclear North Korea unravels the strategic balance of power in the Korean Peninsula and the South Pacific region, and might lead to a serious reconsideration of Japan's post–World War II restrictions as well as the generally pacific emphasis of its Constitution. It might force Japan to seek to get rid of the Article 9 provision of its Constitution—which limits its military action only to matters of "self-defense." In other words, Japan would be more inclined to seek a new mandate to develop "offensive military capabilities." A more assertive Japan as a hemispheric power with an offensive capability will be rejected by China—of course, for historic and geopolitical reasons. While this could lead to a spiraling "arms race" throughout the region, it would also pit the United States' interest against that of China—since China, from its own World War II experience at the hands of Imperial Japan, would not want to see a re-armed and a potentially aggressive nationalist Japan.

But the calculations and political reasoning started to change in 2017 following a series of political tirades and unfriendly exchanges between President Trump and Kim Jong Un. Following intensification of talks between North Korea and South Korea, a Spring 2018 statement by North Korea that it was stopping further nuclear testing and missile launchings, and the participation of North Korean athletes and contingent in the 2018 Winter Olympic Games hosted by South Korea, a new and possibly more promising reality emerged: the Trump-Kim Summit which was held in Singapore on June 12, 2018. The meeting ended on a high but ambivalent note: agreement in principle for the complete, irreversible, and verifiable denuclearization of the Korean Peninsula, the potential removal of sanctions, cessation of hostilities, and a formal end to the (1950–1953) Korean War. As the other regional powers (Russia and China) continue to maneuver themselves into the geopolitics of the Korean Peninsula, it would seem that both sides recognize that the road to "complete" denuclearization' of North Korea or a change in its attitude that would allow it to rejoin the comity of nations, would be a long and arduous one.

But there is already a victory in all of this—that is, both sides have made the political judgment to increase the level and substance of their communication, which, hopefully would lead to a more lasting peace (devoid of war) on the Korean Peninsula with positive implications for the rest of the world. Although some argue that "the prime threat to the security of modern great powers are themselves; their greatest menace lies in their own tendency to exaggerate the dangers they face, and to respond with counterproductive belligerence."[79] As I have alluded to earlier, the North Korean leadership is composed of rational actors; they pretty well understand that they could not use their nuclear weapons on the United States, their regional adversaries, or any other country for that matter without bringing an immediate and suffocating end to the regime. A preemptive nuclear attack on South Korea or Japan would likely invoke a US response which, as part of its extended deterrence doctrine, has security arrangements with both countries under its nuclear protection umbrella.

Amid wrenching economic sanctions, North Korea, like any other country, wants economic development for its own progress and for its people, and may have become convinced that war on the Korean Peninsula (whether conventional or nonconventional) would destroy the very thing it seeks to preserve: the Kim dynasty and its hold on political authority. While South Korea, on the other hand, holds out the promise of an eventual Korean unification, it does not in itself want war because win or lose, it stands to pay a heavy and unacceptable price. In fact, most regional political pundits see a war on the Korean Peninsula as an "unwinnable war." On the basis of the above rationalizations, it would thus seem that there is a greater chance that reason would prevail over emotion. To the extent that it informs the choices political leaders make, it also tells us that extreme choices will, more often than not, lead to extreme results. And this goes to the larger picture of dealing with the environment in which oftentimes fateful judgments are made. "For many everyday judgments, we use heuristic strategies because they are relatively easy in mental effort, and undermost everyday conditions they provide good estimates."[80] It is also true that although "these heuristics may be quite helpful, they oftentimes lead to severe and systematic errors."[81] But there is a simple reason for this. The act of making a judgment involves at the same time making inferences about what is known. It is also about how that which is already known opens up the possibility through which we are able to deal with the irreducible uncertainty of making choices and decisions based on a linear model of what the future may hold. In the end, seemingly good judgments harbor within themselves, potentially bad outcomes.

In chapter 9, I shift the attention a bit by discussing the role (or lack thereof) of multilateral institutions or regimes in shaping conformity and compliance by state actors, particularly in the area of international environmental management and control. The idea is to explore the capacity of institutions in shaping collective sentiments and interests in ways that the common obligations they impose on state actors are brought to bear in addressing collective problems such as climate change, environmental pollution, and the management of public goods and common-pool resources. The chapter also discusses how *ecopolitics*, as played by different states for their own interests, has sought to undermine the regulatory authority of international environmental agreements and regimes, which, to the extent it has been argued, exposes humanity's fate to the seemingly immutable "tragedy of the commons."

NOTES

1. Strauss, Leo. 1999. "What is Political Philosophy?" In *Political Philosophy: Essential Selections*, edited by Aeon J. Skoble and Tibor R. Machan, 433–445, Upper Saddle River, NJ: Prentice Hall, 433.
2. Strauss, Leo. 1999. "What is Political Philosophy?" In *Political Philosophy: Essential Selections*, edited by Aeon J. Skoble and Tibor R. Machan, 433–445, 436.
3. Strauss, Leo. 1999. "What is Political Philosophy?" In *Political Philosophy: Essential Selections*, edited by Aeon J. Skoble and Tibor R. Machan, 433–445, 436.
4. https://www.fpzg.unizg.hr/_download/repository/Punctuated-Equilibrium_Theory.pdf, 97. Accessed on September 25, 2018.
5. https://www.fpzg.unizg.hr/_download/repository/Punctuated-Equilibrium_Theory.pdf, 98. Accessed on September 25, 2018.
6. Menke, Christoph. 2018. "Judging What Cannot be Judged: The Aporia of Aesthetic Critique." In *Judgement and Action: Fragments toward a History*, edited by Vivasvan Soni, and Thomas Pfau, 223–238, 224.
7. Stoessinger, J. G. 2010. *Why Nations go to War*. Belmont, CA: Wadsworth/Thomson Learning.
8. Kalpakgian, Mitchell. 2012. "The Ladder of Knowledge and the Ascent to Wisdom in Boethius' The Consolation of Philosophy." In *Boethius, The Consolation of Philosophy*, edited and translated by Scott Goins and Barbara H. Wyman, 177–185. San Francisco, CA: Ignatius Press, 183. I have purposely paraphrased a few words attributed to Boethius to reflect his universal notion of man as a rational animal.
9. Bates, Robert H. 2010. *Prosperity and Violence: The Political Economy of Development*, 2nd ed., New York: W. W. Norton & Co., 83.
10. Hayek, F. A. 1960. *The Constitution of Liberty*. Chicago, IL: The University of Chicago Press, 69.
11. https://www.britannica.com/topic/political-science#ref848558. Accessed on September 15, 2018.

12. Kalu, Kalu N. 2018. *Political Culture, Change, and Security Policy in Nigeria*. London: Routledge Publishers, 30.

13. Weick, Karl E. 1979. *The Social Psychology of Organizing*, 2nd ed., New York: McGraw-Hill, Inc., 25.

14. Kalu, Kalu N. 2018. *Political Culture, Change, and Security Policy in Nigeria*, 30.

15. Farr, Arnold L. 2009. *Critical Theory and Democratic Vision: Herbert Marcuse and Recent Liberation Philosophies*. Lanham, MD: Lexington Books, 94.

16. Riccucci, Norma M. 2010. *Public Administration: Traditions of Inquiry and Philosophies of Knowledge*. Washington, DC: Georgetown University Press, 50.

17. Merton, Robert K. 1968. *Social Theory and Social Structure*. New York: The free Press, 147.

18. Merton, Robert K. 1968. *Social Theory and Social Structure*, 147.

19. Merton, Robert K. 1968. *Social Theory and Social Structure*, 147.

20. Riccucci, Norma M. 2010. *Public Administration: Traditions of Inquiry and Philosophies of Knowledge*, 50.

21. Weick, Karl E. 1979. *The Social Psychology of Organizing*, 2nd ed., New York: McGraw-Hill, Inc., 59.

22. Weick, Karl E. 1979. *The Social Psychology of Organizing*, 2nd ed., 59.

23. The section titled "Postmodernism: Uncertainty and Doubt" is a revised and updated excerpt from an earlier work by the author titled *Citizenship: Identity, Institutions, and the Postmodern Challenge*. New York: Routledge Publishers, 58–60.

24. Carlton, Eric. 2006. *Politeia: Visions of the Just Society*. Madison, NJ: Farleigh Dickinson University Press, 188.

25. Carlton, Eric. 2006. *Politeia: Visions of the Just Society*, 188–189.

26. Carlton, Eric. 2006. *Politeia: Visions of the Just Society*, 186.

27. Haste, Helen. 2004. "Constructing the Citizen." *Political Psychology* 25, no. 3, 413–439, 22.

28. Aronowitz, Stanley. 1989. "Postmodernism and Politics, *Social Text, No. 21: Universal Abandon?*" *The Politics of Postmodernism*. Durham, NC: Duke University Press, 46–62, 46.

29. Aronowitz, Stanley. 1989. Postmodernism and Politics, *Social Text, No. 21: Universal Abandon? The Politics of Postmodernism*, 55–56.

30. Gilbert, Rob. 1992. "Citizenship, Education and Postmodernity." *British Journal of Sociology of Education* 13, no. 1: 51–68, 52.

31. Aronowitz, Stanley. 1989. Postmodernism and Politics, *Social Text, No. 21: Universal Abandon? The Politics of Postmodernism*, 46–62, 56.

32. Gilbert, Rob. 1992. "Citizenship, Education and Postmodernity." *British Journal of Sociology of Education*, 54. See also J.–F. Lyotard. 1984. *The Postmodern Condition: A Report on Knowledge*. Manchester, U. K: Manchester University Press.

33. Gilbert, Rob. 1992. "Citizenship, Education and Postmodernity." *British Journal of Sociology of Education,* 55.

34. Gorham, Eric. 1995. "Social Citizenship and Its Fetters." *Polity* 28, no. 1: 25–47, 45.

35. Howell, Kerry E. 2013. *An Introduction to the Philosophy of Methodology*. London: Sage Publications, 105.
36. Kolb, David. 1990. *Postmodern Sophistications: Philosophy, Architecture, and Tradition*. Chicago, IL: The University of Chicago Press, 100.
37. Rorty, Richard. 1989. *Contingency, Irony, and Solidarity*. Cambridge: Cambridge University Press, 1989. http://www.equip.org/article/the-postmodern-challenge. Accessed on September 20, 2018.
38. Fox, Charles J. 1996. "Reinventing Government as Postmodern Symbolic Politics." *Public Administration Review* 56, no. 3: 256–262.
39. Fox, Charles J. 1996. "Reinventing Government as Postmodern Symbolic Politics." *Public Administration Review*, 257.
40. Hansen, Phillip. 1993. *Hannah Arendt: Politics, History and Citizenship*. Stanford, CA: Stanford University Press, 116–117.
41. Hansen, Phillip. 1993. *Hannah Arendt: Politics, History and Citizenship*, 117.
42. Glenn, Evelyn. 2000. "Citizens and Inequality: Historical and Global Perspectives." *Social Problems* 47, 1: 1–20, 4.
43. Kymlicka, Will. 1995. *Multicultural Citizenship: A Liberal Theory of Minority Rights*. New York: Oxford University Press.
44. Hansen, Phillip. 1993. *Hannah Arendt: Politics, History and Citizenship*, 118.
45. Fox, Charles J., and Hugh T. Miller. 1995. *Postmodern Public Administration*. Thousand Oaks, CA: Sage, 45.
46. Beiner, Ronald. 2003. *Liberalism, Nationalism, Citizenship: Essays on the Problem of Political Community*. Vancouver, Canada: The University of British Columbia Press, 27.
47. Lipson, Charles. 1994. "Is the Future of Collective Security Like the Past?" In *Collective Security Beyond the Cold War*, edited by George W. Downs, 105–131. Ann Arbor, MI: University of Michigan Press, 114.
48. Mearsheimer, John J. 1994-95. "The False Promise of International Institutions." *International Security* 19, no. 31: 5–49. See also John J. Mearsheimer. 2006. "The False Promise of International Institutions." In Hans J. Morgenthau. 2005. *Politics Among Nations: The Struggle for Power and Peace*, 7th ed., 569–585, 571.
49. Mearsheimer, John J. 2006. "The False Promise of International Institutions." In Hans J. Morgenthau. 2005. *Politics Among Nations: The Struggle for Power and Peace*, 7th ed., 569–585, 571.
50. Kinsella, David, Bruce Russett, and Harvey Starr. 2013. *World Politics: Menu for Choice*, 10th ed., Boston, MA: Wadsworth, 22.
51. Mearsheimer, John J. 2006. "The False Promise of International Institutions." In Hans J. Morgenthau. 2005. *Politics Among Nations: The Struggle for Power and Peace*, 7th ed., 569–585, 573.
52. Mearsheimer, John J. 2006. "The False Promise of International Institutions." In Hans J. Morgenthau. 2005. *Politics Among Nations: The Struggle for Power and Peace*, 7th ed., 569–585, 575.
53. Barkin, Samuel J. 2006. "Realist Constructivism." In Hans J. Morgenthau. 2005. *Politics Among Nations: The Struggle for Power and Peace*, 7th ed., 585–601, 586.

54. Wendt, Alexander. 1999. *Social Theory of International Politics*. New York: Cambridge University Press, 366.

55. Alexander Wendt. 1992. "Anarchy is What States Make of it: The Social Construction of Power Politics." *International Organization* 46: 391–425.

56. Mearsheimer, John J. 1990. "Why We Will Soon Miss the Cold War." *The Atlantic Monthly* 266, no. 2: 35–50, 5.

57. Mearsheimer, John J. 1990. "Why We Will Soon Miss the Cold War." *The Atlantic Monthly* 266, no. 2: 35–50.

58. Waltz, Kenneth. 1979. *Theory of International Politics*. Boston, MA: Addison-Wesley, 161–210.

59. Waltz, Kenneth. 1979. *Theory of International Politics*, 161–210. See also Alexander Wendt. 1999. *Social Theory of International Politics*, 103.

60. Posen, Barry R. 1984. *The Sources of Military Doctrine: France, Britain, and Germany Between the World Wars*. Ithaca, NY: Cornell University Press, 63.

61. Allison, Graham T. 2004. *Nuclear Terrorism: The Ultimate Preventable Catastrophe*. New York: Owl Books/Henry Holt & Company, 130.

62. Allison, Graham T. 2004. *Nuclear Terrorism: The Ultimate Preventable Catastrophe*, 130.

63. Mearsheimer, John J. 2001. *The Tragedy of Great Power Politics*, 15.

64. Bueno de Mesquita, Bruce, and David Lalman. 1992. *War and Reason: Domestic and International Imperatives*. New Haven, CT: Yale University Press, 4.

65. Gartner, Scott Sigmund. 1997. *Strategic Assessment in War*. New Haven, CT: Yale University Press, 9.

66. Bueno de Mesquita, Bruce, and David Lalman. 1992. *War and Reason: Domestic and International Imperatives*, 19.

67. Bueno de Mesquita, Bruce, and David Lalman. 1992. *War and Reason: Domestic and International Imperatives*, 19.

68. Little, Daniel. 1991. *Varieties of Social Explanation: An Introduction to the Philosophy of Social Science*. Boulder, CO: Westview Press, 16.

69. Betts, Richard K. 2015. "Puttering with Primacy." In *The Use of Force*, 8th ed., edited by Robert J. Art and Kelly M. Green, 356–363, 358.

70. Brown, Seyom. 2015. "The Just War Tradition (Jus ad Bellum)." In *The Use of Force*, 8th ed., edited by Robert J. Art and Kelly M. Green, 69–80, 70. See also Thomas Aquinas. 1988. *On Politics and Ethics*. New York: Norton; St. Augustine. 2003. *City of God*. U. K: Penguin Books; Thucydides. 1974. *History of the Peloponnesian War*. UK: Penguin Books; Michael Walzer. 1978. *Just and Unjust Wars: A Moral Argument with Historical Illustrations*. New York: Basic Books.

71. Brown, Seyom. 2015. "The Just War Tradition (Jus ad Bellum)." In *The Use of Force*, 8th ed., edited by Robert J. Art and Kelly M. Green, 69–80, 70.

72. Posen, Barry R. 1984. *The Sources of Military Doctrine: France, Britain, and Germany Between the World Wars*. Ithaca, NY: Cornell University Press, 61.

73. Betts, Richard K. 2015. "The Lost Logic of Deterrence." In *The Use of Force*, 8th ed., edited by Robert J. Art and Kelly M. Green, 98–105, 98.

74. Betts, Richard K. 2015. "The Lost Logic of Deterrence." In *The Use of Force*, 8th ed., edited by Robert J. Art and Kelly M. Green, 98–105, 103.

75. Bell, Mark S, and Nicolas L. Miller. 2015. "Nuclear Weapons and Conflict." In *The Use of Force*, 8th ed., edited by Robert J. Art and Kelly M. Green, 318–332, 328.

76. Carter, Ashton, and William J. Perry. 1999. *Preventive Defense: A New Security Strategy for America*. Washington D. C: Brookings Institution Press, 128–132.

77. Carter, Ashton, and William J. Perry. 1999. *Preventive Defense: A New Security Strategy for America*, 128–132.

78. Carter, Ashton, and William J. Perry. 1999. *Preventive Defense: A New Security Strategy for America*, 128–132.

79. Van Evera, Stephen. 1998. "Offense, Defense, and the Causes of War." *International Security* 22, no. 4: 5–43, 43.

80. Hastie, Reid, and Robyn M. Davies. 2001. *Rational Choice in an Uncertain World: The Psychology of Judgment and Decision Making*. Thousand Oaks, CA: Sage Publications, 76.

81. Tversky, A., and D. Kahneman. 1974. "Judgement under Uncertainty: Heuristics and Biases." *Science* 185: 1124–1131, 1124.

Chapter 9

Governing the International Commons

Ecopolitics and the Limits of Regulation

The physical ecology of the earth has been changing for years due partly to increased economic and industrial activities of humans, as well as what many would consider a lack of multilateral consensus on policy changes needed to develop effective solutions to a persistent global problem with ominous consequences for mankind. To the extent that we can categorize energy and the environment as public goods or as "public property," it has become quite obvious that there are many factors that make it difficult to articulate as well as implement a sustainable global environmental policy. Among these are differences in national interests, economic and trade issues, developmental asymmetry, interest group advocacy, state sovereignty, and a passive appreciation of the urgency needed to craft a global response to contemporary international environmental problems. When different actors (states) frame the problem in different ways and see it through multiple prisms, the result is that we end up creating intractable policy controversies on an important issue that impinge on the welfare of the international system.

While the "tragedy of the commons" offers a compelling illustration of the lack of political capacity to deal with obvious environmental risks of global proportion, this chapter argues that any attempt to resolve the problem of the "commons" must also seek to resolve first, the issue of individual behavior regarding "common" property, the imperatives of state sovereignty, the nature of public goods, and the persistent problem of environmental externalities. Traditionally, national responses to multilateral issues have been driven by a regime model (or a norm-based approach) of policy making, which in most cases, seem to reduce compliance to the discretionary whims of signatory states. Although it has been pointed out that "policy responses to the issue of climate change and the likelihood of effective action, can oftentimes depend on how politicians and governments frame the issue";[1] but to the extent that issue framing influences how people process information and shape public opinion, such tactic has thus become a ready tool in the politics of global environmental policy. But what is lost in all this is that in the end, "while aggregate outcomes of government policies seem to underestimate the synergistic and interdependent nature of social-ecological relationships at different levels of effect, they ironically, also help to increase the government's vulnerability to ecological change."[2] At some point, the cumulative effect of years of neglect and inattention would generate its own set of problems that adds to the original ones, thereby undermining any collective desire and effort to deal with them in an effective manner.

Unfortunately, the advantage of using political guise to escape state responsibility to the global environmental commons is reinforced by a simple reality in interstate relations. While some states may decide to voluntarily take concrete steps in the search for remedies to the problem of global environmental change, they are often dissuaded from doing so without the visible assurance that others will follow suit in the same manner. We have been told, at least from a realist perspective, that because states do not trust the intentions of other states, the reality of international politics means that each state acts based on the general norm of self-help. But then this premise does not work quite well in the context of environmental change and politics, and the reason is quite obvious. If states accept that they have a common interest in environmental control and preservation, or that the problem exists in the first place (and is one that requires collective attention), then "the mutual recognition that each state will have to interact repeatedly with others over the long term might build the trust necessary to provide the assurance that cooperation will be forthcoming and that other states will not free-ride."[3] But the fact is that states do not always recognize the same problem all of the times. Even when they do, they often differ in their interpretation of the scope and implications of the problem, the way it is framed, and the sense of urgency which it may require. Sometimes, they might disagree on whether there is a problem in the first place, even where the ecological reality clearly suggests otherwise.

GLOBAL ECOLOGY AND EVOLUTIONARY CHANGE

According to the World Health Organization, large-scale and global environmental hazards to human health include climate change, stratospheric ozone depletion, loss of biodiversity, changes in hydrological systems and the supplies of freshwater, land degradation and stresses on food-producing systems. Among these hazards are the increasing global carbon emissions from coal and other fossil fuels which recently rose 1.4 percent in 2017—a rise attributed to economic growth and increasing energy demand in Asia and other parts of the industrialized world.[4] There are also other factors that have been pointed to as the root causes of environmental change: developmental inequalities, unsustainable industrial production and growth, and overconsumption that arise from corporate globalization and free trade. Appreciation of this scale and type of influence on human health requires a new perspective which focuses on geographic and cross-border ecosystems and on the recognition that the foundations of long-term solutions rely in great part on the continued stability and functioning of the biosphere's life-supporting systems.

This should not come as a surprise. "For more than fifty years, per capita consumption of natural resources such as wood, energy, fish, and water has been rising much faster than population growth."[5] But despite increases in consumption in places like China and India, the gulf in consumption levels within and between countries continues to demonstrate both the political and economic consequences of the different sets of stress that human activity puts on the earth's declining capacity to provide them.[6] For example, while "the 12 percent of the world's population that lives in North American and Western Europe accounts for 60 percent of private consumption spending, the one-third living in South Asia and sub-Saharan Africa accounts for only 3.2 percent."[7] And "the United States, with less than 5 percent of the global population, uses about a quarter of the world's fossil fuel resources—coal, oil, and natural gas."[8] Not only does it raise the issue of global inequality, it also raises issues of justice when about 1.4 billion people in the developing countries live on less than $1.25 a day; nearly 1 billion people lack access to safe drinking water, and 2.5 billion people live without basic sanitation.[9]

Although it would be somewhat convenient to blame the international community for much of these disparities, that should not be the case. This is the very reason why states are created—to deal with issues concerning the welfare of their citizens, to develop effective institutions, and processes of accountability, and the need to coordinate the affairs of individual states in consonance with the collective welfare of the international community. The United Nations Environmental Programme (UNEP) has convened international negotiations on major environmental conventions for the past two decades:[10] the Vienna Convention for the Protection of the Ozone Layer (1985), the Montreal Protocol on Substances that Deplete the Ozone Layer (1987), the Basel Convention on the Control of Transboundary Movements of Hazardous Wastes and Their Disposal (1989), the Convention on Biological Diversity (1992), the Rotterdam Convention on the Prior Informed Consent Procedure for Certain Hazardous Chemicals and Pesticides in International Trade (1998), and the Stockholm Convention on Persistent Organic Pollutants (2001). But most states and their political leaders, for one reason or the other, have been less willing to satisfy their obligations to these conventions. They are more concerned about the welfare of ruling oligarchs and their clientelist network which maintains effective dominance of the political and economic infrastructure of their states. They have continued to be irresponsible both in the way they govern, and also in the way they respond to issues of global environmental interest.

Although the Brundtland Commission on Environment and Development (1987) worked on the premise that more growth was compatible with a better global environmental management, it also sought for the transfer of environmental technologies and economic assistance to support sustainable development in the South. To the extent that it was sustainable to alleviate poverty, economic development was thus viewed as a positive approach toward environmental management. It followed similar argument of advocates of "open trade" regime that "restricting trade on environmental grounds would be illogical and counterproductive."[11] "Open trade fosters efficient worldwide production as well as the transfer of environmental technologies and higher standards from the North to the South";[12] in the hope that sound policies and incentives within an open trading structure would lead to much better long-term environmental management.

By categorizing environmental management and protection as a public good or as "public property," how then can we overcome such human dispositions which generally contribute to the "tragedy of the commons"? Because the long-term consequences of sociological and environmental change are yet unknown, today's solutions may be inadequate for tomorrow's problems. While the initial objective should be to achieve symmetric policy development in critical segments, the more elusive objective should be to develop a framework that evolves with changing needs, technological developments, and has the potential to contribute to a sustainable future. This chapter explores the varied nature of these environmental issues, why they have remained irreconcilable among major global actors (states, agencies, and environmental groups), and what alternative approaches and/or considerations could help resolve persistent collective action problems.

Drawing upon Aristotle's concept of the commons and its more modern corollary in the works of Garrett Hardin[13] and Elinor Ostrom,[14] I illustrate three central factors that prevent most states from initiating actions conducive to an effective global environmental regime. Hardin argues that resources held in common would be over-exploited since resource-users are individualistic; hence emphasis on private property would offer the only practical strategy to prevent the tragedy of the commons. While Ostrom's work shows that our social, environmental, and personal advancement depends on the well-being of the commons, she argues that we would need the existence of social control mechanisms that regulates the use of the commons without resorting to the exclusiveness of private property rights. But because most mechanisms of social control at the international level are anchored within the sovereign authority of the state (and the state has multiple and diverse interests), it becomes very difficult to arrive at a value-neutral model for global social control and regulation.

INTERNATIONAL REGIMES AS INSTITUTIONS

Because regimes reflect specific principles, norms, rules, and decision-making procedures which form the basis of cooperation on a particular issue in international relations; and by agreeing to it, a government voluntarily accepts external interference in the way it exploits resources within its own sovereign territory.[15] But this is the easiest part, because in the final analysis, independent state action and sovereign authority can affect other states that may, directly or indirectly, be unconnected to the action. Unilateral actions by states, more often than not, have multilateral consequences for others—thus raising the issue of the global commons. To the effect that "state power plays a major role in the decisions that are chosen by international regimes tasked with resolving coordination problems,"[16] matters get even more complicated when states have divergent interests in the solutions that are chosen to resolve them.[17]

Over the years, the combination of a growing scientific consensus on the damaging effects of carbon emission and green-house effects generated the momentum for the international convention on climate change popularly known as the Rio Earth Summit. The "Framework Convention was initially signed by 155 countries in 1992, but entered into force in 1994. While it identified a wide range of measures to enable the international community to stabilize greenhouse gas concentrations at levels that should mitigate climate change; but no firm targets or deadlines were agreed upon, and no one was committed to anything specific."[18] Although originally meant to develop a legally binding forest treaty, it settled for a non-binding statement of principles—a factor that favored the corporate interest more than that of local communities. "Institutional structures may bring opposing parties (including NGOs and other interest groups) to the negotiating table, facilitate co-operation and enhance the capacity of individual governments to implement regime commitments; but the reality of the matter is that some implementation problems lie beyond the reach of institutional solutions."[19] The reason why most states do not follow up on their environmental commitments underlies the power of localized interests and how international agreements are more likely to be held hostage to the political swings and fortunes that prevails at home.

The Kyoto Protocol

Although there has been the Montreal Protocol on *Substances that Deplete the Ozone Layer* (1987), its major weakness lay in the "need to persuade developing countries to participate in the regime, and in the fact that politicians (as was discovered later in the Ozone Trends Panel Report) had signed an agreement in advance of the scientific evidence supporting their action."[20] It was later that the development of the Kyoto Protocol (1997) became the essential framework for the United Nations Convention on Climate Change. It draws into the discussion the average annual carbon emissions by region, and at the same time illustrates the role of industrialization and economic development as central contributing factors in global warming and environmental change. The Kyoto Protocol requires developed countries to reduce emissions of six greenhouse gases, on average, by 5 per cent below 1990 levels between 2008 and 2012."[21] While this benchmark proved problematic for most countries, "the European Union agreed to reduce emissions by 8 percent below 1990 levels; the United States by 7 percent; and Japan and Canada by 6 per cent. The Russian Federation agreed to stabilize emissions at 1990 levels; and Australia negotiated an increase of 8 per cent above 1990 levels."[22]

Eventually, "the United States withdrew its support in 2001, and instead sought to reduce greenhouse gases by 18 percent over the next decade through voluntary, incentive-based, and existing mandatory measures."[23] Although the United States withdrew from the Kyoto Protocol citing its impact on its economic productivity (or rather pressured by the corporate lobby), it remains in no doubt that without United States' ratification (or a review of the exceptions given to countries like China and India), reducing emissions and meeting the stipulated targets in the nearest future will prove to be a daunting task. There was also concern about the idea of "emission trading" (the direct buying or selling emission quotas which are assigned to countries), which, in itself, would allow developing countries to sell some of their emission quotas to developed countries who will, in turn, receive emission credits—which ironically, could allow them to release more emission and pollution into the atmosphere.

The Paris Agreement

In the continuing effort to combat the effects of climate change and to reduce the global emission of greenhouse gases, the Paris Agreement came into effect on November 4, 2016. Since then, more countries have ratified the Agreement reaching a total of 125 states in 2017 (including about 55 countries that account for approximately 55 percent of global emissions), and the number is still growing. As part of the *United Nations Framework Convention on Climate Change*, the Agreement[24] seeks to bring all nations into a common cause to undertake effective measures to combat climate change and adapt to its effects. Its central aim, however, is to "strengthen the global response to the threat of climate change by agreeing to keep a global temperature rise this century well below 2 degrees Celsius above pre-industrial levels and to pursue efforts to limit further temperature increase to 1.5 degrees Celsius."[25] While the Agreement includes a requirement for a "*global stocktake*" to take place in 2023 and every five years thereafter, to assess the collective progress toward achieving the purpose of the agreement and to inform further individual action by signatory states;[26] it also allows each country to decide for itself the range and manner of contributions it would be willing to make.

However, on June 1, 2017, the United States unilaterally announced its withdrawal from the Paris Agreement (although it could only formally do this until four years after it went into effect), citing the economic disadvantages and financial burdens it imposes on the United States and its industrial productivity. "In practical terms, withdrawal from the agreement means little, since it was never submitted to the Senate for ratification";[27] but its political consequences may be reflected in the fact that "other nations are finding it harder to maintain their own commitments in view of increasing domestic political pressures"[28]—reinforced, more or less, by the action of the United States. There is no doubt that meeting the ambitious program of the Paris Agreement is challenging. But the main barrier to reaping the benefits of the transition to clean energy and mitigating severe climate change remains the lack of political will to reconcile the multiple interests for or against various provisions of the agreement.[29] It is also possible to make the case that the political will is driven by the human inclination to preserve their own self-interests, to believe what they want to believe, and to see what they want to see even in the face of competing evidence. Reduced to its implication for policy choices and decision making, the ensuing habit of selective attention often leads to a habit of adverse selection, or no selection at all.

ON THE VEXING QUESTION OF CLIMATE CHANGE

Because the long-term consequences of most environmental problems are yet unknown, today's solutions may be inadequate for tomorrow's problems. For the simple fact that the evolution of our social system does not follow the same mechanism as the evolution of species,[30] we need to develop a dynamic risk analysis matrix based on a prioritization and/or aggregation of basic human needs and their likely environmental consequences. Communicating this information, their potential health impacts and response strategies will itself serve as a policy response to climate change."[31] As conceived, "climate change is caused by the ever growing emissions of greenhouse gases produced by human activities like fossil fuel burning, industrial processes, agricultural activities, and deforestation—which help to reduce the natural absorptive capacity of the earth."[32] As "global population growth creates more people who aspire to modern lifestyles and opportunities, the quest to fulfill these aspirations often leads to unrestrained socioeconomic growth—thereby worsening the climate change phenomenon, and undermining the values that engender appreciation and protections for natural resources."[33]

However, the central issue raised by the above point is that most global environmental problems are incremental in nature and take time to manifest to a degree that must require immediate and consistent action. While scientists may have mustered crucial evidence of changes in the earth's climate and a prospective decline in its carrying capacity including the incidence of ozone depletion, many people just hear and read about these but they rarely feel its intensity in their daily lives. The debate between those who accept the incidence of climate change and those who do not misses what the real issue and imperatives are. Where there is this level of ambiguity and uncertainty, the unknown in this case becomes the most potent obstacle to finding lasting solutions. But while both sides to the debate may have a case to make, they also miss the point about the debate. And no matter which side is correct, it is a debate for which the issue of winners or losers does not and should not arise.

The point that has been missed is that, either way, something should be done to prevent the current stage of ecological decline or degradation from getting worse (accepting the notion that climate change has occurred); or to do something to prevent it from ever happening or becoming a possibility (assuming there is no incidence of climate change at the moment). The first assumption requites a reactive policy initiative, while the later suggests a proactive policy position. Even if there is no climate change in actuality, there is no guarantee that it would not happen. Would it therefore not be wise to actually take concrete steps today to make sure that it does not happen or to mitigate its deleterious effects should it ever become a fait accompli? In the alternative, and if there is climate change, what difference would it therefore make by taking action today to deal with its more empirical manifestations? What has, unfortunately been missed in this is the recognition that, for either side of the debate, there are consequences.

A reasonable person cannot expect that things will naturally remain the same with all the activities going on in our biological and human ecosystem. "The implications of climate change are not simply minor adjustments in lifestyle, increased seasonal discomfort, and shifts of flora and fauna toward the poles, but major disruptions in human life as well as in natural ecology."[34] Because change and adaptation is a natural reaction of all biological and social systems to environmental disturbances, the evolutionary paths in which that change takes is oftentimes unpredictable. Hence "global economic, demographic, and environmental macro trends, can be understood only within the context of the major changes in the physical environment produced by the explosive growth in economic activity and population growth."[35] It is for this reason that scientists have continued to raise concern about the increasing level of society's ecological footprint and the earth's carrying capacity for meeting the individual and social needs of modern society. As Scheraga et al. point out,[36] some climate change will occur as the result of natural climatic variation, and some as the result of human activities that already have altered the atmosphere and committed us to future climate changes.

But regardless of the source of change, systems that are sensitive to changes in climatic conditions (agriculture/food supply) will be affected, including human health; hence, failure to invest in adaptation can only increase the probability of severe consequences for the global future. Furthermore, even as we wrestle with environmental issues one after the other, the problem may yet not be fixed because we are currently caught up in the very habit of doing the same things that caused the problem in the first place. But then, policy action would depend on who is presenting what evidence and who believes who and at what point in time. Because of the deep ideological divide in matters concerning environmental policy making, opponents of climate change have often been more willing to launch "skeptical attacks that consistently mix scientific data, opinion and policy advice; while most public discussions have been polluted on a wide front with language and narrative that encourages negative emotions and distrust of scientific expertise and political leadership."[37] To an extent, "fostering a climate of uncertainty has now become the new normal for creating and maintaining public confusion and official inaction on climate change and for contesting research findings about future consequences of human activities on earth."[38] In the end, this can only help to increase the cognitive gap between the information being provided and the trust and political will critical to making the tough decisions needed to solve them.[39]

THE POLITICS OF ENVIRONMENTAL MANAGEMENT: WHY REGULATION FAILS

While there have been several reasons adduced as to the causes of global climate change, efforts to agree on common solutions to global problems have generally met with resistance. For example, while "the European Union, Japan, and Canada have supported efforts to combat climate change, the United States and Australia have remained skeptical, at times even questioning the science of global warming."[40] The number of international and regional environmental negotiations has been increasing steadily since the 1970s, and today there are over 450 multilateral environmental agreements,"[41] but still many factors and consideration prevent a global consensus both in policy development and implementation. Among these are lack of credible commitments and the problem of mutual monitoring[42]—because states generally seek to keep their aces closer to the chest.

The inherent competitive order of the international system creates a condition of *anarchy* where states look out primarily for their own interests, partly because they do not trust the intentions of the other states. Anarchy, here means the "absence of hierarchy, specifically the absence of a world government with recognized authority to maintain order and make rules."[43] But even where this order may partly exist (such as the United Nations), the will of the majority of the states in the General Assembly can easily be thwarted by the veto power of one or more members of the Security Council. As a result, "this structural conflict has impacted negotiations on global and regional commons issues—such as ozone depletion, climate change, fisheries in the high seas, as well as negotiations on problems where air and water pollution cross national borders."[44] But the more profound aspect of this is that "environmental issues do no wait for the policy process; and as negotiations and disagreements continue, more species become extinct, biodiversity declines, forests are cut down, land is degraded, GHGs (greenhouse gases) are emitted into the atmosphere, toxic chemicals are released and accumulate, and hazardous wastes continue to be disposed improperly."[45] As the process of regime creation and/or modification drags on, environmental problems get worse and their adverse effects become more manifest and pronounced at various levels of intensity and scope.

There is also the case of implementation deficit or situations where states agree on the mechanisms for dealing with a particular environmental issue, but for one reason or the other, they eventually renege or fall short when the time comes for its full implementation. "Given the piecemeal approach to policy issues, the reactive and incremental nature of the policy making process means that most environmental policies lack a comprehensive and cohesive structure; and policy makers are often forced to cobble together disparate policy options in an effort to deal with different challenges."[46] Modifying regulatory structures is very hard and time-consuming, simply because it requires additional funding that may not be readily available; and secondly, it may run head-on to a coalition of interests that could galvanize in opposition to any regulatory changes that seeks to undermine institutionalized economic or political interests. Because individual or social actors are "subject to confirmatory bias in the way they interpret information; the interaction of biased assimilation with differences in the trust an actor ascribes to various other members of a policy system may lead to complex dynamics that in many cases will be antithetical to social learning for sustainability and adaptive management."[47] As a result, compliance with and reducing environmental impacts becomes more challenging or difficult to follow through because they seem to go against a priorily held belief systems or preferences.

On the premise that "environmental problems are typically long-term challenges, with causes that are rooted in well-established patterns and practices, they therefore require similarly long-term thinking and action."[48] To change existing practices to conform to prevailing environmental challenges also requires re-educating and reconditioning individuals and societies into new patterns of behavior and orientations that are oftentimes difficult to sustain in an effective manner. There is also the issue of regulatory fatigue in which too many legal or administrative restrictions generate problems that makes compliance more technically and financially costly. Because interest groups mount continuous pressure on law makers and administrative agencies alike, the strict standards necessary for effective implementation are often compromised. Because administrative flexibility often creates a situation where slippage may occur between policy and implementation,[49] it can also be argued that the implementing agencies themselves can partly be blamed for the ineffectiveness of the policies for which they have been designated.

There is also the crucial issue of trust and how it affects collaborative and compliance actions and the risk-taking propensity of social actors over time. As a critical factor in commons governance, the generation of trust in the scientific information or trust in the viability of the solutions proffered to address long-term effects emanating from the use of common pool resources, can oftentimes work at cross-purposes to undermine the collective confidence needed to build collaborative consensus. Other problems as highlighted by Peter Dauvergen are also of note:[50] States may change their minds even after signing an agreement (or consenting to a regime) and then withdrawing later. Regimes continue to evolve even after implementation begins, strengthening and weakening as norms shift (or as negotiators amend the formal rules).

Many environmental regimes are weak or non-binding, with little influence over the behavior of states and private firms; and ongoing research (and resulting debates) within the scientific community can make it hard to create and maintain a scientific consensus on the causes, consequences, and solutions for particular ecological problems. Furthermore, corporations can exploit the resulting uncertainty common to the scientific method to further delay negotiations or weaken regimes (or to prolong the uncertainty). The domestic political influence of corporations, lobby groups, and bureaucracies may work to weaken national legislation designed to meet international obligations. And above all, the priority of all states in maintaining economic growth can also mean that international negotiators compromise and avoid strict measures entailing economic costs. As Hardin would have it, the cumulative effect of these factors results in a situation where the global community reflects the natural drift of a system of sovereign states toward a tragedy of the commons.

The Logic of the Commons

Garrett Hardin's[51]work paints a vivid portrait of how "ruination is the destination toward which all men rush," as each pursues his own best interest in a society that believes in the freedom of the commons—where without controls, the logic of personal gain will inevitably overfill and destroy the very pasture upon which mankind relies for his common subsistence and well-being. This therefore helps to explain the seemingly intractable problem of environmental degradation in contemporary societies. "The systematic exploitation and pollution of the environment, is set to continue since individual corporations and states, despite a clear collective interest, choose not to impose upon themselves the costs of unilateral environmental action."[52] But instead, the anticipation of free-riding is sufficient to ensure that corporations and states do not burden themselves with additional costs and taxes[53]—thereby preventing the formulation and implementation of effective long-term solutions to a genuinely global problem.

The real question therefore is "why do states refuse to cooperate or choose to renege on their commitments when problems that require genuinely global solutions could also spell adverse consequences for them if nothing is done in time?" A reference to Aristotle's account in Book II of *The Politics* will be illustrative in answering this question. In his critic of the "virtues" of common ownership or public property as advanced in Plato's *Republic*, Aristotle argues that "while it may be an admirable state of affairs where all say the same thing, it would nonetheless be an impossible state of affairs."[54] For him, the foremost drawback to common ownership is that the greater the number of owners, the less the respect for the property; hence people are much more careful of their own possession than those communally owned, and they exercise care over public property only insofar as they are personally affected.

When a "public good" or public property is viewed in light of common ownership (communal possession or as a common pool resource), "the thought that someone else is looking after it tends to make others careless of it; and as a result no person will concern himself very much about any of them."[55] Naturally, people are more likely to be more appreciative as well as take good care of that which they can call "mine" (private property), as opposed to that which they can call "ours" (public property). We can therefore make the case that the problem posed by the tragedy of the commons is a problem deeply ingrained in human behavior, the natural inclination to safeguard self-interest in place of the public interest. It is this disposition that has unfortunately been projected unto the state, hence when states shirk their responsibilities or seek to "free-ride" on multilateral environmental obligations, it offers a mirror though which we can see the downside of collective action and multilateral policy implementation.

But then, the tragedy of the commons also raises not only an existential question for mankind, but also a question of human necessity. Although growth in population would seem to worsen the tragedy of the commons, but then the least of all solutions would be to stop human breeding if that is ever possible. It would thus seem that the whole idea behind the phenomenon of the commons is a graphic illustration of the unavoidable circumstance of man's existence—the finite nature of available natural resources and the likely consequences of the stress which we have come to impose on the earth's carrying capacity. It therefore leaves us little or no choice in mitigating the negative effects, and unless appropriate causal forces can be found to maintain human environmental demands in a sustainable equilibrium, then the incremental destruction of the earth's ecosystem would eventually become tragic—made even worse by everyday human activity.[56] Because every *effect* must naturally have a *cause*, it then suggests that whatever we do in the course of human existence and adaptation must of necessity generate its "own tragedy."

The domestic imperatives of individual states have remained obdurate in shaping national responses to the collective objective of developing effective environmental standards and control; but in order to change the behavior of states, we must first seek to change the behavior of the individuals that make up the state. And it is this behavior which is all-too common projected outward to influence the larger sociopolitical and biological environment in which we live. To address the tragedy of commons, we must start to exert some means of individual and social control as the foundation upon which we can frame a more structured regulatory environmental regime at the local and state levels. Because all aspects of human endeavor is essentially impacted by the tragedy of the commons (even those that are well-intentioned), Hardin's conclusion regarding mankind's fate in light of this situation is quite profound. He concludes that the problem posed by the "commons" has no technical solutions but requires a fundamental extension of morality, "hence if the great powers continue to look for solutions in the areas of science and technology only, the result will be to worsen the situation."[57]

The above sentiment may, in fact, support Elinor Ostrom's argument to the contrary regarding the immutable conditions to which Hardin's tragedy of the commons imposes on mankind. In her assessment, Ostrom does not see the tragedy of the commons as a forgone conclusion to which mankind could not escape or adapt, but she sees it as an "empirical outcome dependent on the institutions governing access, utilization, management, exclusion, ownership and transfer of ownership."[58] These types of institutions and the normative basis for their acceptance already existed in several of the cultural contexts that she studied, hence have been the basis for dealing with the compliance issues (collective action and coordination problems) that have prevented the tragedy of the commons from manifesting; and if well sustained would still do so for the foreseeable future. To the extent that the "tragedy of the commons" offers a compelling logic that explains the lack of political will to dealing with the complex issues surrounding global energy and environmental needs, the central argument is that any effort to reconcile the problem of the "commons" to the practical realities of state sovereignty and interests must also seek to resolve first, the nature of individual behavior regarding "common" property. It should also reconcile that with the imperatives of state sovereignty, the nature of public goods, and the persistent problem of externalities and market failures.

Hardin argues that resources held in common would be over-exploited since resource-users are individualistic; hence emphasis on private property would offer the only practical strategy to prevent the tragedy of the commons. While Ostrom's work shows that our social, environmental and personal advancement depends on the well-being of the commons, she argues that we would need the existence of social control mechanisms that regulate the use of the commons without resorting to the exclusiveness of private property rights. But because most mechanisms of social control at the international level are anchored within the sovereign authority of the state (and the state has multiple and diverse interests), it becomes very difficult to arrive at a value-neutral model for multilateral social control and regulation—a crucial factor that makes it difficult to resolve persistent collection action problems. This argument resonates rather well when considered in terms of the interrelated aspects of the issues. "Environmental issues such as deforestation, climate change, and pollution are impacted by population growth and movements, and these issues also affect people's health and well-being. States competing in a global economy seek economic growth, often at the expense of the environment through the burning of fossil fuels such as coal that emit carbon dioxide into the atmosphere, leading to global warming."[59]

The "interconnectedness of ecosystems means that many problems are non-reducible, hence cannot be resolved by addressing individual parts in isolation."[60] The same goes for the inexhaustible quest by states for development and the inability to delink economic growth from energy (fossil fuel) use. This means that we must correspondingly address the mutually interdependent effects of all three environments (human/individual, sociopolitical/cultural, and physical-biological) in such a way that by strengthening the parts, the whole can survive and endure. Whether by design or default, as soon as we begin to politicize crucial environmental issues, it invariably turns into an argument between opposing political ideologies—thereby inhibiting the timely formulation and implementation of effective long-term solutions to a genuinely multilateral problem.

The Nature of Public Goods

The market analogy implied here is meant to stress the collective utility of viewing healthy environmental management as a *public good*—a good characterized by the lack of ability to create exclusion and the jointness of their consumption. Because anyone can have access to these goods once they are produced (clean air, oil clean up on the beaches, removal of toxic pollutants from the water), consumers (individuals, states, corporations) will misrepresent their demand for such goods as they can obtain them (as well as "free-ride") once they are produced.[61] Hence, a clean and healthy environment construed as a *public good* means that it cannot practically be withheld from an individual (corporation or state) without withholding it from all (the non-excludability criterion) and for which the marginal cost of an additional person consuming or benefiting from it once it has been produced, is zero.[62] Such is the case that whenever one person (or state) cannot be excluded from the benefits that others provide, each person (or state) is motivated not to contribute to the joint effort (at least optimally), but to "free-ride" on the efforts of others; and if all participants chose to "free-ride," then the collective benefit (healthy environmental management) will not be produced.[63]

For an environmental management regime to serve its purpose of sustaining a healthy ecosystem, biodiversity, and quality of life, it has to be maintained for the long term. Because contributions that states make with regard to the maintenance of public goods (the environmental commons) is akin to a form of taxation, should they therefore be held accountable in the same way that individuals are when they happen to shirk the obligation to pay their taxes? But fulfilling such requirements demands credible commitments and a sense of mutual monitoring among state actors in the international community. To the extent that states must solve the commitment problem without resorting to an external enforcer; "they then have to motivate themselves to monitor activities and be willing to impose sanctions to keep conformance high."[64] But states generally lack the political will (or are reluctant) to expend the extra resources needed to monitor compliance. In fact, each of them is equally disposed to take advantage of the very system they seek to monitor should things work against their own self-interest. Ironically, they understand the simple mantra: "states that comply today may, of necessity, be tomorrow's violators."

To address the tragedy of the commons, we must start to exert some means of individual and social control as the foundation upon which we can frame a more structured regulatory energy and environmental regime at the sovereign state level. This means that we must correspondingly address the mutually interdependent effects of all five segments (individual, sociocultural, political, environmental, and economic) in such a way that by strengthening the parts, the whole can survive and endure. But this will also depend on how we can mitigate the relative asymmetry in the developmental capacities of states in the international system which, in itself, raises differential compliance, monitoring, and coordination costs for each of the states. Relative transaction costs may put the burden of compliance on those states that are able and willing to bear them. They may also be dissuaded by the prevailing *assurance problem* in the sense that not only do they want and cherish effective environmental management and are willing and able to pay for it; but they are less sure that others equally likely to benefit from this, would be able to contribute enough or even willing to pay to achieve the objective.

In some ways, the real issue might be less about the differences in compliance costs, but may rest more on existing evidence of demonstrable commitment by all parties involved no matter the difference in relative contributions. And it is, perhaps for this reason, that Ostrom and Ostrom[65] argue that if any action can be taken under a set of decision rules where the benefits to each individual (in this case states) can be expected to exceed the costs, and cost can be fairly proportioned among the beneficiaries, each individual (state) would have an incentive to agree to a form of collective organization (or regime of norms), and would forego holdout strategies and procure the joint consumption good. While some of the above approach may, in fact, be true in the current environmental management and governance protocol, I think the real "holdout" here is the actor's (or a state's) independent and comparative assessment of what is fair or not in terms of proportionality, including acceptance of the measures by which the ideal of fairness has been established. At the moment, we do not have a consensus on what constitutes fairness and under what circumstances and conditions it should mostly apply.

Interdependence and the Problem of Externalities

This argument resonates rather well when we consider the interrelated aspects of human consumption, energy exploration, and environmental issues. "Environmental issues such as deforestation, climate change, and pollution are impacted by population growth and movements, industrial and resource exploration activities, and these issues also affect people's health and well-being; states competing in a global economy seek economic growth, often at the expense of the environment through the burning of fossil fuels such as coal that emit carbon dioxide into the atmosphere, leading to global warming."[66] "The interconnectedness of ecosystems means that many problems are non-reducible, hence cannot be resolved by addressing individual parts in isolation."[67] The same goes for the inexhaustible quest by states for development and the inability to delink economic growth from energy (fossil fuel) use. The point is that "increased interdependence creates novel and difficult-to-foresee vulnerabilities in social-ecological systems, which often appear unrelated and which may have considerable geographic distance between them."[68] Whether by design or default, as soon as we begin to politicize crucial energy and environmental issues, it invariably turns into an argument between opposing ideologies. The result is a level of indifference, negation, and burden-shifting that, in the end, worsens the situation for everyone.

In economic terms, externalities or spillover-effects are considered market failures, simply because they reflect consequences (costs) for society that are not captured in the market price of goods and services. In environmental terms, pollution (for example) results in a negative externality when (as is generally the case) producers do not pay the financial or health costs that their activities impose on society. Because it is very difficult to determine where and how far a case of pollution in one country would be consequential for other countries both near and far—a development generally known as *ecological shadow,*—the transboundary effects of environmental externalities raise both a legal and a sovereignty issue. The "increasingly consolidated structure of global markets creates circumstances of nested vulnerabilities, in which shocks at the global scale cascade down to affect local livelihoods and welfare." That is, as environmental stress moves social-ecological systems nearer to thresholds of critical change, the response of even small communities to economic shocks or to new opportunities and modes of adaptation may trigger relative vulnerabilities elsewhere.[69]

Even though there have been various efforts such as "Principle 21" produced under the 1972 Stockholm Conference that sought to combine sovereignty over national resources with state responsibility for external pollution; and the 1979 Convention on Long-Range Transboundary Air Pollution (LRTAP) which dealt with the problem of acid rain; but still yet, the problem of state culpability arises in situations where the transboundary pollution may have been involuntary, was due to a common mistake, or as a result of private sector economic activities. Furthermore, because the air and the seas have no limiting boundaries when it comes to pollution, no country can accurately determine the extent to which an environmental event (as a result of fossil fuel/energy exploration) in its own territory will affect other "innocent" countries, as well as the short- and long-term effects on human health and quality of life. This has remained an irresolvable dilemma when it comes to fossil fuel/oil exploration.

In a February 2011 environmental meeting in Washington, DC, scientists projected that by the year 2020, there will be about 50 million environmental refugees moving from one country to the other due to food shortages in their home countries. They argue that climate change has impacted food security by making winters warmer, and this has allowed pests that carry plant diseases to survive over the cold months and attack crops in the spring. And they warned that in light of the earth's finite resources, if we continue like we have been doing at the moment both in terms of population growth and in the level of consumption, the planet could be unrecognizable by the year 2050. The alarming discovery of how fast the planet has changed in the last few years (from melting of the polar ice cap, rising sea levels, erosion of low-lying shorelines, and the disappearance of species), hence should be enough to convince us of the pressing need to live not by "more of the same, but by less of the same."

Today, various states, local governments, private sector and nonprofit organizations are taking action (even if miniscule at this point) to address some or the other linkage issues that contribute to adverse environmental outcomes. Even the "World Bank itself stopped financing coal since 2010 because of the hydrocarbon's link to global warming and extreme weather patterns, and many international banks such as Deutsche Bank, and Lloyds Banking Group, are turning away from fossil-fuel projects."[70] The same assessment has also driven some oil and gas companies to join the chorus as part of the solution to addressing climate change. "On September 24, 2018, Oxy Petroleum, Exxon Mobil, and Chevron formally joined a coalition of some of the world's biggest energy companies on the OIL and Gas Climate Initiative (OGCI)."[71] The coalition, "which had committed $1 billion to funding environmental-friendly energy ventures to reduce emissions, announced a goal to cut their release of methane (the second most prevalent greenhouse gas) by one-third by 2025."[72] While this is desirable from a policy perspective, but they still represent volitional and piece-meal reactions to what certainly would require a broader universal commitment to dealing with the effects. The world still needs a consensus on the scope and ramifications of global climate change and the degree to which various phenomena contributes to its intensification. Checkmating the use of coal and hydrocarbon emissions in one category or region, does not prevent its use in other areas or regions. In the final analysis, as the utilization in one region cancels out its non-utilization in another area, the problem still remains as it has ever been and we are back to "square one."

In chapter 10, I reinforce the role of states and governments as governing institutions. Drawing upon matters concerning objects and the ontological and causal questions they raise, I make the case that our understanding of objects or phenomenon is based on our understanding, or at best, perception of the functions they perform. Utilizing the frictional metaphor (as already advanced in chapter 1), I offer an extended discussion on the phenomenon of *interaction* and how it can help in our understanding of various types of social action at different levels of analyses, be they political, sociological, bilateral, multilateral, cognitive, geographical, or structural. The chapter ends by reinforcing the subject of institutions and the institutionalization process, and how these enable the conditions and recursive patterns that engender stability, equilibrium states, and development.

NOTES

1. Singh, Shane. 2017. How Issue Frames Shape Beliefs about the Importance of Climate Change Policy Across Ideological and Partisan Groups. https://journals.plos.org/plosone/article?id=10.1371/journal.pone.0181401. Accessed on September 17, 2018, 1.
2. Adger, Neil, Hallie Eakin, and Alexandra Winkels. 2009. "Nested and Teleconnected Vulnerabilities to Environmental Change." *Frontiers in Ecology and the Environment* 7, no. 3: 150–157, 150–151.
3. Carter, Neil. 2001. *The Politics of the Environment: Ideas, Activism,* Policy, 2nd ed. Cambridge, UK: Cambridge University Press, 244.
4. Salvaterra, Neanda. 2018. "Coal's Global Rebound Heats Up." *The Wall Street Journal* (September 4): B1–B2.
5. Chasek, Pamela S., David L. Downe, and Janet Welsh Brown. 2010. *Global Environmental Politics: Dilemmas in World Politics*, 5th ed. Boulder, CO: Westview Press, 2.
6. Ibid.
7. Ibid.
8. Worldwatch. 2004. *State of the World 2004*. New York: W. W. Norton & Co., 5.
9. United Nations. 2008. *Millennium Development Goals Report* 2008. New York: United Nations, 4.
10. Chasek, Pamela S., David L. Downe, and Janet Welsh Brown.2010. *Global Environmental Politics: Dilemmas in World Politics*, 5th ed., 65.
11. Dauvergne, Peter. 2011. "Globalization and the Environment." In *Global Political Economy*, 3rd ed., edited by John Ravenhill, 450–480. New York: Oxford University Press, 464.
12. World Trade Organization. 1999. "Trade and Environment," *Special Studies* 4 (Geneva: WTO). Press Release: www.wto.org/english/tratop_e/stud99_e.htm. See also E. Neumayer. 2001. *Greening Trade and Investment: Environmental Protection without Protectionism*. London: Earthscan.
13. Hardin, Garrett. 1968. "The Tragedy of the Commons," *Science* 162 (December 13): 1243–1248.
14. Ostrom, Elinor. 1990. *Governing the Commons: The Evolution of Institution for Collective Action*. New York: Cambridge University Press.
15. Carter, Neil. 2001. *The Politics of the Environment: Ideas, Activism, Policy*, 2nd ed., 245.
16. Krasner, S. D. 1991. "Global Communications and National Power: Life on the Pareto Frontier." *World Politics* 43, no. 3: 336–366. See also James A. Caporaso and Mary Anne Madeira. 2012. *Globalization, Institutions and Governance*. London: Sage Publications, 106.

17. Caporaso, James A., and Mary Anne Madeira. 2012. *Globalization, Institutions and Governance*. London: Sage Publications, 106.

18. Carter, Neil. 2001. *The Politics of the Environment: Ideas, Activism,* Policy, 2nd ed., 251.

19. Carter, Neil. 2007. *The Politics of the Environment: Ideas, Activism, Policy*, 2nd ed., 264.

20. Ibid., 248.

21. Dauvergne, Peter. 2011. "Globalization and the Environment." In *Global Political Economy*, 3rd ed., edited by John Ravenhill, 450–480. New York: Oxford University Press, 476.

22. Dauvergne, Peter. 2011. "Globalization and the Environment." In *Global Political Economy*, 3rd ed., edited by John Ravenhill, 450–480. New York: Oxford University Press, 476.

23. Switzer, J. V. 2004. *Environmental Politics: Domestic and Global Dimensions*, 4th eds., Belmont, CA: Thomson/Wadsworth, 293.

24. https://unfccc.int/process-and-meetings/the-paris-agreement/what-is-the-paris-agreement. Accessed on September 20, 2018, 1–6.

25. https://unfccc.int/process-and-meetings/the-paris-agreement/what-is-the-paris-agreement. Accessed on September 20, 2018, 2.

26. https://unfccc.int/process-and-meetings/the-paris-agreement/what-is-the-paris-agreement. Accessed on September 20, 2018, 2.

27. Rinfret, Sara R., Denise Scheberle, and Michelle C. Pautz. 2019. *Public Policy: A Concise Introduction*. Thousand Oaks, CA: CQ Press, 243.

28. Mooney, Chris. 2018. "Trump withdrew from the Paris Climate Deal a Year Ago: Here's What has Changed. Energy and Environment Analysis," *The Washington Post*, June 1, 2018, 2 (Online).

29. https://www.theguardian.com/commentisfree/2018/aug/15/enough-with-the-fairy-tales-about-the-paris-agreement-its-time-for-facts. Accessed on September 15, 2018.

30. Boyd R., and P. J. Richerson. 1985. *Culture and the Evolutionary Process*. Chicago, IL: University of Chicago Press. See also D. T. Campbell. 1975. "On the Conflicts Between Biological and Social Evolution and Between Psychology and Moral Tradition." *American Psychology* 30, no. 11: 1103–1126.

31. Scheraga J. D., K. L. Ebi, J. Furlow, and A. R. Moreno. 2003. "From Science to Policy: Developing Responses to Climate Change." In: *Climate Change and Human Health: Risks and Responses*, edited by A. J. McMichael, D. Campbell-Lendrum, C. F. Corvalan, K. L. Ebi, A. Githeko, J. D. Scheraga, and A. Woodward, 1–333, WHO/WMO/UNEP, 243.

32. Boda, Zsolt. 2003. "Global Environmental Commons and the Need for Ethics." *Society and Economy* 25, no. 2: 213–224, 213.

33. Macpherson, Cheryl Cox. 2012. "Climate Change Matters." *Journal of Medical Ethics* 40, no. 4: 288–290, 288.

34. Keohane, Robert O. 2015. "The Global Politics of Climate Change: Challenge for Political Science." The 2014 James Madison Lecture, *PS: Political Science & Politics* 48, no. 1: 19–26, 19.

35. Chasek, Pamela S., David L. Downe, and Janet Welsh Brown. 2010. *Global Environmental Politics: Dilemmas in World Politics*, 5th ed., 2.

36. Scheraga, J. D., K. L. Ebi, J. Furlow, and A. R. Moreno. 2003. "From Science to Policy: Developing Responses to Climate Change." In *Climate Change and Human Health: Risks and Responses*, edited by A. J. McMichael, D. Campbell-Lendrum, C. F. Corvalan, K. L. Ebi, A. Githeko, J. D. Scheraga, and A. Woodward, 1–333. WHO/WMO/UNEP, 243.

37. Taylor, Maria. 2014. "Influences on a Changed Story and the New Normal: Scientists' Beliefs and Public Scepticism." *Global Warming and Climate Change*. ANU Press, 144. https://www.jstor.org/stable/j.ctt130h8d6.13. Accessed on September 19, 2018.

38. Taylor, Maria. 2014. "Influences on a Changed Story and the New Normal: Scientists' Beliefs and Public Scepticism." *Global Warming and Climate Change*. ANU Press, 146. https://www.jstor.org/stable/j.ctt130h8d6.13. Accessed on September 19, 2018.

39. Smith, Mark Stafford. 2015. "Responding to Global Environmental Change." In *Change*, edited by Gabriele Bammer, 29–42. ANU Press, 36. https://www.jstor.org/stable/j.ctt16wd0cc.7. Accessed on September 19, 2018.

40. Smith, Mark Stafford. 2011. "Globalization and the Environment." In *Global Political Economy*, edited by John Ravenhill, 450–480, 475.

41. Ibid., 470.

42. Ostrom, Elinor. 1990. *Governing the Commons: The Evolution of Institution for Collective Action*. New York: Cambridge University Press.

43. Chasek, Pamela S., David L. Downe, and Janet Welsh Brown. 2010. *Global Environmental Politics: Dilemmas in World Politics*, 5th ed., 272.

44. Ibid., 278.

45. Ibid., 279.

46. Rinfret, Sara R., Denise Scheberle., and Michelle C. Pautz. 2019. *Public Policy: A Concise Introduction*. Thousand Oaks, CA: CQ Press, 260.

47. Henry, Adams Douglas., and Thomas Dietz. 2011. "Information, Networks, and the Complexity of Trust in Commons Governance." *International Journal of the Commons* 5, no. 2: 188:212, 196–197.

48. Bryner, Gary, and Robert J. Duffy. 2012. *Integrating Climate, Energy, and Air Pollution Policies*. Cambridge, MA: The MIT Press, 196.

49. Carter, Neil. 2001. *The Politics of the Environment: Ideas, Activism, Policy*, 2nd ed., 327.

50. Dauvergne, Peter. 2011. "Globalization and the Environment." In *Global Political Economy*, 3rd ed., edited by John Ravenhill, 450–480, 471–472.

51. Hardin, Garrett. 1968. "The Tragedy of the Commons," 1243–1248.

52. Hay, Colin. 2011. "Globalization's Impact on States." In *Global Political Economy*, 3rd ed., edited by John Ravenhill, 312–344. New York: Oxford University Press, 322.

53. Hay, Colin. 2011. "Globalization's Impact on States." In *Global Political Economy*, 3rd ed., edited by John Ravenhill, 312–344, 322.

54. Aristotle. 1962. *The Politics*. Translated by T. A. Sinclair. NY: Penguin Books, 58.

55. Aristotle. 1962. *The Politics*, 58–59.

56. Elliott, Herschel. 1997. "A General Statement of the Tragedy of the Commons." *Population and Environment* 8, no. 6: 515–531, 523.

57. Hardin, Garrett. 1968. "The Tragedy of the Commons," 1243–1248.

58. Forsyth, Tim, and Craig Johnson. 2014. "Elinor Ostrom's Legacy: Governing the Commons and the Rational Choice Controversy." *Development and Change* 45, no. 55: 1093–1110, 1098.

59. Spiegel, Steve L., Jennifer M. Taw, Elizabeth G. Mathews, and Kristen P. Williams. 2012. *World Politics in a New Era*, 5th ed., New York: Oxford University Press, 458.

60. Carter, Neil. 2007. *The Politics of the Environment: Ideas, Activism, Policy*, 2nd ed., 177.

61. Aggarwal, Vinod K, and Cedric Dupont. 2011. "Collaboration and Co-Ordination in the Global Political Economy." In *Global Political Economy*, 3rd ed., edited by John Ravenhill, 67–95. New York: Oxford University Press, 83.

62. Aggarwal, Vinod K, and Cedric Dupont. 2011. "Collaboration and Co-Ordination in the Global Political Economy." In *Global Political Economy* (3rd Ed.), 83.

63. Ostrom, Elinor. 1990. *Governing the Commons: The Evolution of Institution for Collective Action*. New York: Cambridge University Press, 6.

64. Ostrom, Elinor. 1990. *Governing the Commons: The Evolution of Institution for Collective Action*, 44.

65. Ostrom, Vincent., and Elinor Ostrom. "Public Goods and Public Choices. Workshop in Political Theory and Policy Analysis." Indiana University, Bloomington, IN, USA. http://johannes.lecture.ub.ac.id/files/2012/02/Public-Goods-and-Public-Choices.pdf. Accessed on January 12, 2019, 11.

66. Spiegel, Steve L., Jennifer M. Taw, Elizabeth G. Mathews, and Kristen P. Williams. 2012. *World Politics in a New Era*, 5th ed., 458.

67. Carter, Neil. 2007. *The Politics of the Environment: Ideas, Activism, Policy*, 2nd ed., 177.

68. Adger, Neil, Hallie Eakin, and Alexandra Winkels. 2009. "Nested and Teleconnected Vulnerabilities to Environmental Change," 150–157, 151.

69. Adger, Neil, Hallie Eakin, and Alexandra Winkels. 2009. "Nested and Teleconnected Vulnerabilities to Environmental Change," 150–157, 156.

70. Salvaterra, Neanda. 2018. "Coal's Global Rebound Heats Up." *The Wall Street Journal*, September 4, p. B2.

71. Worland, Justin. 2018. "Oil Companies See Green." *Time* 192, no. 14 (October 8): 24.

72. Worland, Justin. 2018. "Oil Companies See Green." *Time* 192, no. 14 (October 8); 24.

Chapter 10

State and Institutions as Organizing Symbols

What I have tried to do in this work is to develop a broad template drawing upon the importance of the social system as a conceptual lens in the function analysis of states, governments, and institutions. In addressing the issue of why some states and governments have not functioned well; that is, they have not or are not doing well in serving the basic needs and requirements of their societies, it is necessary to draw from the sociological foundations and the nature of interactions that shape social and political action in the modern state. Why do some states or governments fail and others endure? In what ways do the personalities (individual behaviors) developed within a social system (a state) at whatever stage in the life-cycle, spontaneously act in ways as to fulfill the functional requisites of the social system of which they are part,[1] and in what ways they do not? These are important questions that also raise issues about how differences in cultural practices, belief systems, educational opportunities, and socialization processes induce varied and patterned orientations toward political objects, symbols, and the nature of interactions within social or political systems.

There is this generic notion that while states may differ in terms of ideology, economic system, and institutional architecture, its role as an organizing framework for system-wide political action and international relations cannot be second-guessed. But what are the undercurrents that sustain the states' role as an organizing framework? To the extent that these *undercurrents* can be attributed to the role of institutions, but then, what are institutions and why do they oftentimes fail? In this work, I have sought in various ways to point us to novel epistemological trajectories for understanding the ontological, social, and political worlds of states and governments and the institutional effects that simultaneously lock in individual and collective choices into patterned and seemingly coordinated responses to political objects, symbols, and their general conformity to prevailing normative structures. As previously alluded to, a "social system is a system of the differentiated actions of individuals organized into a system of differentiated roles."[2] But it is a "condition of the existence of the system that the differentiated roles must be coordinated either negatively, in the sense of the avoidance of disruptive interference with each other; or positively, in the sense of contributing to the realization of certain shared collective goals through collaborative activity."[3]

Part of the functional problem of social systems is the difficulty in deciding what roles are to be institutionalized, who is to perform those roles, and for what purposes?[4] To this end, *structure* matters in the sense that the objective sought should determine the logic and the way the structure is designed to achieve the objective. This should be done in ways that not only seek to differentiate between noncognitive structures (rules, laws, and regulations) and cognitive structures (norms, values, beliefs, and social facts); but also in ways that embed them consistently and recursively into the very fabric of social and political life. By integrating ongoing practices and routines into an authoritatively sanctioned structure of order, obligations, and expectations, we are thus able to construct a self-sustaining framework which, in and of itself, would be capable of directing the motives and actions of individuals in ways that support and reinforce applicable social conventions.

STATE AND STATECRAFT: COMPETING DIFFERENTIALS

The terms *state* and *statecraft* are conceptually different but functionally interconnected; the first exemplifying the institutional design and structure that defines the context within which governance takes place, while the latter denotes the coordination of the various activities or functions undertaken in the management of state affairs. It is therefore to serve the primary interest of the state that the practice of statecraft assumes different dimensions that often result in different consequences or effects. There are many states that are governed well and there are those that are not so governed. The consequence is that some citizens may be happier than others but also seem more optimistic and favorable about their future than citizens of other countries. This is also evident not only between states but also within states. But despite these differences, the common denominator for all states is that the process of governance as an activity creates a dynamic tension between the state and its institutions (structure) and the practice of statecraft (process). It is in the management of these tensions or interactions that we experience differences between states in terms of capabilities (power), levels of development (economy), and citizen satisfaction (legitimacy).

It matters very little whether some states are more endowed than others or whether Fortune has "blessed" some more than the others. Solutions to social problems do not just evolve, they are invented and acted upon. In his enduring admonition to humanity, Boethius cautions us in dealing with matters of this nature because for him "Fortune is of more benefit when she is adverse than when she brings prosperity, for in the latter case she approaches under the guise of happiness. When she seems kind, she lies; but when she shows herself fickle and unstable, she is truthful. In the first case she deceives; in the latter she instructs."[5] But in the administration of states and in the governance process itself, Fortune, in whatever guise or denomination it unfolds, is a matter of timing, inference, and judgment. In the end, what matters most is how states and policy makers are able to muster the resources, skills, and the political will necessary to address such central problems that are naturally in competition with each other. Among these are the need for good education, health care, employment, good roads, electricity, rule of law, equal opportunity, and the more existential needs to safeguard the territorial integrity and security of the state.

Barring any agreement on the central issues of governance, the oftentimes zero-sum nature of political competition can only add to the evolving tension between state and statecraft. One of the tenets of democracy is the emphasis on political competition but this is seen only as a mechanism for making a choice between *means* and *ends*, as well as for adapting to the evolving tension between the state (as an institution) and statecraft (as a process or activity). In democratic politics, "competition for power is focused on contests that are generally carried out in structured settings in which people know they have to abide by certain rules; but also one in which each side seeks to win the argument in the eyes of their constituencies."[6] But in today's world, science and technology have also made it possible to engage in this competition through the media, the Internet, or though other online platforms, further complicating the process by which we interact and compete with each other as well as share knowledge about political objects, symbols, and politics itself. To the extent that democracy may offer us a means for selecting those who would govern, and because it is based on political authority acquired by way of majority rule, it rarely guarantees distributive equality. Although it may guarantee equality to participate in the process, it does not guarantee equality of outcome, particularly when the majority is set to implement its own agenda and programs oftentimes in prejudice to the interests of the minority. Here, I do not mean *minority* in the exclusive context of using ascriptive characteristics such as race, gender, or other denominations. I use the term in the context of a broader social or political engagement in which people, interests, socioeconomic groups, parties, or coalitions, place their individual or collective bets (wagers) on the table as everyone else. Whichever individual or coalition of interests wins, it imposes its will on the others, or at least has the opportunity to do so.

In the end, "democracy offers no guarantee of the pursuit of truth through science and its application to politics";[7] nor does "institutionalizing mechanisms that require people to agree to anything to promote their convergence on the truth."[8] And such is the case that when *politics* enters through the front door, *truth* oftentimes seems to escape through the back door. Political competition has thus become one of the most prominent ways to decide how society is governed, and most importantly, who does the governing. The "distinction as to the nature of the competition is not only between individual and group action but also between *conditions*, on the one hand, in which alternative ways based on different views or practices may be tried; and *conditions*, on the other hand, in which one agency has the exclusive right and the power to prevent others from trying."[9] But it does not end there. As soon as we decide on who would govern, interest groups, individuals, professional bodies, and nongovernmental agencies join the fray in one form or the other, as a way of casting their influence and judgment on existing or future public policies. And the "general reason for seeking such influence is that outcomes of governmental decisions affect the distribution of burdens and benefits throughout society: who pays how much in taxes; whose activities are regulated and in what ways; who receives what services, subsidies, authorizations, exemptions, and so on."[10] In the following sections, I will draw upon much of what has been stated above to reinforce our working notion of functional theory and interactions as equally demonstrated in earlier sections of this book, particularly chapters 1, 2, 3, 5, and 6. I also focus on the issue of ontology and its implication for generating causal explanations regarding what makes "objects" or "things" what they are; and how this translates into our collective understanding of what they actually do (their functions).

FUNCTIONAL THEORY AS ORGANIZING PRINCIPLE: DO OBJECTS HAVE ONTOLOGY?

Objects have ontology, but we lack the capacity to know all of it. We only have partial knowledge of an object by way of what it does (or what we think it does) for us. An apple is an object that we call a fruit (an objective fact justified through language), but it is not just any other fruit. It is a fruit with unique properties akin to the category known as *pome*. Apples have unique properties in shape, color, taste, mealy texture, smell, and seasonality/temporality. By virtue of these properties, I can be able to distinguish an apple from an orange or a mango. Does this then mean that we know everything about what an apple is? My point here is that left alone and at a distance, we cannot fully know what makes an apple an apple except by what it does for us (its utility function). An apple can be used to serve many functions such as apple pie, cider, juice, cobbler, tarts, and so many other delicacies that I cannot, in my very limited knowledge about confectionaries, imagine. On the other hand, an apple can simply be eaten and chewed up literally as both food and nourishment.

But then, does an apple have ontology, and if so, what is it? Yes, an apple has ontology, but it is an ontology that is both internal (inside of it) and external (outside of it). It is one that is both present to the senses but is also metaphysical (transcends what we see as an object). We do not buy an apple just to look at it; we buy it because of the interests we believe it would serve for us in terms of its functional properties such as the nutritional quality, the taste, the pie, and the crunch. All of these are part of the apple's ontology without which it will not be an apple. I notice that in my delineation above of the properties of an apple, I also included the term "seasonality/temporality" in the list. It is my way of simply recognizing the fact that the apple tree grows during specific periods of the year (say mid-September to mid-November, although some species may grow all-year round) in various cold temperate climates. I argue that "seasonality" or temporality" is also part of the constitutive properties of an apple in the sense that it is an essential phenomenon that affects both the apple's size, shape, color, growth, maturity, ripeness, liquid content, mealiness, and taste. Seasonality, though it is a phenomenon that occurs outside of the apple; but by helping to determine much of what happens inside the apple, it cannot be excluded as an extended property of the apple. It is partially locked into the apple (in some ways) as an important feature without which the apple cannot develop and become the object that we see as an apple.

We cannot separate the apple as a fruit from the function it performs for us as an apple. Its ontology is therefore constitutive of the apple as object and the apple as function, each partially included in the other. As John Searle clearly points out, "functions are never intrinsic; they are assigned relative to the interests of users and observers";[11] otherwise we are only left with identifying objects in terms of their internal properties much of which we do not and may never know. The same inductive-deductive mode of analysis could be applied to almost everything that we need to live and coexist in the social world. Examples would include a car and its function of motion, a barber and his function of cutting hair, the podiatrist and his function of fixing the foot, the government, and the function of maintaining law and order, and the function of a dog as a cuddly canine friend. But again, going back to the apple and its constitutive properties, particularly the notion of seasonality, it also teaches us a great lesson about the realities of the social world in which we live. If we extend the proposition that "seasonality" is a constitutive part of what makes an apple what it is, to the role of social actors (individuals) within social systems, we find that sooner than later, *time* (using the term as a surrogate for seasonality) is in everything we do. In fact, time determines and shapes much of what we do in our social world.

As I already alluded to in chapter 5, the value of time does not derive from itself, but only from how it shapes human behavior and in the structuring of social relations such that a sense of order and structure is maintained in the exercise of individual or social action. Because time has extension, durability, and is constantly in eternal motion, it cannot be imagined but can only be reflected in the lived experience of the social world of human beings. A time that has already passed can never be reclaimed. In the same way that nature regulates the occurrence of the seasons (spring, summer, autumn, and winter), and day and night based on immutable laws that are beyond human; worldly time itself, is embedded in the very structure of existence through which humans react to and address essential issues and realities of the human condition. There is a time for attaining puberty, a time for weaning the child off the milk bottle, a time for females to give birth (give and take 9 months) as naturally dictated by their physio-biology, and a time to sleep or wake up in the morning. Even when we are reluctant to sleep, our biological imprinting sends consistent signals throughout our body that would eventually "force" us to go to sleep—without which the persistent dreariness would not wear off. In the social world of human experience, *time* is in everything.

A phenomenon, on the other hand, is an occurrence, event, or a circumstance that we oftentimes construct as a result of our experience about how certain things seem to occur in our worldly experience. Through language and experience, we attach meaning to the phenomenon and this allows us to explain it or to acknowledge it whenever it is experienced again. So, the question is: "Do phenomena (oftentimes an abstraction) have ontology?" My best estimation would be that they do not; but even if they do, we cannot know what it is in the absolute sense of the term. The ontology of abstract phenomena is the meaning we attach to it (as a social collective) through language and reason. I am aware of the fact that oftentimes we ascribe to an object, a thing, or person, the qualification as a phenomenon, even when the explanation, cause, and the reality of what we see is not in doubt. By this definition, it would simply mean that any observable fact, event, or circumstance could qualify as a phenomenon to the extent they are experienced through sensory perception. But my usage of the term *phenomenon* in this context stays away from the conceptual dilemma we have rather inadvertently created for ourselves. I am simply talking about the types of abstract phenomena we conceive in our thoughts, intuition, and/or experience (such as what makes particular seasons of the year a spring, summer, autumn, or gravity, marriage, cultural or ceremonial rites, and indoctrination rituals).

The complex nature of social reality and experience makes it rather difficult for us, sometimes, to separate fact from fiction, symbols from the meanings behind them, and images from the mirrors upon which they are reflected. But then, I am careful to point out here that I am not making any teleological argument nor do I seek to advocate one. All I am saying is that we generally attach meaning or come to know about an object or phenomenon by what we know about its function or purpose. If we agree that *everything* in our social world exists for something (whatever that may be), then we are on a more solid footing to state that we may not know what each of these "everything" is, until we know, or at best, understand what it *does*. Talcott Parsons points to the effect that "by understanding the *function*, we are able to capture the systemic essence of social reality, in a more direct, empirical, or visceral way."[12] In the same way, Tuomela concludes that "social institutions, be they patterns of activity or whatever related, may be characterized by their social functions."[13] What causes the phenomenon or its ontological properties may be difficult or even impossible to know in all its manifestations without foreknowledge of the atomic, neural, or material properties that constitute it.

My point, therefore, is essentially about *knowing*, not about causality. And there is a big difference between knowledge of a thing (knowing), and its causation (what led to that thing being the object we see or experience); although I will admit that on a functional level, knowledge of an object (what it stands for) and its causality could be ontologically locked into each other in some form or the other. And this makes their separation more difficult. Either way, I am more focused on the interactional process where all sorts of manifestations evolve in various ways that often generate predictable as well as unpredictable outcomes at different levels and scale in both time and space. Although much of these have already been discussed extensively in chapter 1, I am persuaded to provide further elaboration in the following sections for the simple fact that a functional analysis of social systems must of necessity take into account the dynamics of the interaction process between the parts or units and its effect on system stability. While interdependence suggests a functional relationship between the parts or units, interaction points to what each of the parts or units do and how the likely consequences of what they do would affect overall system maintenance and durability. The two premises, interdependence and interaction, are different but in fundamental ways.

INTERACTIONALISM AND TENSION MANAGEMENT

The frictional metaphor as developed in this work offers a means for illustrating the fact that interactions within or between social systems involve some level of tension or friction. Interactions generate gradations of friction or life force that is constitutive of the shared properties (body, mass, ontology, texture, etc.) of the interacting units or agents. The outcome of the interaction generally points to the *function* for which the interaction as a process is expected to serve. I made reference to this earlier in chapter 1 as *interactional functionalism*. I set the premise of the argument by making a distinction between *interdependence* and *interaction*, pointing specifically to the fact that while interdependence involves a relationship between parts or system elements; interaction, on the other hand, involves an analysis of the friction or tension that results when the parts or system elements engage or come in contact with each other in the process of performing sets of activities or obligations. The larger picture from this is that whenever there is interaction between two or more elements or parts of a system, there is generally a form of friction. The magnitude of the friction would, however, depend on the material composition of the parts or systems elements, the type of matter and the atomic or cellular properties they are made of, and the temporal duration of the interactional process itself. It does not necessarily matter whether the interaction occurs in the context of mechanical, biological, or social systems; the point is that any form of contact or interaction has some material consequences, even if undetectable to the sight or any of our sensory organs. Interaction always leads to friction and friction has consequences.

I venture to say that interactions do not necessarily have to be in the form of physical contact; it can be psychological, cognitive, or even viscerally constructed or imagined. Let me expand a bit more on the hypothesis I seek to develop along this line. Social action and all kinds of interdependence involve some form of interaction at some level and at different stages in the evolution of the process. The structure of the interaction could be externally conditioned, regulated, or operationally routinized, sequential, or simply spontaneous. But whichever situation applies in this regard, is nonetheless, conditioned by the ontological properties of the interacting parts or system elements as well as the function or purpose for which the interaction (a constitutive phenomenon) is meant to serve. Social systems exhibit a type of collective ontology that depends on system elements or parts as a necessary condition for their maintenance and stability; but the central question posed here is: What is the effect of the interaction process (tension or friction) to the overall workings of the system, and to what extent does it contribute to system maintenance and functionality? At the constitutive or macro level, our main concern should be on determining how social action bridges micro differences in both structured and unstructured episodes in such a way that ensuing selection pressures evolve in a consistent pattern of order and continuity. Depending on the intensity and direction of effect, social interactions can create both incentives and disincentives that, in and of themselves, lead to new patterns of institutional differentiation (or the need for them) as an adaptive mechanism to prevent the whole system from falling apart.

As already alluded to in chapter 1, I made the point that in the functional analysis of states and governments, interdependence, while essential, is not a necessary condition for interaction or for friction to occur. Interactional friction can occur by happenstance (between system elements that temporarily lock onto each other, particularly in situations where a natural disaster or an emergency disrupts or disorganizes the most essential institutions for the delivery of public services and the maintenance of social order), by ad hoc or opportunistic relationships, by formal contracts, obligatory commitments, or simply by accident. Even if this account is challenged, yet it still remains that interdependence only tells us that A and B do share a collective experience or obligation on something that may be valuable to A and B or to the general public. But their *interaction* tells us about the nature, intensity, and purpose and how specific interests are or are not served in that regard. This will thus help to determine how and which existing norms of *interdependence* will be retained, modified, or nullified; and in what ways any modification would spurn new structural features in the effort to restore the original framework in ways that serve contemporaneous or emerging interests.

Most conflicts that emerge in social and political life arise from the inherent instability of the interactional process between and within system elements, and this is more pronounced in circumstances where "alienated groups are activated to seek alterations in the existing terms of exchange"[14] (distribution of political and economic incentives) they hope, would work in their favor. Ironically when and if they are unsuccessful, they then seek, with whatever means and guise, to subvert the very system and government upon which they would eventually need to secure relief from their alienation. The ability of social systems (in this case states and governments) to remain stable and effective is dependent on the resolution of two functional problems: First, in understanding the magnitude and intensity of the interaction among system elements and the development of intervening structures that modulate the effects in the expected or predictable direction; and secondly, understanding the trajectory to which new or emergent institutional configurations point to, so as to encourage or preempt them based on their desirability or undesirability. There are several conditions under which these should take place, and I will provide further illumination below.

Friction, Equilibria, and Recursive Causality

For the sake of this discussion, we can take the state as a social structure and the government as a sub-social structure, since the state provides the over-arching structure within which governments operate. A social structure is not a static body of complex mass, but is the outcome of continuous and reciprocal sets of interactions sustained by a simple logic—its repetitiveness and irreducibility to its constituent parts. So what keeps this simple logic or phenomenon generally stable and in motion? To address this question, I draw upon three essential properties. The first is that there has to be a *collectively intentioned*[15] acceptance of the desirability of the end for which the interaction serves. The second is the role of institutions in imparting shared normative codes and obligations on the human collective; and the third is the conscious (human-based) and unconscious (process-based) adaptive mechanisms that enables the interaction process to generate alternative means (including the creation and maintenance of new pattern orientations) for addressing specific ends. There is certainly a relationship between social structure and the human agency[16] that constitute it, but much of this relationship is located at the locus of interaction between the two. Because "much of the interaction is repetitive, and structured by clear-cut expectations and common definitions of the situation; we must also recognize the potential for new objects to be inserted or old ones altered and abandoned in a situation, with the result that reinterpretation, reevaluation, redefinition, and remapping of behaviors can always occur."[17] Invariably, this will also lead to alterations or changes in the frame of reference or action templates used in the interaction process, thus resulting in new or emergent structures of parallel interactions.

The outcome of an interaction can yield either positive or negative values; or such *modulating values* that only seek to sustain existing equilibria conditions. But the danger zone is the degree or magnitude (intensity) of the oscillations or deviations from the equilibria condition—a general tendency to gravitate toward or away from the mean. This particular observation is important in shedding additional light in our understanding of how equilibria or stable states are maintained and the dynamics that inform it, particularly in the context of social systems. I will henceforth use the words *equilibria* or *equilibrium* interchangeably to mean the same thing. What do we really mean when we aspire to the notion of equilibria or stable states? Functional theorizing, in my opinion, does not seem to make an absolute claim that systems generally, attain stasis or static equilibrium states. What it acknowledges is that systems *tend* toward homeostatic equilibrium, and because they are able to acquire new and needed inputs from the environment, systems are able to adapt or sustain their self-regulatory and maintenance capabilities. In this regard, systems are thus viewed as having "equilibrium points around which normal functioning occur."[18] These "equilibrium points" are continually under attack or eroded by inertial, social, or environmental forces. It should therefore not be a surprise when Jonathan Turner reinforced the views of early functionalists who pointed to systems as harboring competing "normal and pathological states,"[19] even as they continue to gravitate toward equilibrium conditions.

A wholly sustainable equilibrium state constitutes a situation where the magnitude of the frictional tension between system elements or social actors (the positive force) is equal to the magnitude (negative force) working against the system. In a social system where there are both implicit and explicit forces constantly at work, the issue of attaining optimal or enduring equilibrium state is contingent as well as ongoing. Equilibrium states are rarely static. They represent several contingent processes at work in a seemingly endless tug-of-war between the positive forces of continuity and assimilation and the negative forces of discontinuity and dissimilation. Otherwise, one would be implying that every social force (objective and subjective) in the human universe would natural come to a halt (remain static) at the moment of attaining equilibrium state. But this is never the case. The fact remains that even at the point where we perceive the existence of an equilibrium state, integrative and disintegrative forces continue to compete with each other (whether we know this or not), and it is only the modulating influence of these two forces that results in what is generally (or perhaps erroneously) conceived as an equilibrium state. But it is a state that is in continuous motion and one that is indeterminate as to its final status. It is a state that is highly fluid, conditioned, and continuously contested by competing forces of inertia, attributes of the physical world that make up the social structure, material adjustments as a result of frictional wear and tear, and the ever-present draw-down effects of negative entropy.

Optimal equilibrium states do not exist. Conditional equilibrium states continuously evolve through the mutual-balancing of internal and external forces, oftentimes shaped by a transcendental logic that can only be fully expressed in both time and space. They are therefore untenable or at best unsustainable over time. Rather what we have is a contingent equilibrium state or what I have variously referred to as *equilibrium condition*. Equilibrium condition is not the same as a condition of stasis. For an illustration, let us consider a situation where two or more individuals or social actors reach an agreement on an issue of contention. But it could be the case that as soon as the agreement is reached (signed by all parties) and the specific governance mechanism put in place; the basis for the unraveling of that agreement begins exactly at the same time the signatory ink begins to dry—as both internal (feelings of regret, mistakes, misunderstandings, fairness, and equity) and external forces (changes in political and economic situations, alternating coalitions of interest, and new alliance formations) work at cross-purposes to generate new tensions or exacerbate existing ones that could potentially undermine the agreement—unless mitigating measures are in place to prevent such occurrence.

In this regard, I cannot but fail to be reminded of Pierre Bourdieu's concept of *fields*—to which he refers to as the "totality of actors and organizations involved in an arena of social or cultural production and the dynamic relationship between them."[20] Like Bourdieu's *fields*, the notion of *interactional fields* is a situation that occurs between two or more social actors engaged in the act of production or reproduction. It is therefore the case that while interactional fields are not necessarily placid and settled social spaces, they are, in fact, "arenas of conflict in which all players seek to advance their own interests against that of others—a situation in which some are able (though intermittently or for longer periods) to impose their will on others."[21] In international relations (or interstate diplomacy), the dynamics of *interactional fields* can also be deduced from Robert Wuthnow's "discursive fields"[22]—which consists of the fundamental categories (abstract spaces) in which thinking can take place developed over time by an interacting group of individuals (social actors) and organizations.

Whether observed or not, felt or not, interaction generates friction or tension (or what I would call incremental fissures) in the pattern and mechanism of existing relationships. It is simply a matter of degree and the extent to which incremental fissures, inexorably chipping away at the established social order undetected, eventually attain critical mass—in the form of disagreements, unilateral defections, or outright conflict. The point is that under assumed equilibrium conditions, and when social systems seem to be working well; they are, in fact, not working well as they should be working well. There are always competing forces within and outside of the system that continuously drive it toward equilibrium and disequilibrium. Because each of these forces may be competing with, for, or against the other, the centripetal and centrifugal properties they generate end up canceling out each other. The consequence of this scattering effect suggests that free-floating system elements could combine and recombine in ways that the evolving dynamic results in a moving equilibrium condition.

The *field* concept illustrates a "contested arena within which multiple types of players (social actors) pursue their interests and defend their turf."[23] This is the stuff that makes international relations or foreign diplomacy what it is—an arena of contested discourse. It is a competitive arena where radical or even mundane changes can create ruptures and misalignments that often lead to mistrust and increasing reluctance among social actors to engage in mutual accommodation. As new normative codes evolve to replace existing ones, or to reorient them in response to increasing differentiation in the way the *field* is structured, selection pressures often lead to the development of new institutional combinations that has the potential to lock in competing interests of social actors in ways that any emerging prospect of a *win-win* solution would be enough to keep all actors within the *field*—even as the competing interests continue simultaneously to diverge and converge. Each *win-win* solution is a temporary process of collective enactment, and although fleeting in its appearance, it nonetheless provides additional fodder for the consolidation of mutual gains, even if on a temporary basis.

Interactional fields are very active, dynamic, and sometimes dormant; but no matter the prevailing status, they harbor essential ingredients for cooperation, conflict, and opportunities. They exhibit two properties that also make the resolution of competing interests more complex and enduring. The first property I would call a *microstructure*—consisting of the human actors (field participants) and all the idiosyncratic baggage they bring into the interaction process, the structure of relations (shared or competing values) between the actors, and the primary objective for which the interaction process is supposed to serve. The second property is the *macrostructure*—consisting of the external contingencies and imperatives that affect the interaction process, the political system and its laws, interest groups, and prevailing economic conditions. Because of the recursive interdependence of social structures and the activities of social actors,[24] and "the extent of agreement on the *institutional logics* (shared conceptual frameworks that provide guidelines for the behavior of *field* participants) guiding activities within the *field* or on the issues around which participants are engaged,"[25] equilibrium condition (contingent equilibrium) is maintained not only in the international game itself, but also in the relational properties inherent in the evolving social structures and activity sets.

As pointed out by Tuukka Kaidesoja, "social structures which have initially emerged by virtue of the actions of human beings are able to endure and continue to be causally efficacious, even though they are not currently reproduced through the intentional actions of the current agents."[26] When social actors act in the context of interaction with multiple others, they oftentimes "unrandomize free-floating variables, insert vestiges of orderliness, and literally create their own social realities and constraints."[27] What this suggests is that in an interactional encounter, micro and macro structures cross-cut and feed off each other in a nonlinear zigzagging fashion. But because they are partly interwoven into each other, the symbiotic relationship enables each of them to remain active. Instead of killing off the other, they recreate each other. It is this co-creation that sustains the system elements; and in the analogous case of social structures and actors, enables them to maintain equilibrium conditions between competing interests—at least for the time being.

The structure of *interactional fields* does not have to involve close contact or proximity between social actors. It could be anchored on policy issues, competing policy differences, trade and security issues, compliance issues between users of common-pool resources, property rights, diplomatic relations, forms of joint obligations between social actors, states, governments, interest groups, or between individuals located distances apart from each other. In enacting and dealing with each other, "social actors are rarely aware of their own complexity and the numerous recursive loops on which they depend."[28] Interactional fields therefore can evolve either in cyberspace, in the physical world of human experience, in the consciousness and thought processes, in existing social structures, or in the emotional states of social actors. But no matter the context in which it unfolds, the implications are the same. The role of states and governments is to consistently adapt and reinvent the capacity (acquire the energy) to minimize and overcome the draw-down effects of the *static friction* that occur as an integral part of the interactional process. In this way, the activity of governance can be moved forward in a consistent and desirable pattern. In the following section, I will discuss the evolving role of institutions and institutionalization in the maintenance of stable states, as well as processes that make system monitoring and adaptation an enduring practice.

INSTITUTIONS AND INSTITUTIONALIZATION

In chapter 6, I argued that the process of institutionalization can be made more effective and enduring to the extent that the cognitive and noncognitive aspects are properly aligned to each other. This is consistent with Elinor Ostrom's call that we should think more broadly about governance beyond the formal structures we erect in the exercise of public or formal responsibilities. Governance in this regard ought to reflect "the formal and informal rules of the social game that tame, harness and check our passions, and the mechanisms of enforcement that ensure effective governance even in the most unexpected environments."[29] While governance relies on institutions for its legitimation, institutions on the other hand rely on governance for their continuous validation—hence institutions and governance create incentives for each other. They co-create each other.

Institutionalization refers to "relatively stable patterns of interaction among actors in statuses; in such a way that through repeated patterns of exchanges, bargaining or role-taking, norms emerge as actors adjust their orientations to each other."[30] But this can only be effective when actors have come to realize the utility of abiding by these norms as opposed to doing otherwise, particularly in situations where self-enforcement of the conditions of the norm is more desirable for the maintenance of social order. Parsons was very much concerned with the maintenance of the social order and how existing "mechanism of social control reduce the potential for malintegration and deviance."[31] But then, what are those mechanisms and what are they made of? The first part of addressing this question is to view institutions as carriers of norms, values, and ethical judgments. While these factors have self-restraining qualities, they would still not be enough to address the issue of individual choice or the propensity for people to engage in adverse selection, when confronted with a choice in which they are more likely to escape culpability if they violate some rule or the other.

States and governments are institutions, but they also create other institutional structures that make governance possible. Such institutions include the law, agencies, certifications, licensing, monetary systems, and various forms of contractual relations and organizational forms. Apart from the ability to impose social order by brute force, states and government can, to an extent, and by means of ideology engender a common belief system regarding what the role of government is, what it should be, and how what it eventually becomes would be translated into public policy for the benefit of the "people" or those in political authority. When such belief systems are continuously reinforced, they, overtime, become institutionalized, not only as philosophical dogma, but also as a way of life. It becomes a lens through which citizens create and recreate their own social realities. This is the political role of ideology, but is one that does not come without further elaboration. In his *Structure and Change in Economic History*, Douglass North skillfully pointed out that "the stability of any society requires an ideological superstructure to legitimize the rules of the game."[32] But without additional specificity, it is easy to misunderstand the frame of reference or the context in which his use of *ideology* applies. He was actually discussing ideology in terms of neoclassical economics, and its role in mitigating the free-rider problem, shirking, and opportunistic behavior in the context of political and economic organization. He sees ideology as being analogous to "the values inculcated by the family and by schooling that lead individuals to restrain their behavior so that they do not behave like free-riders."[33]

I would, however, rephrase North's postulation to reflect the fact that the stability of any society requires an "institutional" superstructure (more than ideology) to lock in and reinforce the existing rules of the game, including existing mechanisms of interaction and relationships. Ideologies, to an extent, are much like fuzzy sets. They are sometimes vague, with ambiguous boundary definitions. We are still unsure to what extent ideologies shape belief systems and belief systems, in turn, shape ideologies. Ideologies, even in the midst of competing rationalizations about what it is or is not, help to structure the way in which people develop increasing awareness of that which binds as well as obligates one to the other. But then, and "even with a constant set of rules, detection procedures, and penalties, there is immense variation in the degree to which individual behavior is constrained by *ideology*."[34] Ideology may enable us to deal with some aspect of social reality either by imposing our views or interpretation on that reality, or by the reality imposing itself on our views. The line of demarcation between the two is rather difficult to discern. In the following section, I will try to expand our discussion of institutions as it affects the different processes by which states become developed in different ways and with different outcomes.

DEVELOPMENT AND INSTITUTIONS: A FUNCTIONALIST POSTSCRIPT

The role of institutions is very central in the analysis of social, economic, and political action both in the functional integration of resources as well as in the establishment of the structures and boundaries that guide individual and collective behavior. And this always calls into question: How do we get people to abide by institutional imperatives all of the time, but not some of the time? My emphasis draws upon the normative-institutional foundation that explains individual or group commitments to shared values, norms, and practices. Because such commitments are anchored on shared cognitive frames, schemas, and practices which when repeated over time, become institutionalized as the basis for the validation of social action. By facilitating "the emergence of orderly, stable, social integrating patterns out of unstable, loosely organized, or narrowly technical activities; institutionalization constrains conduct in two main ways: by bringing it within a narrow normative order, and by making it hostage to its own history."[35] Because each single action validates the one before it; it also provides prior justification for legitimizing actions that would be taken under similar circumstances in the future. In this regard, we must see institutions as comprising of two broad elements: a macrostructure and microstructure. A *macrostructure* would include the law, political culture, ideology, social conventions, authority systems, as well as administrative institutions; while on the other hand, a *microstructure* would include the values, customs, norms, and idiosyncrasies, and how these cumulatively work on individuals and/or groups to dictate and influence the choices they make or how they act in specific situations. To the extent that development has an institutionalizing effect, both the macrostructure and microstructure must be seen to permeate each other to such a degree that they become functionally inseparable. Without a corresponding symmetry, one without the other would not create the synergy and order necessary for development and growth.

Development is not only about solving central existential problems of society; it is also about the search for creativity and innovation in the provision of public goods and services, and in designing increasingly effective institutional mechanisms of control, coordination, and order. To be successful, the productive forces that drive the development process must generate enough capacity to address or contain the competing forces of social and political mobilization, and related surge in rising expectations and aspirations within the body politic. Contrary to some variants of the classical western model, development does not necessarily follow a unidirectional path from primitive agriculture to advanced industrial systems; instead, development follows a bidirectional path in which inertial forces can pull it in opposite directions, particularly at that stage when the process reaches critical mass. New ideas, innovation, and resources are needed either to stabilize the process or to propel it forward, without which development and growth stunts, or in most cases, retrogresses into a state of anomie, atrophy, or decay.

The literature is a constant reminder of the instance of *failed states* and why it is a problem both in terms of international politics and state legitimacy. But the coinage itself is a misnomer. States do not fail per se, except that the institutions that undergird their public purpose are what can and do often fail. Institutional failure is a function of both internal and external forces that have crystalized overtime in such a way that the burden it imposes on the state itself becomes overbearing and prohibitive, hence prevailing institutions freeze and decay because they no more have the resources, direction, and control to function. Acemoglu and Robinson's account of why nations (states) fail suggest that "extractive economic and political institutions, though their details may vary under different circumstances, are always at the root of state failure"; and reinforced by the patronage politics and clientelism behind them, they destroy not only law and order but also even the most basic economic incentives."[36] And due to the different histories and social structures, differences in the nature of the elite, and in the details of the extractive industries of the countries, the problem creates a vicious circle that persists.[37]

But individuals also have to play a central role in shaping the trajectory of development in their countries. In the same way that "many political systems and the people selected to operate them must transcend the dangerous conflicts of power and ideology in today's world; coping with world problems also is likely to require many people to rethink their moral priorities."[38] "We need to seek new ways of describing progress in terms of diverse growth and development of human capabilities."[39] From developing prudent management and conservation of the earth's natural resources to dealing with the multiple issues of environmental pollution and climate change, we need to chart a new scheme in which the process of development and growth is complementary, but not in opposition, to each other. "Creating new innovations is not enough unless we also expedite giving up the old ways—such as change in consumption habits without which the ecological benefits gained through better technologies would be lost."[40] Because development and modernization have forced all countries (developed and/or developing) into a race with time; it matters very little the scope of difference between them or their relative ability to withstand short-term shocks or interruptions. What may matter to all is that there is only one earth that we know (at least for the time being) and its ecological diversity and carrying capacity are neither infinite nor limitless. And if we accept the simple premise that there is a purpose for everything in the natural order of the world, then suffice it to say that a loss of one or some, would certainly affect the functioning of the whole. And the institutional basis upon which we seek to isolate and deal with these problems would involve not only the state and government, but also individuals and groups acting in their own capacity as part of the larger puzzle that informs all social systems.

In this work, I have tried to draw upon several sources of epistemological and intellectual interests. Because they offer multiple lenses through which we can conceptualize the ways and means by which institutional processes drive social action, I believe they are crucial to understanding existing state of affairs in the ever-changing realities of our social world. Metaphors, analogies, and heuristics are very good at helping us in simplifying much of the complexities inherent in social systems such as states and governments, as well as dealing with various phenomena that occur in the dynamic and unpredictable field of social scientific inquiry. In chapter 4, by applying the thermostatic analogy in support of the emphasis for the development of organizing structures with self-regulatory capabilities, I draw on the simple insight that "across historical epochs and stages of development, self-regulation systems work to discipline the passions of man and turn situations of potential conflict into a reality of social cooperation."[41] This particular emphasis was presented in the broader epistemic tradition encompassing organization theory and behavior, biology, and physics, particularly as they touch on the principles of cybernetics, self-regulation, servomechanisms, and neural systems.

I also discussed the *feedback loop* as a subsystem and as a communication channel that carries various types of messages. But it poses a series of challenges to the workings of the existing order of systemic and sub-systemic relations and interactions. Within feedback loops, we can either interpret the message correctly or we do not. At other times we may conflate the correct message with the wrong response that not only add to an intensification of the problem, but also masks the problem in such a way that it is difficult to make a proper distinction between cause and effect. It therefore matters a lot how we interpret and organize the messages (signals) in such a way that our responses (or adaptive reactions) to them sustains a continuous level of functionality among and within system elements. This is also in recognition of the fact that as a subsystem within an overarching mother system, the feedback loop rarely lays itself bare. Because we only come to know about its hidden secrets after an observed effect has occurred, the feedback loop, more or less, could be the repository of some of the central problems that undermine social systems.

I have already discussed in chapter 6 the issue of artificial intelligence and man-machine interaction, and how these open up new possibilities and novel ways for carrying out contemporary and future responsibilities of state and government. Although technology, and its applications, is changing the format and pace by which functional roles relate to each other; it is also changing the characteristics of the objects upon which work itself is performed, thereby creating enduring dependencies on the part of humans. I am under no illusion that the reality of our social world is changing and is changing very fast. Such a change would have consequences. But what I am more concerned about is whether policy makers (those who lead) and most citizens (those who are led), actually have a clear sense of where the wind is blowing, the intensity, the velocity, and how much debris it unleashes and where the scattering effects may land them.

NOTES

1. Parsons, Talcott. 1951. *The Social System*. Glencoe, IL: The Free Press, 31.
2. Parsons, Talcott and Edward A. Shils. 2001. *Toward a General Theory of Action: Theoretical Foundations for the Social Sciences*. New Brunswick, NJ: Transaction Publishers, 197.
3. Parsons, Talcott and Edward A. Shils. 2001. *Toward a General Theory of Action: Theoretical Foundations for the Social Sciences*, 197.
4. Parsons, Talcott and Edward A. Shils. 2001. *Toward a General Theory of Action: Theoretical Foundations for the Social Sciences*, 198.
5. Kalpakgian, Mitchell. 2012. "The Ladder of Knowledge and the Ascent to Wisdom in Boethius' The Consolation of Philosophy." In Boethius, *The Consolation of Philosophy*, edited and translated by Scott Goins and Barbara H. Wyman), 177–185. San Francisco, CA: Ignatius Press, 179.
6. Shapiro, Ian. 2003. *The Moral Foundations of Politics*. New Haven, CT: Yale University Press, 204.
7. Shapiro, Ian. 2003. *The Moral Foundations of Politics*, 207.
8. Shapiro, Ian. 2003. *The Moral Foundations of Politics*, 204.
9. Hayek, F. A. 1960. *The Constitution of Liberty*. Chicago, IL: The University of Chicago Press, 37.
10. Graham, Lawrence S, Richard P. Farkas, Robert C. Grady, George Joffé, Donley T. Studlar, and Alan M. Wachman. 2007. *The Politics of Governing: A Comparative Introduction*. Washington, D.C.: CQ Press, 310.
11. Searle, John R. 1995. *The Construction of Social Reality*. New York: The Free Press, 19.
12. Parsons, Talcott. 1937. *The Structure of Social Action*. New York: McGraw-Hill, Inc.
13. Tuomela, Raimo. 2002. *The Philosophy of Social Practices: A Collective Acceptance View*. Cambridge, UK: Cambridge University Press, 157.

14. North, Douglass. 1981. *Structure and Change in Economic History*. New York: W. W. Norton & Co., 183.

15. See John R. Searle. 2010. *Making the Social World: The Structure of Human Civilization*. New York: Oxford University Press.

16. Emami, Zohreh., and Timothy Riordan. 1998. "Tony Lawson on Critical Realism: What's Teaching Got to Do with it?" *Review of Social Economy* 56, no. 3: 311–323, 311.

17. Turner, Jonathan H. 1982. *The Structure of Sociological Theory*. Homewood, IL: The Dorsey Press, 329.

18. Turner, Jonathan H. 1982. *The Structure of Sociological Theory*, 26.

19. Turner, Jonathan H. 1982. *The Structure of Sociological Theory,* 36.

20. Bourdieu, Pierre. 1971. "Systems of Education and Systems of Thought." In *Knowledge and Control: New Directions for the Sociology of Education*, edited by M. K. D. Young, 189–207. London: Collier Macmillan. See also Paul DiMaggio. 1979. "Review Essay: On Pierre Bourdieu." *American Journal of Sociology* 84: 1460–1474, 1463.

21. See Pierre Bourdieu, and Loic J. D. Wacquant. 1992. *An Invitation to Reflexive Sociology*. Chicago, IL: University of Chicago Press, 96. See also W. Richard Scott. 2014. *Institutions and Organizations: Ideas, Interests, and Identities*, 4th ed., Thousand Oaks, CA: Sage Publications, Inc., 221.

22. Wuthnow, Robert. 1989. *Communities of Discourse: Ideology and Social Structure in the Reformation, the Enlightenment and European Socialism*. Cambridge, MA: Harvard University Press.

23. See Fligstein, Neil, and Doug McAdam. 2012. *A Theory of Fields*. Oxford, UK: Oxford University Press. See also W. Richard Scott. 2014. *Institutions and Organizations: Ideas, Interests, and Identities*. Thousand Oaks, CA: Sage Publications, Inc., 235

24. Giddens, Anthony. 1979. *Central Problems in Social Theory: Action, Structure, and Contradiction in Social Analysis*. Berkeley, CA: University of California Press.

25. W. Richard Scott. 2014. *Institutions and Organizations: Ideas, Interests, and Identities*. Thousand Oaks, CA: Sage Publications, Inc, 235. See also Stephen D. Krasner. 1988. "Sovereignty: An Institutional Perspective." *Comparative Political Studies* 21: 66–94.

26. file:///C:/Users/kkalu/Downloads/The_Concept_of_Social_Structure_in Roy_B.pdf, 8. Accessed on January 12, 2019. See also Tuukka Kaidesoja. 2007. "The Concept of Social Structure in Roy Bhaskar's Critical Realism." *Sosiologia* 44, no. 2: 79–94.

27. Weick, Karl E. 1979. *The Social Psychology of Organizing*, 2nd ed., New York: McGraw-Hill, Inc., 164.

28. Morgan, Gareth. 2006. *Images of Organization*. Thousand Oaks, CA: Sage Publications, 249.

29. Boettke, Peter. 2010. "Is the Only Form of 'Reasonable Regulation' Self Regulation? Lessons from Lin Ostrom on Regulating the Commons and Cultivating Citizens." *Public Choice* 143: 283–291, 287.

30. Turner, Jonathan H. 1982. *The Structure of Sociological Theory*, 44–46.

31. Turner, Jonathan H. 1982. *The Structure of Sociological Theory*, 60.

32. North, Douglass. 1981. *Structure and Change in Economic History*, 182.

33. North, Douglas. 1981. *Structure and Change in Economic History*, 46–47.

34. North, Douglas. 1981. *Structure and Change in Economic History*, 47.

35. Selznick, Philip. 1992. *The Moral Commonwealth: Social Theory and the Promise of Community*. Berkeley, CA: University of California Press, 232. See also Scott, W. Richard. 2014. *Institutions and Organizations: Ideas, Interests, and Identities*, 4th ed., Thousand Oaks, CA: Sage Publications, 146.

36. Acemoglu, Daron, and James A. Robinson. 2012. *Why Nations Fail: The Origins of Power, Prosperity, and Poverty*. New York: Crown Business, 372.

37. Acemoglu, Daron, and James A. Robinson. 2012. *Why Nations Fail: The Origins of Power, Prosperity, and Poverty*, 399.

38. Graham, Lawrence S, Richard P. Farkas, Robert C. Grady, George Joffé, Donley T. Studlar, and Alan M. Wachman. 2007. *The Politics of Governing: A Comparative Introduction*, 319.

39. Neuvonen, Aleksi. 2017. *Sitra Memorandum: Rewriting Progress*. Helsinki, Finland: Sitra-The Finnish Innovation Fund, May 31, p. 26.

40. Neuvonen, Aleksi. 2017. *Sitra Memorandum:* Rewriting *Progress*, 4.

41. Boettke, Peter. 2010. "Is the Only Form of 'Reasonable Regulation' Self Regulation? Lessons from Lin Ostrom on Regulating the Commons and Cultivating Citizens." *Public Choice* 143, 283–291, 289.

Bibliography

Abrahamson, Mark. 1978. *Functionalism*. Englewood-Cliff, NJ: Prentice Hall, Inc.
Acemoglu, Daron, and James A. Robinson. 2012. *Why Nations Fail: The Origins of Power, Prosperity, and Poverty*. New York: Crown Business.
Adger, Neil, HallieEakin, and Alexandra Winkels. 2009. "Nested and Teleconnected-Vulnerabilities to Environmental Change." *Frontiers in Ecology and the Environment* 7, no. 3: 150–157.
Aggarwal, Vinod K., and Cedric Dupont. 2011. "Collaboration and Co-Ordination in the Global Political Economy." In *Global Political Economy*, 3rd ed., edited by John Ravenhill. New York: Oxford University Press.
"Alfred Radcliffe-Brown," accessed December 8, 2018, https://en.wikipedia.org/wiki/Alfred_Radcliffe-Brown.
Aquinas, Thomas. 1988. *On Politics and Ethics*. New York: Norton.
Alesina, Alberto, and Paolo Giuliano. 2015. "Culture and Institutions." *Journal of Economic Literature* 53, no. 4: 898–944.
Almond, Gabriel A., and Sidney Verba. 1963. *The Civic Culture: Political Attitudes and Democracy in Five Nat*ions. Princeton, NJ: Princeton University Press.
Allison, Graham T. 2004. *Nuclear Terrorism: The Ultimate Preventable Catastrophe*. New York: Owl Books/Henry Holt & Company.
American Bar Association, "Model Rules of Professional Conduct," Rule 3.4.
Ampére, A.M. 1884. *Essay on the Philosophy of the Sciences* (Trans). Paris, France.
Andersen, Lotte Bøgh, Torben Beck Jørgensen, Anne Mette Kjeldsen, Lene Holm Pedersen, and Karsten Vrangbæk. 2012. "Public Values and Public Service Motivation: Conceptual and Empirical Relationships." *The American Review of Public Administration* 43, no. 3: 292–311.
Andrewes, Antony. 1971. *The Greeks*. New York: Alfred A. Knopf.
Aquino, K., and A. Reed. 2002. "The Self-Importance of Moral Identity." *Journal of Personality and Social Psychology* 83: 1423–1440.
Arnopoulos, P. 1993. "Dialectics, Politics, and Cybernetics: The Sociophysics of Complex Systems." *Cyberntica* XXXVI, no. 4: 345–353.

Arendt, Hanna. 1958. *The Human Condition*. Chicago, IL: The University of Chicago Press.

Argyris, Chris. 1982. *Reasoning, Learning and Action: Individual and Organizational*. SanFrancisco, CA: Jossey-Bass.

Argyris, Chris, and Donald Schon. 1996. *Organizational learning II: Theory, Method and Practice*. Reading, MA: Addison Wesley.

Aristotle, *Rhetoric* I, 1354a31-b11. https://plato.stanford.edu/entries/aristotle-rhetoric/

Aristotle. 1962. *The Politics*. Translated by T. A. Sinclair. New York: Penguin Books.

Aristotle. 1985. Nicomachean Ethics. Translated by Terence Irwin. Indianapolis, IN: Hackett Publishing Company.

Aronowitz, Stanley. 1989. "Postmodernism and Politics." *Social Text, No. 21: Universal Abandon? The Politics of Postmodernism*. Durham, NC: Duke University Press.

"Artifact," accessed July 27, 2018, https://www.merriam-webster.com/dictionary/artifact.

Ashby, W. Ross. 1952. *A Design for a Brain*. New York: John Wiley.

———. 1960. *An Introduction to Cybernetics*. London: Chapman & Hall.

———. 1972. "Setting Goals in Cybernetic Systems." In *Cybernetics, Artificial Intelligence, and Ecology: Proceedings of the Fourth Annual Symposium of the American Society for Cybernetics*, edited by Herbert W. Robinson and Douglas E. Knight, 33–44. Spartan Books. http://aunilo.uum.edu.my/Find/Record/id-ui-lib.88/Description.

———. 2010. "Psychiatry, Synthetic Brains, and Cybernetics." In *The Cybernetic Brain*, edited by Andrew Pickering, 91–170. Chicago, IL: The University of Chicago Press.

Ball, Molly, and Tessa Berenson. 2018. "The Cost to the Court." *Time* 192, no. 14 (September): 28–32.

Barkin, Samuel J. 2006. "Realist Constructivism." In *Politics Among Nations: The Struggle for Power and Peace*, 7th ed., edited by Hans J. Morgenthau, 585–601. New York: McGraw-Hill Higher Education.

Bates, Clifford Angell, Jr. 2003. *Aristotle's "Best Regime:" Kingship, Democracy, and the Rule of Law*. Baton Rouge, LA: Louisiana State University Press.

Bates, Robert H. 2010. *Prosperity and Violence: The Political Economy of Development*, 2nd ed., New York: W. W. Norton & Co.

Beaudry, P. 2003. *The Economic Policy that made the Peace of Westphalia*. Washington, DC: The Schiller Institute.

Becker, G. S. 1968. "Crime and Punishment: An Economic Approach." *Journal of Political Economy* 76: 169–217.

Beer, Stafford. 1956. "A Technical Consideration of the Cybernetic Analogue for Planning and Programming." *Operational Research Quarterly* 7, no. 4: 143. https://www.jstor.org/stable/i353492

———. 1959. *Cybernetics and Management*. New York: John Wiley & Sons, Inc.

"Behavioralism," accessed September 15, 2018, https://www.britannica.com/topic/political-science#ref848558.

Beiner, Ronald. 2003. *Liberalism, Nationalism, Citizenship: Essays on the Problem of Political Community*. Vancouver, Canada: The University of British Columbia Press.

Bell, Mark S., and Nicolas L. Miller. 2015. "Nuclear Weapons and Conflict." In *The Use of Force*, 8th ed., edited by Robert J. Art and Kelly M. Green, 318–332. Lanham, MD: Rowman & Littlefield Publishers, Inc.

Beninger, James R. 1986. *The Control Revolution: Technological and Economics Origins of the Information Society*. Cambridge, MA: Harvard University Press.

Berger, Peter L., and Thomas Luckmann. 1967. *The Social Construction of Reality*. New York: Doubleday Anchor.

Bertalanffy, Ludwig Von. 1968. *General Systems Theory: Foundations, Development, Applications*. New York: George Braziller.

Betts, Richard K. 2015. "The Lost Logic of Deterrence." In *The Use of Force*, 8th ed., edited by Robert J. Art and Kelly M. Green, 98–105. Lanham, MD: Rowman & Littlefield Publishers, Inc.

———. 2015. "Puttering with Primacy." In *The Use of Force*, 8th ed., edited by Robert J. Art and Kelly M. Greenhill, 356–363. Lanham, MD: Rowman & Littlefield Publishers, Inc.

Bhaskar, Roy. 2007. "Theorising Ontology." In *Contributions to Social Ontology*, edited by Clive Lawson, John Latsis, and Nuno Martins, 192–204. London: Routledge.

Bocchiaro, Piero, and Adriano Zamperini. 2012. "Conformity, Obedience, Disobedience: The Power of the Situation." In *Psychology: Selected Papers*, edited by Gina Rossi, 275–294. Rijeka, Croatia: InTech Europe.

Boda, Zsolt. 2003. "Global Environmental Commons and the Need for Ethics." *Society and Economy* 25, no. 2: 213–224.

Boettke, Peter. 2010. "Is the Only Form of 'Reasonable Regulation' Self Regulation?: Lessons from Lin Ostrom on Regulating the Commons and Cultivating Citizens." *Public Choice* 143: 283–291.

Boulding, Kenneth E. 1985. *The World as a Total System*. Beverly Hills, CA: Sage Publications.

Bourdieu, Pierre. 1971. "Systems of Education and Systems of Thought." In *Knowledge and Control: New Directions for the Sociology of Education*, edited by M. K. D. Young, 189–207. London: Collier Macmillan.

Bourdieu, Pierre, and Loic J. D. Wacquant. 1992. *An Invitation to Reflexive Sociology*. Chicago, IL: University of Chicago Press.

Boyd R., and P. J. Richerson. 1985. *Culture and the Evolutionary Process*. Chicago, IL: University of Chicago Press.

Bozeman, Barry. 2007. *Public Values and Public Interest: Counterbalancing Economic Individualism*. Washington, DC: Georgetown University Press.

Bravin, Jess. 2015. "Ruling." *The Wall Street Journal*, Saturday/Sunday June 27–28, A6.

Brinkerhoff, Derick W. 2005. Rebuilding Governance in Failed States and Post-Conflict Societies: Core Concepts and Cross-Cutting Themes. *Public Administration and Development* 25: 3–14.

Brown, Seyom. 2015. "The Just War Tradition (Jus ad Bellum)." In *The Use of Force*, 8th ed., edited by Robert J. Art and Kelly M. Green, 69–80. Lanham, MD: Rowman & Littlefield Publishers, Inc.

Bryner, Gary, and Robert J. Duffy. 2012. *Integrating Climate, Energy, and Air Pollution Policies*. Cambridge, MA: The MIT Press.

Buckley, Walter. 1967. *Sociology and Modern Systems Theory*. Upper Saddle River, NJ: Prentice-Hall.

———. 1972. "A Systems Approach to Epistemology." In *Trends in General Systems Theory*, edited by George J. Klir, 188–202. New York: John Wiley & Sons, Inc.

Bueno de Mesquita, Bruce, and David Lalman. 1992. *War and Reason: Domestic and International Imperatives*. New Haven, CT: Yale University Press.

Burn, A. R. 1965. *The Penguin History of Greece*. London: Penguin Books.

Burrell, Gibson, and Gareth Morgan. 1979. *Sociological Paradigms and Organizational Analysis*. Aldershot, UK: Ashgate.

Burton, John W. 1975. "Functionalism and the Resolution of Conflict." In *Functionalism: Theory and Practice in International Relations*, edited by A. J. R. Groom and Paul Taylor, 238–249. New York: Crane, Russak & Company.

Calabresi, Massimo. 2018. "The Spy Masters." *Time* 191, no. 22 (June 11): 43.

Caporaso, James A., and Mary Anne Madeira. 2012. *Globalization, Institutions and Governance*. London: Sage Publications.

Carlton, Eric. 2006. *Politeia: Visions of the Just Society*. Madison, NJ: Farleigh Dickinson University Press.

Carter, A. 2001. *The Political Theory of Global Citizenship*. New York: Routledge.

Carter, Ashton, and William J. Perry. 1999. *Preventive Defense: A New Security Strategy for America*. Washington, DC: Brookings Institution Press.

Carter, Neil. 2001. *The Politics of the Environment: Ideas, Activism,* Policy, 2nd ed., Cambridge, UK: Cambridge University Press.

Campbell, D. T. 1975. "On the Conflicts Between Biological and Social Evolution and Between Psychology and Moral Tradition." *American Psychology* 30, no. 11: 1103–1126.

Caspary, William R. 2000. *Dewey on Democracy*. Ithaca, NY: Cornell University Press.

"Characteristics of Sociotechnical Systems," accessed December 2, 2017, http://moderntimesworkplace.com/archives/ericsess/sessvol2/STS_Emery.pdf.

Chasek, Pamela S., David L. Downe, and Janet Welsh Brown. 2010. *Global Environmental Politics: Dilemmas in World Politics*, 5th ed., Boulder, CO: Westview Press.

Chazan, Naomi, Robert Mortimer, John Ravenhill, and Donald Rothchild. 1992. *Politics and Society in Contemporary Africa*. Boulder, CO: Lynne Rienner Publishers.

Cicero. 1928. *De Re Publica and De Legibus*. With an English Translation by Clinton Walker Keyes. London: William Heinemann.

———. 1960. *Selected Works*. Translated by Michael Grant. Harmondsworth, Middlesex, England: Penguin Books Limited.

———. 1993. *On Government*. Translated by Michael Grant. London: Penguin Books.

Clair, Judith A. 2015. "Procedural Injustice in the System of Peer Review and Scientific Misconduct." *Academy of Management Learning & Education* 14, no. 2: 159–172.

Clift, Ben. 2006. "The New Political Economy of Dirigisme: French Macroeconomic Policy, Unrepentant Sinning and the Stability and Growth Pact." *British Journal of Politics and International Relations* 8, no. 3: 388–409.

Conant, R. C., and W. R. Ashby. 1970. "Every Good Regulator of a System Must Be A Model of That System." *International Journal of Systems Science* 1: 89–97.

Corley, Pamela, Artemus Ward, and Wendy L. Martinek. 2016. *American Judicial Process: Myth and Reality in Law and Courts*. New York: Routledge.

Costa, Antonio Carlos Da Rocha, Jose Mauro Volkmer De Castillo, and Dalcidio Morales Claudio. 1995. "Toward a Constructive Notion of Functionality." *Cybernetics and Systems: An International Journal* 26: 443–480.

Cooper, Terry. 1984. "Citizenship and Professionalism in Public Administration." *Public Administration Review* 44 (Special Issue): 143–149.

Crossley, N. 2001. "Citizenship, Intersubjectivity and the Lifeworld." In *Culture and Citizenship*, edited by N. Stevenson, 33–46. Thousand Oaks, CA: Sage Publications.

"Cybernetics," accessed June 1, 20188, https://politicsofsoul.org/tag/cybernetics, 1.

"Cybernetics," accessed June 1, 2018, https://politicsofsoul.org/tag/cybernetics, 2.

Daft, Richard L. 2016. *Organization Theory & Design,* 12thed., Boston, MA: Cengage Learning.

Dahl, Robert A. 1982. *Dilemmas of Pluralist Democracy: Autonomy vs. Control*. New Haven, CT: Yale University Press.

Dahrendorf, R. 1959. *Class and Class Conflict in Industrial Society*. London: Routledge and Kegan Paul.

Damon, W., and D. Hart. 1992. "Self-Understanding and Its Role in Social and Moral Development." In *Development Psychology: An Advanced Textbook*, 3rd ed., edited by M. H. Bornstein and E. Michael, 421–464. Hillsdale, NJ: Lawrence Erlbaum Associates Inc.

Daugherty, Paul R., and H. James Wilson. 2018. *Human + Machine: Reimagining Work in the Age of Artificial Intelligence*. Cambridge, MA: Harvard Business Review Press.

Dauvergne, Peter. 2011. "Globalization and the Environment." In *Global Political Economy*, 3rd ed., edited by John Ravenhill, 450–480. New York: Oxford University Press.

Davidson, Donald. 1994. "Actions, Reason, and Causes." In *Readings in the Philosophy of Social Science*, edited by Michael Martin and Lee C. McIntyre, 675–686. Cambridge, MA: MIT Press.

Dechert, Charles R. 1966. "The Development of Cybernetics." In *The Social Impact of Cybernetics*, edited by Charles R. Dechert, 11–37. Notre Dame, IN: University of Notre Dame Press.

Dempsey, Gary. 2001. The Folly of Nation-Building in Afghanistan. The Cato Insti tute. http://www.cato.org/pub_display.php?pub_id=3870, 1–2.

De Tocqueville, Alexis. 2000. *Democracy in America*. Translated and Annotated by Stephen D. Grant. Indianapolis, IN: Hackett Publishing Company.

Deutsch, Karl W. 1966. *The Nerves of Government: Models of Political Communication and Control*. New York: The Free Press.

Diamond, Jared. 2015. *Collapse: How Societies Choose to Fail or Succeed*. New York: Viking.

Dickovick, J. Tyler, and Jonathan Eastwood, ed. 2016. *Comparative Politics: Classic and Contemporary Readings*. New York: Oxford University Press.

———. 2016. *Comparative Politics: Integrating Theories, Methods, and Cases*, 2nd ed., New York: Oxford University Press.

———. 2019. *Comparative Politics: Integrating Theories, Methods, and Cases*, 3rd ed., New York: Oxford University Press.

DiMaggio, Paul. 1979. "Review Essay: On Pierre Bourdieu." *American Journal of Sociology* 84:1460–1474.

"Dirigisme," accessed July 3, 2015, http://www.britannica.com/topic/dirigisme, 1.

Dore, R. P. 1994. "Function and Cause." In *Readings in the Philosophy of Social Science,* edited by Michael Martin and Lee McIntyre, 377–389. Cambridge, MA: MIT Press.

Dowding, Keith. 2004. "Are Democratic and Just Institutions the Same?" In *Justice and Democracy: Essays for Brian Barry*, edited by Keith Dowding, Robert E. Goodin, and Carole Pateman, 25–39. New York: Cambridge University Press.

Drack, Manfred. 2015. "Ludwig von Bertalanffy's Organismic View on the Theory of Evolution." *Journal of Experimental Zoology (B) Molecular and Development Evolution* 324, no. 2: 77–90.

Ducat, Craig R. 2013. *Constitutional Interpretation*, 10th ed., Boston, MA: Wadsworth Cengage.

Durkheim, Emile. 1912/1961. *The Elementary Forms of Religious Life*. New York: Collier Books.

———. 1933. *Division of Labor in Society*. Translated by G. Simpson. New York: Macmillan.

———. 1938. *The Rules of Sociological Method*. Glencoe, IL: Free Press.

———. 1957/1992. *Professional Ethics and Civic Morals*. London: Routledge.

———. 1968. "The Development of the Theory of Social Control." In *The Structure of Social Action: A Study in Social Theory with Special Reference to a Group of Recent European Writers*, edited by Talcott Parsons, 376–408. New York: The Free Press.

———. 1994. "Social Facts." In *Readings in the Philosophy of Social Science*, edited by Michael Martin and Lee C. McIntyre, 433–440. Cambridge, MA: The MIT Press.

Eagan, Jennifer L. 2007. "Is Authority in Public Administration Separable from Authoritarianism? Personalities, Institutions, and Resistance." *Administrative Theory & Praxis* 29, no. 1: 83–101.

Eckstein, Harry. 1977. "Authority Patterns." In *Comparative Politics: Notes and Readings*, 5th ed., edited by Roy C. Macridis and Bernard E. Brown, 271–299. Homewood, IL. The Dorsey Press.

Edgerton, David. 2009. "The Shock of the Old." In *Technology and the Future*, edited by Albert H. Teich, 63–73. Boston, MA: Wadsworth.

Elliott, Herschel. 1997. "A General Statement of the Tragedy of the Commons." *Population and Environment* 8, no. 6: 515–531.

Emami, Zohreh, and Timothy Riordan. 1998. "Tony Lawson on Critical Realism: What's Teaching Got to Do with it?" *Review of Social Economy* 56, no. 3: 311–323.

Emery, F. 1959. "Characteristics of Sociotechnical Systems." Tavistock Institute of Human Relations, Document 527.

Emery, Fred E., and E. L. Trist. 1965. "The Causal Texture of Organizational Environments." *Human Relations* 18: 21–32.

"Entropy," accessed June 30, 2018, https://www.merriam-webster.com/dictionary/entropy.

"Equipotentiality," accessed June 21, 2018, https://en.wikipedia.org/wiki/Equipotentiality.

Fay, Brian. 1994. "General Laws and Explaining Human Behavior." In *Readings in the Philosophy of Social Science*, edited by Michael Martin and Lee McIntyre, 91–110. Cambridge, MA: MIT Press.

Fagence, M. 1977. *Citizen Participation in Planning*. New York: Pergamon Press.

Farr, Arnold L. 2009. *Critical Theory and Democratic Vision: Herbert Marcuse and Recent Liberation Philosophies*. Lanham, MD: Lexington Books.

Faundez, Julio. 2016. "Douglas North's Theory of Institutions: Lessons for Law and Development." *Hague Journal of Rule of Law* 8: 373–419.

Fligstein, Neil, and Doug McAdam. 2012. *A Theory of Fields*. Oxford, UK: Oxford University Press.

Flood, Robert L., and Ewart R. Carson. 1988. *Dealing with Complexity: An Introduction to the Theory and Application of Systems Science*. New York: Plenum Press.

Forsyth, Tim, and Craig Johnson. 2014. "Elinor Ostrom's Legacy: Governing the Commons and the Rational Choice Controversy." *Development and Change* 45, no. 5: 1093–1110.

Fox, Charles J. 1996. "Reinventing Government as Postmodern Symbolic Politics." *Public Administration Review* 56, no. 3: 256–262.

Frank, Robert H., and Ben S. Bernanke. 2007. *Principles of Macroeconomics*, 3rd ed., Boston, MA: McGraw-Hill.

Follesdal, Dagfin. 1994. "The Status of Rationality Assumptions in Interpretation and in the Explanation of Action." In *Readings in the Philosophy of Social Science*, edited by Michael Martin and Lee C. McIntyre, 299–310. Cambridge, MA: MIT Press, p. 307.

"For European Recovery: The Fiftieth Anniversary of the Marshall Plan," accessed July 29, 2018, https://www.loc.gov/exhibits/marshall/marsh-overview.html.

Fox, Charles J., and Hugh T. Miller. 1995. *Postmodern Public Administration*. Thousand Oaks, CA: Sage.

Frederickson, H. George. 2000. "Can Bureaucracy Be Beautiful?" *Public Administration Review* 60, no. 1: 47–53.

Fritz, Kurt Von, and Ernst Kapp. 1974. *Aristotle: Constitution of Athens and Related Texts*. NewYork: Hafner Press.

"Functionalism," accessed November 30, 2017, https://www.britannica.com/topic/functionalism-social-science.

"Functionalism," accessed December 8, 2017, http://anthropology.ua.edu/cultures/cultures.php?culture=Functionalism.

"Functionalism and Parsons," accessed November 15, 2017, http://uregina.ca/~gingrich/n2f99.htm.

Gaddis, John Lewis. 2004. *Surprise, Security, and the American Experience*. Cambridge, MA: Harvard University Press.

Gannon, Martin J. 2014. *Understanding Global Cultures: Metaphorical Journeys Through 28 Nations, Clusters of Nations, and Continents*. Thousand Oaks, CA: Sage Publications.

Gartner, Scott Sigmund. 1997. *Strategic Assessment in War*. New Haven, CT: Yale University Press.

George, Frank H. 1959. *Automation, Cybernetics, and Society*. New York: Philosophical Library.

———. 1958. Probabilistic Machines. *Automation Progress* 3, no. 1: 19–21.

———. 1965. *Cybernetics and Biology*. San Francisco, CA: W. H. Freeman & Co.

Georgiadis, Constantine. 1987. "Equitable and Equity in Aristotle." In *Justice, Law and Method in Plato and Aristotle*, edited by Spiro Panagiotou, 159–172. Edmonton, Alberta: Academic Printing & Publishing.

Giddens, Anthony. 1979. *Central Problems in Social Theory: Action, Structure, and Contradiction in Social Analysis*. Berkeley, CA: University of California Press.

———. 1984. *The Constitution of Society: Outline of the Theory of Structuration*. Berkeley, CA: University of California Press.

Gilbert, Rob. 1992. Citizenship, Education and Postmodernity. *British Journal of Sociology of Education* 13, no. 1: 51–68.

Gingrich, P. 1999. "Functionalism and Parsons." In *Sociology 250 Subject Notes*, November 9. Canada: University of Regina. http://uregina.ca/~gingrich/n2f99.htm. Accessed on December 13, 2017.

Glenn, Evelyn. 2000. "Citizens and Inequality: Historical and Global Perspectives." *Social Problems* 47, no. 1: 1–20.

Godo H., G. Gulbrandse, S. Herstad, A. Mariussen, R. Roset, O. R. Spilling, and F. Orstavik. 2008. *Innovation Systems, Innovation Modes, and Processes of Commercialization*. NIFU STEP-Studies in Innovation, Research and Education, Oslo, Norway: 1–174.

Goodin, Robert E. 2004. "Democracy, Justice, Impartiality." In *Justice and Democracy: Essays for Brian Barry*, edited by Keith Dowding, Robert E. Goodin, and Carole Pateman, 97–111. New York: Cambridge University Press.

Goffman, Erving. 1974. *Frame Analysis*. Cambridge, MA: Harvard University Press.

———. 1983. "The Interaction Order." *American Sociological Review* 48: 1–17.

Gorham, Eric. 1995. "Social Citizenship and Its Fetters." *Polity* 28, no. 1: 25–47.

Graham, Lawrence S., Richard P. Farkas, Robert C. Grady, George Joffé, Donley T. Studlar, and Alan M. Wachman. 2007. *The Politics of Governing: A Comparative Introduction*. Washington, DC: CQ Press, 310.

Greene, Kenyon B. 1973. *Sociotechnical Systems: Factors in Analysis, Design, and Management*. Englewood Cliffs, NJ: Prentice- Hall Inc.

Groom, A. J. R. 1975. "Functionalism and World Society." In *Functionalism: Theory and Practice in International Relations*, edited by A. J. R. Groom and Paul Taylor, 93–111. New York: Crane, Russak & Company.

Haas, Ernst B. 1990. *When Knowledge is Power: Three Models of Change in International Organizations*. Berkeley, CA: University of California Press.

Habermas, Jurgen. 1975. *Legitimation Crisis*. Boston, MA: Beacon Press.

Hall, Peter, and Rosemary C. R. Taylor. 1998. "Political Science and the Three New Institutionalisms." In *Institutions and Social Order*, edited by Karol Soltan, Eric

M. Uslander, and Virginia Haufler, 15–43. Ann Arbor, MI: The University of Michigan Press.

Hamalainen, Timo. 2013. *Building blocks for a new socioeconomic model*. Helsinki, Finland: SITRA, Version 10, 10.

Hamilton, Lee V., and Joseph Sanders. 1995. "Crimes of Obedience and Conformity in the Workplace: Surveys of Americans, Russians, and Japanese." *Journal of Social Issues* 51, no. 3: 67–88.

Hansen, Phillip. 1993. *Hannah Arendt: Politics, History and Citizenship*. Stanford, CA: Stanford University Press.

Hanson, Donald. 1984. "Thomas Hobbes' Highway to Peace." *International Organization* 38:329–354.

Hardin, Garrett. 1968. "The Tragedy of the Commons," *Science* 162 (December 13): 1243–1248.

Hart, David K. 1984. "The Virtuous Citizen, the Honorable Bureaucrat as Public Administrator." *Public Administration Review* 44 (Special Issue): 111–120.

Harvard Law Review. 1990. "Constructing the State Extra-Territorially: Jurisdictional Discourse, the National Interest and Transnational Norms." *Harvard Law Review* 103, no. 6: 1273–1305.

Harrison, Michael I. 2005. *Diagnosing Organizations: Methods, Models, and Processes*. Thousand Oaks, CA: Sage Publications.

Hassan, H., and C. Dwyer. 2010. Was the Copenhagen Summit Doomed from the Start? Some Insights from Green IS Research. Paper presented at the Americas Conference on Information Systems (AMCIS 2010), Lima, Peru.

Haste, Helen. 2004. "Constructing the Citizen." *Political Psychology* 25, no. 3: 413–439.

Hastie, Reid, and Robyn M. Davies. 2001. *Rational Choice in an Uncertain World: The Psychology of Judgment and Decision Making*. Thousand Oaks, CA: Sage Publications.

Hay, Colin. 2011. "Globalization's Impact on States." In *Global Political Economy*, 3rd ed., edited by John Ravenhill, 312–344. New York: Oxford University Press.

Hayek, F. A. 1960. *The Constitution of Liberty*. Chicago, IL: The University of Chicago Press.

Heimann, Eduard. 1938. *Communism, Fascism, or Democracy*? New York: W. W. Norton & Co.

Hempel, Carl G. "The Function of General Laws in History." In *Readings in the Philosophy of Social Science,* edited by Michael Martin and Lee McIntyre, 43–53. Cambridge, MA: MIT Press.

———. 1994. "The Logic of Functional Analysis." In *Readings in the Philosophy of Social Science*, edited by Michael Martin and Lee McIntyre, 349–375. Cambridge, MA: MIT Press.

Henry, Adams Douglas, and Thomas Dietz. 2011. "Information, Networks, and the Complexity of Trust in Commons Governance." *International Journal of the Commons* 5, no. 2: 188–212.

Herman, Gabriel. 2006. *Morality and Behavior in Democratic Athens: A Social History*. Cambridge, UK: Cambridge University Press.

Herring, Peter. 2003. "Inspired by Ideas." *High Technology Finland* 2003. Helsinki, Finland: High Technology Finland.

High Technology Finland. 2003. "Communications and Information." *High Technology Finland* 2003. Helsinki, Finland: High Technology Finland.

Hilsenrath, Jon, and Brian Blackstone. 2015. "Cheaper Currency has Global Impact." *The Wall Street Journal*, August 12, A1.

Hill, Carolyn J., and Laurence E. Lynn, Jr. 2016. *Public Management: Thinking and Acting in Three Dimensions*, 2nded., Thousand oaks, CA: Sage Publications.

Hirokawa, Randy Y. 2005. *Introduction to Theories of Human Communication*. University of Hawaii, Hilo.

Hobbes, Thomas. 1994. *Leviathan*, edited by Edwin Curly based on the Latin edition of 1668. Indianapolis, IN: Hackett Publishing Company, Inc.

Holcombe, Randall G. 1997. "A Theory of the Theory of Public Goods." *Review of Austrian Economics* 10, no. 1: 1–22.

Howell, Kerry E. 2013. *An Introduction to the Philosophy of Methodology*. London: Sage Publications.

Hoover, Kenneth, and Todd Donovan. 2011. *The Elements of Social Scientific Thinking*, 10th ed., Boston, MA: Wadsworth.

Hulin, Charles L., and M. Roznowski. 1985. "Organizational Technologies: Effects on Organizations' Characteristics and Individuals' Responses." In *Research in Organizational Behavior* 7, edited by L.L. Cummings and Barry M. Staw, 39–84. Greenwich, CT: JAI Press.

Hummel, Ralph P. 1987. *The Bureaucratic Experience*, 3rded., New York: St. Martin's Press.

Huntington, Samuel P. 1977. "Postindustrial Politics: How Benign?" In *Comparative Politics: Notes and Readings*, 5thed., edited by Roy C. Macridis and Bernard E. Brown, 501–516. Homewood, IL: The Dorsey Press.

"Infrastructure," accessed December 24, 2017, https://www.merriam-webster.com/dictionary/infrastructure.

Ingraham, Patricia W., and Laurence E. Lynn, Jr., ed. 2004. *The Art of Governance: Analyzing Management and Administration*. Washington, DC: Georgetown University Press.

Jacobs, Walter. 1972. "How a Bug's Mind Works." In *Cybernetics, Artificial Intelligence, and Ecology: Proceedings of the Fourth Annual Symposium of the American Society for Cybernetics*, edited by Herbert W. Robinson and Douglas E. Knight, 95–125. Spartan Books. http://aunilo.uum.edu.my/Find/Record/id-ui-lib.88/Description

Jacobson, David. 1996. *Rights Across Borders: Immigration and the Decline of Citizenship*. Baltimore, MD: The Johns Hopkins University Press.

———. 1998. "State and Society in a World Unbound." In *Public Rights, Public Rules: Constituting Citizens in the World Polity and National Policy*, edited by Connie L. McNeely, 41–57. New York: Garland Publishing Inc.

Jarvie, I. C. 1973. *Functionalism*. Minneapolis, MN: Burgess Publishing Company.

Jepperson, R. L. 1991. "Institutions, Institutional Effects, and Institutionalization." In *New Institutionalism in Organizational Analysis*, edited by W. W. Powell and Paul J. DiMaggio, 143–163. Chicago, IL: University of Chicago Press.

Jolls, Christine, Cass R. Sunstein, and Richard Thaler. 1998. "A Behavioral Approach to Law and Economics." *Stanford Law Review* 50, no. 5: 1471–1550.

Kalu, Kalu N. 2008. *State Power, Autarchy, and Political Conquest in Nigerian Federalism*. Lanham, MD: Lexington Books.

———. 2011. "Institution-Building, not Nation-Building: A Structural-Functional Model." *International Review of Administrative Sciences* 77, no. 1: 119–137.

———. 2017. *Citizenship: Identity, Institutions and the Postmodern Challenge*. New York: Routledge.

———. 2017. *Technology, Culture, and Public Policy: Critical Lessons from Finland*. New York: Routledge.

———. 2018. *Political Culture, Change, and Security Policy in Nigeria*. New York: Routledge.

Kaidesoja, Tuukka. 2007. "The Concept of Social Structure in Roy Bhaskar's Critical Realism." *Sosiologia* 44, no. 2: 79–94.

———, accessed January 12, 2019, https://www.academia.edu/4218954/The_Concept_of_Social_Structure_in_Roy_Bhaskars_Critical_Realism, 8.

Kalpakgian, Mitchell. 2012. "The Ladder of Knowledge and the Ascent to Wisdom in Boethius' The Consolation of Philosophy." In *Boethius, The Consolation of Philosophy*, edited and translated by Scott Goins and Barbara H. Wyman, 177–185. San Francisco, CA: Ignatius Press.

Kay, Sean. 2015. *Global Security in the Twenty-First Century: The Quest for Power and the Search for Peace*. Lanham, MD: Rowman & Littlefield Publishers.

Kellner, Douglas. 1989. *Critical Theory, Marxism, and Modernity*. Baltimore, MD: The Johns Hopkins University Press.

Keohane, Robert O. 1988. "International Institutions: Two Research Programs." *International Studies Quarterly* 32 (December).

———. 2015. "The Global Politics of Climate Change: Challenge for Political Science." The 2014 James Madison Lecture. *PS: Political Science & Politics* 48, no. 1: 19–26.

Kincaid, Harold. 1994. "Assessing Functional Explanations in the Social Sciences." In *Readings in the Philosophy of Social Science*, edited by Michael Martin and Lee McIntyre, 415–428. Cambridge, MA: MIT Press.

King, Gary, Robert O. Keohane, and Sidney Verba. 1994. *Designing Social Inquiry: Scientific Inference in Qualitative Research*. Princeton, NJ: Princeton University Press.

Kinsella, David, Bruce Russett, and Harvey Starr. 2013. *World Politics: Menu for Choice*, 10th ed., Boston, MA: Wadsworth.

Knapp, Peter. 1994. *One World-Many Worlds: Contemporary Sociological Theory*. NewYork: Harper-Collins.

Kolb, David. 1990. *Postmodern Sophistications: Philosophy, Architecture, and Tradition*. Chicago, IL: The University of Chicago Press.

Koslenlaakso, Leena. 2018. Making the Most of AI. *This is Finland* 2018–2019, 6.

Krasner, Stephen D. 1988. Sovereignty: An Institutional Perspective. *Comparative Political Studies* 21: 66–94.

———. 1991. "Global Communications and National Power: Life on the Pareto Frontier." *World Politics* 43, no. 3: 336–366.

Kreps, Gary L. 1986. *Organizational Communication: Theory and Practice*. New York: Longman.

Kreuzer, Marcus. 2001. *Institutions and Innovation: Voters, Parties, and Interest Groups in the Consolidation of Democracy – France and Germany, 1870–1939*. Ann Arbor, MI: The University of Michigan Press.

Kymlicka, Will. 1995. *Multicultural Citizenship: A Liberal Theory of Minority Rights*. NewYork: Oxford University Press.

Lawson, Tony. 2003. "Theorizing Ontology." *Feminist Economics* 9, no. 1: 161–169.

———. 2012. "Ontology and the Study of Social Reality: Emergence, Organization, Community, Power, Social Relations, Corporations, Artefacts and Money." *Cambridge Journal of Economics* 36: 345–385.

Laszlo, Ervin. 1972. *The Systems View of the World: The Natural Philosophy of the New Developments in the Societies*. New York: George Braziller.

Levi-Faur, David. 2012. From Big Government to Big Governance? *The Oxford Handbook of Governance*, Online, September.

Linklater, Andrew. 2007. *Critical Theory and World Politics: Citizenship, Sovereignty and Humanity*. New York: Routledge.

Lipson, Charles. 1994. "Is the Future of Collective Security Like the Past?" In *Collective Security Beyond the Cold War*, edited by George W. Downs, 105–131. Ann Arbor, MI: University of Michigan Press.

Little, Daniel. 1991. *Varieties of Social Explanation: An Introduction to the Philosophy of Social Science*. Boulder, CO: Westview Press.

Lynn, Laurence E., Jr., Carolyn J. Heinrich, and Carolyn J. Hill. 2001. *Improving Governance: A New Logic for Empirical Research*. Washington, D.C: Georgetown University Press.

Luhman, Niklas. 1982. *The Differentiation of Society*. New York: Columbia University Press.

———. 1987. Rechtssoziologie, Opladen: WestdeutscherVerlag. http://www.lawandmethod.nl/tijdschrift/lawandmethod/2015/04/lawandmethod-D-15-00001.pdf. Accessed on September 2, 2018.

Lupia, Arthur, and Mathew W. McCubbins. 1995. Who Controls? Information and the Structureof Legislative Decision Making. In *Positive Theories of Congressional Institutions*, edited by Kenneth A. Shepsle and Barry R. Weingast, 201–233. Ann Arbor, MI: The University of Michigan Press.

Lyotard, J.F. 1984. *The Postmodern Condition: A Report on Knowledge*. Manchester, U. K: Manchester University Press.

MacIntyre, Alasdair. 1988. *Whose Justice? Which Rationality?* Notre Dame, IN: University of Notre Dame Press.

———. 1992. "Justice as Virtue." In *Communitarianism and Individualism*, edited byShlomoAvineri and Avner de-Shalit, 51–64. New York: Oxford University Press.

Macintyre, Andrew. 2003. *The Power of Institutions: Political Architecture and Governance*. Ithaca, NY: Cornell University Press.

Macpherson, Cheryl Cox. 2012. "Climate Change Matters." *Journal of Medical Ethics* 40, no. 4: 288–290.

Macridis, Roy C., and Steven L. Burg. 1991. *Introduction to Comparative Politics: Regimes and Change*. New York: Longman.

Mahler, Gregory S. 2013. *Principles of Comparative Politics*. Upper Saddle River, NJ: Pearson.

Manning, E. C. 1967. *Political Realignment: A Challenge to Thoughtful Canadians*. Toronto/Montreal, Canada: McClelland & Steward Ltd.

March, James, and Johan Olsen. 1986. "Garbage Can Models of Decision Making in Organizations." In *Ambiguity and Command: Organizational Perspectives on Military Decision Making*, edited by James March and Roger Weissinger-Baylon. Marshfield, MA: Pitman.

———. 1989. *Rediscovering Institutions: The Organizational Basis of Politics*. New York: The Free Press.

Marshall, Gary S. 2007. "Commanded to Enjoy: The Waning of Traditional Authority and Its Implications for Public Administration." *Administrative Theory & Praxis* 29, no. 1: 102–114.

Martin, Michael. 1994. "Taylor on Interpretation and the Sciences of Man." In *Readings in the Philosophy of Social Science*, edited by Michael Martin and Lee C. McIntyre, 259–279. Cambridge, MA: MIT Press.

Mathew McCubbins, and Frances Rosenbluth. 1995. "Party Provision for Personal Politics: Dividing the Vote in Japan." In *Structure and Policy in Japan and the United States*, edited by Peter Cowhey and Mathew McCubbins, 35–55. Cambrideg, UK: Cambridge University Press.

Maxwell, J. Clark. 1864. *Proceedings of the Royal Society* 13. London.

Mayhew, David. 1974. *Congress: The Electoral Connection*. New Haven, CT: Yale University Press.

Mead, George Herbert. 1967. *Mind, Self, and Society from the Standpoint of a Social Behaviorist*, edited with an Introduction by Charles W. Morris. Chicago, IL: University of Chicago Press.

Mearsheimer, John J. 1990. "Why We Will Soon Miss the Cold War." *The Atlantic Monthly* 266, no. 2: 35–50.

———. 1994–95. "The False Promise of International Institutions." *International Security* 19, no. 31:5–49.

———. 2001. *The Tragedy of Great Power Politics*. New York: W. W. Norton & Co.

———. 2006. "The False Promise of International Institutions." In Hans J. Morgenthau, *Politics Among Nations: The Struggle for Power and Peace*, 7th ed., 569–585. New York: McGraw-Hill Company.

Melloan, George. 2018. "Is 'First, Kill All the Lawyers' the Democrats' New Credo?" *The Wall Street Journal*, October 13–14.

Menke, Christoph. 2018. "Judging What Cannot be Judged: The Aporia of Aesthetic Critique." In *Judgement and Action: Fragments toward a History*, edited by Vivasvan Soni, and Thomas Pfau, 223–238. Evanston, IL: Northwestern University Press.

Merton, Robert K. 1957. *Social Theory and Social Structure*. Glencoe, IL: Free Press.

———. 1968. *Social Theory and Social Structure*. New York: The Free Press.

Mesthene, Emmanuel G. 2009. "The Role of Technology in Society." In *Technology and the Future*, edited by Albert H. Teich, 77–86. Boston, MA: Wadsworth.

Mill, John Stuart. 2007. "Utilitarianism." In *Justice: A Reader*, edited by Michael J. Sandel, 14–47. New York: Oxford University Press.

Miller, Fred D. 1995. *Nature, Justice, and Rights in Aristotle's Politics*. Oxford: Clarendon Press.

Midgal, Joel S. 1994. "The State in Society: As Approach to Struggles for Domination." In *State Power and Social Forces: Domination and Transformation in the Third World*, edited by Joel S. Midgal, AtulKohli, and Vivienne Shue, 7–34. New York: Cambridge University Press.

Mitrany, David. 1948. "The Functional Approach to Organization." *International Affairs* 24, no. 3: 350–363.

———. 1966. *A Working Peace System*. Chicago, IL: Quadrangle Books.

———. 1975. *The Functional Theory of Politics*. New York: St. Martin's Press.

Montesquieu, Baron de. 1989. *The Spirit of the Laws*. Translated and edited by Anne M. Cohler, Basia Carolyn Miller, and Harold Samuel Stone. Cambridge, UK: Cambridge University Press.

Morgan, Gareth. 2006. *Images of Organization*. Thousand Oaks, CA: Sage Publications.

Morin, Amy. 2018. What is Behavior Modification? Use Behavior Modification Strategies to getyour Child to Follow the Rules. https://www.verywellfamily.com/what-is-behavior-modification-1094788. Accessed on October 15, 2018.

Morone, James A., and Rogan Kersh. 2018. *By the People: Debating American Government*, 3rd ed., New York: Oxford University Press.

Morse, Chandler. 1961. "The Functional Imperatives." In *The Social Theories of Talcott Parsons: A Critical Examination*, edited by Max Black, 100–152. Englewood Cliffs, NJ: Prentice-Hall, Inc.

Mooney, Chris. 2018. "Trump Withdrew from the Paris Climate Deal a Year Ago: Here's What Has Changed." Energy and Environment Analysis, *The Washington Post* (June 1): 2 (Online).

Mueller, Get H. 1989. *Sociology and Ontology: The Analytical Foundations of Social Theory*. Lanham, MD: University Press of America.

Nabatchi, Tina. 2012. "Putting the "Public" Back in Public Values Research: Designing Participation to Identify and Respond to Value." *Public Administration Review* 72, no. 5: 699–708.

Nadler, D., and M. Tushman. 1980. "A Model for Diagnosing Organizational Behavior." *Organizational Dynamics* 9, no. 2: 35–51.

Neumayer, E. 2001. *Greening Trade and Investment: Environmental Protection without Protectionism*. London: Earthscan.

"New Generation Merkava Battle Tank," accessed July 22, 2018, https://defence-blog.com/army/israel-reveals-details-next-generation-merkava-main-battle-tank.html.

Noonan, Peggy. 2018. "Voices of Reason –and Unreason," *The Wall Street Journal*, October 13–14.

North, Douglass C. 1981. *Structure and Change in Economic History*. New York: W. W. Norton & Co.

———. 1991. "Institutions." *The Journal of Economic Perspectives* 5, no. 1: 97–112.

Nozick, Robert. 1974. *Anarchy, State and Utopia*. New York: Basic Books.

Neuvonen, Aleksi. 2017. *Sitra Memorandum: Rewriting Progress*. Helsinki, Finland: Sitra-The Finnish Innovation Fund (May 31).

"Obedience to Authority," accessed October 18, 2018, http://www.psicosocial.net/grupo-accion-comunitaria/centro-de-documentacion-gac/psicologia-y-tecnicas-de-control-social/operaciones-psicologicas/627-obedience-to-authority-an-experimental-view/file.

Offe, Claus. 2006. "Political Institutions and Social Power: Conceptual Explorations." In *Rethinking Political Institutions: The Art of the State*, edited by Ian Shapiro, Stephen Skowronek, and Daniel Galvin. New York: New York University Press.

Oldfield, Adrian. 1998. "Citizenship and Community: Civic Republicanism and the Modern World." In *The Citizenship Debates: A Reader*, edited by Gershon Shafir, 75–89. Minneapolis, MN: University of Minnesota Press.

Olsen, Marvin E. 1978. *The Process of Social Organization: Power in Social Systems*, 2nd ed., New York: Holt, Rinehart and Wilson.

Olson, Mancur. 1977. "Rapid Growth as a Destabilizing Force." In *Comparative Politics: Notesand Readings*, 5th ed., edited by Roy C. Macridis and Bernard E. Brown, 437–452. Homewood, IL: The Dorsey Press.

Onuf, Nicholas. 1989. *World of Our Making*. Columbia, SC: University of South Carolina Press.

Ornston, Darius. 2006. Reorganizing Adjustment: Finland's Emergence as High Tech Leader. *West European Politics* 29, no. 4: 784–801.

Ostrom, Elinor. 1982. "Beyond Positivism: An Introduction to this Volume." In *Strategies of Political Inquiry*, edited by Elinor Ostrom, 11–28. Beverly Hills, CA: Sage.

———. 1990. *Governing the Commons: The Evolution of Institutions for Collective Action*. Cambridge, UK: Cambridge University Press.

———. 2005. *Understanding Institutional Diversity*. Princeton, NJ: Princeton UniversityPress.

———. 2011. "Background on the Institutional Analysis and Development Framework." *The Policy Studies Journal* 39, no. 1: 7–27.

Ostrom, Vincent, and Elinor Ostrom. "Public Goods and Public Choices. Workshop in Political Theory and Policy Analysis." Indiana University, Bloomington, IN, USA. http://johannes.lecture.ub.ac.id/files/2012/02/Public-Goods-and-Public-Choices.pdf. Accessed on January 12, 2019.

Page, Scott. 2007. "Making the Difference: Applying the Logic of Diversity." *Academy of Management* 21, no. 4: 6–20.

Pangle, Thomas L. 1980. *The Laws of Plato*. Translated, with Notes and Interpretive Essay, by Thomas L. Pangle. New York: Basic Books.

Parsons, Talcott. 1937. *The Structure of Social Action*. New York: McGraw-Hill, Inc.

———. 1947. "Introduction: Weber's Methodology of Social Science." In *The Theory of Social and Economic Organization*, edited by Max Weber, 8–29. New York: The Free Press.

———. 1949. *Essays in Sociological Theory, Pure and Applied*. Glencoe, IL: Free Press.

———. 1949. *The Structure of Social Action: A Study in Social Theory with Special Reference to a Group of Recent European Writers*, Volume II. New York: The Free Press.

———. 1951. *The Social System*. Glencoe, IL: The Free Press.
———. 1954. *Essays in Sociological Theory*. New York: The Free Press.
———. 1960. *Structure and Process in Modern Societies*. Glencoe, IL: The Free Press.
———. 1961. *Theories of Society: Foundations of Modern Sociological Theory*. New York: Free Press.
———. 1967. *Sociological Theory and Modern Society*. New York: The Free Press.
———. 1977. *Social Systems and the Evolution of Action Theory*. New York: The Free Press.
———. 2007. *The American Society: A Theory of the Societal Community*. Edited and Introduced by Giuseppe Sciortino. Boulder, CO: Paradigm Publishers.
Parsons, Talcott, Robert F. Bales, and Edward Shils. 1953. *Working Papers in the Theory of Action*. Glencoe, IL: Free Press.
Parsons, Talcott, and Edward A. Shils. 2001. *Toward a General Theory of Action: Theoretical Foundations for the Social Sciences*. New Brunswick, NJ: Transaction Publishers.
Pickering, Andrew. 2010. *The Cybernetic Brain: Sketches of Another Future*. Chicago, IL: The University of Chicago Press.
Pilon, Roger. 2018. "When the Supreme Court is Everything." *Time* 192, no. 14: (September), 32.
Pitts, Walter, and Warren McCulloch. 1943. "A Logical Calcula of the Ideas Imminent in Nervous Activity." *Bull, Math, Biophys* 5: 115–133.
Plato. 1955. *The Republic*. New York: Penguin Books.
———. 1969. *The Last Days of Socrates*. Translated by Hugh Tredennick. New York: Penguin Books.
Plato. *The Laws of Plato*, accessed February 2, 2019, https://oll.libertyfund.org/pages/plato-s-the-laws-jowett-s-analysis.
———. 1974. *The Republic*, 2nd ed. Translated with an Introduction by Desmond Lee. New York: Penguin Books.
"Political Culture," accessed February 14, 2016, http://www.encyclopedia.com/topic/Political_culture.aspx, 1.
"Political Culture," accessed August 10, 2017, http://study.com/academy/lesson/political-culture-definition-theory-types-examples.html.
Porter, Arthur. 1969. *Cybernetics Simplified*. London: The English Universities Press Limited.
Posen, Barry R. 1984. *The Sources of Military Doctrine: France, Britain, and Germany Between the World Wars*. Ithaca, NY: Cornell University Press.
"Process Reimagined," accessed July 19, 2018, https://www.accenture.com/us-en/insight-process-reimagined.
PubMed Central, accessed March 8, 2018, http://www.ncbi.nim.nih.gov/pmc/articles/PMC4657461/, 5-6.
Quackenbush, Stephen L. 2015. *International Conflict: Logic and Evidence*. Thousand Oaks, CA: Sage-CQ.
Radcliffe-Brown, Reginald. 1952. *Structure and Function in Primitive Society*. New York: The Free Press.

Raadschelders, Jos C. N. 2003. *Government: A Public Administration Perspective.* Armonk, NY: M. E. Sharpe.

Raadschelders, Jos C. N., and Richard J. Stillman II. 2007. Toward a New Conceptual Framework for Studying Administrative Authority. *Administrative Theory & Praxis* 29, no. 1: 4–40.

Rainey, Hall G. 2009. *Understanding and Managing Public Organizations*, 4thed., San Francisco, CA: Jossey-Bass.

Rapoport, Anatol. 1956. *General Systems.* Washington, DC: Society for General Systems Research.

Rawls, John. 1971. *A Theory of Justice.* Cambridge, MA: Harvard University Press.

———. 2007. "Justice as Fairness." In *Justice: A Reader*, edited by Michael J. Sandel, 203–221. New York: Oxford University Press, p. 203.

Riccucci, Norma M. 2010. *Public Administration: Traditions of Inquiry and Philosophies of Knowledge.* Washington, DC: Georgetown University Press.

Rittel, H. W. J., and M. M. Webber. 1973. Dilemmas in a General Theory of Planning. *Policy Sciences* 4, no. 2: 155–169.

Rinfret, Sara R., Denise Scheberle, and Michelle C. Pautz. 2019. *Public Policy: A Concise Introduction.* Thousand Oaks, CA: CQ Press.

Roermund, Berat van. 2015. Law and Functionalism: The Limited Function of Law. *ReM* 2015-04, accessed September 2, 2018, http://www.lawandmethod.nl/tijdschrift/lawandmethod/2015/04/lawandmethod-D-15-00001.pdf.

Room, Graham. 2011. *Complexity, Institutions, and Public Policy: Agile Decision-making in a Turbulent World.* Cheltenham, UK: Edward Elgar.

Rorty, Richard. 1989. *Contingency, Irony, and Solidarity.* Cambridge: Cambridge University Press.

Rosenblum, N. N. 1978. "Citizen Participation and Democratic Theory." In *Participation in American*, edited by S. Langston, 43–54. Toronto, Canada: D. C. Heath & Co.

Rosenbloom, David H., and Howard E. McCurdy. 2006. *Revisiting Waldo's Administrative State: Constancy and Change in Public Administration.* Washington, DC: Georgetown University Press.

Rotberg, Robert. 2006. Failed States in a World of Terror. In *Global Politics in a Changing World*, 3rded., edited by Richard W. Mansbach and Edward Rhodes, 131–137. Boston, MA: Houghton-Mifflin.

Rutgers, Mark R. 2015. As Good as It Gets? On the Meaning of Public Value in the Study of Policy and Management. *American Review of Public Administration* 45, no. 1: 29–45.

Salvaterra, Neanda. 2018. Coal's Global Rebound Heats Up. *The Wall Street Journal* (September 4), B1–B2.

Salvi, Steve, "The Original List of Sanctuary Cities, USA," accessed October 13, 2015, http://ojjpac.org/sanctuary.asp.

Sandel, Michael J. 1982. *Liberalism and the Limits of Justice.* New York: Cambridge University Press.

———. 1998. *Liberalism and the Limits if Justice*, 2nd ed., New York: Cambridge University Press.

———. 2007. *Justice: A Reader*, ed. New York: Oxford University Press.

———. 2009. Justice: *What's the Right Thing to Do*? New York: Farrah, Straus and Giroux.

Sartre, Jean-Paul. 1965. *The Philosophy of Jean-Paul Sartre*. Edited and Introduced by R.D. Cumming. New York: Vintage Books.

Sayers, Sean. 1999. *Plato's Republic: An Introduction*. Edinburgh, Great Britain: Edinburgh University Press.

Schein, Edgar H. 1992. Organizational Culture and Leadership, 2nded., Homewood, IL: Richard D. Irwin.

Schneider, David. 1976. "Notes Toward A Theory of Culture." In *Meaning in Anthropology*, edited by Keith M. Basso and Henry L. Silby, 197–220. Albuquerque, NM: University of New Mexico Press.

Scheraga, J. D., K. L. Ebi, J. Furlow, and A. R. Moreno. 2003. "From Science to Policy: Developing Responses to Climate Change." In *Climate Change and Human Health: Risks and Responses*, edited by A. J. McMichael, D. Campbell-Lendrum, C. F. Corvalan, K. L. Ebi, A. Githeko, J. D. Scheraga, and A. Woodward A. WHO/WMO/UNEP, 243.

Scott, W. Richard. 2001. *Institutions and Organizations*, 2nded., Thousand Oaks, CA: SagePublications.

———. 2014. *Institutions and Organizations: Ideas, Interests, and Identities*, 4thed., Los Angeles, CA: Sage Publications.

Scott, W. Richard, and Gerald F. Davis. 2007. *Organizations and Organizing: Rational, Natural, and Open Systems Perspectives*. Upper Saddle River, NJ: Pearson-Prentice Hall.

Searle, John R. 1995. *The Construction of Social Reality*. New York: The Free Press.

———. 2006. "Social Ontology: Some Basic Principles." *Papers 80*: 51–71.

———. 2010. *Making the Social World: The Structure of Human Civilization*. New York: Oxford University Press.

Seidl, David. 2004. Luhmann's Theory of Autopoietic Social Systems, No. 2004-2. Munich Business School, Germany.

———. "Luhmann's Theory of Autopoietic Social Systems," accessed June 18, 2018, https://www.zfog.bwl.uni-muenchen.de/files/mitarbeiter/paper2004_2.pdf.

Selznick, Philip. 1992. *The Moral Commonwealth: Social Theory and the Promise of Community*. Berkeley, CA: University of California Press.

"Servomechanism," accessed June 21, 2108, https://www.britannica.com/technology/servomechanism.

Shapiro, Ian. 2003. *The Moral Foundations of Politics*. New Haven, CT: Yale University Press.

Siaroff, Alan. 2005. *Comparing Political Regimes: A Thematic Introduction to Comparative Politics*. Toronto, Canada: Broadview Press.

Sica, Alan. 2000. "Rationalization and Culture." In *The Cambridge Companion to Weber*, edited by Stephen Turner, 42–58. Cambridge, UK: Cambridge University Press.

Silverman, D. 1970. *The Theory of Organizations*. London: Heinemann.

Simon, Herbert A. 1957. *Administrative Behavior: A Study of Decision-Making Processes in Administrative Organization*. New York: The Free Press.

Simonsen, W., and M. D. Robbins. 2000. *Citizen Participation in Resource Allocation*. Boulder, CO: Westview Press.

Simmons, Robert H., and Eugene P. Dvorin. 1977. *Public Administration: Values, Policy, and Change*. Port Washington, NY: Alfred Publishing Co.

Smith, Alan G. 2017. *A Comparative Introduction to Political Science: Convention and Cooperation*. Lanham, MD: Rowman & Littlefield.

Sommerville, Ian. 2006. *Software Engineering*, 8th ed. (chapter 2). Boston, MA: Addison Wesley.

Singh, Shane. 2017. How Issue Frames Shape Beliefs about the Importance of Climate Change Policy Across Ideological and Partisan Groups. https://journals.plos.org/plosone/article?id=10.1371/journal.pone.0181401. Accessed on September 17, 2018, p. 1.

Shoemaker, Pamela J., James William Tankard, Jr., and Dominic L. Lasorsa. 2004. *How to Build Social Science Theories*. Thousand Oaks, CA: Sage Publications.

Skocpol, Theda. 1979. *States and Social Revolutions: A Comparative Analysis of France, Russia, and China*. Cambridge, UK: Cambridge University Press.

"Smart Factories," Lulea University of Technology, Sweden, accessed September 25, 2018, https://www.ltu.se/org/ets/Smarta-fabriker-staller-nya-krav-pa-arbetet-1.177938?l=en

Smith, Mark Stafford. 2015. "Responding to Global Environmental Change." In *Change*, editedby Gabriele Bammer, 29–42. ANU Press, 36, accessed September 19, 2018, https://www.jstor.org/stable/j.ctt16wd0cc, 7.

"Sociotechnical Systems," accessed December 21, 2017, https://www.researchgate.net/publication/240239070_A_Review_of_Sociotechnical_Systems_Theory_A_Classic_Concept_for_New_Command_and_Control_Paradigms.

"Sociotechnical Systems," accessed December 21, 2017, http://mysite.du.edu/~lbarne28/SE/Slides/Ch2.pdf.

Spiegel, Steve L., Jennifer M. Taw, Elizabeth G. Mathews, and Kristen P. Williams. 2012. *World Politics in a New Era*, 5th ed., New York: Oxford University Press.

Spencer, Herbert. 1898. *The Principles of Sociology*, 3 Volumes. New York: D. Appleton.

St. Augustine. 2003. *City of God*. U. K: Penguin Books.

Starr, Chester G. 1961. *The Origins of Greek Civilization* (1100–650 B.C). New York: W. W. Norton & Co.

Steinbruner, John. 1974. *The Cybernetic Theory of Decision*. Princeton, NJ: Princeton University Press.

Stepan, Alfred. 1978. *The State and Society: Peru in Comparative Perspective*. Princeton, NJ: Princeton University Press.

Stephens, Otis H. Jr., John M. Scheb II, and Colin Glennon. 2015. *American Constitutional Law Volume II: Civil Rights and Liberties*, 6th ed., Stamford, CT: Cengage Learning.

Steward, Dan. 2018. "Autocrats Grow Bolder." *Time* 192, no. 16: 21–22.

Stoessinger, J. G. 2010. *Why Nations Go to War*. Belmont, CA: Wadsworth/Thomson Learning.

Strand, Paul S. 2009. "Religion as Schedule-Induced Behavior." *The Behavior Analyst* 32: 191–204.

Strauss, Leo. 1999. "What is Political Philosophy?" In *Political Philosophy: Essential Selections*, edited by Aeon J. Skoble and Tibor R. Machan, 433–445. Upper Saddle River, NJ: Prentice Hall.

Strauss, Leo, and Joseph Cropsey. 1972. "Montesquieu." In *History of Political Philosophy*, edited by Leo Strauss and Joseph Cropsey, 487–508. Chicago, IL: Rand McNally & Co.

Swinth, Robert L. 1974. *Organizational Systems for Management: Designing, Planning and Implementation*. Columbus, OH: Grid.

Switzer, J. V. 2004. *Environmental Politics: Domestic and Global Dimensions*, 4th ed., Belmont, CA: Thomson/Wadsworth.

"Synergy, Cybernetics, and the Evolution of Politics," accessed April 15, 2018, http://complex systems.org/publications/the-evolution-of-politics.

Tarr, G. Alan. 2014. *Judicial Process and Judicial Policymaking*, 6th ed., Boston, MA: Wadsworth Cengage.

Tawney, R. H. 1926. *Religion and the Rise of Capitalism: A Historical Study*. New York: MentorBooks/Harcourt, Brace & World.

Taylor, Maria. 2014. "Influences on a Changed Story and the New Normal: Scientists' Beliefs and Public Scepticism." *Global Warming and Climate Change*. ANU Press, 144, accessed September 19, 2018, https://www.jstor.org/stable/j.ctt130h8d6.13.

Taylor, James C., and David F. Felten. 1993. *Performance by Design: Sociotechnical Systems in North America*. Englewood Cliffs, NJ: Prentice Hall, Inc.

"The Bretton Woods System," accessed July 29, 2018, http://www.brettonwoodspr oject.org/2005/08/art-320747/.

The CIA World Factbook, "Japan," https://www.cia.gov/library/publications/the-world-factbook/geos/ja.html. Accessed on February 25, 2019.

"The Coefficient of Static Friction," accessed December 31, 2018, http://physics.bu.edu/~duffy/semester1/c6_measuremus.html

The Economist, The People's Bank of China, November 22, 2014.

The Economist, What China wants, August 23, 2014.

The Economist. 2017. "Vorsprungdurch Angst." *The Economist* 424, no. 9048 (July 8): 18–20, 20.

The Wall Street Journal, Thursday July 26, 2018, A6.

The Economist, Russia's Wounded Economy, November 22, 2014, 9.

The Economist. 2017. "Nowhere to Hide." *The Economist* 424, no. 9057 (September 9), 11.

"The Law of Requisite Variety," accessed February 12, 2017, http://pespmc1.vub.ac.be/REQVAR.html.

"The New Deal," accessed July 3, 2015, http://www.history.com/topics/new-deal, 1–7.

"The Paris Agreement," accessed September 15, 2018, https://www.theguardian.com/commentisfree/2018/aug/15/enough-with-the-fairy-tales-about-the-paris-agreeme nt-its-time-for-facts.

"The Postmodern Challenge," accessed September 20, 2018, http://www.equip.org/article/the-postmodern-challenge.

Thompson, James D. 1967. *Organizations in Action*. New York: McGraw-Hill.

Thompson, Dennis F. 2005. *Restoring Responsibility: Ethics in Government, Business, and Healthcare*. Cambridge, UK: Cambridge University Press.

Thucydides. 1974. *History of the Peloponnesian War*. UK: Penguin Books.

Time. 2017. "The Best Invention of 2017: For the Future, for Life, for Good, for Play." *Time* 190, nos. 22–23 (November 27–December 4): 69–93.

Trice, Harrison M., and Janice M. Beyer. 1993. *The Cultures of Work Organizations*. UpperSaddle River, NJ: Prentice Hall, Inc.

Triclot, Mathieu. 2006. Norbert Wiener's Politics and the History of Cybernetics. The Globaland the Local: The History of Science and the Cultural Integration of Europe. Proceedings of the 2nd ICESHS, edited by M. Kokowski, Krakow, Poland, September 6–9. https://halshs.archives-ouvertes.fr/halshs-00514062/document. Accessed on March 25, 2018.

Trist E. L., and K. W. Bamforth. 1951. Some Social and Psychological Consequences of the Longwall Method of Coal Getting. *Human Relations* 4: 3–38.

True, James L., Bryan D. Jones, and Frank R. Baumgartner. "Punctuated Equilibrium Theory," accessed September 25, 2018, https://www.fpzg.unizg.hr/_download/repository/Punctuated-Equilibrium_Theory.pdf, chapter 5, 97.

Tuchman, Barbara. 1984. *The March of Folly: From Troy to Vietnam*. New York: Ballantine Books.

Tucker, Robert C., ed. 1978. *The Marx-Engels Reader*. New York: W. W. Norton & Co.

Tuomela, Raimo. 2013. *Social Ontology: Collective Intentionality and Group Agents*. New York: Oxford University Press.

Turner, Jonathan H. 1982. *The Structure of Sociological Theory*. Homewood, IL: The Dorsey Press.

———. 2003. *Human Institutions: A Theory of Societal Evolution*. Lanham, MD: Rowman & Littlefield Publishers.

Turner, Jonathan H., and Alexandra Maryanski. 1979. *Functionalism*. Menlo Park, CA: The Benjamin/Cummings Publishing Company.

Turner, Bryan S. 1957/1992. "Preface to the Second Edition: Interpreting Emile Durkheim." In Emile Durkheim *Professional Ethics and Civic Morals*. Translated by Cornelia Brookfield. London: Routledge, xiii–xlii.

Tuomela, Raimo. 2002. *The Philosophy of Social Practices: A Collective Acceptance View*. Cambridge, UK: Cambridge University Press.

———. 2013. *Social Ontology: Collective Intentionality and Group Agents*. New York: Oxford University Press.

Tversky, A., and D. Kahneman. 1974. Judgement under Uncertainty: Heuristics and Biases. *Science* 185: 1124–1131.

Tyran, Jean-Robert., and Lars P. Feld. 2001. Why People Obey the Law: Experimental Evidence from the Provision of Public GoodsFile:///C:/Users/kkalu/Downloads/Why_do_people_Obey-the-Law.pdf. Accessed on October 17, 2018.

"Understanding Functionalist Theory," accessed December 2, 2018, http://www.thoughtco.com/functionalist-perspective-3026625.

United Nations. 2008. *Millennium Development Goals Report* 2008. New York: United Nations, 4.

Urone, Paul Peter, and Hinrichs, Roger. 2017. *College Physics*. Houston, TX: OpenStax.

Uttley, A. M. 1954. The Classification of Signals in the Nervous System. *Neurophysio* 6: 479–494.

Valpola, Harri. 2018. Researching the Third Wave of AI. *This is Finland* 2018–2019.

Van Evera, Stephen. 1998. "Offense, Defense, and the Causes of War." *International Security* 22, no. 4: 5–43

Van Wart, Montgomery. 1998. *Changing Public Sector Values*. New York: Garland Publishing, Inc.

Verba, Sidney. 1965. "Comparative Political Culture." In *Political Culture and Political Development*, edited by Lucian W. Pye and Sidney Verba, 512–560. Princeton, NJ: Princeton University Press.

Voegelin, Eric. 1957. *Plato and Aristotle*. Baton Rouge, LA: Louisiana State University Press.

Walker, Guy H., Neville A. Stanton, Paul M. Salmon, and Daniel P. Jenkins. 2008. "A Review of Sociotechnical Systems Theory: A Classic Concept for New Command and Control Paradigms." *Theoretical Issues in Ergonomics Science* 9, no. 6: 479–499.

Michael Walzer. 1978. *Just and Unjust Wars: A Moral Argument with Historical Illustrations*. New York: Basic Books.

Weber, Max. 1922. *Wirtschaft und Gesellschaft (Economy and Society)*. Tubingen: Verlag Von J.C.B. Mohr.

———. 1947. *The Theory of Social and Economic Organization*. Translated by A. M. Hendersonand Talcott Parsons. New York: The Free Press.

———. 1958. *The Protestant Ethic and the Spirit of Capitalism*. Translated by Talcott Parsons. New York: Charles Scribner's Sons.

———. 1968. *Economy and Society: An Outline of Interpretive Sociology*, edited by Guenther Ross and Claus Wittich. New York: Bedminster Press.

———. 1968. *On Charisma and Institution Building*. Chicago, IL: The University of Chicago Press.

Wiechmann, Thorsten. 2007. "Induced versus Autonomous Behavior in Regional Development: A Process Model for Regional Strategy Formation." Association of European Schools of Planning, 1–13. See also https://docplayer.net/48524581-Induced-versus-autonomous-behaviour-in-regional-development-a-process-model-for-regional-strategy-formation.html. Accessed on October 19, 2018.

Weick, Karl E. 1979. *The Social Psychology of Organizing*. New York: McGraw-Hill.

———. 1979. Cognitive Processes in Organizatioins. *Research in Organizational Behavior* 1: 44–74.

Wells, H. G. 1936. *The Shape of Things to Come*. New York: The Macmillan Company.

Wendt, Alexander. 1992. "Anarchy is What States Make of It: The Social Construction of Power Politics." *International Organization* 46: 391–425.

———. 1979. *Theory of International Politics*. Boston, MA: Addison-Wesley.

"What is the Paris Agreement?" accessed September 20, 2018, https://unfccc.int/process-and-meetings/the-paris-agreement/what-is-the-paris-agreement, 1-6.

Wiener, Norbert. 1948. *Cybernetics*. Cambridge, MA: MIT Press.

Williamson, Oliver. 1996. *The Mechanisms of Governance*. New York: Oxford University Press.

Wood, Neal. 1988. *Cicero's Social and Political Thought*. Berkeley, CA: University of California Press.

Worland, Justin. 2018. "Oil Companies See Green." *Time* 192, no. 14 (October 8): 24.

World Bank. 2000. *Reforming Public Institutions and Strengthening Governance: A World Bank Strategy*. Washington, DC: World Bank's Poverty Reduction and Economic Management Network.

Worldwatch. 2004. *State of the World 2004*. New York: W. W. Norton & Co.

World Trade Organization. 1999. Trade and Environment, Special Studies 4 (Geneva: WTO). Press Release: www.wto.org/english/tratop_e/stud99_e.htm.

Wuthnow, Robert. 1989. *Communities of Discourse: Ideology and Social Structure in the Reformation, the Enlightenment and European Socialism*. Cambridge, MA: Harvard University Press.

Yolles, Maurice. 2003. The Political Cybernetics of Organizations. *Kybernetics* 32, nos. 9/10:1253–1282.

Young, John F. *Cybernetics*. London: Iliffe Books Limited.

Ziegenfuss, James T. Jr. 2002. *Organization & Management Problem Solving*: *A Systems and Consulting Approach*. Thousand Oaks, CA: Sage Publications.

Index

About the Author

Kalu N. Kalu is Distinguished Research Professor of Political Science & National Security Policy at Auburn University Montgomery, USA; Docent Professor, Tampere University, Finland; and a Fulbright Scholar. He has been a research affiliate at The Whitney and Betty Macmillan Center for International and Area Studies (Yale University); FDD Academic Fellow, on Counterterrorism and Intelligence (Israel); and a senior research fellow at the Nigerian Institute of International Affairs, Lagos. He is a recipient of two certificates in *Joint Strategic Leadership* (2010) and *National Security Decision Making* (2011) from the United States Air War College (MAFB).

His research emphasis is in the areas of comparative institutions and development, organizational theory and change, citizenship and administrative theory, technology-culture interface, complex adaptive systems, national security policy, and healthcare politics and policies. He has been invited and participated in several international learned conferences and fellowships in several countries around the world including Canada, Germany, Italy, Norway, Finland, Switzerland, Israel, Saudi Arabia, United Arab Emirates, Nigeria, China, Singapore, and India.

His articles have appeared in leading peer-reviewed journals such as *Public Administration Review*, *Administrative Theory & Praxis*, *International Review of Administrative Sciences*, *Administration & Society*, *Contemporary Politics, Systematic Practice and Action Research, Defence Studies, Air & Space Power Journal*, *International Journal of Organization Theory & Behavior, and Journal of Political and Military Sociology*. He has authored several books including *State Power, Autarchy and Political Conquest in Nigerian Federalism* (Rowman & Littlefield Publishers, 2008); *Citizenship:*

A Reality far From Ideal (coedited with Nada Kakabadse and Andrew Kakabadse, Palgrave Macmillan Publishers, 2009); *Technology, Culture, and Public Policy: Critical Lessons From Finland* (Routledge Publishers 2017); *Citizenship: Identity, Institutions, and the Postmodern Challenge* (Routledge Publishers 2017); and *Political Culture, Change, and Security Policy in Nigeria* (Routledge 2018).